Small Worlds:

Provinces and Parties
in Canadian Political Life

Methuen: Canadian Politics and Government

Small Worlds:
Provinces and Parties in Canadian Political Life

David J. Elkins
University of British Columbia

Richard Simeon
Institute of Intergovernmental
Relations, Queen's University

with the collaboration of
Donald E. Blake
University of British Columbia

Mike Burke
University of British Columbia

Richard Johnston
University of British Columbia

Robert Miller
Queen's University

Methuen

Toronto   New York   London   Sydney   Auckland

Canadian cataloguing in Publication Data

Main entry under title:

Small worlds

ISBN 0-458-94270-7

1. Canada—Politics and government—Addresses, essays,
lectures. 2. Political parties—Canada—Addresses, essays,
lectures. 3. Regionalism—Canada—Addresses, essays,
lectures. I. Elkins, David J., 1941—   II. Simeon,
Richard, 1943—

JL65 1980.S63   320.971   C80-094070-9

Printed and bound in Canada

1 2 3 4 5   80   83 82 81 80

Contents

Preface

Five years ago, we published our article "Regional Political Cultures in Canada." While flattered by the amount of attention it attracted, we were surprised at the variety of responses. Some criticized the article for exaggerating the degree of regional difference in Canada; others welcomed it as confirmation of their image of a regionalized country. Both sides took us to be saying much more than we actually did. "Regional Political Cultures" quite explicitly explored only one dimension of a varied, complex and multidimensional phenomenon. And while confirming the importance of provincial and language differences in some basic attitudes towards politics, it also confirmed the strength of other sources of belief, such as class, which interact with territory in complex ways.

This book is in part a response to the earlier reactions. We have tried to provide a more complete and rounded analysis of regional and provincial cleavages in Canada — at the level of feelings, perceptions, preferences and political cultures, as well as at the level of concrete actions such as voting, party policies and government expenditures. There is still much left unsaid here, but we hope that this book will more accurately convey our view that although regionalism is a profound and fundamental feature of Canada, it is only one of many features which contribute to Canada's diversity. We also believe that we have demonstrated some respects in which regional diversity is a strength and not a liability.

Most readers will assume that the other — or the major — reason we have written this book concerns the "crisis of national unity" symbolized by the election of the Parti Québécois on November 15, 1976. Although we applied for research support at that time, we prefer to consider the two events as fortuitously related rather than as cause and effect. We, like many Canadians, consider that election and its attendant causes and consequences as momentous and significant, and our book has been modified inevitably by our thoughts and feelings about "national unity." Nevertheless, Quebec and its many aspirations constitute only one of several dimensions of Canadian unity and diversity. If Quebec disappeared tomorrow, most of what we have to say about Canadian political parties and regions would remain valid. Thus we hope that readers will approach the book not only as a means of understanding national unity, but several other aspects of Canada as well. We do not, thereby, wish to minimize the importance of what happens to or in Quebec; instead, we wish to offer our understanding of Quebec within the broader context of Canadian federal and provincial politics.

These two "causes," or inspirations, for our work share a double theme. Regionalism and Quebec are both more and less important in some ways than many other observers have suggested. We hope that we have succeeded in showing that cleavages, conflict and diversity are not all of a piece. One reaches very different conclusions, prognoses and prescriptions depending on whether one examines citizens' attitudes, political parties and participation, or policies and governmental practices. Likewise, an objective assessment of trends in these features shows, we feel certain, that on some issues the country is increasingly divided, while on others convergence is occurring. We cannot predict the outcome of current controversies, except to suggest that none of the possible outcomes will be as simple as either the optimistic or pessimistic commentators allege. Many people would be well advised to heed Alfred North Whitehead's dictum: "Seek simplicity, and when you find it, distrust it."

In the mixed pleasures and pains of authorship, we have incurred many debts. As always, we owe most to friends and colleagues who have endured our repeated requests for help. Without our co-authors (Blake, Burke, Johnston and Miller), we could have produced this book more quickly, but we are certain it would have been a lesser creation. Not only did they produce good chapters; they also helped to clarify our own.

Other people who shared ideas and critical remarks with us include (in no order of precedence): Keith Banting, Brenda Beck, Alan Cairns, Ken Carty, Roff Johannson, Jean Laponce and Stephen Milne, at the University of British Columbia; and John Meisel, Edwin R. Black, Douglas Brown, Peter Leslie, W.P. Irvine and Michel Ben-Gara at Queen's University. Dorothy Holman, Patti Candido and Joan Prentice not only typed and retyped endless drafts; they tied up countless loose ends and lightened our burden.

For data, we gratefully acknowledge the value of the national election studies: John Meisel made available the 1965 and 1968 studies; and Harold Clarke, Jane Jensen, Larry LeDuc and Jon Pammett quickly offered the 1974 study. The Data Library at the University of British Columbia and the Computing Centres at Queen's and U.B.C. were invaluable allies in handling the data sets. Special thanks are necessary to the Canadian Institute of Public Opinion, for the data which made Chapter III possible. We express our gratitude to the institute. The CIPO is, of course, not responsible for the analysis and interpretations we have provided. As a consequence of its copyright to the original data, the CIPO also claims a shared copyright to Chapter III, and permission for copying any substantial part of it should be sought from CIPO.

Academic research is crippled without money, and we were fortunate in drawing upon several sources. Elkins thanks the Canada Council (now the Social Science and Humanities Research Council) for research grant S76-1391 in 1977–78 and a Leave Fellowship in 1978–79. He also thanks U.B.C. for several small research grants which were essential to specific chapters. Simeon thanks the Economic Council of Canada for support of the early stages of the research for Chapter III. This and Chapters VIII and IX were carried out as part of the research program of the Institute of Intergovernmental Relations at Queen's University.

We appreciate the permission of the Canadian Political Science Association to reprint portions of "Regional Political Cultures in Canada" in Chapter II and "The Perceived Structure of the Canadian Party Systems" in Chapter VII.

Although it appeared too late to use as fully as we would have liked, the CBC/Radio-Canada survey "Confederation/Referendum" (March 1979) encouraged us by demonstrating that our primary data were not as dated as some people had feared. The survey was thoughtfully designed, and we recommend that interested readers examine it for themselves. We are grateful to Radio-Canada for making an extensive summary available to us.

None of the individuals or organizations mentioned above bear any responsibility for our use of their ideas or data. We take the credit for what is good and we accept the blame for what is wrong, as do our co-authors in their respective chapters.

DAVID J. ELKINS
RICHARD SIMEON
September 1979

Introduction

This book explores some of the many dimensions of regionalism in Canada.It does so from several perspectives and with a variety of intellectual tools. It is rooted in the belief that "regionalism" is at once the greatest strength of and greatest challenge to the broader Canadian system; and that Canada grows and survives as a creative interaction of diverse communities — or as we will call them "small worlds." The richness and multiple dimensions of regional diversity mean that no vision of a homogeneous "One Canada" is either possible or desirable.

The perception of Canada as a regionalized country is well established. Distinctive regional societies with unique histories and economies have flourished. Political cleavages, whether at the level of elections, party systems, judicial cases or intergovernmental conflict, have turned on inter-regional and federal-provincial conflict. "National unity" has been a constant preoccupation of Canadian politicians. Today the fabric of the Canadian system itself is challenged as perhaps never before by the clash between the rival development strategies of Quebec nation builders, province builders and country builders.

The expectations — or hopes — of many who see regionalism as obsolete in the contemporary world have been confounded. Thus it was once believed that the inevitable process of "modernization" implied increasing "nationalization," centralization and integration. Postwar Canadian observers felt that war and depression had combined not only to strengthen vastly the human and fiscal resources of the central government, but also had led to a nationalization of sentiment, the formation of a national economy, of nationally organized interest groups, and so on. Cleavages in the future would be organized along horizontal functional or class lines, not along the vertical lines of region, province, territory and culture. In this, Canadian observers were echoing a widespread interpretation of the unidirectional character of nation-building, a view which is now challenged not only in Canada, but in many other western countries which have seen a resurgence of ethnonationalist and regional movements.

While regionalism has received as much attention from political scientists as it has from political leaders — indeed, in Porter's view, has been an "obsession" — its full dimensions remain elusive and not fully charted. Indeed, it is as important to probe the limits of regionalism as it is to understand its extent. Similarly, we need to know a great deal more about its causes as well as the possible mechanisms by which a political system which is *both* regional and national can creatively reconcile its diverse communities.

The term *regionalism* is itself unclear, and in many ways unsatisfactory. Obviously it calls to mind the political salience of the spatial dimension of politics, that politics is somehow about the relationship among regions. But "region" is a somewhat arbitrary concept; by itself it signifies very little. "Regions" do not have identities, aspirations or interests nor, in themselves, do they have any theoretical context. Indeed, the number of ways regions can be mapped is probably as great as the number of theoretical concerns: a geological region will be drawn differently from a climatic region, and so on. Regions may be subprovincial, cross-provincial or, at the other extreme, supranational.

To gain content, the spatial concept *region* must be associated with some other politically relevant differences: in attitudes, identities, economic or other interests, and so on. Similarly, even a linguistic difference does not in itself create political conflict; it does so only when language is associated with differential access to power, status or economic advantages. Hence one major purpose of these studies is to slice into "regions," to ask what other differences are strongly associated with them.

But which regions? In Canada we talk of regions in a variety of ways: Cape Breton and the Annapolis Valley; the lower mainland and the interior; the "Golden Horseshoe" and northern Ontario; or the Prairies, Atlantic Canada or the West. Within provincial politics, the subprovincial regions have considerable political relevance. At the other level, several political leaders have urged a "five-region Canada," and it may be institutionalized in Senate representation or in constitutional amendment formulas. Some issues do seem to provoke the broader regional divisions. And analysts often group provinces together in regions, perhaps as much to build up respectable sample numbers as anything else.

But whether or not regions in this sense have much meaning is an empirical question, one which several of these essays touch on. Several writers have warned against the dangers of too quickly lumping together provinces which may be close together geographically, but have little else in common. But a further powerful reason leads us to concentrate most of our attention on *provinces*. To rise much above folklore, and to become mobilized as political forces, regional differences must become institutional-ized, to have an institutional focus. In Canada, the provincial governments provide such a centre. They are important decision makers in their own right; they play an important part on the national stage. They are the institutional framework around which parties, elections and other political activities are organized; political office is a vital political prize. It is, to a large degree, regionalism which gives provinces their strength in the Canadian political system, but it is, in turn, provinces and their political elites which shape, mould and reinforce this regionalism. Most of the time, therefore, we will be probing *provincial* differences.

That provinces are complex systems in their own right, and at the same time participants in the national system, suggests two distinct lines of inquiry.

First is an exercise in comparative politics. Here we treat each of the provinces as a distinct unit, and ask whether they are similar or dissimilar, and why. Are their cleavage patterns, voting behaviour, party systems, policy outputs, cultures, and so on alike? If they are not, how are the differences to be explained: by reference to differences in demography, history, level of economic development, or other factors? Are provinces on these and other dimensions converging or diverging? Such differences are interesting in their own right. They also permit us to formulate and test hypotheses for which the comparative method is required. These interprovincial differences also define the magnitude of a principal task of the national system. How broad are the differences which it must reflect and accommodate? Before asserting a gross failure of national institutions to act as effective integrative and conflict-managing devices, one should consider the possibility that the reason lies not in institutional weakness, but in the magnitude of the challenge.

When we look at provinces and their populations in the country-wide political system we focus directly on these integrative mechanisms. They are of many types. Perhaps the most important is the individual himself, and the balance in his own mind between loyalty to and identification with national and provincial politics. As we shall see, Canadians have a high degree of awareness of a "regionalized" Canada, but they tend also to have positive feelings about both levels. Dual loyalties are not incompatible — and indeed, by definition, federalism requires them. An important matter for inquiry is to find out when the loyalties come into conflict, and which prevails in that case.

But political parties which operate in both federal and provincial governments can also be highly important integrative mechanisms, linking together politics at two levels. Indeed, the classic brokerage model of Canadian politics assigns to parties a central role in managing regional cleavages. By appealing to voters in all regions parties would be coalitions of regional support; party decision-making in caucus and cabinet would be the arena in which regional leaders worked out their differences. In recent years, as Richard Johnston demonstrates, this integrative capacity appears to have declined; each major party fails to win substantial numbers of seats in a crucial region. Moreover, unlike the case in Germany or the United States, provincial and national parties are weakly linked: they have different ideas, different organizations, and there is very little mobility of leaders from one level to another. We explore the varying patterns of federal and provincial support which underlie these phenomena.

We thus include in the concept *regionalism* two broad dimensions: the dimension of interprovincial difference, and the dimension of interregional and regional-national interaction.

We conceive regionalism to be a multidimensional concept: its elements are logically distinct, and their association is a matter of empirical investigation. We do not intend to examine all the dimensions here.

First are interregional differences in demographic makeup: in ethnic and religious background, in occupational structure, age profiles, the pattern of urban and rural growth, and so on.

Second are interregional differences in history and earlier development. The historical memory of Quebecois or Maritimers who look to a long experience prior to Confederation is quite different from some of the western provinces where the pioneer experience is that of parents and grandparents.

Third are differences in economic structure. We refer here not simply to disparities in wealth, important as they are, but rather to differences in more structural terms — the reliance on primary or secondary industry, the role of different natural resources, the nature of foreign ownership, and so on.

More generally, political economists have begun to explore differences in class structure which arise out of these economic differences. Macpherson's analysis of the "one-class" structure of Alberta is the pioneer study. Other political economists have recently explored the possibility that a regionally fragmented capitalist class, based on regionally diversified industries, has formed alliances with provincial governments, against elements of a "national" bourgeoisie centred on Ottawa. Much needs to be done before these relationships can be fully traced out, and we do not do so here. This analysis, however, has an important implication. In much earlier debate class and regional politics were seen to be antagonistic; scholars debated which was more "real," or whether one was supplanting the other. Now the two levels may be integrated: interprovincial conflict may have a class basis; "class politics," in turn, will differ from region to region.

The demographic, historical and economic differences can be seen as the underlying bases of politics, which in turn give rise to variations in attitude and behaviour. Thus, while we do not describe such differences at length, we shall draw heavily on them as possible explanations for the more overtly "political" factors we do look at. The first of these are attitudinal differences. Attitudes can be categorized in an infinite variety of ways. We focus on three aspects:

(1) Conceptions of Community

Here we refer to the complex of attitudes and identifications which define for a person his political community: the system with which he identifies, and to which he feels loyalty, and the set of people whom he includes in his sense of "us"— with whom he feels common citizenship and to whom he feels obligation. In a regionalized political system, such feelings are a crucial underpinning for unity or disunity. It is at the heart of current political debate in Quebec; it is equally important to understanding what an Albertan means when he says "our oil." In this book, we examine the extent to which Canadian citizens think in terms of regions — and which ones they refer to — and explore their feelings about federal and provincial governments: to which do they feel closest, and so on. To what extent is the country torn apart by the pre-eminence of provincial identifications?

(2) Orientations to Politics

Here we explore some of the variations in citizens' basic conceptions of politics and of themselves as political actors. We focus on three primary elements of such beliefs: political involvement, trust in governments and sense of political efficacy. Whereas conceptions of community are intimately related to national integration and to federal-provincial conflict, the orientations we explore here are related more to comparative politics, to explaining variations in provincial party systems or policy decisions.

(3) Policy Preferences

People may differ profoundly about their sense of community, but share common views about the purposes or interests they wish governments to serve; similarly, the community itself may not be in question, but it may be rocked by many intense policy disagreements. A country's unity will be most threatened if strong identification with provincial units is combined with a pattern of policy cleavage in which the major divisions follow territorial rather than class or other lines. We therefore explore policy disagreements on a large number of issues to discover whether interprovincial disagreements are greater or lesser than other divisions — or, to put it another way, do provincial populations tend to have different policy preferences? Do some issues mobilize opinion on regional dimensions, and others on other dimensions?

Attitudes become politically relevant when they are mobilized or organized into politics, or when they are translated into action. In western political systems this role falls primarily on elections, parties and interest groups. Voters elect provincial and federal governments; parties contest at both levels. We look at these relationships from three perspectives. First, from the voters' perspective we examine patterns of voting and party identification — to what extent do citizens vote one way provincially and another federally? To what extent do different social groups divide differently in each province? Second, we look at parties and elections as national institutions. Are the electoral cleavages primarily territorial? Can the parties act as nationally integrative institutions? Can they win support nationally, or are they confined to some regions? Federal-provincial conflict, in turn, will be related to whether or not the electoral coalition of the national party is reproduced by its counterparts in each province. Third, the results of these cleavages and party strategies will be manifested in party systems: how do provincial party systems — as defined by such factors as numbers, competitiveness, ideology — differ among themselves or from the national party systems?

Differences in behaviour and attitudes, in turn, should be manifested in government policy and behaviour. Our final chapters explore these questions, first comparatively and then in terms of interaction of national and provincial political systems. First, we explore some important aspects of variation in policy outputs from province to province and relate them to variations in political and environmental characteristics. Second, in the conclusion we examine some aspects of the contemporary crisis in Canadian politics which can be defined as fundamental conflict, or lack of consensus, about the character and purpose of the Canadian community. On its surface, it is a clash between rival state-building governments, but much of what we have found shows it has a deeper base. On the other hand, our findings offer some hopeful notes: despite the pervasiveness of regional differences, there are very important unifying factors, and, indeed, the regional differences may not be quite as profound as the concentration on elite conflict has led us to believe.

We thus move up a ladder; from basic differences, to attitudes, to behaviour, and finally to governments themselves. Each level is related to the previous one, but there are many intervening variables at each step.

Two other issues need exploration. The first is whether the regional divisions are equally great in each of the dimensions we explore. The more we find regional differences occurring in every dimension, the more realistic it becomes to speak of "provincial societies," characterized by a distinct history, economy, ethnic makeup, sense of community, network of social and political institutions, and so on. In fact, we will see interprovincial variations are not consistent across all dimensions. They are greater, for example, at the level of attitudes than they are at the level of policy, where the similarity of problems facing all governments, together with the equalizing effect of federal grants, produce rather small variations around a common theme. Similarly, policy preferences of provincial populations differ rather sharply on some issues, but very little on others.

Second is the question of interprovincial divergence or convergence over time. As we have seen, much earlier theorizing, Canadian and otherwise, argued that modernization embodied a unidirectional movement to larger and larger units. In part this stemmed from a nationalization of culture; in part from a growing need for rationalization, given the complexity of modern policy and the interdependence between governments. But, in contrast to this viewpoint, most Canadian commentators have pointed to what Donald Smiley calls the "attenuation of federal power" in the postwar period. Disaffection from the central government and the assertion of province-centred desires for control over development have risen tremendously especially since the 1960s. Quebec led this movement but by no means monopolizes it. It is vital both to measure and to account for these developments. Several essays therefore have an important time dimension: we look at policies since World War II, and measure policy preferences since the late 1940s. We look at the success of national parties over an even longer period. This allows us to illuminate an important controversy in contemporary Canadian political science. The primary evidence for the continuing pre-eminence of territorial cleavages and for a growing provincialization of sentiment comes from watching the political competition between federal and provincial *governments*. We know very little about the underlying support for these contending political elites. It could be that the institutions systematically exaggerate the conflict. Our data will help answer that question, and allow us to trace whether provincial populations are becoming more similar or more diverse.

The essays in this book do not provide definitive answers and leave unexplored many dimensions of regionalism in Canada. Together, however, they provide a rich sense of diversity and commonality, a diversity which is both unlikely to disappear and is a defining characteristic of the Canadian community itself.

I
The Sense of Place[1]

David J. Elkins

One of the primary reasons for creating a federal rather than a unitary state concerns the prior existence of several independent or quasi-independent states, colonies or territories. Typically, residents of such political or administrative units have developed emotional attachments which cannot be easily ignored; thus, federalism rests in part on the tenacity of affective ties to political units. By their very nature, moreover, federal systems usually serve to perpetuate loyalties to their constituent elements.[2] If federalism is an expedient device for responding to strong local loyalties, the enshrinement of these loyalties in legally defined provinces assures their longevity.

One intriguing question, then, concerns the ways and degree to which new loyalties to the nation and to the federal system develop and coexist with feelings of affection for the political "building blocks" from which a federation was constructed. For federal systems to succeed, therefore, citizens should have positive feelings about both the federal and provincial levels of organization.

Although this conclusion seems obvious when stated so baldly, much commentary on federalism rests on a contrary assumption — namely, that to strengthen the federation one must undermine the feelings people have about their province, that citizens must choose one identity and discard all others. This perspective is not confined to studies of Canada. Two examples out of many will have to suffice.

> But contintentalism is merely the upper millstone; the lower millstone, parochialism or provincialism, is its complement; and it is the attrition by these two powerful forces that has ground down the solid fabric of Canadian nationalism.[3]
>
> The problems which Indian federalism faces stem from the need of her people, to have a government armed with sufficient powers . . . to combat the strong sentiments of regionalism found throughout the land.[4]

A corollary of multiple loyalties to province and nation concerns the development strategies employed by governments. Each of the ten provincial governments in Canada has increasingly come to emphasize its own development, while the eleventh government — the federal government in Ottawa — has increasingly viewed its role as the equalizer of fiscal resources among provincial governments and the equalizer of governmental and social services throughout the country. Needless to say, national development and equalization are frequently viewed by provincial governments as an unjustified encroachment on provincial jurisdictions and as obstacles to the smooth implementation of provincial development strategies.[5] Equally obvious is the fact that "rich" provinces (mainly Ontario, Alberta and British Columbia) resent federal policies more than "poor" provinces which receive a substantial portion of their revenues from direct transfer payments. As in so many instances, provincial and regional differences in specific situations hinder consensus and also hinder a united front among provincial governments in regard to federal government policies. While this diversity may be a complicating factor in national development, the local loyalties on which it is based are an integral part of Canadian identity.[6]

Even without a federal structure, Canada would be diverse and would contain antagonistic elements — such as the linguistic and ethnic hostility between French-speakers and the speakers of English and other languages. Under a system of federalism, however, these points of contrast are heightened and emphasized, because of the natural desire of provincial governments to pursue policies beneficial to the unique populations each represents.

Canada'a history cannot be viewed solely from the perspective of nation building, as important as that has surely been. Equally important has been the parallel and contemporaneous process of province building.[7] Provincial governments are responsible, according to the Canadian constitution, for most of the activities of direct concern to citizens in their daily lives — education, roads, medical services and social welfare, to name a few. There has been continual conflict as a result of each province's attempts to pursue its own planned development and the other contradictory attempts of the federal government to achieve minimum standards of services on a national basis. Poorer provinces, for example, have been forced to accept federal transfer payments in order to finance these services, and to try to catch up economically with the richer provinces. The result is an intermingling of responsibilities not envisioned in the constitution, and a degree of dependence of some provincial governments on federal largesse which undermines the normal operations of federalism.

As a result of basic differences compounded by the complex varieties of federal-provincial relations, each of the provinces constitutes a "small world" within the wider context of Canada as a subcontinental nation. It should hardly occasion surprise, therefore, to find that citizens have loyalties to their province and region, as well as that the populations of different provinces have different mixes of feelings about Canada.

Like the fabled ten blind men who touch the trunk or tail or belly of an elephant and report quite different animals, Canadians are in touch with different parts of Canada and they report what they know. Each report, not surprisingly, is unique; and our job consists in trying to gain an overview of this elephant from contrasting reports. Also like the blind men, Canadians are quite definite about the veracity of their reports, and all clearly believe they react to Canada rather than to another beast. Hence, a sense of identity does exist even though the exact content of that identity or "nationalism" varies a great deal among groups.

An awareness of "Canada" as a concept, or entity, coexists with clear awareness of provinces and regions. There is little apparent conflict between these cognitions, though the balance of affections for one or the other, naturally, varies from person to person. Canadians have highly differentiated images of their country. They distinguish between Canada and its constituent geographic and social parts, between federal and provincial governments, between the land and the people, and between society and government. What Northrop Frye calls "the imaginative sense of locality"[8] does not, for most people, obscure the sense of a continental country any more than the pleasure of a spring day makes us forget the changing cycle of the seasons.

The rich variety of perceptions and cognitions has a pattern. Differences follow the lines of province-language cleavages, and they reflect little patterning along other socioeconomic dimensions. Except for province/language groups, diversity of images within groups overwhelms the diversity between groups, with only a few exceptions noted below. Interestingly, one form of social patterning reinforces province-language differences: the longer immigrants reside in Canada, the more "provincially" oriented they become; native-born Canadians are at least as "provincial" in their orientations. Yet all these groups score relatively high on several measures of identification with Canada.

Readers will no doubt have their own images of Canada which they will compare to those outlined in this chapter. Perhaps it would be useful to pause and ask yourself about some of these aspects before inspecting the data. How many regions are there in Canada, and what are they? What kind of society is Canada: English, bicultural, a mosaic, a colony of the United States, or what? Is there another country in which you would prefer to live? Is there another province which you would prefer to your current place of residence? Which level of government do you care about most? Which level of government affects your life the most?

It is possible to have, as some people do, a Canadian identity and images of the country which are almost wholly devoid of geographic, regional or provincial demarcations. The underlying theme of the data we present, however, concerns the profound importance of geography and its associated history. Our analysis did not ordain this conclusion. Other scholars have reached similar conclusions with different data, and our data were capable of revealing quite different patterns. Nevertheless, it is abundantly clear that Canadians have a deep and abiding sense of place — of their area, province or region, and of Canada as a country.

National Character and National Identity

Scholars, journalists, historians and literary critics have tried to define and describe the "national character" of Canadians. All have found it an extremely difficult endeavour. The concept of national character, for one thing, is nebulous and difficult to specify in terms of observable qualities.[9] For another, everyone agrees that the French and English parts of Canada should be studied separately, so that at best Canada could be described as having a dual national character.[10] In addition, there is the problem of generalization. Studies of literary products, painting, films and the like may reveal traits and patterns not characteristic of many people.[11] Such studies also inevitably lead to the view that national character differs in important respects in different parts of the country, among ethnic groups and in different historical periods.

A more historical approach, such as that of Louis Hartz, Kenneth McRae and Gad Horowitz, overcomes some of these problems by emphasizing the intermingling of antecedent forces, the "fragment societies" which Hartz postulates.[12] Even so, we must conclude that French Canada differs strongly from the rest of the country, since it derived from a "feudal fragment," whereas the rest of Canada derived from a "liberal fragment."

Another approach focuses on values and value-patterns. To some extent, analysis in this vein can draw upon systematic social-psychological evidence, but much of it seems destined to be impressionistic; and different people have different impressions.[13]

A more political orientation rests on a secure foundation of analysis of the actual operation of institutions and of the policies and goals of governments and public spokesmen.[14] To some extent, this approach supplements those of Hartz and Lipset. By focusing mainly on federal or nationwide institutions and policies, however, one can form an unrealistic image of the unity of Canada. Such a perspective is a useful corrective to those analysts who emphasize the diversity and fragility of Canada, but both sides of the coin are essential for a comprehensive and accurate portrait of national character.

National identity is not the same thing as national character, though the two may influence each other.[15] The feeling of being a Canadian, as distinct from attachment to other nations, may be easier to assess because it does not require the isolation of *common* patterns. Identity is personal or group-based, and this focus can reveal either homogeneity or heterogeneity on a national scale. Furthermore, identity, or a sense of "nationalism" or "patriotism," can be based on quite various features — different people can be proud of different aspects of Canada and yet all may share a *positive* feeling.[16]

For all these reasons, we have restricted our attention in this chapter to a few specific aspects of national identity. This accords with our theoretical and descriptive focus on provincial, regional and linguistic cleavages and on partisan divisions.

Cognitive Maps

Let us begin by ascertaining Canadians' images of the geography of Canada. While it would be useful to have evidence about whether perceptions of provincial and regional divisions have changed over time, the only solid quantitative evidence derives from the 1974 national election survey.[17] Each respondent was asked what region he lived in, with no prompting as to whether region meant town, subprovincial region, province or larger area. Subsequently, each person was asked to name all the other regions of Canada.[18] There were approximately 700 different combinations of regions named by the 2562 respondents. Many of these combinations were quite similar, of course, and they can be regrouped into a more manageable typology. Thus we can see the extent to which respondents vary in naming particular regions or provinces, in the total numbers named, in the types of classifications used, and in the relative occurrence of the response that there are no regions in Canada. We can also see how persons in different provinces and social groups vary in their response patterns.

It is important to note that any response counted as a region, whether unusual or not. The investigators imposed no preconceptions about "correct" regional boundaries. Many people simply mentioned a few provinces or broad regional categories like the Maritimes, central Canada or the North. Others were extremely detailed, such as the person who said "the other regions" were "Atlantic and along the St. Lawrence to Lakes between Windsor and Quebec City, northern Ontario, northern Quebec, northern half of Yukon to the Territories." What requires attention are the ways in which the details seem to be organized cognitively and how many details are mentioned.

Underlying the answers given by almost every respondent was an important assumption, namely, that "Canada" consists of the political unit with that name. Only one respondent in more than 2500 included part of the United States in his list of regions. Some respondents did not *explicitly* include all of Canada's territory in their answer. For example, regions labelled "west, east, and north" may be too vague to prove that the respondent intended to include everything. Yet the impression one forms by reading these varying answers is quite distinct: people were thinking of Canada as currently defined in political and territorial terms, not something larger and only rarely something smaller.[19]

Furthermore, geographical imagery predominates over functional, topological or climatic characterizations. In discussing their own regions, slightly more than 6 per cent of respondents defined regions in nongeographic terms (such as rich or poor, French or English, dry or rainy, flat or mountainous). This figure rises only to 10.3 per cent in discussing regions other than the respondent's own.

It might seem natural to many observers, in answering these questions, to list all the provinces. Only 3.7 per cent of the sample did so, however, and there was some variation among provincial and language groups in the rate of doing so. Many respondents named regions larger than a single province, particularly when discussing the regions other than their own. There was no uniformity of perception in this regard, however, since there were divisions of opinion over whether the Atlantic region was a single region or several, over whether the Prairies included British Columbia, and over whether "the North" was a distinct region. A modest number of respondents named as regions areas smaller than a province. About 7 per cent of the national sample did so in referring to their own region, and about 5 per cent did so in reference to other regions. A higher proportion of residents of Quebec or Ontario referred to subprovincial regions; and for many of them, the "other regions" named besides their own were also within their own province. In other words, for some people, "Canada" consists of their own province; even though they limit their responses to one province, it is still true that they think in regional terms.

The principal sources of variation in these measures of awareness of regions are provincial and linguistic. Each provincial population manifests a different pattern of responses; and French-speaking Canadians (especially in Quebec) differ from those who speak English or other languages. If one looks at how many people named regions (or how many did not), Ontario and the four western provinces were more likely than Quebec or the four Atlantic provinces to respond in regional terms. Similarly, the English were more "regionally conscious" than the French. If one looks only at those people who named any regions at all, however, the situation is more or less reversed: people from the East who referred to any regions named more regions than did those from west of the Ottawa River. Language differences were reduced but not reversed by this procedure. Thus French and eastern Canada appear more polarized than the rest of the country into two categories — those who "see regions" (and see more regions) and those who do not think regional divisions important.

Other social and demographic variables were largely unrelated to thinking of Canada in regional terms, except for education and age. More highly educated people and younger people were more likely to say Canada was composed of regions, and they were more likely to name a larger number of regions than were the less educated or older Canadians. Since the young are, on the average, much more highly educated than their parents or grandparents, and since they have also travelled and lived in more parts of Canada, it is fair to say that this represents a generational difference, and not a matter of life cycle.

Most speculation concludes that modernization should result in a decline of regionalism, or at least a decline in its perceived importance. If the above observations about generational differences are correct, then the opposite process is at work in Canada. As is true for other aspects of regionalism discussed below, exposure (through education, mass media, travel or business) to other parts of Canada enhances one's awareness of regional variation. For example, people who are involved in Canadian political life — as evidenced by high scores on political efficacy and political involvement — perceive more regions and are more likely to think of Canada in regional terms than those less involved. Paradoxically, perhaps, respondents who are least "parochial" in orientation are most "provincial" or "regional" in their perceptions.

If there is variation in the awareness of regional variety, there is also great variation in the exact content of the perceptions and how they are organized into "cognitive maps" of Canada. In part, of course, this reflects the wording of the questions in terms of one's own region and the other regions. If one names British Columbia, for example, as his region, then it will not appear in the list of other regions. Surprisingly, however, there is great variety among provincial populations in the way they define their own and other regions. In no province does a majority define its own region as the province of residence, though Quebec, Ontario and British Columbia have substantial minorities who "think provincially" in this way. In every province, about 5 to 15 per cent perceive "the North" as a distinct region. Besides these two similarities, differences are more common.

Residents of Atlantic Canada distinguish among the four provinces of Newfoundland, Prince Edward Island, Nova Scotia and New Brunswick relatively infrequently. Most residents there tend to think of that area as a region, and the rest of the country concurs.[20] Similarly, residents of Manitoba, Saskatchewan and Alberta make few distinctions among themselves, sometimes including British Columbia in "the West" or Prairies but more often seeing British Columbia as separate. The central and eastern provincial populations reciprocate by making almost no distinctions among the three Prairie provinces and also by being ambivalent about whether British Columbia should be thought of as part of a general western region or as separate from the Prairies.[21]

Quebec and Ontario respondents see each other as separate regions, and this is a common perception throughout the country. Despite that, quite a few people in the West refer to "central Canada" in a way which might include both Ontario and Quebec. Some western Canadians also speak of "the East" in a way which includes Ontario and Quebec with the Atlantic region. Since there were no follow-up questions ascertaining what provinces or areas the respondent intended to include in these rough categories, we cannot be sure of the content. What is certain, however, is the relative frequency of use of category labels.

Canada's diversity is manifested clearly in the results summarized in this section. Different kinds of people focus their attention on different parts of the country and on different aspects of the regional composition of Canada. Furthermore, the systems of classification — or cognitive maps — diverge across certain social categories as well as from one province/language group to another.

Not everyone agrees, however, that Canada consists of regions. We saw that this belief was founded, in part, on ignorance or on the lack of cognitive skills. It is worth considering the possibility that those who deny the regionalization of Canada believe that another form of "conflict," or social differentiation, is more important. The most obvious alternative conceptualization concerns a social-class analysis. We have information on whether individuals "feel close to other people in the same class as you" (where the respondent has specified his own class) and on whether they feel that class conflict is inevitable.

If this alternative hypothesis is correct, we should expect that people who believe class conflict is inevitable (particularly if they also feel close to their class peers) will be less likely to state a regional classification. Although there are minor exceptions, the short answer is that there is no relationship — positive or negative — between perceptions of possible class conflict and denying the regional character of Canada. In fact, Canada reveals its regional character in this respect just as so many others. Although the relationships are tenuous and of varying magnitude, several province/language groups manifest a slight tendency for those persons who envision no class conflict to assert also that there are no regions in Canada. In other provinces no differences exist among respondents according to their beliefs about class conflict compared to whether there are regions or not.

When we divide the population according to language alone, there is a slight pattern. English respondents reveal a weak positive relationship: those who name regions think class conflict is inevitable and those who do not mention regions see no possibility of class conflict. Bilingual respondents, on the other hand, exhibit a weak negative relationship. For Francophones and "other language" respondents, no pattern emerges at all.

In short, it seems safe to reject the hypothesis that respondents have been forced to "see" regions by the nature of the questions asked, and have thereby been denied an opportunity to present a cognitive map of Canada along wholly nonregional lines. We have seen that a few respondents think of functional rather than geographic regions, many do not name any regions and apparently deny the regional nature of Canada. But there is no evidence that these latter types of respondents have a class-based image of Canada. For most Canadians, Canada consists of several regions or several provinces, and the variety occurs in the particular regions on which they focus their attention and in the classification schemes they use to organize these perceptions.

What are the consequences for Canadian unity and Canadian politics of these regional cleavages and the vast variety of perceptions of Canadian regions? Our answers to this question, in so far as it can ever be answered, will be given throughout the chapters of this book.[22] No single answer suffices, because Canada's geographic diversity and "provincialization" have different kinds of effects on different types of attitudes and behaviour.

Canadian National Identity

Canadians have by several criteria a strong sense of themselves as a nation. Considering the pervasive influence and proximity of the United States, its mass media, its economic ties with Canada and the exchange of immigrants and tourists across their borders, one should perhaps be surprised there is a Canada at all and that nationalism is as strong as it is.[23] Several types of data support the view, however, that Canadian national identity is viable even if not as strident or boastful as some Canadians would prefer.

Six variables from a nationwide survey during the 1968 federal election have been recoded and combined into an index of Canadian national identity, with results shown in Table 1.[24] Crude as this indicator may be, it has a clear face validity. To score low, one must favour the merger of Canada and the United States, one must believe that some people in Canada have more important ties with other countries than with each other, and one must have a self-image which does not emphasize Canadian-ness. High scores indicate the opposite of these traits.

These six components were positively correlated with each other, in varying degree, and with an overall index which cumulated the scores in a range of zero to twelve. The distribution was skewed towards the higher scores, indicating perhaps the relatively widespread sentiments the index was intended to assess.[25] Since neutral or ambiguous responses were scored as "one," it would be theoretically possible (although uncommon) to score as high as six out of twelve without evidencing any positive feelings about Canada. Thus the index has been collapsed for some purposes as follows: low = 0 to 6 (32.4% of the sample), middle = 7 to 9 (39.5%) and high = 10 to 12 (28.0%). Thus the middle and high categories contain people who differ only in the *degree of positive affect* toward Canada, whereas the low category contains people with both neutral and negative affect. The proportions scoring in these categories, and the means and standard deviations, are given in Table 1 for various province and language groups. "Province" here indicates the non-French-speaking respondents in all cases except "Quebec French" and "non-Quebec French," so that one may compare language as well as provincial cleavages. Several features of this table deserve emphasis.

Table 1
Canadian National Identity Index by Province/Language Groups—1968
(Percentage across; Means)*

	Canadian National Identity					
	High (10-12)	Middle (7-9)	Low (0-6)	Mean Score	Standard Deviation	N
National	28.0%	39.5	32.4	7.85	2.39	2767
Newfoundland	4.2%	43.8	52.1	6.06	2.46	48
P.E.I.	35.3%	41.2	23.5	8.71	2.34	17
Nova Scotia	26.4%	36.4	37.3	7.55	2.61	110
New Brunswick	36.8%	39.5	23.7	8.33	2.31	76
Ontario	31.8%	43.4	24.8	8.23	2.29	927
Manitoba	36.1%	41.4	22.6	8.56	2.17	133
Saskatchewan	30.1%	43.4	26.5	8.20	2.25	136
Alberta	22.1%	44.3	33.6	7.72	2.12	235
B.C.	27.9%	34.4	37.7	7.72	2.37	247
Quebec English	48.8%	37.7	13.9	9.25	2.17	122
Quebec French	18.8%	31.6	49.5	6.94	2.41	632
Non-Quebec French	33.3%	53.6	13.1	8.38	1.74	84

*Note: Percentages are based on trichotomized index; means and standard deviations are based on full range of scores (0-12).

First, language alone does not divide the population on this measure. Although the French in Quebec do not score "high" as much as most English Canadians, the non-Quebec French are strongly Canadian in orientation. Non-French residents of Newfoundland, on the other hand, score quite low on this index.

Second, all population groups have average scores above the cut-off point between "low" and "middle." None have averages in the "high" range (10-12), though the Quebec English approach this point most closely.

Third, there is considerable variation within each province/language group, judging by standard deviations. The non-Quebec French are most homogeneous on this indicator, as on many others, reinforcing the view that they should be analyzed as a separate category. This is especially noteworthy since they are geographically so dispersed. Nevertheless, given these indications of heterogeneity, it is worth asking about social, economic, political and demographic correlates of scores on the national identity index.

Status variables correlate positively with scores on this index. As education and income increase, so does the score on the index, indicating clearer national orientation. Similarly, higher status occupational groups — and farmers — score higher than other groups. The differences between classes (as designated by respondents) are small but consistent with these status differences. In religious terms, the highest scores are found among Jews and persons avowing no religion. The lowest scores occur among Roman Catholics, with Protestants and Greek Catholics in between. Scores on the index increase as rate of church attendance declines. There is also a slight decline in national identity scores as age increases, except that the youngest age cohort (18-29) also scores relatively low. There are no consistent differences among categories on several variables including gender, community size, country of birth, country of ancestors, year immigrated to Canada or union membership.

Political variables do relate moderately strongly to national identity scores. Those who favour the separation of Quebec, or who think it likely, score much lower than those who oppose separatism. As feelings of political efficacy or political trust increase, so do scores on the index of national identity. In partisan terms, supporters of the NDP and Liberal parties score highest in orientation to Canadian nationalism, Créditiste, Union Nationale and "other" party groups score lowest, with Social Creditors and Progressive Conservatives in the middle.

An interesting sidelight concerns feelings about the monarchy. In 1968, respondents were asked to agree or disagree with the statement "Canada should abolish the monarchy." Nationally, 44 per cent favoured (strongly or mildly) the abolition of the monarchy, while 44 per cent opposed abolition. (The remainder were undecided.) When broken down into province/language groups, however, the range of opinion is very wide, from Newfoundlanders' apparently intense devotion to the Queen to the Quebec French's equally strong opposition to the monarchy. Clearly this symbol of statehood arouses important and openly expressed feelings.[26] This may be a case, however, where the gap between feelings and actions must be remembered. One doubts that there are many occasions for those feelings to eventuate in political action.[27]

These feelings about the Queen as head of state bear no relationship to the index of national identity just presented. Although for some Canadians the Queen is a significant element of national identity, in the population as a whole the monarchy appears to play no systematic role. There are a few significant social and political correlates of attitude towards the monarchy, with opponents of this institution coming mainly from French, Catholic, Liberals, Créditistes and the young. Supporters are more likely to be English, Protestant, elderly and Progressive Conservative. Education, class, gender and occupation bear virtually no relationship to these feelings. Those who in 1968 favoured separation of Quebec or who believed it likely were only slightly more likely to wish to abolish the monarchy than anti-separatists.

It appears, therefore, that a person's orientation on this matter results less from explicitly political ideology and more from his ethnic or linguistic community or from provincial or regional norms. In any case, both supporters and opponents of the monarchy score, on average, equally high on our index of national identity.

Table 2
How Canadians Feel About Canada in General Compared
to Other Countries*
by Province/Language Groups (1974)

	Percentage Preferring Three Countries to Canada (0)	Percentage Who Have Mixed Assessments** (scores of 1-5)	Percentage Preferring Canada to All Three Countries (6)	Mean Score (out of 6)	N
National	0.8%	17.6%	81.6%	5.59	2034
Newfoundland	0%	31.3%	68.7%	5.28	67
P.E.I.	0%	9.8%	90.2%	5.80	51
Nova Scotia	0%	19.8%	80.2%	5.60	126
New Brunswick	0%	13.0%	87.0%	5.77	77
Ontario	0.7%	11.2%	88.1%	5.76	547
Manitoba	0%	14.6%	85.4%	5.71	82
Saskatchewan	0%	13.3%	86.7%	5.83	83
Alberta	0.7%	15.9%	83.4%	5.62	151
B.C.	0%	18.6%	81.4%	5.67	221
Quebec English	0.8%	18.7%	80.5%	5.60	118
Quebec French	1.8%	26.6%	71.6%	5.23	457
Non-Quebec French	3.7%	7.4%	88.9%	5.59	54

*This index compares scores on "feeling thermometers" for the concept "Canada in general" and for the concepts "England," "France" and "United States." The maximum possible range is 0 to 6, with higher scores indicating greater "warmth" felt for Canada in general than for the other three countries.

**"Mixed feelings" encompasses a wide variety of orientations. Nearly half of these 17.6% of the respondents give equal scores to Canada and one of the other countries but rate Canada higher than the other two. Another quarter of this group (4.7%) rate all the countries the same or, at most, give one country a higher score than Canada. Only about 2% of the sample place Canada lower than both of the three other countries.

Although Canadians vary in their sense of identity as just measured, on another measure comparing Canada to other countries, they uniformly prefer Canada. Respondents were asked to express their "warmth" towards "Canada in general," "England," "France," and "the United States" on the feeling thermometer.[28] An index was constructed from these scores as follows. If an individual felt more "warmly" towards Canada in general than towards England, he was scored as a "two"; if more warmly towards England, as a "zero"; if the same for both, as a "one." And so on for France and the United States. Adding these scores together yields an index ranging from zero (prefers or feels more warmly towards all three countries than to Canada) to six (warmer towards Canada than to all three other countries). The results are displayed in Table 2. It should be emphasized that these results pertain to 1974, whereas the national identity index derived from 1968 data.

The main point to note concerns how high the mean scores are, and what large proportions score the maximum six out of six on the index. Canadians almost without exception prefer Canada. Less than 1 per cent of the sample express greater warmth of feeling about all of these three other countries than about Canada.

In addition, there is almost no difference from one province/language group to another in feelings of warmth about Canada in general. It is true that the Quebec French have a marginally lower average score than any other province, and they are also more internally divided than most other groups.

Although we have not reported the data here, when we compare feelings of warmth about "Canadian government" to these same scores for England, France and the United States, a similar pattern emerges. The mean scores are lower (4.46 nationally), and there is more variation across province/language groups. The support for Canada, however, is higher than some might expect; and intergroup differences are small compared to some of the variables presented in previous sections.

As with several other aspects of images of Canada, many "background" variables are unrelated to these measures of attachment to Canada. Partly this may reflect the fact that it is easy to give high scores on the feeling thermometer. When one considers, however, that no direct comparison of Canada and other countries was asked for, it is probably remarkable how uniform all groups are in their greater feelings of warmth for Canada than for England, France or the United States. This holds true, except for very small and irregular differences, even when one compares people in terms of their country of birth or country of ancestral origin. Respondents born in the United States or the United Kingdom score slightly lower on both indices; but among those born in Canada, people of British origin score slightly higher. All in all, social background plays a minor role, if any, in explaining these feelings.

To some extent, attitudes about Canada reflect one's experiences in Canada, as we have noted before. This is true here as well, especially as regards warmth towards Canadian government. On average, people who have lived in more than one province score *lower* on our index comparing Canadian government to other countries, while they tend to score *higher* on the index involving Canada in general than do people who have always lived in the same province.

When respondents are classified by years they have lived in Canada, a clear pattern emerges. Those born here score lowest on the index involving Canada in general, long-term immigrants (those who came here in 1945 or earlier) score higher, and post-1945 immigrants score highest of all. On average, people who have lived in more than one province score higher on this index of attachment to Canada compared to people who have always lived in the same province. As the number of provinces in which one has lived increases above one or two, one becomes even more favourable to Canada in general. These "mobile" Canadians are also the people in our survey who evinced the greatest awareness of Canadian regionalism, yet they are the most oriented to Canada as a whole.[29]

People who favour separatism score lower on our index about Canada in general than opponents of separatism on this index, but more than 70 per cent of the separatists still score at the highest point (six out of six), compared to about 84 per cent of the opponents of separatism. It will be recalled that these data were collected in 1974, before the Parti Québécois was elected as the government in Quebec. Nevertheless, this survey occurred well after that party had gained a substantial following and only a year after it had become the official opposition in the Quebec National Assembly.

In 1968, respondents were asked to give thermometer scores to "French Canadians," "English Canadians," "Englishmen" and "Americans." We can thus compare how different types of Canadians feel about each other and about citizens of two other countries. The national mean scores for these four categories of people were: French Canadians (75), English Canadians (79), English(72) and Americans (72). There were few interesting social or regional variations in these scores. French Canadians rated the English and Americans slightly lower than did English Canadians. English Canadians rated themselves higher than they did French Canadians, and the French Canadians returned the favour by rating themselves more "warmly" than they did the English Canadians.

Since these ratings of people were collected in 1968 and the ratings of countries were collected in 1974, no direct comparison is possible. Nevertheless, some speculations come to mind.[30] First, these thermometer scores suggest that Canadians feel quite warmly about the citizens of other countries, and yet they apparently prefer Canada as a country to other places. Second, Canadians can prefer Canada to England and the United States even while feeling as warmly about Englishmen and Americans as they do about themselves or members of ethnic groups here in Canada. Third, respondents clearly are capable of distinguishing among classes of objects they have been asked to rate. These different patterns of responses about countries, governments and peoples argue for the meaningfulness of these answers; they do not reflect simply "response sets" where everything is rated favourably or everything unfavourably.

One element of the index of national identity deserves special attention. Respondents were asked to agree or disagree (strongly or mildly) with the statement that "Canada and the U.S.A. should join together as one country." Although a clear majority of every province-language group in Table 3 opposes annexation or merger, the proportions do vary somewhat. In particular, French-speaking Canadians, Nova Scotians and Newfoundlanders — in 1968 at least — expressed a somewhat greater willingness to join the United States.

Furthermore, some will be surprised to find as many as 20 per cent of the sample either mildly or strongly in favour of annexation. Is this evidence, for example, of a dislike for Canada, a lack of nationalism, a strong dose of realism about who already owns Canada, or what? Unfortunately, respondents were not asked to explain their views on this matter, but some speculations are in order. First, given the increasing concern expressed in the media about American domination of Canada, we might expect a significant drop in support for annexation if this were asked today. Second, some respondents may have had in mind that Canada would take over the United States, not vice versa. At the very least, they could have been imagining a situation like the European Common Market, in which national identity is not lost even when closer international ties are established. Third, in the light of Tables 1 and 2 above, which reveal a very high level of national feeling, these opinions about annexation or merger might be best interpreted as an attempt to have the "best of both worlds": support for joining the United States comes from the economically weakest sectors of Canada and not from British Columbia, Alberta or Ontario which probably have had the closest economic ties with the United States.[31]

Table 3
"Canada and the USA should join together as one country"
by Province/Language (1968)*

	Strongly Agree	Mildly Agree	Mildly Disagree	Strongly Disagree	N
National	10%	10	12	61	2767
Newfoundland	23%	19	17	29	48
P.E.I.	6%	6	53	24	17
Nova Scotia	16%	12	9	49	110
New Brunswick	4%	9	12	63	76
Ontario	6%	8	11	71	927
Manitoba	10%	6	14	65	133
Saskatchewan	10%	4	18	58	136
Alberta	4%	11	13	66	235
B.C.	6%	9	11	73	247
Quebec English	8%	7	10	67	122
Quebec French	17%	14	12	45	632
Non-Quebec French	17%	12	11	45	84

*Note: Percentages do not add to 100 per cent because of the omission of "no opinion" responses.

Regardless of the construction one puts on these responses, it is interesting that one in five Canadians in 1968 would contemplate joining the United States en bloc. We would need to know the proportions of such "anti-nationalists" (if they are that) in other countries (such as Mexico, Finland, Holland, Belgium and Portugal) which are contiguous to larger, wealthier, more powerful countries. Only then could we assess whether these figures are unusual.

When social, economic and demographic groups are examined, a strong majority in every category opposes annexation or merger. A few interesting patterns emerge, however, with differences nearly as large as for province/language groups. Language and language-related categories, of course, follow the pattern in Table 3; the French are less opposed to joining the U.S.A. than are the English-speakers, even though they are overall opposed to such a development. Similarly, Catholics, those of French origin, and those who favour Quebec separation also are somewhat more likely to favour a North American union. The differences, however, are modest; and a majority in every case is opposed. It is perhaps ironic that "separatists" (at least in 1968) should express greater willingness to amalgamate two countries at the same time that they seek to disentangle themselves from one of them.

Age, gender, class, occupation and union membership bear no clear or consistent relationship to this issue. Years of education and income, on the other hand, are fairly clearly related negatively to annexation: high income or highly educated individuals oppose such a merger even more than lower income or less educated persons.

The clearest differences in attitude toward annexation occur among the political variables. Partisanship is clearly patterned — the NDP opposes union with the United States very strongly, Créditistes oppose it least of all, with other parties occupying a middle position. As scores on political efficacy and political trust increase, so do the proportions who oppose this merger of countries. All of this suggests that involvement in Canadian political life — by opposing separatism, by feeling efficacious, by trusting the government — has a strong bearing on one's attitudes toward Canadian sovereignty. These same factors, we have seen, appear important in the other measures of attachment to Canada presented in this section. Social factors other than language, on the other hand, have less relevance or none at all. This pattern should be clearly established by now: those people who are most knowledgeable, most involved, and most sensitive to regional and linguistic considerations are precisely the people who have the strongest sense of themselves as Canadians.

Provincial Identifications

Despite their very high level of attachment to Canada compared to other countries, Canadians diverge a great deal in their orientation to their province. In this section we examine how warmly Canadians feel about their own province compared to Canada and how important they think provincial governments are compared to the federal government.[32]

Table 4 summarizes salient features of an index measuring relative "warmth" of feelings about Canada and the provinces. The index has been constructed in a manner analogous to that in Table 2. Scores on the feeling thermometer were compared for "Canada in general" minus "your province in general," "Canada as a place to live" minus "your province as a place to

Table 4
Relative Attractiveness of Canada and the Provinces
by Province/Language Groups (1974)*

	Percentage Most Oriented to Provinces	Percentage Most Oriented Nationally	Mean Scores	Standard Deviations	N
National	4.9%	18.4%	3.64	1.70	2383
Newfoundland	5.9%	3.9%	2.74	1.47	90
P.E.I.	4.2%	2.1%	2.89	1.45	84
Nova Scotia	1.7%	10.9%	3.45	1.48	147
New Brunswick	4.3%	21.5%	4.01	1.65	85
Ontario	0.9%	25.9%	4.29	1.44	651
Manitoba	5.3%	18.6%	3.79	1.69	108
Saskatchewan	6.9%	12.9%	3.53	1.72	94
Alberta	12.0%	6.3%	2.72	1.68	166
B.C.	6.0%	13.5%	3.42	1.67	242
Quebec English	1.5%	37.9%	4.78	1.37	126
Quebec French	9.3%	11.6%	3.21	1.78	531
Non-Quebec French	1.7%	20.0%	3.61	1.65	59

*Note: This index compares "Canada in general" to "your province in general," "Canada as a place to live" to "your province as a place to live," and "Canadian government" to "government in your province." The range is 0-6, with zero being most favourable to your province, and six being most nationally oriented. Percentages do not add to 100 per cent because of the omission of scores 1-5.

live," and "Canadian government" minus "the government in your province." For each comparison, if the Canada score exceeded the provincial score, a code of "two" was given; if they were equal, a "one"; if less for Canada than for the province, a "zero." Hence, cumulating the scores yields an index with a range from zero to six, with *higher scores indicating an orientation more favourable to Canada and less to one's province.* In Table 3, besides the mean and standard deviation, we have included the per cent of each group scoring zero (most provincial) and six (most national in orientation).

On a seven-point (0-6) scale, the numerical midpoint is 3.0, which is only slightly lower than the mean for the entire weighted sample. This suggests that the distribution of views about national and provincial units follows a roughly symmetric curve nearly evenly divided between favouring the province of residence and Canada as a whole. Despite this balance overall, province/language groups exhibit wide variations in mean scores and in the proportions scoring zero or six. Interestingly, Alberta had the largest proportion scoring extremely favourable to the province and the lowest mean score, considerably lower even than the Quebec French. Apparently the anti-federal and pro-independentist feelings in Quebec, at least among the Francophones, were not manifested in liking their province as much as for Albertans and their province. In part, this may reflect dissatisfaction with the Bourassa government in Quebec, which was subsequently defeated in 1976 after this survey was conducted, but it surely also reflects strong positive feelings in Alberta.

Several sociodemographic characteristics correlate with these national and provincial orientations. If a respondent has ever lived in another province, he scores slightly higher in national orientation; and as the number of provinces increases in which he has lived, there is a steady increase in Canadian national orientation. Clearly provincial orientations result, in part at least, from lack of knowledge or familiarity with other parts of the country.[33] As knowledge and experience of other parts of Canada increase, one is more likely to feel more warmly about Canada than about a particular province; but, as we have seen, these factors also increase awareness of ιegional differences. This reinforces the argument that for the majority of respondents regional and national identities are complementary rather than contradictory.

Although there are some minor variations among social and economic groups in relative warmth for Canada compared to the provinces, these are overshadowed by the provincial variations just documented. Some political variables do reveal an interpretable pattern of scores on this index. As expected, respondents who favour the separation of Quebec also score very provincially oriented in this index. Those with no opinion or a qualified position score higher; and the highest (most national) scores occur among those who strongly oppose separation. Similarly, partisan differences probably reflect partisan feelings as much as feelings about governments or political units in the abstract. For example, Liberal supporters are the most strongly federal in orientation, and the Liberal party formed the federal governing party at the time of this survey as it had since 1963. Progressive Conservative supporters are much less federally oriented, though hardly negative about Canada. Similarly, the NDP formed the government in three of the four western provinces at the time of this survey, and its supporters were more likely to feel warmly about provincial units than were the other major party supporters.

Turning now to a direct measure of the perceived importance of the federal and provincial governments,we have in Table 5 data for 1965, 1968 and 1974 on this orientation. The index contains questions about which government has the most effect on "how you lead your life," about which government you are most interested in, and the like.[34]

Nationally and in the case of every province/language group, there has been a decline in the orientation federally from 1965 to 1974. Ontario and the English in Quebec registered a slight increase from 1968 to 1974, but even these two groups are more provincially oriented by 1974 than in 1965.

On a scale from zero to eight, four is the logical midpoint. In 1965 every group scored four or higher, indicating on balance a somewhat greater federal than provincial orientation. By 1974 every group except Ontario and the Quebec English had scores below four, indicating that the balance of perceptions had shifted to one more favourable to the provinces, though still near the midpoint.[35]

Since there is variation within each group, reflected in the standard deviations, we have examined the proportions scoring 0-3 out of 0-8, that is, the most "provincially" oriented respondents. The same conclusions obtain in this analysis as in the mean scores. Ontario (10.6%) and the Quebec English (8.3%) have the fewest provincially oriented respondents by 1974, compared to 22.6 per cent as a national average and much higher proportions in British Columbia (40.6%), Alberta (38.3%), Saskatchewan (33.7%), Prince Edward Island (44.2%), Newfoundland (31.4%) and the Quebec French (26.8%).

Table 5
Perceived Importance of Federal and Provincial Governments
by Province/Language Groups (1965, 1968, 1974)

| | Means and Standard Deviations | | | | | | | | |
| | 1965* | | | 1968* | | | 1974* | | |
	Means	S.D.	N	Means	S.D.	N	Means	S.D.	N
National	4.9	1.8	2118	4.2	1.5	2767	3.9	1.8	2562
Newfoundland	4.5	1.3	24	4.3	1.7	48	3.6	1.7	102
P.E.I.	5.7	1.2	24	3.5	1.2	17	3.3	1.6	95
Nova Scotia	5.1	2.0	72	4.3	1.3	110	3.8	1.7	174
New Brunswick	4.7	1.8	75	3.9	1.3	76	3.8	1.7	93
Ontario	5.4	1.8	693	4.4	1.5	927	4.6	1.7	696
Manitoba	5.1	1.6	123	4.4	1.5	133	3.7	1.9	113
Saskatchewan	5.1	1.7	92	4.2	1.4	136	3.5	1.7	101
Alberta	5.2	1.8	170	4.2	1.6	235	3.4	1.6	175
B.C.	5.0	1.7	127	4.0	1.5	247	3.3	1.6	251
Quebec English	5.3	1.7	84	4.3	1.4	122	4.5	1.6	132
Quebec French	4.0	1.6	559	3.8	1.7	632	3.7	1.7	570
Non-Quebec French	5.2	1.7	75	4.1	1.5	84	3.8	1.6	60

*Zero for each year indicates most provincially oriented and the higher the score, the more federal the orientation; maximum range is zero to eight.

In Table 4 we saw that many groups scored more "warmly" towards the federal than the provincial level, but in Table 5 we can see that, despite that, most groups have come to view the provincial governments as important and the federal government as relatively less important.[36] Apparently respondents can distinguish between realistic assessments of "importance and their own feelings. This distinction must be borne in mind, because it makes it difficult to state unequivocally that people have *exclusive* orientations to one or another level. Their evaluations obviously depend on the issues raised and on the context of the question.

Most sociodemographic variables are unrelated to this assessment of the importance of the levels of government. Several of our earlier measures also suggested that people of many different types shared similar views, with the variation occurring among provinces, between parties, and only slightly among social categories. Other than political attitudes like separatism or partisanship itself, the major correlate of provincialism versus nationalism is residence. People who have lived in several provinces are slightly more national, believe the federal government is more important, and score higher on our index of national identity. Likewise, among immigrants, the longer one has lived in Canada, the more "provincial" he is; and Canadian-born respondents are the most strongly "provincial" according to all of the measures we have presented so far.

Supplementary data about the prevalence of federal and provincial orientations come from a survey conducted by the CBC and Radio-Canada in February and March 1979.[37] Respondents were asked, "When you think of *your* government, which government comes to mind first, the government of Canada or the government of (province)?" The proportion saying "province" ranged from 19 per cent in Ontario to 48 per cent among the Quebec French, with 32 to 41 per cent in the rest of English Canada. In every province but Quebec "Canada" came to mind more often than "province," but in Quebec "both" was a much more common response (18%) than in the other nine provinces (7%).

The question, "which government looks after your interests and needs the best" was also asked. For non-Quebec respondents, 25 per cent said Canada, 47 per cent said their province, and 13 per cent said both equally. In Quebec, the English looked to the Canadian government (54%) or both (22%) and only 11 per cent to the provincial government. French Quebeckers named Canada (30%) or both (21%) less often than province (39%). Despite a Quebec government strongly committed to Quebec interests, more Quebec residents — whether French or English — thought the federal government looked after their interests better than did the residents of Ontario or the West, with only Atlantic Canada (35%) scoring higher. Even in the Atlantic region, however, Canadians clearly put more faith in their provincial governments than in the federal.

When asked which governments should have increased powers if the Canadian constitution were revised, all the groups except the Quebec English favoured the provincial over the federal governments. Except for the Quebec (French and English) respondents, however, the modal response (roughly half) thought the division of powers should be left as they are now.

Questions were asked about whether it was desirable for the respondent's province to put its own interests before the interests of Canada. First, respondents were asked whether this actually happened. Then they were asked if this *should* be done. In Quebec, 61 per cent thought it either was the case or should be; 27 per cent thought the interests of Canada should come first; and 11 per cent did not have an opinion. In the other nine provinces, the results were: provincial interests (50%), national interests (32%), and "don't know" (18%). The modal orientation clearly favoured provincial governments dealing with local interests regardless of national consequences.

These recent poll results indicate, if anything, even greater support for provincial governments, provincial interests and provincial powers than we found in our earlier surveys. Of course, it is difficult to draw sound conclusions when such different types of questions are posed and when new events — such as the election of a separatist government — have intervened. Nevertheless, it seems likely that Canadians of all sorts (except the Quebec English) have come to focus their attention more on provincial levels of government and may identify themselves as much by their provincial residence as by their national citizenship.

The question this raises, of course, is whether the "sense of place" has grown so strong as to be incompatible with a sense of national identity. Several pieces of evidence support the view that these powerful provincial loyalties — even in Quebec — are not really anti-Canadian but are part of what it means to be a Canadian. For one thing, we saw above that "your government" more often meant the federal government than provincial; especially if we combine "Canada" and "both Canada and province," every group in Canada appears more nationally than provincially oriented.

Second, respondents were asked whether their province would have the right to leave Confederation if their provincial government were unable to resolve "some extremely important issues" ("des points extrêmement importants") with the federal government. A distinct minority in every province and language group agreed, ranging from 11 to 20 per cent among the provinces other than Quebec, through 16 per cent of English-Quebeckers, to 35 per cent of French Quebeckers. The modal response for every group was "no," their province did not have the right to leave Confederation under those circumstances.

Finally, these provincial loyalties are negatively related to national loyalties only for Quebec separatists. In the following section, we explore more fully the reinforcing nature of national and provincial feelings on the basis of the 1974 survey.

Multiple Loyalties in Canada

From the facts that provinces elicit strong attachments from many of their residents, and that provinces differ in so many ways from each other, one might conclude that these loyalties override any sense of nationalism or national identity. This conclusion is totally unwarranted, except in the case of a minority of Quebec French respondents with separatist sentiments. We have, for example, seen that the sense of national identity is high, as measured in 1968, at least; and a clear majority of each province/language group in 1974 (even those who favour Quebec separatism) prefers Canada to other countries and feels more warmly towards members of the opposite language groups in Canada than towards citizens of England or the United States.

Further and more impressive evidence can be gleaned from the images of Canada summarized here. Canadians perceive that this country is extremely diverse: it has many regions and it contains many distinct types of people of varying ancestry or origins. There is little sense that Canada should be radically different in these respects from what it is.[38] To identify, therefore, with a region or a language or ethnic group may be equivalent to asserting one's unique identity *within the context of a diverse whole*. To be a special type of person or to live in one region or province rather than another need not be an affirmation of an exclusive identity, but of a partial identity within a grander whole.[39]

The extent to which these particular loyalties and affections reinforce national loyalty may be seen from the correlations in Table 6. We have correlated the scores on the feeling thermometer for different groups of Canadians in 1974 for "Canada" and the respondent's own province for the dimensions of "in general," "as a place to live," and "government." With only very minor exceptions, the correlations are large, significant and positive — those who feel most warmly towards any aspect of their province also feel especially warm towards Canada on that same dimension. Of course, there are individuals who love Canada or their province and dislike the other, but overall these individuals are the exception and not the rule.

Let us clarify what we are measuring here. We are not asserting that most people have the *same* feelings or the *same* degree of warmth towards both Canada and their province. As we saw in Table 4, there are large variations among groups in the extent to which "warmth" of feeling for Canada is greater or less than for their province; nevertheless, this variation occurs in a restricted range, since Table 6 reveals that high (or low) scores on one thermometer are related positively to high (or low) scores on the other. Thus the relatively higher or lower scores for Canada in Table 4 reflect differences within either a generally favourable or a generally unfavourable outlook.

Similarly, the variation in Table 5 reflects assessments of the relative importance for the respondent's life of the federal government compared to that of his province. This estimate of importance has been made by each respondent in the context of his generally positive or generally negative evaluation of *both* levels of government.

Let us examine briefly the distribution of these multiple loyalties. There are many ways in which to approach this question. The one chosen here involves dividing the scores on "Canada in general" for the feeling thermometer into those above and those below the median. This is then cross-tabulated with a division of scores for "your province in general," where each provincial subsample has been segmented at its own median. Thus people who score "low" on both measures may still have a wide range of

Table 6

Correlations between "Warmth" for Canada and for Province of Residence
on "Feeling Thermometer" for Various Subsamples (1974)

	Correlations between "Canada" and "your province"					
	"in general"		"as a place to live"		"government"	
	r*	p*	r	p	r	p
National (weighted)	.30	.001	.41	.001	.28	.001
Atlantic region	.47	.001	.55	.001	.35	.001
Quebec	.16	.001	.31	.001	.51	.001
Ontario	.27	.001	.40	.001	.26	.001
Prairies	.32	.001	.36	.001	.17	.001
B.C.	.20	.001	.44	.001	.04	.29
Non-French	.31	.001	.41	.001	.22	.001
French	.24	.001	.36	.001	.56	.001
Quebec French	.23	.001	.37	.001	.57	.001
Non-Quebec French	.19	.108	.25	.05	.36	.007
Quebec English	.32	.001	.21	.02	.43	.001

* "r" means Pearson correlation coefficient.
* "p" means significance level; .001=.001 or less.

scores, and many even score higher than fifty out of one hundred; but they overall stand as less positive about both Canada and their province than the other groups. The national figures are: 32.9 per cent score above average on both measures, 27.3 per cent score below average on both, 25.5 per cent are above average on "Canada" but below average for their province, and only 14.3 per cent are less "warm" than average for Canada but more warm than average for their province.

Needless to say, these proportions vary somewhat from province to province, but in no province does the group "low" in warmth for Canada and "high" for the province constitute the largest group. The more interesting question is: what kinds of people exhibit these different patterns of competing or reinforcing loyalties?

As we have found repeatedly in this chapter, most social categories play a very small role in accounting for these loyalties, except for language and variables (like religion) closely related to it. Age, gender, country of birth, education, social class and occupation lack any clear and consistent relationship to this typology of loyalties or feelings of warmth.

Respondents who are unilingual English or who use English and a language other than French score higher on Canada and the provincial dimensions and low in the categories of below average on both. The opposite is true for French and bilingual (French and English) respondents. Similarly, Protestants more than Catholics fall into the category of above average for both dimensions.

The most consistent explanatory variables are political. Respondents who feel efficacious are more likely to have strong positive loyalties to both province and Canada. Political involvement, interestingly, reveals no clear pattern, because many "separatists" score high on this variable in 1974.

The strongest relationship is between provincial party affiliation and the typology of loyalties. As expected, supporters of the Parti Québécois score extremely high on the category of provincial loyalty but low on warmth for Canada. The Union Nationale partisans score overwhelmingly in the category of disaffected from both Canada and province, as do the Créditistes and Social Creditors. Progressive Conservatives, Liberals and the NDP — in that order — display the most extensive set of reinforcing loyalties to both Canada and their province.

There is some evidence that personality may play a role in explaining these loyalties, although the data are quite indirect. As we move from above average on both dimensions through conflicting loyalties to below average on both aspects, the feeling thermometer scores decline for all of the following objects: Canadian government, provincial government, the United States, England and France. We speculate — and it is no more than speculation — that part of the roots of these loyalties, or lack thereof, is a general misanthropy factor. People who have cool feelings about any of these objects also have cool feelings about all of them. They are perhaps people who have no clear feelings of acceptance, security and rootedness in Canada or anywhere else.

Of course, these are not independent dimensions. Low self-esteem or misanthropy may relate to low sense of efficacy and to the choice of political outlook and partisanship. All in all, however, it appears that there is a syndrome of discontent with all political objects or a satisfaction with all of them. The Parti Québécois stands as an exception here, since its supporters in 1974 were quite positive about Quebec, despite their generally low sense of attachment to other political objects.

Multiple loyalties or affections clearly exist in Canada. We have tapped only two here — province and country. No doubt there are others as well — local geography, race, language, ethnic group, religion, party and others.[40] It is perhaps easier to see why a strong attachment to a party or a religion need not conflict with a loyalty to Canada; by the same logic, however, an attachment to provinces as places to live, as governments, or in general may reinforce Canadian national identity. After all, they are *Canadian* provinces, and recognized as such by most respondents.

For Canada and Canadians, ". . . a sense of unity is the opposite of a sense of uniformity."[41] In the vast spaces and endless variety of Canada, "what held such people together was not love for each other, it was love of the land itself, the vast empty land in which, for more than three centuries, a certain type of man has found himself uniquely at home."[42] Perhaps Carl Berger's assessment of W. L. Morton's writings on the Canadian West can stand as the best summary of the complex mixture of attachments to Canada and to province or region: that he exemplified ". . . a formula by which loyalty to one was reconciled with affection for the other."[43]

Conclusions and Speculations

Successful federations, by their structure, require and encourage multiple identities and loyalties. There is no logical reason why there must be a hierarchy of feelings such that nationalism blots out regional attachments, or vice versa. Particularistic identities are nurtured within a context provided by the nation as a whole. It is, judging by these data, not even necessary that all people or groups share the same images of that whole within which they are unique parts.

This is a cautiously optimistic conclusion and perspective. Optimistic because it emphasizes that diversity may help to hold Canada together, may be a feature of which most Canadians are proud. But cautious because there can clearly be circumstances in which citizens feel that they must choose between identities and loyalties, however painful that choice may be. The separatist political movement in Quebec exemplifies this danger. The reason a choice appears necessary is not hard to find: many Quebecois sense that the diversity of Canada is not sufficiently broad or sufficiently respected to harbour and protect their identity as Francophones. Perhaps they are correct in their assessment. It is apparent, however, that such fears will be encouraged rather than dampened by policies which imply that provincial and local loyalties must be eradicated in order to strengthen Canadian national identity. One can hope that the evidence in this chapter and throughout this book will help citizens and political leaders resist temptations to suppress diversity in the pursuit of unity.

This conclusion is optimistic for another reason. The multiple and reinforcing identities outlined here are strongest among those people who are most knowledgeable about Canada. Most Canadians know a great deal about the United States and feel quite warmly towards Americans, yet they prefer Canada. Similarly, the more extensive their familiarity with several parts of Canada and the more sensitive Canadians are to regionalism, the more they favour the federal government over their provincial governments and the higher they score on the measure of national identity, regardless of provincial, linguistic or social backgrounds. Stanley Morse found in Saskatchewan that those respondents who had had the most contact with foreigners and who had had the most opportunity to travel abroad were the ones who most frequently stressed that being a Canadian and being a resident of Saskatchewan were integral elements of their self-image.[44]

The literature on ethnocentrism reveals other possibilities.[45] In-group solidarity and identity have frequently been found to be positively related to out-group stereotyping and hostility. Perhaps Canada is unusual, but the evidence presented here suggests that ignorance of other nations — and ignorance of one's own nation — are associated with parochial and localistic sentiments. Canadian nationalists, by comparison, are very cosmopolitan and feel warmly towards several other nations.

In the persistent wrangling which characterizes relations among provincial governments and between federal and provincial governments in Canada, there is a common frame of reference: Canada.[46] The poorer provinces did not take kindly to former Prime Minister Trudeau's repeated remarks that they should be content because they are so much better off than most nations throughout the world. No, they asserted that the relevant point for them concerned being relatively less advantaged than certain other Canadian provinces or regions. Surely this contains an element of rhetoric, but it also manifests the potency of reinforcing identities within a Canadian nation-state.

It is particularly appropriate that provincial leaders exhibit a concern for this national frame of reference within which to pursue their particular — and often divergent — goals of economic and social development. The evidence is clear that federal policies and the spread of information have reduced regional disparities in the provision of services of important types.[47] Any Canadian who moves from one province to another will experience much less dislocation and suffer much less change in amenities like health and medical care, pensions, social services and education than if he were to leave Canada and settle in any other country in the world.

This is hardly novel or surprising. And yet so many analysts and politicians in Canada speak as though these vivid regional sentiments were illicit, as though by themselves they accounted for the high or low standard of living in various parts of Canada or were responsible for the weakness of the Canadian dollar. My assessment is quite different. Without a "sense of place," without "the imaginative sense of locality," without the pride in one's region, there would be much less support for and affect toward Canada. I do not know which is correct: "I am a British Columbian, and therefore I am a Canadian," or "I am a Canadian, and this makes me part of British Columbia." But either way it works, there can be for most Canadians no pleasure in being forced to choose between one identity and another.[48] Multiple loyalties can have, therefore, a civilizing result, since they encourage us to reject absolute choices and teach us to give assent and express dissent in graduated and qualified terms.

Notes

1. Grateful acknowledgment is hereby given to Brenda Beck, Donald E. Blake, Richard Simeon and especially Alan C. Cairns for comments on an earlier draft of this chapter.

2. Richard Simeon, "Regionalism and Canadian Political Institutions," *Queen's Quarterly*, 82 (Winter 1975): 499-511.

3. Donald Creighton, *Towards the Discovery of Canada: Selected Essays* (Toronto: Macmillan, 1972), p. 281.

4. Benjamin N. Schoenfeld, *Federalism in India* (Washington, D.C., 1960), p. 21, cited by Norman D. Palmer, *The Indian Political System*, 2d ed. (Boston: Houghton Mifflin, 1971), p. 104.

5. Anthony Careless, *Initiative and Response: The Adaptation of Canadian Federalism to Regional Economic Development* (Montreal: McGill-Queen's University Press, 1977).

6. J.M.S. Careless, "'Limited Identities' in Canada," *Canadian Historical Review*, 50 (1969): 1-10, makes a similar argument.

7. Edwin R. Black and Alan C. Cairns, "A Different Perspective on Canadian Federalism," *Canadian Public Administration*, 9 (1966): 27-44; Cairns, "The Governments and Societies of Canadian Federalism," *Canadian Journal of Political Science*, 10 (December 1977): 695-725; and Larry Pratt, "The State and Province-Building: Alberta's Development Strategy," in *The Canadian State*, ed. Leo Panitch (Toronto: University of Toronto Press, 1977).

8. Northrop Frye, *The Bush Garden: Essays on the Canadian Imagination* (Toronto: Anansi, 1971), p. iii.

9. Alex Inkeles and Daniel Levinson, "National Character: The Study of Modal Personality and Sociocultural Systems," in *The Handbook of Social Psychology*, 2nd ed., ed. Gardner Lindzey and Elliot Aronson (Reading, Mass.: Addison-Wesley, 1969), 4: 418-506.

10. John Porter, "Canadian Character in the Twentieth Century," *The Annals of the American Academy of Political and Social Science* (March 1967), 370: 48-56; Ted G. Harvey, Susan K. Hunter-Harvey, and W. George Vance, "Nationalist Sentiment Among Canadian Adolescents: The Prevalence and Social Correlates of Nationalistic Feelings," and Paul G. Lamy, "Political Socialization of French and English Canadian Youth: Socialization into Discord," both in *Socialization and Values in Canadian Society*, ed. Elia Zureik and Robert M. Pike (Toronto: McClelland and Stewart, 1975), 1: 232-262, 263-280. For discussions of ways in which the language cleavage is more complex, encompassing more than "dual character," see John Meisel, *Working Papers on Canadian Politics*, 2d ed. (Montreal: McGill-Queen's University Press, 1975), chap. 3, and H.D. Forbes, "Conflicting National Identities Among Canadian Youth," in *Foundations of Political Culture: Political Socialization in Canada*, ed. Jon H. Pammett and Michael S. Whittington (Toronto: Macmillan, 1976), chap. 15, pp. 288-315.

11. Margaret Atwood, *Survival: A Thematic Guide to Canadian Literature* (Toronto: Anansi, 1972); Northrop Frye, *The Bush Garden*.

12. Louis Hartz, ed., *The Founding of New Societies* (New York: Harcourt, Brace & World, 1964); Kenneth D. McRae, "The Structure of Canadian History," in *The Founding of New Societies*, ed. Hartz; Gad Horowitz, "Conservatism, Liberalism and Socialism in Canada," *Canadian Journal of Economics and Political Science*, 32 (May 1966): 141-71; Gad Horowitz, "Notes on 'Conservatism, Liberalism and Socialism in Canada,'" *Canadian Journal of Political Science*, 11 (June 1978); 383-99.

13. Seymour Martin Lipset, "Revolution and Counterrevolution: The United States and Canada," in his *Revolution and Counterrevolution*, rev. ed. (Garden City, N.Y.: Anchor Books, 1970), pp. 37-75; S.M. Lipset, "Value Differences, Absolute or Relative: The English-Speaking Democracies," chap. 8 of his *The First New Nation* (Garden City, N.Y.: Anchor Books, 1967); Tom Truman, "A Critique of Seymour M. Lipset's Article, 'Value Differences, Absolute or

Relative: The English-Speaking Democracies,'" *Canadian Journal of Political Science*, 4 (December 1971): 497-525; Charles Taylor, *The Pattern of Politics* (Toronto: McClelland and Stewart, 1970).

14. Donald V. Smiley, *The Canadian Political Nationality* (Toronto: Methuen, 1967); Philip Resnick, *The Land of Cain: Class and Nationalism in English Canada, 1945-1975* (Vancouver: New Star Books, 1977).

15. For a sensitive discussion of the concept of national identity, see John Meisel's contribution to *Options Canada* (Proceedings of the Conference on the Future of the Canadian Federation, University of Toronto, 1977), pp. 14-33, which contains many interesting observations about the specific content of Canadian identity. See also Mildred Schwartz, *Public Opinion and Canadian Identity* (Don Mills, Ont.: Fitzhenry & Whiteside, 1967), chap. 2.

16. Forbes, "Conflicting National Identities among Canadian Youth."

17. For further detail on the matters summarized below, see "Regional Consciousness in Canada," chap. 2 of H.D. Clarke et al., *Political Choice in Canada* (Toronto: McGraw-Hill Ryerson, 1978), Jon H. Pammett, "Public Orientation to Regions and Provinces," in *The Provincial Political Systems: Comparative Essays*, ed. D.J. Bellamy, J.H. Pammett, and D.C. Rowat (Toronto: Methuen, 1976).

18. The questions were: "People often think of Canada as being divided into regions, but they don't always agree on what the regional divisions are. We would like to know if you think of Canada as being divided into regions? (If yes) What region do you live in? What are the other regions of Canada?"

19. Mildred Schwartz, *Politics and Territory: The Sociology of Regional Persistence in Canada* (Montreal: McGill-Queen's University Press, 1974), p. 311, makes the useful point that "regions" exist only as parts of a broader perceptual field, which in this case is Canada. H.D. Forbes, "Conflicting National Identities Among Canadian Youth," in *Foundations of Political Culture: Political Socialization in Canada*, ed. Pammett and Whittington, contains some interesting observations on the use of "North American" as a description of self.

20. Schwartz, *Politics and Territory*, p. 325, summarizes Gallup Poll data showing that most parts of the country favour "Maritime union," although in the Maritime provinces themselves somewhat more oppose than favour this merger of provinces into one political unit.

21. Schwartz, ibid., summarizes Gallup Poll data showing that, while a majority in each region opposed the unification of the Prairie provinces, a substantial minority favours this idea in each region.

22. Schwartz, ibid., chaps. 1 and 12, has an extensive discussion of some of the consequences based on her analysis of the 1965 Canadian national election study.

23. Allan Smith, "The Continental Dimension in the Evolution of the English-Canadian Mind," *International Journal*, 31 (Summer 1976): 442-469.

24. Six variables were recoded into trichotomous categories, with zero indicating a non-Canadian orientation, one indicating a neutral or ambivalent orientation, and two indicating a clear Canadian orientation. For example, respondents were asked "Who would you say have more in common: French Canadians and French people from France, or French Canadians and English Canadians, that is to say, English-speaking peoples of British ancestry?" Only those respondents who thought French Canadians and English Canadians were most alike were scored as "two"; those who alleged the similarity of French Canadians and French were scored as "zero"; and all others were scored as "one." A similar question and scoring procedure were used for ascertaining the perceived similarity of English Canadians compared to French Canadians and to residents of Britain. A third question compared English Canadians to French Canadians and to Americans. A fourth question asked how Canadians think of their society. "Canadian" responses (scored "two") included "multicultural" or "mosaic," "French and English partnership," or "just Canada." Zero scores were assigned to those responses indicating ties to another

country — such as "an English country," "part of the Commonwealth," "a satellite of the U.S.A.," or "a French country." An analogous question was asked about the respondent's self-image: "two" was assigned to respondents who replied "simply Canadian" or "Canadian"; zeros were given to answers like English Canadian, French Canadian, Quebecois, or another "ethnic" answer (such as Swedish), which indicated a relatively exclusive orientation to a part rather than to the whole of Canada; with neutral, DK or "other" responses scoring as "one." Finally, those who agreed (strongly or mildly) that Canada should merge with the U.S.A. were coded as "zero"; those who disagreed were coded as "two"; and those who had no opinion were coded as "one."

25. Although not quite comparable, a nationwide poll of urban dwellers recently found overwhelming feelings that Canada is "the best country in the world." For example, 87% of English-speaking and 75% of French-speaking Canadians agreed that Canada was best. There was some regional variation, but a clear majority everywhere agreed. See "The Weekend Poll" in *Weekend Magazine* (July 1, 1978), p. 3. The poll of 1139 people was conducted in 32 of the largest urban centres in mid-1978.

26. Similar conclusions may be drawn from John Johnstone, *Young People's Images of Canadian Society* (Ottawa: *Study*, No. 2, Royal Commission on Bilingualism and Biculturalism, 1969), p. 14; Ronald Manzer, *Canada: A Socio-Political Report* (Toronto: McGraw-Hill Ryerson, 1974), pp. 153-5; Schwartz, *Public Opinion and Canadian Identity*, pp. 114-116; and Michael S. Whittington, "Children and the Monarchy: Canadian Perceptions of the Queen," in *Foundations of Political Culture*, ed. Pammett and Whittington, pp. 240-250.

27. See the discussion in Whittington, "Children and the Monarchy."

28. The "feeling thermometer," which was used to assess these feelings of "warmth," asks the respondents to assign a score between 0 and 100 to each object, with low scores representing "coolness," 50 meaning "neutral," and higher scores signifying degrees of "warmth."

29. See Chapter 4 of this book, "The Horizontal Mosaic," for discussions of immigrants and migrants in the Canadian political cultures.

30. See also J. Alex Murray and Mary C. Gerace, "Canadian Attitudes Toward the U.S. Presence," *Public Opinion Quarterly*, 36 (Fall 1972); 388-97; and Forbes, "Conflicting National Identities Among Canadian Youth."

31. Of course, a generalized attachment to Canada or opposition to merger with the United States does not entail rejection of material or intellectual products of the U.S. See, for example, Manzer, *Canada: A Socio-Political Report*, pp. 110-15, 125, 130, 135.

32. See Edwin R. Black, *Divided Loyalties: Canadian Concepts of Federalism* (Montreal: McGill-Queen's University Press, 1975) for an extensive discussion of how Canadian conceptions of federalism have changed over time.

33. Fred Schindeler, "Perceptions of Federal-Provincial Relations in Ontario," (Paper presented at the Annual Meeting of the Canadian Political Science Association, Montreal, June 1972), p. 37, found that Ontario respondents who received at least some of their schooling outside Ontario were the most "federal" in orientation.

34. In interpreting the figures, two things must be borne in mind. First, some questions were asked in all three years, but several were asked only once or twice. Hence, part of the variation across time may reflect the effects of question changes rather than changes in attitude. Second, the 1974 figures were calculated in a slightly different fashion from those in 1965 and 1968. In the two earlier surveys, there were only four relevant questions, yielding an index with a range from 0-8, whereas in 1974 the range was 0-10, since the index on that year was based on five questions. Scores for 1974 have been adjusted to a 0-8 range to make them comparable to 1965 and 1968.

35. Schwartz, *Public Opinion and Canadian Identity*, p. 93, presents Gallup Poll data for 1943 to 1960, which shows that the balance of opinion even then was quite solidly opposed to taking more power away from the provinces and centralizing it in Ottawa. People were particularly

strong in rejecting the notion that provinces should be "abolished and the whole country governed from Ottawa."

36. This greater weight given to provinces in general and to provincial governments in particular may stem from a realistic assessment of trends in the size of governments and in the assertiveness of provincial leaders in an era of "big government." See the perceptive discusssion in Alan C. Cairns, "The Other Crisis of Canadian Federalism," an inaugural address as Visiting Professor of Canadian Studies, University of Edinburgh, November 17, 1977.

37. Canadian Broadcasting Corporation and Société Radio-Canada, Confederation/Referendum (March 1979), mimeographed.

38. Forbes, "Conflicting National Identities Among Canadian Youth," p. 303, in summarizing the English-Canadian students' view of themselves as more similar to Americans than to French Canadians, but opposed to merger with the U.S., states: "The assumption implicit in these opinions is that cultural differences need not be a barrier to national unity, nor cultural similarities necessarily grounds for political union."

39. But see Forbes, "Conflicting National Identities Among Canadian Youth," pp. 309-313, for some cautious remarks about the assimilative tendencies of English-Canadian students.

40. Forbes, "Conflicting National Identities Among Canadian Youth," pp. 293-295, 308-313, discusses the ambiguous nature of "hyphenated-Canadian" labels like French-Canadian or Italian-Canadian. For suggestive data on French-English relations and attitudes toward "other ethnic" groups, see John W. Berry, Rudolf Kalin, and Donald M. Taylor, Multiculturalism and Ethnic Attitudes in Canada (Ottawa: Supply and Services Canada, 1976).

41. Frye, The Bush Garden, p. vi.

42. Blair Fraser, The Search for Identity: Canada, 1945-1967 (Toronto: Doubleday, 1967), p. 314.

43. Carl Berger, The Writing of Canadian History (Toronto: Oxford University Press, 1976), p. 256.

44. Stanley J. Morse, "Being a Canadian: Aspects of National Identity Among a Sample of University Students in Saskatchewan," Canadian Journal of Behavioural Science, 9 (1977): 265-273.

45. Robert A. Levine and Donald T. Campbell, Ethnocentrism: Theories of Conflict, Ethnic Attitudes, and Group Behaviour (New York: Wiley, 1972).

46. For a classic study, see Richard Simeon, Federal-Provincial Diplomacy: The Making of Recent Policy in Canada (Toronto: University of Toronto Press, 1972).

47. Richard Simeon and Robert Miller, "Regional Variations in Public Policy," Chapter 8 below, and Dale H. Poel, "The Diffusion of Legislation among the Canadian Provinces: A Statistical Analysis," Canadian Journal of Political Science, 9 (December 1976): 605-626.

48. See the poignant remarks of Solange Chaput Rolland, My Country, Canada or Quebec? (Toronto: Macmillan, 1966), such as p.18: "Though a resident of Halifax is a Maritimer first, he resents me for being, as a French Canadian, a Quebecer first." To be a Maritimer or a Quebecker first clearly implies that although second, Canadian identity is also important.

II

Provincial Political Cultures in Canada[1]

Richard Simeon, David J. Elkins

The Framework of Analysis

Canadian politics is regional politics; regionalism is one of the pre-eminent facts of Canadian life, whether reflected in the principles of cabinet-building, the acrimony of federal-provincial conferences, or the virtual elimination of class voting on at least a national scale.[2] The concept of regionalism has been given a wide range of different meanings in the study of Canadian politics. It has been used to refer to regional differences in basic social and economic characteristics, such as economic bases, levels of income or religious and ethnic makeup. It has also been employed as a summary of patterns of cleavage and conflict — the West versus central Canada, and so on. It has most recently been understood as referring to the regional character of electoral behaviour, party strength and party systems.[3] In all of these senses, though, it has had a descriptive, rather than an explanatory, role.

We explore another dimension of regionalism. To what extent do the populations of the Canadian provinces differ in some basic orientations to politics? What are the sources of such differences? Do they indicate the persistence of what may be called "regional cultures"?

Regional or provincial differences in sense of efficacy, in the degree of citizens' trust in their governments, and in the degree and type of involvement in political matters, the dimensions we examine, may be the result of cultural variation, broadly conceived — in other words, of the ethos or community norms of an area deriving from particular historical forces and events. But three other explanations have also been advanced to account for these differences in attitude.

First, writers like Lane see the relevant explanation in terms of personality characteristics: efficacy emerges from a general sense of personal competence; trust in government from a general sense of trust in mankind and an experience of benign social relations in one's own life.[4] Second, these

31

attitudes may be linked to various socioeconomic and demographic indicators, such as age, education or class.[5] Thus, for example, Maritimers might have a lower sense of efficacy than British Columbians because on the whole Maritimers are less educated, less affluent and more rural than the latter group. Third, trust, efficacy and involvement may stem from the actions and effectiveness of the political authorities themselves — that is, they may not always reflect anything personal about the citizens but represent more or less realistic responses to the "objective" realities of political life. For example, survey researchers have found a striking decline in trust in the government among Americans in recent years, presumably stemming at least partly from involvement in Vietnam and from the failure to deal adequately with social tensions.[6]

In most instances there are probably complex interactions among these types of explanation. Nevertheless, in so far as regional differences in attitudes can be explained in any of these ways, one hesitates to call them cultural differences or to attach any independent causal potency to them. If any of the above explanations hold true, then regionalism simply reflects varying mixes of categories of individuals who have fundamentally similar orientations but who populate different regions in different proportions. For example, the NDP appears to be basically an urban party, and the greater incidence of that party in Ontario and British Columbia, compared to the Maritimes, may reflect no more than the widely differing demographic composition of these regions. We will therefore speak of regional political cultures only where substantial interprovincial differences remain or are enhanced after plausible control variables are introduced.[7]

Our suggestion, then, is that over and above regional differentiation in terms of the above three factors there exist in Canada what may justly be termed regional political cultures. More specifically, there are substantial regional divergences in some of the basic attitudes towards politics and political activity displayed by mass publics which cannot be accounted for by any plausible control variables. Differences in history, patterns of settlement, ethnic composition and even institutions make it likely that we can isolate such cultural attitudes and beliefs. Many writers have described the differing political ethos of Canada's regions and provinces: among them are E.R. Black on British Columbia's "politics of exploitation,"[8] C.B. Macpherson on Alberta,[9] S.M. Lipset on Saskatchewan,[10] and P.E. Trudeau and the Tremblay Report on Quebec.[11]

Two further caveats are necessary. The first concerns the explanatory status of the concept *culture*. We do not mean to imply by the above discussion that cultures are not caused. Instead, we wish to emphasize that routine differences in the distribution of personal, social and demographic characteristics, and in the distribution of political institutions and events, do not constitute culture. Only where these factors do not account for regional variation will we entertain the use of culture as a label for these phenomena.

Second, we use the term regionalism simply as a descriptive statement about the way provinces or other areas differ. It is not an explanation. Regions are containers, and other factors are necessary to account for variations in their contents.[12]

In spite of these limitations, and other constraints posed by the data available, it is useful to explore the range of regional differences in some basic orientations to political life in Canada and to see what accounts for them. The three sets of attitudes we have chosen — efficacy, trust and involvement — are important components of most definitions of political culture.[13] It has been argued frequently that political life should be affected by the extent to which citizens trust the government, by whether they feel a sense that the government is important in their lives, and by the extent to which they feel they can influence it. However, we use these concepts somewhat differently from Gabriel Almond and Sydney Verba. For them, these orientations are the basic components of political culture itself. We treat them instead as attitudes which may be explained by culture or by other factors.

Unfortunately, the question of the causal significance of cultural variables has never been squarely faced. Almond and Verba go no further than suggesting that the "civic culture" is "congruent with" democratic political life.[14] Their implicit model is that political culture, as part of a wider societal culture, is largely shaped by extra-political factors such as family and school socialization patterns and that political culture in turn shapes political life. As Brian Barry and others point out, however, the causal arrow may in fact run the other way, especially when "culture" is operationalized in questions such as Almond and Verba and other writers have used.[15] The effectiveness and responsiveness of governments, the actions of political elites and parties, the structure of political competition and conflict, and related features may determine whether people have a sense of efficacy, whether they trust the government, and whether they think it important to them.[16] A recent study suggests that differences between blacks in Newark and blacks in Detroit on some of these dimensions are most easily explained by differences in the actions of the two city governments.[17] Villagers in Laurence Wylie's Peyrane felt the government to be remote, hostile and arbitrary, perhaps because it was indeed all of those things.[18] In the data below we shall see that residents of Quebec view their provincial government as more important to them than residents of other provinces see their provincial governments — no doubt in part because it does have more impact on its citizens than do other provincial governments on theirs.

By restricting our analysis to regional differences which remain after major alternative explanatory variables are controlled, we implicitly define cultural variation in terms of the pattern of relationships among variables. If a control for class, for example, has not reduced interregional variation on some dependent variable, then obviously the remaining variance reflects the fact that class is associated with the dependent variable in different ways, or to different degrees, in these regions. This approach must be interpreted with considerable caution, because it will be easy for readers to conclude too much from our analysis. For example, we do not wish to imply that descriptive differences between regions are unimportant because they are "eliminated" by appropriate control procedures or that only cultural variables are of political interest. Quite the contrary. The greater urbanization and industrialization of some regions and the differing demographic features of regional populations are undoubtedly important in shaping the issues dominant in their respective areas. All we say is that we are concerned with a conceptually different problem. Regionalism and cultural variation are both important; but what they mean in terms of concrete political actions awaits analysis informed by more ample and more sophisticated data.

Since regions may be defined in a variety of ways, it is important that we clarify at the outset how we approached this problem. We shall look in this chapter primarily at differences among the Canadian provinces, which can be seen as analytically distinct political systems. We treat the provinces comparatively, asking first how their populations differ in patterns of political orientations and, second, what explains the differences. But because language is such an important cultural dimension in Canada, we have added a language component to the basic ten-province division. Hence, for most of the analysis, we employ twelve "province/language" regions: the non-French-speaking in the ten provinces and two French-speaking groups (those in Quebec and those outside of Quebec).[19] Because of the small samples in most regions it was not feasible to examine French-speakers separately except in Quebec. We have had to eliminate Prince Edward Island from some of the tables, again because of the small number of respondents. Furthermore, when extensive control variables are introduced, cell sizes dwindle rapidly in the smaller provinces. Accordingly, tables grouping the Atlantic and Prairie provinces were prepared to supplement the twelve-region tables. But, because it is dangerous to assume citizens of geographically proximate areas share the same attitudes,[20] only the twelve-region tables are presented. The loss of numbers seemed less severe than the submergence of provinces.

This way of defining regions, while adequate for exploratory purposes, has the peculiar result that evidence of regionalism and of cultural divergences is somewhat reduced compared to other procedures. For example, to find differences, as we do, between the non-French-speaking residents of Quebec and the Francophones there can be interpreted simply as an interesting regional difference. But, of course, if one recalls that both groups are part of the same provincial political system, then that fact sets both groups off more sharply from other provinces. In other words, the relative proportions of French and non-French-speakers is a contextual feature which is masked by our means of distinguishing regions. Given the data limitations, we cannot overcome this problem; instead, we call the reader's attention to it.

Data and Procedures

As noted in the introduction, we have relied on data from nationwide electoral surveys in 1965, 1968 and 1974.[21] In addition, we have created special merged data files in order to have sufficient cases in each province-language group.[22] One consequence of that procedure, of course, is the loss of historical variation among the time periods. To compensate for this loss, we have included a few tables summarizing the 1965 or 1968 data. In those tables, as well as in the tables not reproduced here, there are no substantial or theoretically interesting differences between the year-by-year results and the merged data. In addition we must note that these studies were directed primarily at understanding national politics, whereas our interest lies more in the provincial context; and only a small part of the original studies was concerned with the cultural dimensions we discuss.

The data must therefore be assessed with considerable caution. It is difficult to know what questions on trust and efficacy are measuring.[23] It is especially hard to gauge the intensity of feelings expressed, or to know the extent to which respondents are making ritualistic responses to what, after all, are rather common clichés about politics. They may also respond on the basis of transitory events in their provinces. Moreover, the questions may have somewhat different meanings, and the answers may express somewhat different types of feelings, from province to province.[24] Many of the questions direct the respondent to nothing more specific than government in general; they do not distinguish between federal and provincial governments in all cases, or between elected politicians and bureaucrats.[25]

These cautionary notes may be construed as a further "explanation" of observed regional differences. In other words, in addition to personality, social and demographic characteristics, and political events, provincial differences may in part reflect response errors because of nonequivalence of questions and responses across social and regional lines. We have taken steps to try to assess this possibility. For one thing, we have built complex indicators of the basic variables, as explained below, rather than relying on single item measures of efficacy, trust and involvement. Perhaps of equal importance, we have compared the results for 1965, 1968 and 1974. In so far as response error or related matters account for provincial differences, they should be reduced by combining answers to several items, often worded in quite different formats, since it is unlikely that misunderstanding would follow the same lines on different types of questions. It is also implausible that the same misunderstandings and response errors should follow the same regional lines in consecutive samples utilizing different respondents.[26] Since we obtained virtually identical results for all three samples, we are satisfied that such differences as remain can be only in the very slightest degree manifestations of these artifactual problems. In fact, the results were so similar that in most instances we have presented only those for the merged data set so as not to burden the text unduly with extraneous material.

Although we outline the technical details of scales and types of analysis when we present the findings, it may be useful to outline here the general steps taken in constructing the basic measures of efficacy, trust and involvement. We first examined every question asked in each year to compile a master list of all possible items of relevance, plus some that we did not expect to be relevant. The purpose of the latter items was to see if our procedures could separate out these items, or whether our preconceptions "built in" the results.[27] We are happy to say that the procedures discriminated satisfactorily. Factor analyses were performed on the total sample for each year, and for each of seven subgroups as follows: five regional groups of non-French-speakers (Maritimes, Quebec, Ontario, Prairies and British Columbia), and two French-speaking groups (Quebec and non-Quebec). The small samples made it impracticable to do factor analyses for each province separately.

With minor variations in the loadings of a few items, each regional and national analysis yielded the same structure. There were basically three factors of interest, which were fairly clearly interpretable as follows: a combined efficacy-trust factor (with a large number of items), an involvement factor, and a miscellaneous factor containing a few items we had thought might be in the first two factors plus the extraneous items mentioned above.

Guttman scaling procedures showed that the efficacy and trust items could be treated either separately or combined. We report them separately, but we have conducted all of the analyses on a combined scale as well, with similar results which are not reported to avoid duplication. We do not report the details of these Guttman procedures for several reasons. First, we are not satisfied that they are the most appropriate tests of scalability, since they assume unidimensionality which appears to us to be an excessively stringent requirement in cultural analysis. Second, the number of items is relatively small compared to what Guttman feels is required for satisfactory tests.[28] This, we might note, is a feature of most scales using the procedures, and is not a peculiarity of our study. Finally, the questions and items were chosen for the original study for different reasons, with no apparent expectation of their use in this manner. Had we designed the study, the focus would have been quite different and we would feel more confident applying these statistical procedures. The reader will note, however, that the patterns of relations in the findings constitute a form of construct validation which appears to us to satisfy the needs of an exploratory study.[29]

We have reported no chi-square tests for the tables, since they are all significant — a reflection of the large numbers of respondents as well as of the very substantial regional differences. We have, however, included confidence intervals in Tables 1, 2, 5, 8 and 9; similar confidence intervals are also relevant in the other tables where the Ns and proportions are the same. It is important to note that confidence intervals alone do not provide an adequate picture of the magnitude and reliability of differences. For one thing, we are concerned mostly with the range of differences across all regions and not just with the comparison of any two regions.[30] Second, most of the differences withstand a double test, namely, application of control variables and replication in three different years. We do not present the 1965 or 1974 results in most cases because the two years were so nearly identical to 1968. Third, as noted above, interprovincial differences are muted by the removal of the French-speaking groups to separate categories. Were they grouped with their provincial fellow citizens, this would raise the Ns as well as heighten certain contrasts. Finally, this is an exploratory study, and while significance tests are useful they are only aids in forming hypotheses. They would help, for example, to guide future researchers' decisions about the size of samples needed in the Maritimes and whether the Atlantic provinces can usefully be grouped into a common region. The significance of regional differences in the Prairies has the same purpose and result.

Regional Contrasts in the Basic Dimensions

Sharp differences between provincial and language groups emerge from the data. Most striking is the division into two main groups. One is made up of the respondents living in poorer, less economically developed areas, whether English- or French-speaking. It includes people from the Atlantic provinces and French Canadians both inside and outside Quebec. At the other extreme are residents of the then two wealthiest provinces, Ontario and British Columbia. Ranged between, but closer to the second group on most dimensions, are residents of the Prairie provinces. The non-Quebec Francophones provide an interesting case study of a group under cross-pressure. They score very low on efficacy and trust but very high on political involvement. In later chapters we will discover other fascinating features of this unusual group. The analysis to follow will focus mainly on the two polar groups, but some quite large differences within each group must be noted. The English-French differences have received much more attention from Canadian scholars and will not be the central focus of this analysis.[31]

We will first examine the gross differences between regions or what we have called "regionalism."

Political Efficacy

Political efficacy refers to a sense that one can be personally influential in politics, can make one's voice heard, and can be effective. Table 1 presents the 1968 distribution of responses on a scale divided into three categories.[32] It also presents mean scores and standard deviations for each province. Table 2 gives the pattern of responses on the merged data set which combines 1968 and 1974. (In 1965 there were too few items to form a satisfactory scale.)

The basic divisions are dramatically illustrated. Among the Atlantic provinces and both French-speaking groups, between half and two-thirds of the respondents rank low on the efficacy scale in 1968 and in the merged data

Table 1
Efficacy Scores by Province-Language Groups, 1968 (Percentage Down)*

	NAT	NFLD	NS	NB	QE**	QF**	ONT	MAN	SASK	ALTA	BC	Non-QFR**
Low	44	65	59	64	42	58	34	38	48	40	24	63
Medium	45	31	35	29	46	36	50	50	42	50	63	33
High#	11	4	6	7	12	6	15	13	10	9	13	4
Means***	1.79	1.23	1.41	1.24	1.90	1.39	2.09	1.98	1.71	1.83	2.29	1.11
Standard deviation	1.28	1.21	1.21	1.23	1.27	1.21	1.25	1.26	1.32	1.23	1.10	1.15
N =	2767	48	110	76	122	632	927	133	136	235	247	84
Confidence intervals†	1.85	13.49	9.19	10.79	8.84	3.85	3.22	8.50	8.40	6.39	6.02	10.32

* Prince Edward Island has been eliminated because there were only 17 respondents.

** The abbreviations in this and other tables refer to provinces: QE refers to English-speaking residents of Quebec; QF to French-speaking Quebeckers; and non-QFR to French-speakers living outside Quebec.

The small proportions scoring "high" reflect the fact that a respondent had to "pass" every item in the scale to obtain that score.

*** The means and standard deviations are based on the raw scores, 0–4.

† These are 95 per cent confidence intervals on the proportion nearest 50 per cent in each column. The confidence interval bounds the area of variability around the regional scores; 95 per cent of any random variation will fall within the stated interval. For example, Newfoundland and Nova Scotia differ by less than either of their confidence intervals, whereas they are both significantly different from Ontario and the western provinces.

Table 2

Efficacy Scores by Province-Language Groups, Merged Data (1968 and 1974) (Percentage Down)

	NAT	NFLD	PEI	NS	NB	QE	QF	ONT	MAN	SASK	ALTA	BC	Non-QFR
Low	40	52	52	45	56	39	54	31	39	39	38	21	55
Medium	49	44	41	45	37	49	40	53	50	50	53	64	40
High	11	4	8	10	7	12	7	16	11	12	9	15	5
Means*	1.72	1.53	1.56	1.65	1.50	1.72	1.53	1.85	1.72	1.73	1.71	1.94	1.50
Standard deviations	0.66	0.58	0.64	0.66	0.62	0.66	0.62	0.67	0.65	0.66	0.62	0.60	0.60
N =	3970**	97	66	196	121	183	912	1269	192	188	320	374	111
Confidence intervals***	1.56	9.95	12.06	6.96	8.84	7.24	3.24	2.75	7.07	7.15	5.47	4.86	9.26

* Means and standard deviations are based on scores of "low" equals "one," "medium" equals "two" and "high" equals "three." We could not use the full range of scores since the items differ somewhat in 1968 and 1974.

** The 1974 national sample is weighted; all provincial samples are unweighted.

*** These are 95 per cent confidence intervals, as explained in Table 1.

set. In British Columbia the figure is less than one-quarter, rising to about one-third in Ontario. On the Prairies and among the Quebec English, about four out of ten persons rank low. At the other end of the scale, we find fairly large proportions in Ontario, British Columbia and among the Quebec English ranking high; somewhat lower levels on the prairies; and much lower levels in the rest. Variations in the mean scores tell the same story.

Individual items reinforce these impressions. Asked what they thought they could do to influence the federal government if it were considering a bill they felt wrong or unfair, only one out of five British Columbians in 1968 answered "nothing" or said they did not know. (In British Columbia, at least, western alienation, if it exists, does not seem to imply a sense of power-lessness.) In the Maritimes over two-thirds said they could do nothing. This question is very similar to one asked by Almond and Verba in their five-nation study.[33] The gap between the two Canadian extremes, Newfoundland and British Columbia, appears to be even larger than that between Italy and the United States.

The other items follow a similar pattern, with only minor variations. For example, in the English-speaking sections west of New Brunswick, generally less than 45 per cent agree with the statement that people like them have no say in what the government does. Among Maritimers and the French-speaking, 60 per cent or more feel they have no say.

In addition to the basic groupings, some variations stand out. British Columbia seems to have the greatest proportion of respondents with a strong sense of efficacy. On the Prairies, respondents in Manitoba have higher levels of efficacy than those in either Alberta or Saskatchewan. In the Atlantic region, the proportions in Nova Scotia contrast somewhat with those in Prince Edward Island, New Brunswick and Newfoundland. French Canadians in Quebec, perhaps because they control "their" government in the province, seem more likely to be efficacious than their confreres outside the province.

One of the simplest but most vexing questions to ask of figures like these is, how impressed should one be? What is striking — how large the regional differences are, or how small? Whether we regard the glass as half full or half empty, and whatever the perspective, these figures are striking. That a minority (24 per cent) in British Columbia has only a low sense of efficacy, but that in several other provinces a substantial majority do, suggests a quite different political centre of gravity. It is hard to believe that differences of this magnitude do not reflect or contribute to important differences in the nature of politics across Canada.

Political Trust

Here we ask: to what extent do citizens feel government and politicians to be competent, concerned for, and interested in their welfare and worthy of

Table 3
Political Efficacy: Responses to Individual Questions by Province-Language Group (Percentage)

	NAT	NFLD	PEI	NS	NB	QE	QF	ONT	MAN	SASK	ALTA	BC	Non-QFR
*1974**													
1. MP acts on problem (percentage "No" or DK)	48	33	61	45	47	57	60	40	51	29	53	44	52
2. People like me have no say (percentage agree and strongly agree)	53	67	65	44	51	51	70	45	66	58	51	37	48
3. Politics too complicated (percentage agree and strongly agree)	65	86	63	57	80	66	63	62	85	71	75	56	82
4. So many voters, no use in voting (percentage agree and strongly agree)	14	18	20	20	27	18	22	10	19	10	14	6	4
1968													
1. "What could you do . . . ?" (percentage saying "Nothing" or DK)	43	88		63	71	38	55	32	40	51	41	22	71
2. People like me have no say (percentage agree)	47	54		57	61	42	56	41	35	42	43	38	69
3. Politics too complicated (percentage agree)	69	65		78	68	69	73	64	76	72	72	69	73
4. Elections make government pay attention (percentage saying, "A good deal.")	47	52		46	37	48	32	55	56	47	47	60	39
1965													
1. People like me have no say (percentage agree)	50	38		64	73	52	50	47	50	57	41	43	64

(See Table 1 for confidence intervals.)

*In 1974, because of over sampling of some provinces and under sampling of Ontario and Quebec, the national averages are weighted averages; the provincial percentages are based on unweighted Ns.

respect? Political trust is conceptually related not to potential activity, but to support for and satisfaction with the political regime.[34]

Table 4 summarizes the 1968 distribution of scores and gives the means and standard deviations for each region. Once again, the regional differences are clear, though the magnitude appears somewhat smaller than with efficacy. Residents of British Columbia, Manitoba and Ontario, rank high in levels of trust. Maritimers, especially New Brunswickers, rank low. Alberta seems somewhat out of place, with almost half of its respondents scoring low, along with those in Nova Scotia and the non-Quebec French. The French-speaking groups, which were very close to the Atlantic provinces on the efficacy dimension, are more likely to trust the government.

The merged data for 1965 and 1968 follow these general lines quite closely, except that Saskatchewan scored much less trusting in 1965, giving it a middling score in the merged data. (There were no political trust items in the 1974 study.)

The individual items reveal similar patterns, as seen in Table 6. In each of the English-speaking areas outside the Maritimes more than 55 per cent of respondents felt they could "trust the government to do the right thing" all or most of the time. The figure was about 10 per cent lower for the French-speaking, and another 10 per cent lower for the Atlantic provinces. The proportions agreeing with the statement that there are hardly any crooks in the government ranged from 40 per cent in British Columbia to 7 per cent in New Brunswick. French Canadians were slightly less likely than any others to agree that the government wastes a lot of money; on this question the variations were small. British Columbians were most likely, Prince Edward Islanders and New Brunswickers least likely, to consider government officials generally able and competent. The striking fact about the final question is not the regional difference, but the virtual unanimity across the country that the government pays special attention to "the big interests." Interestingly enough, the responses to the other questions suggest that many voters do not see this as rendering the government less trustworthy in other respects.

Supporters, Critics, Deferentials and the Disaffected: a Typology

Political efficacy or citizen competence refers to a respondent's own perception of his ability to influence the course of governmental affairs. Trust refers to his sense that the government is generally helpful, beneficial, trustworthy and capable. On both dimensions we have found wide variations within Canada. But how are the two related? Logically, it is easy to see that they may be independent: those who trust the government may or may not feel that they themselves are able to influence it; they may either see themselves as political actors shaping policy or as the recipients of policies developed by persons better and wiser than themselves. Similarly, one who distrusts the government may either feel powerlessness to change it or be

Table 4
Trust Scores by Province-Language Groups, 1968 (Percentage Down)

	NAT	NFLD	NS	NB	QE	QF	ONT	MAN	SASK	ALTA	BC	Non-QFR
Low*	41	58	49	64	39	44	37	34	37	47	32	49
Medium	44	33	38	28	50	45	45	44	48	40	47	38
High	15	8	13	8	11	11	18	23	15	14	21	13
Means	1.96	1.42	1.68	1.33	1.99	1.81	2.11	2.27	2.00	1.80	2.28	1.74
Standard deviations	1.37	1.27	1.37	1.39	1.30	1.28	1.39	1.39	1.37	1.39	1.36	1.44
N =	2767	48	110	76	122	632	927	133	136	235	247	84

(See Table 1 for confidence intervals.)
*On a scale from 0-5, low=0-1; medium=2-3; high=4-5.

Table 5
Trust Scores by Province-Language Groups, Merged Data (1965 and 1968) (Percentage Down)

	NAT	NFLD	PEI	NS	NB	QE	QF	ONT	MAN	SASK	ALTA	BC	Non-QFR
Low	41	44	59	43	65	40	44	36	38	43	43	34	43
Medium	45	36	37	42	29	47	45	46	44	47	42	48	44
High	15	19	5	15	7	13	11	18	18	11	15	18	13
Means*	1.75	1.75	1.46	1.73	1.42	1.73	1.67	1.83	1.80	1.68	1.73	1.84	1.69
Standard deviations	0.70	0.76	0.60	0.71	0.61	0.68	0.66	0.71	0.73	0.66	0.71	0.71	0.68
N =	4885	72	41	182	151	206	1191	1620	256	228	405	374	159
Confidence intervals	1.39	11.48	15.08	7.19	7.61	6.81	2.83	2.43	6.08	6.47	4.81	5.06	7.72

*The means are scored as in Table 2.

confident of his ability to do so. There are thus good grounds for believing that trust and efficacy are analytically independent.

Indeed, the location of individuals along these two dimensions may provide important clues about their roles as citizens and political actors. We can imagine a typology of four citizen types. The first consists of those who profess both a positive sense of political efficacy and a sense of trust. These "supporters," as we term them, come closest to the conventional ideal model of the trusting and active citizen. Second are those at the other extreme, who have neither faith in the government nor a sense of being able to do much to influence it. We would expect them to be apathetic and disengaged from politics, though perhaps available for mobilization under some conditions. We shall call them the "disaffected."[35] Third are those who trust the government, but who do not feel much ability to influence it. This comes close to what is meant by the notion of deference: government looks after one's interests, but it is something to be left to others, something which is remote from the ordinary citizen. They are labelled "deferentials." Finally, there are those who do not really trust the government but who do have some confidence about their ability to affect it. They may be actual or potential activists, easily mobilized to support protest activity. As William Gamson points out, "A combination of high sense of political efficacy and low political trust is the optimum condition for political mobilization."[36] They will be labelled "critics." If these suggestions are correct, and if we find differing distributions of the citizen types in the various provinces, we should have some important clues about differences in the conduct of politics.

The typology was operationalized by dichotomizing the trust and efficacy scales, then relating them to each other.[37] In the national sample, 26 per cent fall in the supporter category, 34 per cent in the disaffected, 10 per cent in the deferential and 30 per cent in the critic group, as may be seen in Table 7. There is a significant association between the two dimensions. The Pearson correlation coefficient between efficacy and trust is .35 in the national sample. Supporting the possibility of regional cultural differences is the fact that the relationship varies among the provinces, though it is positive in all cases. The Pearson correlation is .47 in Alberta, .25 in British Columbia and .31 in Ontario.

Some support for the characterization of the political types given above is available. Tables not reported here show that critics and supporters are considerably more likely to vote and otherwise participate in politics than are the other two categories. Nationally, supporters and deferentials were considerably more likely to support the Liberals than were the other two categories. The critics were much more likely to support the NDP than were the others.

The regional distribution follows the pattern found before. In New-foundland, New Brunswick and Nova Scotia a majority of respondents are disaffected. About 45 per cent of French Canadians, in or out of Quebec, are

Table 6
Political Trust: Responses to Individual Questions by Province-Language Groups, Merged Data (1965 and 1968)

	NAT	NFLD	PEI	NS	NB	QE	QF	ONT	MAN	SASK	ALTA	BC	Non-QFR
1. Trust government to do what is right (percentage always or most of the time)	58	56	37	49	43	60	49	65	65	55	61	62	53
2. People running government are crooked (percentage hardly any)	28	28	7	31	15	26	17	34	39	25	28	40	30
3. People running government are smart (percentage all)	44	38	24	39	27	44	46	46	47	44	43	48	36
4. Government gives everyone a fair break (percentage everyone)	12	17	12	12	9	13	11	14	14	8	10	10	13
5. Government wastes a lot of money (percentage some, not much)	55	56	46	53	36	56	59	54	45	51	51	60	52
N =	4885	72	41	182	151	206	1191	1620	256	228	405	374	159

Table 7
Four Citizen Types by Province-Language Groups, 1968 (Percentage Down)

	NAT	NFLD	NS	NB	QE	QF	ONT	MAN	SASK	ALTA	BC	Non-QFR
Supporter	26	8	17	10	29	17	31	32	26	30	38	14
Deferential	10	13	6	10	11	13	8	11	10	4	9	17
Critic	30	27	24	25	30	25	35	31	26	29	38	23
Disaffected	34	52	53	54	30	44	26	26	38	36	15	46
Total percentage	100	100	100	99	100	99	100	100	100	99	100	100
N =	2767	48	110	76	122	632	927	133	136	235	247	84

(See Table 1 for confidence intervals.)

in this category. The figure drops to about 37 per cent in Alberta and Saskatchewan, 26 per cent in Ontario and Manitoba, and to only 15 per cent in British Columbia. The order is reversed among the supporters: British Columbia has the greatest proportion, at 38 per cent, and the Maritimes, especially Newfoundland and New Brunswick, the least.

Regional differences in the proportion of critics and deferentials are much less sharp. The French Canadians, especially those from outside Quebec, were somewhat more likely than other groups to be deferential. The lowest levels were in Alberta and Nova Scotia. Critics were most common in British Columbia (38 per cent) and in Ontario (35 per cent). They were least prominent in the Maritimes and among the French Canadians.

Involvement

The substantial differences among the provinces on the trust and efficacy dimensions would lead us to expect parallel findings when we examine political activity and involvement, since many studies suggest there is a positive relationship between activity and the other elements. In order to examine differences in political involvement, a scale was constructed using data from the 1965 and 1974 studies.[38] There were few activity and involvement questions in 1968, so it was impossible to construct a scale.

The results in Tables 8, 9 and 10 are surprising. Provincial differences are very small and, if anything, suggest a higher level of involvement in the Maritimes than anywhere else. The 1965 mean score for the Maritimes as a whole was 3.38, compared with 3.33 among the Quebec French, 3.31 in Ontario, and 3.26 in British Columbia. Slightly fewer ranked high on involvement in the Maritimes than elsewhere, but considerably fewer Maritimers were ranked low.

The regional patterns of responses varied considerably from question to question.[39] People in Prince Edward Island were the most likely to report having voted in all federal elections, and the other Maritime provinces were close behind. Most surprisingly, the French Canadians, both inside and outside Quebec, were considerably more likely to report voting in all federal elections than the non-French-speaking populations in Ontario, British Columbia or Manitoba. Frequency of voting in provincial elections was led by the French-speaking and Maritimers. There was little variation in the attendance at election meetings, but the highest proportion was in the Maritimes. Differences in reported interest in the election were small, though the New Brunswick respondents and the Quebec French were considerably more likely to report little interest.[40]

The expected regional differences did show up on questions asking whether the respondents tried to influence other voters and whether they read party literature, but even here the magnitude of differences was considerably less than with trust and efficacy.

Table 8
Political Involvement by Province-Language Groups, 1965 (Percentage Down)

	NAT	NFLD	NS	NB	QE	QF	ONT	MAN	SASK	ALTA	BC	Non-QFR
Low*	36	29	35	27	38	33	36	37	40	45	38	31
Medium	41	50	44	49	36	42	40	48	30	38	38	40
High	23	21	21	24	26	24	24	15	29	18	24	29
Means	3.29	3.50	3.25	3.37	3.27	3.33	3.31	3.10	3.47	2.91	3.26	3.43
Standard deviations	1.90	1.35	1.77	1.72	2.03	1.91	1.88	1.73	2.42	1.83	2.02	1.90
N =	2118	24	72	75	84	559	693	123	92	170	127	75
Confidence intervals	2.09	20.00	11.47	11.31	10.38	4.09	3.65	8.83	10.01	7.48	8.44	11.09

*On a scale from 0-11, low = 0-2; medium = 3-4; high = 5-11.

Table 9
Political Involvement by Province-Language Groups, Merged Data (1965 and 1974) (Percentage Down)

	NAT	NFLD	PEI	NS	NB	QE	QF	ONT	MAN	SASK	ALTA	BC	Non-QFR
Low	34	32	15	30	26	30	31	35	36	40	46	37	27
Medium	43	48	51	42	49	43	44	42	48	33	37	41	45
High	24	21	34	29	25	27	25	24	16	28	18	21	28
Means*	1.89	1.89	2.19	1.99	1.99	1.97	1.93	1.89	1.80	1.88	1.73	1.84	2.02
Standard deviations	0.75	0.72	0.68	0.77	0.72	0.76	0.75	0.76	0.70	0.82	0.75	0.75	0.74
N =	3321**	73	73	158	120	145	839	1035	182	144	255	254	102
Confidence intervals	1.68	11.46	11.47	7.69	8.94	8.05	3.36	3.00	7.26	7.99	6.11	6.06	9.66

* The means are scored as in Table 2.
**The 1974 national sample is weighted; provincial samples are unweighted.

Table 10
Political Involvement: Responses to Individual Questions, Merged Data (in Percentages)

	NAT	NFLD	PEI	NS	NB	QE	QF	ONT	MAN	SASK	ALTA	BC	Non-QFR
1965, 1968, and 1974:													
1. Very interested in politics	29	24	16	27	22	37	16	35	34	34	31	33	26
2. Voted in all federal elections	58	53	70	59	59	64	63	59	52	59	44	49	62
3. Voted in all provincial elections	51	51	65	55	53	51	64	48	40	50	36	42	56
N =	7330*	174	136	356	244	338	1761	2316	369	329	580	625	219
1965 and 1974:													
1. Tried to influence others	22	14	16	21	17	23	21	24	17	24	24	21	27
2. Attended political meetings	17	19	33	23	23	16	20	14	13	21	16	15	26
3. Read about politics	71	67	81	67	64	77	60	77	78	69	73	75	63
4. Helped in campaign	7	6	14	13	13	9	7	7	4	10	5	7	9
N =	3321*	73	73	158	120	145	839	1035	182	144	255	254	102

*The 1974 national sample in both analyses is weighted; provincial samples are unweighted.

On questions tapping activity and political behaviour, then, French Canadians and Maritimers rank at least as high as the others, despite a much more pervasive cynicism about politics and a sense that there is little the individual can do to influence government. Nor is this anomaly explained by a greater belief that what governments do has serious consequences. On this more psychological dimension of involvement, the differences once again mirror those on trust and efficacy. Thus the 1968 survey asked respondents how much difference they felt the government in Ottawa made in their lives. In Ontario, Alberta, British Columbia and Manitoba about 70 per cent reported that Ottawa made a great deal of difference, and less than 10 per cent responded "not much." As expected, the Quebec French-speakers perceived the least federal impact: only 26 per cent reported a good deal, and 41 per cent said not much. In the three Atlantic provinces, and among the French outside Quebec, between 22 and 31 per cent reported the federal government had little impact, despite the rather large federal role in the welfare of these provinces.

Since the highest voting turnout is in the Maritimes, we would expect this area to display the greatest partisanship, and sense that important consequences flowed from the results of elections.[41] Respondents in 1968 were asked how much difference it made which party was in power at each level. The *least* sense of partisan difference was found in the Maritimes and among the French-speaking groups. British Columbians were most likely to perceive important differences at *both* levels. Only 19 per cent in British Columbia felt it made no difference which party was in power federally. This rose to 35 per cent among the non-Quebec French, 42 per cent in Nova Scotia, 48 per cent among the French-speaking in Quebec and 51 per cent in New Brunswick. At the provincial level, 12 per cent in British Columbia said it made no difference, as did 22 per cent in Ontario, 30 per cent in Nova Scotia, 37 per cent in New Brunswick, 38 per cent in Newfoundland and 43 per cent among the Quebec French. The last figure suggests French Canadians are remote not just from federal politics, but from all politics. British Columbians, on the other hand, see politics at both levels as being important.

We have thus an interesting anomaly: actual participation patterns seem to contradict what would be expected from efficacy, trust and psychological involvement. The reason is unclear. One possibility is that for many in the Maritimes and Quebec, political activity is in a sense non-political; rather, it is a ritual or a social activity carried on with little reference to the affairs of state. In the absence of adequate data to test this supposition, we pose it as a hypothesis for future research.

Summary

The data on efficacy, trust and involvement suggest some characterizations of the patterns of orientations to politics found in the mass populations of the

Canadian provinces. British Columbia, Manitoba, Ontario and English Quebec are what might be called citizen societies. In all of them, though most strongly in British Columbia, we find relatively high levels of both trust and efficacy. Only in Ontario, British Columbia and Manitoba do supporters outnumber the disaffected. In addition, in these latter provinces a substantial proportion of those who distrust the government are confident of their ability to do something about it: they are much more likely to be critics than to be disaffected. This is not to say these provinces have perfectly homogeneous populations: many British Columbians are passive and disaffected too. Each type is found in each province; it is the proportions which differ.

At the other extreme are the disaffected societies: Newfoundland, New Brunswick and, to a lesser extent, Nova Scotia.[42] Here the proportions of citizens who neither trust their government nor feel able to influence it are very large. The relatively small proportion of critics suggests that hostility to the government is less likely to be translated into political action. Both French-speaking groups lie close to the Atlantic provinces: the major difference is that levels of trust are higher, with the result that there are fewer in the disaffected category and somewhat more in the deferential group. Saskatchewan and Alberta are quite similar to each other, which is especially interesting given their quite different political traditions and levels of wealth. Together they seem to lie about midway between the polar groups, though there is considerable variation in their positions from question to question. Finally, we have seen that the variation in the basic dimensions of trust and efficacy do not lead as expected to sharp differences in mass political activity.

On most of the measures used, British Columbia stands out as the province with the highest levels of trust and efficacy and the greatest degree of psychological involvement in politics, though not the highest activity levels.[43] Given the widespread discussion of western alienation, this is perhaps all the more striking since the questionnaire, while usually not specifying any particular level of government, was administered in the context of a federal election. New Brunswick stood out at the opposite extreme, and this impression is reinforced when we consider that a large proportion of the non-Quebec French are also New Brunswickers.

There is some affinity among regional groupings of provinces, but geographical proximity by no means coincides with similar patterns of orientations. The quite striking difference between Manitoba and its two Prairie neighbours is one example. Nova Scotia's position also differs considerably from that of its neighbours.

Regional Differences Resulting from Control Variables

What lies behind these differences between the Canadian provinces and language groups? Several possibilities immediately present themselves. The most plausible is that they are a reflection of some other differences between provinces. We know that the Canadian provinces differ in basic demographic characteristics, such as ethnic backgrounds, distribution of the population between rural and urban areas and predominance of different religious affiliations. We also know that there are large variations in the socio-economic characteristics of provincial populations — in educational, income and occupational distributions. All of these factors have been found in other contexts to correlate with the dimensions examined here. Indeed, we may ask, are the regional differences merely artifacts of these other differences?

In order to test this possibility, we introduced a variety of control variables to ascertain whether, once their effects were eliminated, regional differences remained. If so, the search for explanations would have to move to some less easily quantifiable variables, such as historical background and experience, traditional community norms and variations in the actual performance and responsiveness of political authorities in the different parts of the country. It is only if these latter types of variable seem important that we can begin to talk with confidence of regional political cultures; this is, in fact, what we find.

Introduction of the control variables also permits us to look at the simultaneous effects of regional and socioeconomic variables. We can ask whether variations *within* provinces follow similar patterns, or whether a control variable with major effects in one province has little or a different impact elsewhere.

The effects of the control variables were examined in two ways. First, we prepared cross-tabulations of the control variables with the dependent variables within each province. The controls introduced here include self-defined class,[44] objective class as indicated by education, federal and provincial party identification,[45] age, gender and community size. Second, an analysis of variance procedure was used to help sort out the separate and joint effects of the regional factor and the socioeconomic ones.

A major debate in the literature of Canadian political science is between those who advocate a class interpretation of Canadian politics and who see regionalism as exaggerated and artificial, and those who argue that class is uniquely unimportant in Canada and that region and language are the crucial variables.[46] Much of the time this debate is cast in either/or terms, as if one or the other is *the* factor. This is obviously shortsighted: class may explain some dependent variables better than regionalism does and vice versa. More important, *both* sorts of variables are likely to have an effect on Canadian attitudes and political behaviour. That is certainly the case here: class is important; region is important — and each has an effect when the other is controlled for. Given the importance of the debate, our analysis will focus on the joint effects of class and region.

Efficacy

The importance of class identification is immediately evident in Table 11. In each province, except New Brunswick, the mean score on efficacy declines as

Table 11

Mean Efficacy Scores by Province-Language Groups Controlling for Subjective Class and Education, Merged Data (1968 and 1974)

	NAT	NFLD	PEI	NS	NB	QE	QF	ONT	MAN	SASK	ALTA	BC	Non-QFR
A. Subjective Class*													
Upper	2.05	—**	2.00	1.67	—	1.92	1.91	2.19	—	—	2.10	2.40	—
Middle	1.80	1.63	1.50	1.82	1.66	1.72	1.59	1.91	1.80	1.89	1.86	1.94	1.75
Working	1.59	1.49	1.56	1.53	1.42	1.60	1.38	1.71	1.66	1.55	1.53	1.87	1.50
B. Education													
0-3 years	1.23	1.33	—	1.57	—	—	1.13	1.27	1.00	—	1.18	—	1.42
4-7	1.41	1.45	1.25	1.61	1.48	1.52	1.36	1.55	1.40	1.29	1.20	1.79	1.28
8-10	1.60	1.48	1.38	1.44	1.35	1.52	1.51	1.70	1.66	1.66	1.55	1.73	1.58
11-13	1.89	1.66	1.75	1.85	1.75	1.87	1.68	1.96	1.84	1.91	1.88	2.04	1.67
14-17	2.04	—	2.33	—	—	1.93	1.85	2.08	1.94	2.25	2.10	2.15	—
Over17	2.29	0***	—	—	0	1.78	2.18	2.36	—	—	—	2.25	0

* We have combined "upper-" and "upper-middle-class" identifiers as "upper," and "lower-" and "working-class" identifiers as "working."

** Dashes indicate 5 or fewer respondents in the cell.

*** Zero is not a mean score; it indicates no cases in the cell.

Table 12

Mean Efficacy Scores by Province-Language Groups Controlling for Federal Party Identification, Merged Data (1968 and 1974) (Percentage Down)

	NAT	NFLD	PEI	NS	NB	QE	QF	ONT	MAN	SASK	ALTA	BC	Non-QFR
Party Identification*													
Liberal	1.76	1.54	1.60	1.68	1.59	1.75	1.56	1.88	1.87	1.88	1.94	1.99	1.59
Conservative	1.71	1.64	1.50	1.65	1.45	1.73	1.47	1.86	1.52	1.76	1.67	1.90	1.33
NDP	1.81	—	—	1.86	—	—	1.76	1.85	1.76	1.64	1.67	2.00	1.14
Social Credit–Créditiste	1.53	0***	0	0	0	—	1.44	—	—	0	1.44	1.86	0
Other	—**	0	0	0	0	0	—	0	—	—	0	0	0
None	1.61	1.30	1.56	1.55	1.52	1.61	1.50	1.73	1.60	1.53	1.57	1.82	1.36

* Only federal identification is presented, since controlling for provincial party identification yields the same conclusions.

** Dashes indicate 5 or fewer respondents in the cell.

*** Zero is not a mean score; it indicates no cases in the cell.

one moves from upper through middle to working class. At the same time, as one looks horizontally across the table, the provinces differ from each other in all class categories. Within any one class the mean score varies, just as we expect on the basis of the provincial norms in Tables 1 and 2. In fact, in the highly efficacious provinces like Ontario and British Columbia, the working-class respondents score higher than do the upper- or middle-class respondents in less efficacious provinces like Nova Scotia. In other words, provincial averages cannot simply reflect the proportions of upper-class or working-class identifiers, since these groups vary so much from one province to another.

Education has the same effect as class. With only minor exceptions, a greater amount of education means a greater sense of efficacy. The gap between educational categories, however, varies from province to province. In different provinces the critical point at which educational level affects the sense of efficacy seems to vary too. In every educational category, and most especially in the middle ones, provincial differences persist. At the lower and upper ends of the scale there seems to be somewhat of a convergence, but regional differences are still noticeable even there.

Party identification, reported in Table 12, is rather weakly related to efficacy in the national sample. NDP identifiers are the most likely to have a strong sense of efficacy, followed in fairly even steps by Liberals, Conservatives and others. Region makes a much greater difference than party. In several areas there is very little distance between members of different parties: Quebec, Ontario and British Columbia stand out. In other provinces, most notably Alberta and Manitoba, the distance between Liberals and Conservatives is very great.

Contiguous provinces sometimes reveal markedly different patterns. For example, contrast Social Credit identifiers in Alberta and British Columbia or Liberals and Conservatives in the Atlantic provinces.

An interesting finding concerns those persons who profess no party identification at all. Their mean scores parallel very closely the provincial averages in Table 2. This reinforces the conclusion that regions are as important as party, if not more so, in shaping the sense of efficacy.

Controlling for party, it is clear that any party identifier is more likely to share the feelings of his provincial fellow citizens than he is those of his party colleagues across the country. This no doubt affects intraparty politics as well as provincial interparty relations. This is one of our central themes, and we shall return to it repeatedly in later chapters.

Trust

The relationship between political trust and class or education is almost identical to that for efficacy. As we see in Table 13, with the exception of British Columbia, higher class equals higher degree of trust. Similarly, again excepting British Columbia, the more education, the greater the sense of trust

Table 13

Mean Trust Scores by Province-Language Groups Controlling for Class and Education, Merged Data (1965 and 1968)

	NAT	NFLD	PEI	NS	NB	QE	QF	ONT	MAN	SASK	ALTA	BC	Non-QFR
A. Subjective Class													
Upper	1.85	—*	—	1.80	—	1.83	1.83	1.85	2.07	—	2.00	1.79	1.67
Middle	1.81	1.75	1.42	1.90	1.67	1.72	1.73	1.87	1.90	1.77	1.81	1.86	1.75
Working	1.68	1.70	1.41	1.63	1.31	1.70	1.60	1.79	1.72	1.61	1.66	1.85	1.66
B. Education													
0-3 years	1.41	1.25	—	1.11	—	—	1.38	1.57	1.25	1.13	1.44	1.50	1.50
4-7	1.59	1.76	—	1.61	1.38	1.60	1.60	1.69	1.39	1.35	1.51	1.72	1.55
8-10	1.72	1.79	1.39	1.63	1.40	1.75	1.69	1.80	1.81	1.68	1.71	1.72	1.77
11-13	1.84	1.86	—	2.00	1.39	1.68	1.81	1.85	1.84	1.84	1.76	1.98	1.93
14-17	1.89	—	—	1.71	1.88	1.91	1.77	1.94	2.21	1.88	1.84	1.86	1.63
Over17	1.98	0**	0	—	—	1.89	1.94	2.00	—	—	2.29	1.63	—

* Dashes indicate 5 or fewer respondents in the cell.

**Zero is not a means score; it indicates no cases in the cell.

Table 14
Mean Trust Scores by Province-Language Groups Controlling for Federal Party Identification,
Merged Data (1965 and 1968)

	NAT	NFLD	PEI	NS	NB	QE	QF	ONT	MAN	SASK	ALTA	BC	Non-QFR
Party Identification													
Liberal	1.85	1.80	1.55	1.85	1.60	1.81	1.76	1.90	2.06	1.84	1.91	2.06	1.70
Conservative	1.72	1.61	1.38	1.72	1.34	1.71	1.70	1.85	1.65	1.67	1.61	1.72	1.68
NDP	1.64	0*	0	—	1.17	1.63	1.73	1.67	1.49	1.53	1.64	1.76	1.64
Social Credit— Créditiste	1.56	0	0	0	—	—	1.45	—	—	—	1.67	1.73	—
Other	1.58	0	0	0	0	0	1.44	—	0	0	—	—	0
None	1.64	1.88	—**	1.56	1.35	1.53	1.59	1.71	1.85	1.54	1.78	1.63	1.71

* Zero is not a mean score; it indicates no cases in the cell.

**Dashes indicate 5 or fewer respondents in the cell.

in government and elected officials. On the whole, the absolute differences between classes or between educational categories, nationally or in any province, are somewhat less than for efficacy, but the pattern is quite clear. Trustful provinces reflect their trust in each class or education level.

Higher status individuals appear to converge slightly relative to regional norms, while working-class or less well-educated respondents reveal wide variation from province to province.

Party identification is clearly related to trust in Table 14, as it is at the provincial level which has not been included to save space. Since they support the governing party in this period, the Liberal identifiers generally score as more trusting than other parties. Nevertheless, even they are far from homogeneous, ranging from 2.06 in British Columbia to 1.55 in Prince Edward Island. As in Table 12, those repondents with no party identification follow the provincial norms quite closely.

Citizen Types

Nationally, class and education are related to the classification of four political types. Table 15 shows that the proportion of supporters and critics rises as one moves from working to upper classes. Working-class citizens are much more likely to be deferentials or disaffected.

Among the supporters this relationship holds in each province, though the magnitude of class differences again varies somewhat from province to province: six percentage points separate middle and working classes in British Columbia and only slightly more in Ontario and French Quebec. Nineteen points separate the classes in Nova Scotia, and seventeen in Alberta and Saskatchewan. Within each class, regional variations persist; and in each class British Columbia has the largest proportion of supporters and Newfoundland the smallest.

In each province the working class is likely to feel more disaffected than the middle or upper classes. But in British Columbia, which has the fewest disaffected, the gap is virtually nonexistent. The sharpest class differences are, as before, in the Maritimes and on the Prairies. The range among the provinces is considerably larger within the working class than in the middle class.

The small overall proportion of deferentials makes it harder to isolate provincial and class variation, but it appears that deference decreases with rising status and varies among regions.

Overall class differences in the critic category are rather small: they are almost invisible in Quebec, Ontario, Manitoba and Saskatchewan. By far the highest proportion of critics is found in British Columbia's working class. Regional variations exist but they are generally smaller than those found previously.

Objective class differences, as evidenced by the control for education in Table 16, yield the same message: there are considerable differences between

Table 15
Citizen Types Controlling for Class by Province, 1968

	NAT	NFLD	NS	NB	QE	QF	ONT	MAN	SASK	ALTA	BC	Non-QFR
1. Supporter												
Upper	38	—	20	—	30	29	41	—	—	59	53	—
Middle	31	7	31	21	32	19	34	40	35	38	41	24
Working	20	10	12	9	19	11	26	25	18	21	34	14
2. Deferential												
Upper	5	—	0	—	15	3	6	—	—	6	0	—
Middle	8	7	6	36	10	12	6	10	8	3	7	6
Working	12	10	7	2	15	17	12	15	10	5	10	16
3. Critic												
Upper	39	—	40	—	30	42	43	—	—	29	41	—
Middle	32	40	25	7	31	26	36	33	29	33	37	29
Working	28	23	20	26	31	22	32	32	25	24	40	22
4. Disaffected												
Upper	18	—	40	—	25	26	10	—	—	6	6	—
Middle	29	47	39	36	27	43	24	17	29	26	15	41
Working	40	57	62	63	35	50	30	28	47	49	16	47
N =	2613	46	101	61	117	614	883	122	131	216	237	69

Table 16
Citizen Types Controlling for Education by Province, 1968

	NAT	NFLD	NS	NB	QE	QF	ONT	MAN	SASK	ALTA	BC	Non-QFR
1. Supporter												
Less than 10 years	17	5	11	10	20	12	23	21	16	17	22	9
10-13	36	10	30	7	38	26	37	37	37	36	51	20
13+	45	—	29	—	35	33	44	63	50	59	52	—
2. Deferential												
Less than 10 years	13	16	8	12	10	15	13	15	8	7	14	20
10-13	6	0	3	7	10	11	4	7	15	2	5	7
13+	5	—	0	—	17	6	4	6	0	0	3	—
3. Critic												
Less than 10 years	26	24	15	17	25	23	30	31	23	22	43	20
10-13	36	40	33	50	38	25	40	35	28	40	34	33
13+	37	—	71	—	26	42	38	19	50	30	36	—
4. Disaffected												
Less than 10 years	45	54	66	61	44	50	34	32	54	54	22	51
10-13	23	50	33	36	15	38	20	22	20	22	11	40
13+	4	—	0	—	22	19	15	13	20	11	9	—
N =	2767	48	110	76	122	632	927	133	136	235	247	84

Table 17
Citizen Types Controlling for Party Identification by Province, 1968

	NAT	NFLD	NS	NB	QE	QF	ONT	MAN	SASK	ALTA	BC	Non-QFR
1. Supporter												
Lib.	31	4	28	21	31	20	36	44	30	44	49	17
PC	23	13	14	9	31	17	29	14	26	24	34	0
NDP	25	—	—	—	—	53	22	25	29	11	27	0
Other	18	—	8	0	17	10	26	26	12	26	28	18
2. Deferential												
Lib.	11	19	5	17	13	14	9	16	11	6	9	19
PC	10	0	7	11	15	20	9	10	13	3	11	14
NDP	5	—	—	—	—	0	7	4	4	0	0	29
Other	8	—	8	0	4	11	8	5	6	5	10	0
3. Critic												
Lib.	28	26	20	21	27	22	32	23	30	39	32	29
PC	31	38	26	23	31	24	35	38	34	28	40	0
NDP	40	—	—	—	—	6	44	54	18	44	55	14
Other	29	—	27	40	38	32	31	16	12	20	39	9
4. Disaffected												
Lib.	29	52	48	42	29	44	23	16	30	11	10	36
PC	36	50	52	57	23	39	27	38	28	44	14	86
NDP	31	—	—	—	—	41	27	17	50	44	18	57
Other	44	—	58	60	42	48	35	53	71	50	23	73
N =	2767	48	110	76	122	632	927	133	136	235	247	84

classes which are consistent in direction but not in magnitude in each province; and within each educational category, interprovincial differences remain apparent. Indeed, when one decomposes each province into educational categories it appears that the regional differences loom larger than they do when each province is taken as a whole. For example, in the whole disaffected group, the range between highest and lowest province taken as a whole is 38 points; for those with less than 10 years in school, it is 44 points; and for those with 10 to 13 years it is 39 points. The gap closes only among those who have been to university. The spread among supporters is 27 points when whole provinces are compared but is 44 points in the 10 to 13 years of schooling group. In each educational category of critics, the gap between the provinces is about twice that of the gap between the provinces as a whole. This control variable, then, sharpens rather than mutes the originally observed provincial differences.

In Table 17 we find that in most provinces Liberal identifiers provide the largest proportion of supporters and the smallest proportion of the disaffected. As well, the Liberals are slightly less likely than others to be critics, and more likely to be deferentials.

In each province where the party provides significant competition, NDP supporters are the more likely to be critics, with one striking exception: Saskatchewan NDP identifiers were less likely to be critics in 1968 than were Conservatives or Liberals. Quebec Créditistes were also more likely to be critics than were the supporters of other parties. Conservatives did not differ greatly from Liberals nationally—but there were rather striking party differences in some areas, like Manitoba, and very small differences in others, such as Quebec. Once more the regional differences within parties, especially the two largest ones, exceed those between parties nationally.

Other Control Variables

If class, education and party identification fail greatly to reduce regional variations, it seems unlikely that other standard control variables will do so, since previous studies suggest their relationship to these dependent variables is generally weaker. That is indeed the case: gender, age and size of place of residence had little effect on the regional variations, and the results are not reported here in detail.

But as Table 18 shows, these variables have another characteristic. Like those we have previously examined, they tend to have different effects in different provinces. Table 18 reports the extent of under- or overrepresentation of different groups in each province in the high efficacy and high trust categories. In this table a score of more than 1.00 means the group in question (for example, men) have more high scores on efficacy or trust than their size in the overall sample would indicate.

Looking first at gender, we find men are more likely than women to feel efficacious, except in New Brunswick and among the Quebec non-French and

Table 18
Degree of Over- or Underrepresentation of Selected Groups on Efficacy and Trust Scales,
By Province-Language Groups, Merged Data

	Efficacy, 1968-74					Trust, 1965-68				
	Males	Age 36-45	500,000+ and Suburbs	10,000 to 500,000	Farm, rural up to 10,000	Males	Age 36-45	500,000+ and Suburbs	10,000 to 500,000	Farm, rural up to 10,000
Nation	1.24	1.52	1.21	1.01	0.81	0.95	1.03	1.06	1.06	0.91
Newfoundland	1.05*	[0.76]*	[no cases]	1.18*	0.95*	0.81*	[0.84]*	[no cases]	1.36*	0.69*
P.E.I.	1.45*	[0.69]*	[no cases]	1.37*	0.86*	[1.41]*	[1.07]*	[no cases]	[2.41]*	0.89*
Nova Scotia	1.30	[1.69]	[no cases]	1.33*	0.85*	1.07	[1.20]	[no cases]	1.62	0.72
New Brunswick	0.96*	0.93*	[no cases]	1.55*	0.83*	0.86*	1.22*	[no cases]	[1.76]*	0.88*
Quebec Non-French	0.98	1.89	0.95	[0.68]	[1.36]	1.17	0.97*	1.07	[0.59]	[0.89]
Quebec French	1.20	1.93	1.07	1.12	0.80	1.03	1.14	0.87	1.21	0.90
Ontario	1.25	1.40	1.22	0.85	0.93	0.96	0.98	1.00	0.98	1.02
Manitoba	1.26	1.11	1.16*	[1.39]*	0.76*	0.85	[0.61]	1.53	0.79	0.77
Saskatchewan	1.39	1.58	[no cases]	0.95	1.04	0.88	[1.19]	[no cases]	[0.61]	1.28
Alberta	1.07	1.52	[no cases]	1.19	0.73	0.95	1.54	[no cases]	1.05	0.92
B.C.	1.34	1.50	1.14	0.92	0.73	0.87	1.22	1.11	0.89	1.02
Non-Quebec French	0.91*	[1.05]*	[1.11]*	1.42*	0.87*	[0.71]	1.01*	[0.0]	1.38	0.86

Representation Index = percentage of "high" scorers who are in group X / percentage of sample who are in group X

*High plus middle scores were used in efficacy and/or trust.
[ ] indicates fewer than ten cases.

the non-Quebec French. Nevertheless, there are very substantial variations among the provinces. On the trust dimension, women generally score higher than men, with a few exceptions. Socialization into sex roles, then, appears to produce differing results in different areas, whether we examine efficacy or trust.[47]

Similarly with age: the group aged 36 to 45 are greatly overrepresented in the high efficacy category nationally, and especially so in both groups in Quebec. In the Atlantic provinces, except Nova Scotia, they are underrepresented. In most areas age makes little difference when it comes to trust. But, for some reason, in Alberta those aged 36 to 45 are very much *more* likely to

Table 19

Analysis of Variance—Province-Language, Class, Education, Federal Party Identification, and Provincial Party Identification—with Efficacy, Trust, and Involvement as Dependent Variables (Merged Data)

	F-probabilities		
	Province	Class	Interaction
A. Province-Language by Subjective Social Class			
1. Efficacy (N = 4029)	.001	.001	.144
2. Trust (N = 4885)	.023	.001	.627
3. Involvement (N = 3380)	.033	.001	.267
	Province	Education	Interaction
B. Province-Language by Education			
1. Efficacy (N = 4029)	.001	.001	.010
2. Trust (N = 4885)	.001	.001	.095
3. Involvement (N = 3380)	.002	.001	.298
	Province	Federal Party	Interaction
C. Province-Language by Federal Party Identification			
1. Efficacy (N = 4029)	.001	.001	.191
2. Trust* (N = 4885)	.001	.001	.027
3. Involvement (N = 3380)	.005	.001	.281
	Province	Provincial Party	Interaction
D. Province-Language by Provincial Party Identification			
1. Efficacy (N = 4029)	.001	.016	.312
2. Trust* (N = 4885)	.001	.001	.054
3. Involvement (N = 3380)	.043	.002	.475

*The Atlantic provinces were combined because of small Ns in some cells.

be trusting than others, while in Manitoba the same age group is *less* likely to be trusting. The effects of the control for age, then, vary from province to province, even though the effects of age on trust are not large overall.

Residents of large cities everywhere, except in Manitoba (meaning, in this case, Winnipeg), are somewhat overrepresented in the high efficacy group. In most cases, those living on farms and in communities of less than ten thousand are underrepresented. An exception tends to confirm what Lipset has written about social organizations in Saskatchewan, with its large emphasis on cooperative organization among farmers at the rural level. In Saskatchewan, residents of small communities are overrepresented in the high efficacy groups as compared with residents of larger centres.[48] Community size seems to make less difference on the trust dimension, but the patterns are generally similar to those with efficacy.

This analysis demonstrates that some of the conventional control variables do not operate in the same direction everywhere in the country. The practical effect, of course, is that looking at effects in a whole national sample obscures as much as it illuminates.

More fundamentally, Table 18 suggests another aspect of regional differences. Not only do provinces differ in patterns of basic orientations to politics, but also provincial populations respond differently to the impact of various social forces.[49] This may be either because a factor like urban or rural represents a different phenomenon in different areas; or that cultural or other differences predispose populations to perceive and respond to it in different ways. The problem is fascinating and demands much further research.

Analysis of Variance
Regional differences remain substantial after controls are introduced. At the same time most of the control variables had strong effects, albeit ones of varying direction and magnitude in different provinces. The question then arises: do these variables account for as much variance in efficacy and trust as does region? Ideally we would like to report that X per cent of the variance is due to class, Y per cent to party identification, and so on. This is impossible, mainly because of the small cell sizes in some cases and zero cells in some regions.

It was possible, however, to test for the statistical significance of the relationships through an analysis of variance procedure, and to gain from this some idea of the relative importance of the explanatory variables.[50] Given the problem of cell sizes, no more than a two-way analysis of variance is possible, so we have tested region against class, region against education, and region against party identification.[51] This allows us to ascertain the significance of each variable when the other is controlled, and also to examine the interaction effect. The results are displayed in Table 19. Since an efficacy scale could be constructed only for the 1968 and 1974 samples, trust only for

1965 and 1968, and political involvement only for 1965 and 1974, the Ns vary accordingly. The reader should bear in mind, as well, that these results collapse together events of very different periods. Nevertheless, we believe the results are clear and meaningful, since the control variables are all significantly related to efficacy, trust and involvement; and of course the province-language groups account for a significant amount of variation in all cases.

Since the table reports only the statistical significance levels of the independent variables for each of our basic dimensions, the smaller the number, the more significant the variable in accounting for basic orientations. We find significant effects for all independent variables with all of the measures of political culture. Some are more significant than others, but all are so unequivocally strong that it is fair to conclude that no one variable predominates. In other words, in an important sense there are not only regional cultures in Canada, but also class and party cultures (or subcultures) as well.

Very few of the interaction effects are significant. This implies that the effects of region and the other variables are indeed independent of each other.

Class, as indicated by respondents' own self-placement or by education, is significant in every comparison and for every dependent variable. This suggests that previous analyses questioning the role of class in voting must be qualified in two ways: first, class does affect basic orientations, and, second, its effect seems to be different in different regions. We shall examine the role of class in detail in a later chapter.

Summary

We began this section by asking whether the provincial differences originally observed were by-products or artifacts of other differences between provinces, rather than a result of some factors more intrinsic to regional cultures themselves. If they were by-products of these control variables then that would have explained the differences. The provincial differences still might have important consequences for politics in the regions, but as social, demographic and economic changes took place within provinces we would expect to find corresponding changes in patterns of orientation.

The analysis shows unequivocally that political trust and efficacy are indeed related to a good many variables: no single factor explains all the variations. It shows that class and education especially have a strong and independent effect on the basic orientations of citizens. In the light of previous research in other countries we would be very surprised if this were not the case, but it is perhaps salutary in the Canadian context to underline the salience of class: regionalism does not eliminate its effect on citizen attitudes. But, equally, class, party identification and the other control variables do not wash out the wide variations between regions. These persist within all categories of all the control variables. For example, working-class citizens in British Columbia are much more likely to share the attitudes of middle- and upper-class individuals in British Columbia on most questions than they are to share the views of French-Canadian or Maritimes workers. There does appear, therefore, to be a clear "regional effect" whose dimensions are yet to be fully explored.

A second lesson of this analysis is that controlling for these variables alters our perception of the regional differences. We may find that controls, rather than reducing differences, increase them within each control category. More often, the provinces seem to converge at the upper-status levels, while the differences remain the same or even become accentuated at lower levels. Thus, if we can speak of a national pattern of attitudes at all, we can do so only among those who are both objectively and subjectively near the top of the status scale. In one or two cases, there appeared also to be a slight convergence at the lowest educational level. Further research is needed to pursue this finding, but it does suggest the possibility that for those at the top and bottom the immediate social conditions of life—poverty or affluence, ignorance or higher education—are the basic determinants of political attitudes. But in the middle ranges the effects of social conditions are more ambiguous, or conflicting, so that there is more "room," so to speak, for community norms to operate.

The third lesson is that within the provinces the control variables seem to have different effects. In most cases, the direction of their effect was the same, but their impact was different. In several cases, such as gender and community size, though, the variables acted in directly contradictory ways. The provincial context within which broad social and economic forces operate, then, conditions the impact these forces will have on citizens.

It is also important to note that class or status cleavages in the basic orientations to politics are quite distinct from cleavages as measured by voting. Indeed, in the Maritimes, the very sharp differences in trust and efficacy that separate social groups are not parallelled by sharp differences between classes in voting behaviour. Disaffection in the Maritimes working class does not translate itself into voting for protest parties. In British Columbia, on the other hand, a strong tradition of class cleavage and working-class protest goes hand in hand with few class differences in basic orientations to politics. In British Columbia, with its strong NDP, populist-tinged Social Credit party and militant unions, there exist strong and active organizations who see it their role to mobilize and express the views of the dissatisfied. Hence hostility is directed at political opponents, not at the system itself. Where such mobilizing agencies are weak or do not exist, hostility cannot be expressed effectively, so it is manifested in a generalized rejection and distrust of the whole political system.[52]

To say that provincial variations remain after other factors are taken into account does not, of course, mean that the provinces are homogeneous.

Divisions within them vary widely, from the relatively homogeneous British Columbia to the more divided Maritimes or Prairie provinces. Nor, of course, are class or other groups homogeneous across regions. What we have found instead is a complex pattern of interaction between regional and other factors: a full explanation of why some individuals are supporters or deferentials and others critics or disaffected requires awareness and explication of this interaction.

Conclusions

This study has demonstrated that there are strong differences among the citizens of Canadian provinces and among those of different language groups in some basic orientations to politics. Variations in political efficacy and political trust were especially marked. Political involvement proved puzzling. Some data related to a sense of the importance of politics closely paralleled the efficacy and trust findings, but a scale measuring actual political activity yielded contradictory results. A simple classification of political types suggests that quite different sorts of individuals predominate in different parts of the country. While all types are found in all provinces, the proportions vary widely. The polar regions are Ontario, British Columbia and Manitoba, where we find high levels of trust and efficacy, and the Atlantic provinces, characterized by a pervasive disaffection from the political process. The other English-speaking groups fall close to the Ontario-British Columbia-Manitoba pattern, though there are some differences between them. French-speaking Canadians fall nearer to the Maritimes pattern. These variations are not a function of demographic or socioeconomic differences between the populations of provinces or language groups, even though such factors do independently affect the kinds of orientation we have analyzed.

Given these variations in basic orientation among the provinces, the analyst may ask two kinds of questions. The orientations may be seen as dependent variables: what explains them? But they may also be independent variables: the question then becomes do they in turn explain other political phenomena?

We sought to account for the provincial differences in these attitudes by asking whether the differences disappeared when some basic socioeconomic and demographic factors were held constant. The persistence of differences within all categories of the control variables strengthens our confidence that, independent of these other social and economic forces, there are indeed differences between the provinces which may be called cultural, which are rooted in the matrix of historical and sociological factors unique to each province. These contextual elements give rise to differences in political ethos, which we would expect to be relatively constant and which would be passed on through the socialization process.

What are the sources of these cultural variations? Here we must depart from the survey data and begin to speculate more widely. The first source might be the differing historical experiences of the Canadian provinces — differences in colonial background, ethnic sources of population and settlement patterns. We might contrast, for example, the effects of the society and ideas imported by the Loyalists to the Maritimes with those imported to British Columbia by radical American miners and Labourite Englishmen.

Another important possibility is that the dividing line formed by the Ottawa River separates rich from poor, developed from undeveloped. George Perlin suggests that Newfoundland and New Brunswick can be seen socially, economically and politically as less modern than other provinces.[53] John Wilson argues that the basic source of regional cultures is in levels of industrialization and economic development.[54] The relative poverty of the Maritimes, together with the lack of large urban concentrations and the presence in the labour force of high proportions of primary workers, supports such interpretations. The low level of immigration may mean little importation of new ideas; the high level of emigration may mean that some of the most "modern" individuals, especially from the lower class, have left. In Chapter IV we examine the nature and effects of migration patterns in Canada, and these patterns appear to account for at least part of the sense of inefficacy and distrust in the Atlantic region.

The economic weakness of the Maritimes may explain the distinctive patterns found there, even though the controls for class and other socioeconomic variables did not reduce regional differences. The fact that poor and ill-educated citizens make up such a large proportion of the Atlantic area population may mean that their feelings come to pervade the whole society. The overall economic weakness and vulnerability of the economy may well engender feelings of distrust and lack of efficacy even among those who are well off. Moreover, the size of the work place, degree of unionization, patterns of communication and other such factors not examined here are related to economic modernization and, perhaps, to basic political orientations. Finally, a sense of distrust and lack of efficacy, as well as the feeling that the government has little beneficial impact on one's life, are likely to be stronger when governments have been unable to control economic forces or prevent long-term depression. Thus the political hopelessness so prevalent in the Maritimes may stem from the historical failure of either federal or provincial governments to solve the economic problems of the area. One is likely to be a critic, rather than disaffected, only if there is a reasonable hope something can be achieved. In contrast, whether or not because of greater governmental competence, citizens in British Columbia and Ontario have not undergone long periods when governments have seemed unable to engineer relative prosperity for large numbers of citizens.

If this interpretation is plausible it suggests that the Maritimes pattern is less that of the traditional society than of the traditional enclave surrounded by and subordinate to a more modern metropolis. The Maritimes, and to a lesser extent Quebec, could therefore be seen as the "small town in mass society" writ large: the dominant central Canadian and American metropolis is remote, distant and difficult to affect, but at the same time has an even more fundamental impact on the lives of Maritimers than do their own governments. Maritimers are likely to have a complex mixture of attraction to and rejection of this metropolis. A similar though weaker sense of insecurity and of being on the periphery may account for the Alberta and Saskatchewan patterns.

A study of an analogous set of regional differences in Italy, with its developed north and underdeveloped south, suggests some findings very similar to the Canadian pattern. In the south, interclass differences in attitudes such as involvement and interest were much larger than in the north. In the south, a relatively high level of political consciousness and contact with politicians (in a patron-client relationship) was accompanied by a great deal of distrust and cynicism towards politics.[55]

Another possible explanation, though not a cultural one, is that the patterns we have found stem not so much from accumulated historical experience passed on through the socialization process, but rather from the much more immediate experiences that individuals have had with governmental authorities. This implies more British Columbians may feel a sense of efficacy because they indeed have more opportunity to influence the government; they may trust their government because it deserves it. Undoubtedly something of this sort is at work, as illustrated by the fact that Liberals were more likely to be supporters at a time when there was a Liberal government in Ottawa. On the other hand, we saw very little evidence that "western alienation," an issue in British Columbia in 1968, had much effect on British Columbia attitudes. Very little comparative analysis of the responsiveness of the provincial governments or of the responsiveness of Ottawa to the interests of the different regions has been undertaken. In the absence of such data and analyses, it would be invidious to make judgments about their relative effectiveness, responsiveness or trustworthiness. We feel sure that the data do tap rather more deeply rooted attitudes, but there is rich scope for future enquiry on this question.[56]

A final and related cause of the variations we have found lies in the structure of political institutions. Where patterns of party leadership, electoral competition and the like permit effective political expression of the viewpoints of diverse groups, rather than damping and stifling them, we would expect greater levels of trust, efficacy and involvement.

What are the consequences of these differences between provinces: do they help shape other features of provincial politics? To ask this question raises again the problem of the causal arrow: the orientations of citizens may shape the character of the government, but at the same time the attitudes may be responses to the government's behaviour. Most of the literature in political culture, while recognizing that mutual causation exists, tends to see culture as the prior and independent variable and other elements of political life as the dependent ones. Without trying to solve that puzzle, one can suggest some possible links between the attitudes we have examined and politics in the provinces.[57]

For example, politics in the Maritimes — and Quebec before the Quiet Revolution — has been characterized as more personalistic and more patronage-oriented than politics in other areas. The pattern of distrust and lack of efficacy together with relatively high participation we found in the Maritimes and Quebec is perhaps consistent with this kind of politics. Group and issue-based politics implies much higher levels of political competence.

Regional variations in attitudes may also help to explain why third parties and protest groups seem to have widely varying degrees of success. Despite being the poorest and most economically backward part of Canada, and despite the dominance of such elite groups as the fish merchants of St. John's or New Brunswick's K.C. Irving, no large-scale radical or protest movement or party has achieved much support in the Maritimes, though a short-lived Farmer-Labour movement formed the Nova Scotia opposition after the 1920 election, and there have been one or two other equally brief spasms of radical activity elsewhere. The existing elites and parties seem solidly entrenched. This pattern might be changing, as suggested by the recent organization of fishermen's unions. But the quiescence, even docility, of the Maritimes population in the face of economic deprivation remains a striking fact. Perhaps this is partly due to the relatively small stratum in Maritimes society of critics — those, who, as we have suggested, are likely to act on their grievances and are likely to be available to be mobilized by new parties and groups. Disaffection from government and politics is very widespread, but this is not translated into political action. Neither the disaffected nor the deferentials pose much threat to existing elites. It would be tempting to say that these data provide one explanation of why the New Democratic party has never gained much support in the Maritime provinces. No third-party member has been elected in New Brunswick since 1920.

British Columbia and Ontario are at the other extreme. Their politics are characterized by a much higher level of support and by a widespread belief even among the dissatisfied that they can be politically effective. In British Columbia especially we find, along with much satisfaction, a more radical politics—both historically and in the present. The British Columbia New Democrats seem to be more radical than those in any other province. Trade union organization is widespread, and the unions appear to be more militant than elsewhere (except for Quebec recently). Here the large proportion of British Columbians who are critics may become important. More than two-thirds of British Columbians who distrust the government think they can do something about it. But more than four-fifths of the Maritimers who distrust the government do *not* think they can.

Quebec may appear to qualify this interpretation, since the province has obviously had a major upsurge in radical politics in recent years; yet it appears to be rather closer to the Maritimes on the dimensions discussed here than it does to British Columbia. One explanation may be that until relatively recent years, Quebec mass politics appeared to be much like that in the Maritimes. Mobilization of the disaffected is a recent, and still incomplete, development. Thus it may be that we would find French Canadians moving from the disaffected to the critic category at an increasing rate. This development might be both a result and a condition of the success of the leadership of Quebec movements such as the Parti Québécois, the Créditistes, the Front d'Action Politique, the CNTU and community action groups. Little such leadership has emerged in the Maritimes. The distrust, and hostility to the government, is there but not the sense of power to change it. "Disaffection leads to action only if it finds leadership and organizational support."[58]

Notes

1. This chapter is a revised and updated version of our article published in the *Canadian Journal of Political Science*, 7 (September 1974): 397-437. We are indebted to Mike Burke for data processing.

2. See, for example, Mason Wade, ed., *Regionalism in the Canadian Community, 1867-1967*, (Toronto: 1969).

3. See Donald E. Blake, "The Measurement of Regionalism in Canadian Voting Patterns," *Canadian Journal of Political Science*, 5 (March 1972): 55-81, and the references he cites; John Meisel, *Working Papers on Canadian Politics* (Montreal: McGill-Queen's University Press, 1975), especially chap. 1; Mildred Schwartz, *Politics and Territory: The Sociology of Regional Persistence in Canada* (Montreal: McGill-Queen's University Press, 1974); and John Wilson, "The Canadian Political Cultures," *Canadian Journal of Political Science*, 7 (September 1974): 438-83.

4. Robert E. Lane, *Political Life* (Glencoe, Ill.: Free Press, 1959): 164.

5. This parallels closely the distinction between "demographic" and "cultural" explanations by Arthur Stinchcombe, *Constructing Social Theories* (New York: Harcourt, 1969), chap. 3.

6. William Gamson, *Power and Discontent* (Homewood, Ill.: Donsey, 1968); and Jack Citrin, *Political Disaffection in America, 1958-1970* (Englewood Cliffs, N.J.: Prentice-Hall, forthcoming).

7. This conception of political culture has been expounded in more detail in our article, "A Cause in Search of Its Effect, or What does Political Culture Explain?" *Comparative Politics*, 11 (1979), 127-145.

8. "British Columbia: The Politics of Exploitation," in *Social and Cultural Change in Canada*, ed. W.E. Mann (Toronto: Copp Clark, 1970), I, 112-29.

9. C.B. Macpherson, *Democracy in Alberta* (Toronto: University of Toronto Press, 1953).

10.S.M. Lipset, *Agrarian Socialism* (Garden City, N.Y.: Anchor Books, 1968).

11. "Some Obstacles to Democracy in Quebec," in P.E. Trudeau, *Federalism and the French Canadians* (Toronto: Macmillan, 1968); and Quebec Royal Commission of Inquiry on Constitutional Problems, *Report* (Quebec: Queen's Printer, 1956).

12. Regionalism seems to us to be on a par with "nation" as an unspecified intervening variable rather than an explanatory variable. See the extensive discussion of this problem in Adam Przeworski and Henry Teune, *The Logic of Comparative Social Inquiry* (New York: Wiley-Interscience, 1970), especially pp. 24-30.

13. Gabriel Almond and Sydney Verba, *The Civic Culture* (Princeton, N.J.: Princeton University Press, 1963), are mainly responsible for popularizing this conception.

14. Ibid., p. 493.

15. Brian Barry, *Sociologists, Economists and Democracy* (London: Collier-Macmillan, 1970); and Jack Citrin and David J. Elkins, *Political Disaffection Among British University Students: Concepts, Measurement, and Causes* (University of California, Berkeley: Institute of International Studies, Research Monographs, No. 23, 1975).

16. Theodore Lowi, *The Politics of Disorder* (New York: Basic Books, 1971), pp. 109-19.

17. Joel Aberbach and Jack Walker, "Political Trust and Racial Ideology" (Paper presented to the American Political Science Association, 1969), p. 6.

18. Laurence Wylie, *Village in the Vaucluse* (Cambridge, Mass.: Harvard University Press, 1957).

19. This means that characterizations of "New Brunswick" in this chapter actually refer only to the English two-thirds of the population. However, on virtually all indicators French-speaking New Brunswickers seem to be like the English, though slightly less involved and efficacious and slightly more trusting. This appears to show that *regional* political cultures may override linguistic divisions, though this conclusion is highly tentative.

20. Note the differences between Alberta and Saskatchewan found by Macpherson, *Democracy in Alberta*, and Lipset, *Agrarian Socialism*. At several points in later chapters we shall have occasion to emphasize how diverse the Prairie provinces are.

21. We wish to thank the principal investigators for making these data sets available and to thank the U.B.C. Data Library for storing them and providing invaluable service in easing the difficulties of access.

22. This merged data set and codebook are available through the U.B.C. Data Library to interested scholars.

23. A more detailed study in Great Britain throws some light on the cognitive elements involved in efficacy and trust: Citrin and Elkins, *Political Disaffection*.

24. Of course, if one knew what these different interpretations of the question were, they could be used as indicators of the effects of culture on perceptions and responses.

25. Citrin and Elkins, *Political Disaffection*, found sharp differences between views of British politicians and British bureaucrats. See also Canada, *Report of the Task Force on Government Information* (Ottawa: Queen's Printer, 1969).

26. This assumes that "errors" are random. If they are not random, then they are of interest in cultural analysis.

27. Donald Campbell and D.W. Fiske, "Convergent and Discriminant Validation by the Multitrait-Multimethod Matrix," *Psychological Bulletin*, 56 (1959): 81-105.

28. L. Guttman, "Principles of Scalogram Analysis," in *Measurement and Prediction*, ed. S. Stouffer et al., vol. 4, *The American Soldier* (Princeton: Princeton University Press, 1950).

29. L. Cronbach and P.E. Meehl, "Construct Validity in Psychological Tests," *Psychological Bulletin*, 52 (May 1955): 281-302; and Jane Loevinger, "Objective Tests as Instruments of Psychological Theory," *Psychological Reports*, 3 (1957): 635-94, Monograph Supplement 9.

30. Note that most regions in Table 1, for example, differ significantly from the national average.

31. For this, see the perceptive chapters in Meisel, *Working Papers*.

32. The scale is made up of the following individual items in the 1968 survey: "What do you think you could do if the federal government were considering a law which you felt to be unfair or wrong?" Dichotomized between those who said "nothing" or "don't know" and the rest.

"People like me don't have any say about what the government does." Agree-disagree.

"Sometimes government and politics seem so complicated that a person like me can't really understand what's going on." Agree-disagree.

"How much do you feel that having elections makes the government pay attention to what the people think? A good deal, some, or not very much?" Dichotomized between "not very much" and the two other responses.

It should be noted that this scale differs slightly from that employed by John Meisel using the same data. His includes items which form part of the trust scale outlined later.

In 1974, two items were identical to those in 1968: "People like me don't have any say about what the government does," and "Sometimes government and politics seem so complicated that a person like me can't really understand what's going on." In addition, we used the following two items which parallel fairly closely the intent of the other 1968 items:

"So many other people vote in federal elections that it doesn't matter very much whether I vote or not." Agree-disagree.

"If you wrote him [your Member of Parliament] about a specific problem, do you think he would try to do something about it?" Yes-no.

33. Almond and Verba, *The Civic Culture*, p. 185, asked about a law which was unjust or harmful, rather than unfair or wrong.

34. The scale is made up of responses to the following items in the 1965 as well as the 1968 survey:

"How much of the time do you think you can trust the government to do what is right?" Dichotomized between "just about always" or "most of the time" and "some" or "none of the time."

"Do you think that quite a few people running the government are a little crooked, not very many are crooked, or do you think hardly any of them are crooked?" Dichotomized between "hardly any" and the rest.

"Do you feel that almost all of the people running the government are smart people who usually know what they are doing, or do you think there are quite a few of them who do not know what they are doing?" Dichotomized between "almost all know what they are doing" and the rest.

"Do you think that all of the people who are high in the government give everyone a fair break — big shots and ordinary people alike — or do you think some of them pay more attention to what the big interests want?" Dichotomized between "fair to everyone" and the rest.

"Do you think that people in the government waste a lot of money we pay in taxes, waste some of it, or don't waste very much of it?" Dichotomized between "don't waste very much" and the rest.

35. Giuseppe Di Palma defines "disaffection" to include an absence of close ties to the polity, a posture of estrangement, remoteness and rejection relating to the whole system. See *Apathy and Participation: Mass Politics in Western Societies* (New York: Free Press, 1970), chap. 2. Our term disaffection is also close to R.E. Lane's notion of alienation. See *Political Ideology* (New York: Free Press, 1962), p. 42.

36. Gamson, *Power and Discontent*, p. 48.

37. Only in 1968 were there sufficient items to construct both efficacy and trust scales. Hence we cannot present figures for 1965, 1974, or the merged data set, thus greatly limiting the reliability of our analysis.

38. The scale is made up of the following items on the 1965 survey:

1. "How much interest do you generally have in what is going on in politics — a good deal, some, or not much?" Dichotomized between "not much" and the rest.
2. Recall correctly the name of the winning candidate.
3. "Did you, on your own, talk to any people and try to show them why they should vote for one of the parties or candidates?"

4. "Did you attend any political meetings or gatherings during the campaign?"

5. "Did you read any party leaflets or reports of election speeches during the campaign?"

6. Report voting in all federal elections since you have been old enough to vote.

7. Report voting in all provincial elections since you have been old enough to vote.

8. Help in an election campaign.

9. Make a financial contribution to a party or candidate.

10. Canvass for financial contributions.

11. Belong to a political club.

In 1974 the items were only seven in number, but were quite similar to the above. Besides 1, 6, 7 and 8 above, which were identical, we utilized: "How often did you try to convince friends to vote the same as you?" (Often or sometimes).

"How often did you spend time working for a political party or a candidate?" (Often or sometimes).

"How often do you read about politics in the newspapers?" (Often or sometimes).

39. See also Rick Van Loon, "Political Participation in Canada: the 1965 Election," *Canadian Journal of Political Science*, 3 (September 1970): 376-99.

40. The regional differences in 1968 were larger. Asked about their interest in the 1968 election, the proportion saying they had *no* interest ranged from 11 to 13 per cent among all the English-speaking groups west of Quebec. It rose to 24 per cent in the Maritimes as a whole, 31 per cent among French-speakers outside Quebec, and 40 per cent among the Quebec French. Just over 53 per cent of Ontarians reported "very much" interest; only 39 per cent of Maritimers did. The figures for the Maritimes and Quebec are especially striking, since the former had a "native son" as leader of the Conservatives, and the latter had a French Canadian as Liberal leader, and Confederation as a major issue.

41. This is the agreement of P.J. Fitzpatrick. See "New Brunswick; The Politics of Pragmatism," in *Canadian Provincial Politics*, ed. Martin Robin (Scarborough, Ont.: Prentice-Hall, 1971), especially pp. 119, 122.

42. After describing the issue-free, patronage-oriented, ethnically tense politics of New Brunswick, Fitzpatrick concludes that there is general satisfaction: "the people prefer their political system the way it is." Our data suggest a very different interpretation. See Fitzpatrick, ibid., p. 133.

43. This interpretation contrasts strongly with the more impressionistic view of Martin Robin, who argues that rampant patronage, low political morality and disregard of democratic rules and procedures have bred mass resentment and apathy. See his "British Columbia, the Politics of Class Conflict," in *Canadian Provincial Politics*, pp. 27-68, especially p. 38.

44. The question was: "Which of the following five social classes would you say you were in — upper class, upper-middle class, middle class, working class or lower class?" A probe forced respondents to choose. In the tables, upper and upper-middle were combined as "upper," and "working" and "lower" were combined as "working."

45. The party identification coding used here is not the same as in the codebook for the 1965 or 1968 study. Instead we have combined that question with the follow-up questions about whether the individual was thinking of the federal or provincial level and, if provincial, we then used the next question on what his federal identification was and conversely for provincial identification.

46. The literature here is too large to summarize fully. Notable examples of the class interpretation are John Porter, *The Vertical Mosaic* (Toronto: University of Toronto Press, 1965); Charles Taylor, *The Pattern of Politics* (Toronto: McClelland and Stewart, 1970); the work of Robert Alford is the most closely identified with the non-class view. See *Party and Society* (Chicago: Rand McNally, 1963); and "Class Voting in the Anglo-American Democracies," in *Party Systems and Voter Alignments: Cross-National Perspectives*, ed. S.M. Lipset and Stein Rokkan (New York: Free Press, 1967), pp. 67-93.

47. But note that in Table 18 each provincial sample is considered separately. It is not possible from the table to make interprovincial comparisons, such as whether men in New Brunswick are more likely to have a strong sense of efficacy than are men in Ontario.

48. Lipset, *Agrarian Socialism*, especially pp. 244-68.

49. Blake, "Measurement of Regionalism," has also found that the ethnic and religious correlates of party voting depend significantly on the province in which the group is located.

50. For further information on the nature of analysis of variance, see William L. Hays, *Statistics for Psychologists* (New York: Holt, Rinehart and Winston, 1963), chaps. 12 and 13; and H. Scheffé, *The Analysis of Variance* (New York: Wiley, 1959).

51. Given the numbers of cases in the smaller provinces, an analysis of variance involving more than two control variables requires that one collapse the Maritimes together as one region and the Prairies and British Columbia as another; or that one collapse the control variables to the point of meaninglessness—for example, Liberals and Conservatives as one group and "all other parties" as another. We have, therefore, not been able to conduct an analysis of variance which would take account simultaneously of all the relevant variables.

52. In the same way, status differences in turnout have been found to be smaller in European countries with strong socialist parties than in the United States where such parties do not exist. See also Giuseppe Di Palma, "Disaffection and Participation in Western Democracies," *The Journal of Politics*, 31 (November 1969): 984-1015.

53. See George Perlin, "Social Change, the Mobilization of Electoral Support and Political Development in Newfoundland" (Paper presented at the Workshop on Community Political Development, Institute of Social and Economic Research, Memorial University, 1972).

54. John Wilson, "The Canadian Political Cultures."

55. Sydney Tarrow, "The Political Economy of Stagnation: Communism in Southern Italy, 1960-70," *Journal of Politics*, 34, no. 1 (February 1972): 120-22.

56. Di Palma in *Apathy and Participation* has argued strongly for the need to link levels of apathy and participation to government performance and party activity. See "Conclusion."

57. John Wilson has argued that differences in provincial party systems can in part be traced to differences in regional cultures. See "The Canadian Political Cultures." For United States studies, see Raymond Wolfinger, "Why Political Machines Have Not Withered Away and Other Revisionist Thoughts," *Journal of Politics*, 34, no. 2 (May 1972): 365-98; Raymond Wolfinger and Fred I. Greenstein, "Comparing Political Regions: The Case of California," *American Political Science Review*, 63 (March 1969): 74-86; James Prothro and Charles Grigg, "Fundamental Principles of Democracy: Bases of Agreement and Disagreement," *Journal of Politics*, 22 (1960): 276-94; and Herbert McClosky, "Consensus and Ideology in American Politics," *American Political Science Review* 58 (June 1964), 361-82.

58. Di Palma, *Apathy and Participation*, p. 116.

III
Regional Preferences: Citizens' Views of Public Policy

Richard Simeon, Donald E. Blake

Citizens' attitudes and orientations to region and country, we have argued, logically divide into three different categories. In previous chapters we have examined two of them: orientations to political life in a very general sense; and attachments, identities and loyalties to the two primary levels of government. In this chapter we examine the third dimension: the extent of differences in policy preferences across the various Canadian regions. By policy preferences we mean beliefs and desires about what governments — any governments — should actually do. Should Canada have a guaranteed annual income, should it restore the death penalty, should it do more to control or restrain foreign investment, should it extend official bilingualism? There are good reasons to expect that the three dimensions are, at least in principle, distinct from each other: we would not expect the level of political efficacy to determine support for or hostility to the welfare state. Nor would a citizen's commitment to, say, legalizing marijuana necessarily carry any implications for which level of government should make the decision. To believe that "government" should provide a service is to be open about which should do so.

In fact, citizens probably seldom couple their belief that "there ought to be a law" with a statement that a particular government should pass it. Most often, one assumes, citizens would be happy if any government did — and would likely support whichever level seemed most likely to do so. Ample evidence suggests that most citizens, and this is probably true even for relatively sophisticated groups, have little knowledge about how jurisdiction and responsibility are shared in the Canadian federal system.[1] Given the massive interpenetration of federal and provincial activities, such confusion is understandable.

On the other hand, it may be that policy preferences are, on occasion, linked with an orientation to government. Citizens may place an independent value on a service being provided by the government closest to them, even if the actual character of the service is likely to be the same whichever level does it. Moreover, it may be that in some cases a given preference logically entails action by one level or another: for example, a strong desire for a high level of development assistance to poorer provinces might be coupled with the reasonable belief that only Ottawa has the resources to provide it.

Nevertheless, our concern here is with preferences, expressed largely independently of government levels. We ask: do the populations of the Canadian regions differ sharply among themselves in their policy preferences? Do they differ in the substance of what they want government to do? If so, what is the magnitude of the differences, and which areas stand out? Second, following the logic used in previous chapters, we ask whether the interregional differences we find are larger or smaller than the differences generated by other potential cleavages. In other words, is region a more or less important line of division on policy issues than are religion, language, age, education, and so on? Since many policy issues facing the country are not themselves expressed in regional terms, we would expect, at least on some issues, to find that region is not the most salient line of division.

Third, we are interested in change. Is the regional cleavage on policy growing or declining? Are provinces and regions becoming more similar or more dissimilar? And, as a corollary, do we find opinion *within* regions becoming more or less homogeneous.

We explore these questions using a unique data source. The Canadian Gallup poll has for more than thirty years regularly asked Canadians not only how they intend to vote, but also what their opinions are on a host of contemporary policy issues. We examine responses to 248 of these questions, the first asked in May 1949, the last in October 1975 — though we also look briefly at a few questions asked since then. Thus we have the opportunity to examine the evolution of opinion over a long period, and to use surveys as a tool for studying history as well as for today's immediate issues. The questions asked run the gamut, from the use of the strap in schools to the weightiest foreign policy questions. In several cases we are able to trace out changes in detail through the use of identical questions asked at several different times; in other cases we examine trends by pooling the responses to a large number of varied questions in a given issue area for different time periods.

We approach this mass of material with contradictory expectations. On the one hand, we might expect to find increasing convergence among the provinces, and to find regions becoming internally more heterogeneous, while the country as a whole would be more homogeneous. We would expect to find that differences other than region, especially those associated with class, would become more salient than regional differences.

Why? First, S.M. Lipset, Stein Rokkan and others have argued that the process of social and economic development involves a shift from cleavages based on conflict between centre and periphery, and on cultural (religious, linguistic) differences towards a cleavage pattern based on functional or economic cleavages.[2] The persistence of region and language divisions, they suggest, is largely a holdover from the past. Hence, if Canada is to follow this model, we would expect small differences on region, religion and language, and larger ones on economically based divisions. However, the recent growth of regionalist and ethnonationalist movements in many countries, including some of the most developed, calls the model into question even for countries other than Canada.[3] Moreover, Michael Hechter, Tom Nairn and others have shown how developmental processes may sustain and even exacerbate centre-periphery conflicts and may lead to exploitation of the peripheral regions by the metropolis.[4]

Second, a version of the developmental model has been applied to federal countries, not least Canada. For example, J.A. Corry and others in the postwar period anticipated a growing "nationalization" of Canadian political life and, with it, a growth in the power of the central government and a decline in the provinces.[5] There are several elements to this argument. As provinces developed they would become economically and socially more alike: therefore they were likely to manifest increasingly similar patterns of division. At the level of identities and attachments to government, the mixing and the common cause brought on by wartime experience, the growth of national media and other developments, would promote a "national" orientation. At the level of policy, the experience of the Depression had shown the inadequacy of provincial governments in responding to severe economic problems. The new postwar commitment to Keynesian economics and the welfare state would naturally be based on central government activity. Most important, the development of large national and multinational corporations, oriented to serving national markets, and to manageability, predictability and stability, would lead to the need for effective central governments. Samuel Beer[6] makes a similar argument for the United States: the move from localistic politics to a politics of class-related economic issues, to the contemporary politics of managing technocracy is accompanied by a progressive strengthening of central over local governments, and of national cleavages over regional ones. National and international media are likely to enhance the trend to diminution of interregional differences.

Yet, on the other hand, we have reason to expect not convergence but *divergence*. Studies of political behaviour, especially voting, conducted against the background of the developmental model offer support to this point of view. The partisan preferences of Canadians are shaped to a very large extent by region, and while little is known about the links in Canada between party affiliation and positions on major policy questions, if they have any relationship at all we would expect regional variations in policy attitudes too. Moreover, regional disparities and differences in regional economies have not only persisted, but in some ways become more pressing. Provincial governments have come to control much greater proportions of public spending, and have become much more assertive in policy development. Moreover, federal-provincial conflict on a large number of issues has become more intense. All this suggests that the regional, provincial or territorial cleavage has become more salient and more important. In turn, it might be expected that this should be accompanied by an increasing divergence between the policy preferences of citizens in different regions.

One of the more interesting questions concerning the apparent growth of provincial power and assertiveness, and the accompanying "attenuation of federal power," is where the drive for provincialism originates. Does it follow public opinion or lead it? Thus one possibility is that growing alienation from Ottawa, growing divergence in the policy goals of provincial populations and growing attachments to provincial governments, all lead to provincial governments developing greater political support, and greater resources for bargaining with the central government.

But another approach suggests that the impetus and initiative are likely to come from provincial government elites themselves, striving to exploit the constitutional and fiscal resources at their disposal to maximize their own influence and freedom of action. To do this, they are encouraged to stress and magnify the provincial/territorial dimension of issues and to downplay issues which cut across region.[7] They are likely to try to enlist public opinion and group interests in the province in support of this province-building drive. Moreover, the highly visible process of policy-making through federal-provincial negotiation, in which rival national and provincial elites work out their differences, is also likely to stress the public significance of regional divisions. Because of the institutionalized power of both levels of government, it may be hard to mobilize groups and opinion on issues other than regional ones.

Thus the political observer coming to Canada for the first time will be struck most forcibly by the dominance of territory in Canadian political debate. But it is most unclear how much this visible conflict at the elite level is reflected in mass opinion. Does our focus on highly publicized conflict among regional leaders in fact exaggerate the intensity of regional differences; does it blind us to larger similarities which find little expression mainly because they lack the leadership to express themselves? In short: is federal-provincial conflict at the government level paralleled by a similar division in the policy preferences of citizens?

The answer to this question is not without contemporary political import. The central question in the debate on the future of the Canadian constitution is the distribution of powers between the federal and provincial governments.[8] Many of the proposals put forward call for further decentralization of powers, reflecting the strength of the provincial governments which are such central participants in the bargaining.[9] It is important to ask, however, whether such proposals are in fact congruent with opinion as we find it expressed in the public at large. Before accepting large-scale decentralization, we might want to ask: is that consistent with our knowledge of public orientations? The data reported here permit one such test.

Indeed, they suggest one criterion for deciding on the appropriate distribution of powers in a new constitution.[10] All other things being equal, where interprovincial differences are large, persistent and more significant than other possible bases of division, then responsibility for the relevant policy areas should be allocated to the provinces. This is because the opinion data would suggest that each provincial population wanted to do different things. If the power were left with Ottawa, then at least some regional populations would be frustrated by a national majority. In such a situation, frustration and conflict are minimized if the provincial populations each have the freedom to do what they want.

On the other hand, where we find regional differences small, and declining, and where cleavages other than region seem to lie behind policy divisions, then a strong case can be made for *federal* power, since only the federal government encompasses and bridges the various divisions. Moreover, if the population is basically homogeneous across regions, then economies of scale follow from federal responsibility.

No one would claim that the kinds of public opinion we examine here should be the only criterion for allocating powers. Many other factors would have to be considered. Yet one would want to think carefully before allocating powers to one government when there does not appear to be any popular basis for it. Public opinion can be an important touchstone for the debate—one which has not been considered prominently so far.

Data and Method

The data employed here consist of responses to virtually every policy question asked by the Canadian Institute of Public Opinion, now the Canadian Gallup poll, in its periodic surveys from 1949 to 1975.[11] In order to qualify for inclusion in our analysis, a question had to call for a specific choice for or against a given policy option. Thus questions seeking favourable or unfavourable reactions to "government immigration policy" were excluded, but those asking for an opinion on whether or not immigration should be increased were included. Similarly, judgments about the "seriousness" of a given issue or problem were not analyzed, but specific proposals to deal with such issues or problems were.

Occasionally questions had to be ignored because the answers were not present in the data available to us or because of gaps in the demographic data provided. It is also possible that in combing through several hundred questions we inadvertently missed some which met our criteria. However, unlike most analysts of this type of data, we did not restrict our attention to questions with identical wording. This step is unusual, though not unprecedented, and requires some elaboration.[12]

Our strategy is to group particular policy *questions* into generally recognizable policy *areas*. For example, there are many Gallup poll questions about "blue laws," such as laws governing Sunday sports and store openings, which might be grouped with a wide variety of questions on "moral issues." In comparing the views of different groups of the population we can then make judgments about the relative acceptance of traditional moral views based on the pooled results of many questions. Similarly, responses favouring or opposing bilingual labels and signs can be considered compatible with, among others, those favouring or opposing the protection of French language rights in the more general category of endorsing or opposing conciliatory policies towards French Canada.

This not only helps to compensate for changes in question wording and for random variations resulting from sampling error, but also gives a truer picture of real policy differences than can be obtained by focusing on specific questions. This has long been recognized in academic survey research as a rationale for the building of scales from a number of discrete items. The parallel is not exact because we have to combine individuals and surveys, but the principle is the same.

Ultimately, 248 questions were grouped into 12 policy areas, with response categories collapsed where necessary to produce the following "policy dichotomies":

Role of government	Favour/oppose expansion, size, intervention
Foreign policy	Liberal, internationalist/ conservative, isolationist
Social policy	Expand, support/restrict, curtail
Moral issues	Progressive/traditional
Defence	Pro-military, western alliance/not
Ties with British past	Maintain/weaken, sever
Federal-provincial relations	Pro-federal/neutral, pro-provincial
French-English relations	Conciliatory/not
Foreign influence, investment	Oppose, curtail/favour, expand
Labour	Anti-, critical/pro-, sympathetic
Immigration	Favour, expand/oppose, restrict
Women's rights	Favour/oppose.

These categories of response, plus "don't know," were used in cross-tabulating each policy question against current party choice, religion, language, education, age, union membership and region. Our method requires us to dichotomize the variables. We examine Liberal vs. Conservative supporters; Protestants vs. Catholics; French vs. English speakers; least educated (Grade 8 or less) vs. most educated (some university); young (under 30) vs. old (50 or over); union members vs. non-members; and a number of regional divisions, especially Quebec vs. the rest of Canada. All these divisions might logically be associated with conflicting policy views. As in so many studies we are plagued by highly inadequate measures of class position. In this we are prisoners of our data and we have had to rely on education and union membership.[13]

Difference scores, also employed in later chapters in the analysis of political divisions, were used to compare the magnitude of differences between groups divided by a particular cleavage. The scores were calculated according to the following formula:

$$DI(\text{difference index}) = \tfrac{1}{2} \sum_{i=1}^{n} | p_i - q_1 |$$

where p_i is the proportion of group p (e.g. young) selecting alternative i, and q_i is the proportion of group q (e.g. old) selecting that alternative. These differences are summed over the three response alternatives (e.g. agree, disagree, don't know). Scores can vary between zero and one, with large numbers indicating greater differences between two distributions of opinion. This type of statistic has proven useful in other studies of public opinion and has a certain intuitive appeal.[14] A given score indicates what proportion of a given group would have to change its opinion in order to produce a distribution of opinion identical to that in the group to which it is being compared.

The difference scores were calculated for each question and each independent variable and then averaged across questions in each of our policy categories. Then, in order to detect possible trends in the magnitude of differences, averages were calculated for the time periods 1949-1969 and 1970-1975. This dividing line is an arbitrary one, since there is no reason to believe that 1969-1970 marked a turning point in the evolution of Canadian public opinion or that even if such a watershed existed it appeared in all policy areas simultaneously. However, it has the virtue of dividing the set of questions approximately in half and does not produce results substantially different from those obtained with a 1965-1966 cutting point (the approximate chronological midpoint ignoring the very few questions prior to 1954). Moreover, in a number of cases we have been able to verify our results by examining other bodies of data as well as Gallup polls conducted since 1975.

The Gallup questions themselves provide a fascinating glimpse of the changing public agenda — and of the preoccupations of the poll designers. For example, in the fifties and early sixties questions about the Cold War, nefarious Communists and a nuclear holocaust were common, but they disappeared almost entirely in later years. When Gallup asked about "women's rights" in the fifties and sixties, the questions were about whether or not women should receive equal pay with men, but later, consensus on that apparently assumed, the issue was whether or not there should be publicly supported day care for the children of working mothers. The first question related to environmentalist and conservationist concerns — asking about the seal hunt — did not appear until 1971. The Gallup poll has apparently been almost obsessed by issues related to unions and collective bargaining, with the result that we have a rich array of questions on that over the whole period. On some other issues of great contemporary significance, however, such as the future of Canadian federalism, we are hard put to find questions before the 1970s.

As in all survey research, especially that depending on secondary analysis, we have had to make trade-offs. The pooling of results from large numbers of questions adds greatly to our confidence in the results and overcomes some of the dangers of the small Gallup sample sizes. The price is sometimes a lack of detail. The techniques we can use to summarize an almost unprecedented array of data are limited by the nature of these data; the gain, however, is to be able to discuss with some confidence the sweep of opinion over a critical period of Canadian history.

I. Societal Divisions and Policy Differences: An Overview

Our expectations about the impact of region of residence on the policy preferences of Canadians are mixed. While there is considerable indirect support for the view that policy attitudes continue to be shaped by region, there is some theoretical support for convergence. But what about the other social divisions which might also be expected to generate differing policy views? One possibility, following the "end of ideology" school, is that these other differences too have declined, a result of the supposed levelling effects of geographic and social mobility, mass media exposure, urbanization, the welfare system and universal public education.[15] But another possibility, suggested by a social mobilization perspective, is that class and other functional divisions would come to replace region and language as sources of conflict on policy.

Previous studies of voting behaviour and public opinion in Canada have, on the whole, found little evidence for a decline of regional cleavages nor for a growth in class cleavage.[16] Most such studies, however, have asked few questions about policy except those tied to immediate events like elections, and none, with the exception of Mildred Schwartz's study of national identity, have examined issues over a long period. Her study, the most comprehensive one to date, looked at Gallup poll data up until 1962. While she did not restrict her attention to policy *preference* questions as we have done, she explored a similar range of policy areas. Her conclusion attests to the strength of region in comparison to other divisions and to its continuing importance:

> It is apparent from the distribution of opinions reported in this study and from information and generalizations derived from other studies, that the major divisions in Canadian society, those based on region and origin and tied to economic factors seriously weaken national consensus. Moreover, there are few signs of a reversal in this trend.[17]

Table 1
Dimensions of Difference on Policy Issues: 1949-1975*

Issue Area	Socio-Economic Division							Average Regional DI**	Date of First Question	Number of Questions
	Liberal/ Tory	Protestant/ Catholic	English/ French	Primary/ University	Young/ Old	Union/ Non-Union	Quebec/ Non-Quebec			
Role of government	.081	.057	.121	.181	.104	.076	.091	.084	1949	32
Foreign policy	.079	.125	.158	.214	.076	.051	.138	.102	1954	23
Social policy	.070	.088	.109	.105	.075	.051	.105	.090	1951	21
Moral issues	.067	.123	.114	.156	.125	.059	.144	.109	1949	51
Defence	.110	.116	.214	.211	.096	.040	.144	.100	1955	7
Ties with Britain	.184	.327	.383	.179	.173	.108	.313	.177	1956	6
Federal-provincial relations	.071	.057	.134	.205	.081	.066	.113	.102	1957	7
French-English relations	.161	.257	.324	.280	.118	.041	.340	.183	1961	13
Foreign influence	.072	.096	.160	.198	.111	.055	.123	.096	1956	23
Labour	.065	.090	.098	.149	.100	.149	.099	.083	1959	46
Immigration	.076	.114	.157	.294	.064	.054	.114	.086	1954	13
Women's rights	.050	.085	.110	.147	.097	.068	.109	.090	1954	9

*Table entries are difference indices, calculated as described in the text, averaged over the total number of policy questions in a given issue subset.

**Calculated over all comparisons of each region (Atlantic, Quebec, Ontario, Prairies, B.C.) with the rest of Canada.

Table 1 presents the mean indices of difference for each issue and each independent variable in our analysis. The average regional DI for each policy area is calculated by averaging the difference scores for each region versus the rest of Canada. The scores for Quebec versus the rest of Canada are included in these calculations, but have also been reported separately. While each series (with the exception of defence issues) contains at least one question from the 1970s, the starting dates differ somewhat, as can be seen from the final column in the table.

Perhaps because the two categories represent the extremes of the most and least educated, the primary/university dichotomy produces the highest difference scores across most of the issue areas. The educational division is followed by the English-speaking–French-speaking dichotomy. The average regional differences of opinion rank third, just ahead of religion, and considerably ahead of party and union membership. Thus over the whole time period, the regional and linguistic dimensions are important sources of issue differences.

The regional differences vary considerably by issue area. They are strongest (DI = .183) on matters which relate to English-French relations — a category which groups questions about bilingualism, the use of the English and French languages, and so on. They are also strong on a group of questions which concern the monarchy, the Canadian flag and other symbols of nationhood. It is this category which also most sharply differentiates French- and English-speakers and Quebeckers from residents of the other provinces. Federal-provincial relations and foreign policy also yield high scores. Taken together, these categories suggest that regional differences are greatest on those issues which relate to Canada's character as a society or nation, and to values and symbols which they evoke.

The other category in which the overall regional DI is more than .100 is our large group of "moral" questions, those having to do with life style and with moral judgments about things like the death penalty, abortion and the use of drugs. The regional difference here seems to capture a dimension of more traditional versus more open secular cultures — a perception which is reinforced by the sharp differences by age and religion in this category.

The categories which capture divisions on social and economic policy, and on the traditional left-right dimensions of government are "role of government," "social policy" and "labour." Here regional differences are much less pronounced. Role of government and labour exhibit the lowest differences among the twelve categories; social policy is close, along with immigration and questions about the role of women.

The same pattern is found with Quebec versus the other provinces, with much the sharpest divisions, as expected, on English-French relations and the symbols of nationhood. The DI drops below .100 on the role of government and labour and is only slightly above that level on social policy.

Table 2
Dimensions of Difference on Policy Issues: 1949-69, 1970-75*

Issue Area	Socio-Economic Division							Average Regional DI	Minimum Number of Questions
	Liberal/ Tory	Protestant/ Catholic	English/ French	Primary/ University	Young/ Old	Union/ Non-Union	Quebec/ Non-Quebec		
Role of government	.069/ .094	.065/ .055	.171/ .078	.201/ .163	.099/ .108	.097/ .055	.106/ .071	.088/ .078	12/ 13
Foreign policy	.066/ .131	.140/ .076	.170/ .104	.210/ .232	.073/ .091	.053/ .042	.152/ .071	.109/ .072	13/ 3
Social policy	.063/ .074	.103/ .080	.130/ .098	.122/ .097	.046/ .091	.037/ .058	.115/ .099	.091/ .091	6/ 12
Moral issues	.074/ .059	.173/ .072	.146/ .084	.148/ .168	.106/ .149	.060/ .059	.168/ .113	.118/ .097	21/ 22
Ties with Britain	.130/ .220	.281/ .358	.350/ .405	.179/ .179	.180/ .166	.093/ .124	.259/ .367	.152/ .202	3/ 3
French-English relations	.102/ .229	.265/ .246	.336/ .311	.149/ .150	.098/ .141	.054/ .026	.369/ .306	.193/ .171	6/ 6
Foreign influence	.094/ .058	.087/ .101	.181/ .141	.185/ .210	.084/ .133	.063/ .048	.123/ .123	.102/ .090	7/ 10
Labour	.067/ .062	.100/ .073	.106/ .086	.154/ .139	.093/ .113	.152/ .144	.105/ .083	.087/ .077	24/ 17
Immigration	.077/ .073	.088/ .150	.201/ .122	.357/ .216	.061/ .070	.059/ .048	.124/ .097	.088/ .083	4/ 5

*See notes to Table 1. The first number in each pair in a given table entry is the mean DI calculated over questions in the period 1949-1969, the second over questions from 1970-75.

These observations are based on the aggregation of questions over a thirty-year time span. What changes have occurred in that time? Table 2 shows the mean indices of difference for two time periods — 1949-69 and 1970-75 — though it should be noted that the bulk of questions in the first time period were asked during the 1960s. The results provide some evidence for the "convergence" hypothesis. In seven of the nine categories, the DI for the regions declined; only in one did it increase. The greatest convergence was in foreign policy and moral issues. Three areas — defence, women's rights and federal-provincial relations — contained too few questions to justify a division.

This convergence hypothesis is even more striking when we look at the French-English and Quebec/non-Quebec cleavages. In both of these, too, there is convergence on all but one or two dimensions and, in general, the magnitude of convergence is even greater than with all regions. For example, the DI for foreign policy declined by .081 for Quebec/non-Quebec and for French-English relations by .063. There was also a striking convergence on moral issues. Among the left-right issues, there is also sharp convergence on the role of government, social policy, labour and immigration. Here we see the attitudinal impact of Quebec's Quiet Revolution — it was Quebeckers' attitudes which were changing most, and these changes were bringing their attitudes closer to those of their English-Canadian fellow citizens.

There is one major exception to this pattern of convergence: a much *sharper* division across every one of our independent variables on the character and symbols of nationhood. The English-French scores here increased from .350 to .405, the highest score obtained throughout the analysis; it rose by about the same amount in the Quebec/non-Quebec comparison.

Comparison of the magnitude and direction of changes in the importance of various cleavages is facilitated by examining Table 3, which reports the arithmetical differences between mean DIs in the two time periods. The differences have been calculated so that a positive result signifies a greater difference on a given cleavage and issue in 1970-75 compared with the earlier period, and a negative result a reduction in the magnitude of difference.

Overall, there is some evidence for a decline in the tendency for political disagreement to be rooted in social divisions. Over all the categories, declines in the difference index outnumbered increases by 37 to 24. In only one category, ties with Britain, did increases in the DI outnumber decreases. The general convergence among social groups was most evident in two categories which appear to tap traditional left-right divisions: role of government and labour. But it was less evident in social policy, where age differences, ties with unions and partisan affiliations all produced sharper differences in recent years. Immigration also produced greater consensus, in all divisions except for age and religion, where there were modest increases. Again we find that it

Table 3

Changes in Magnitude of Differences Between Period 1 and Period 2
by Issue Area and Cleavage*

Issue Area	Socio-Economic Division							Average Regional DI
	Liberal/ Tory	Protestant/ Catholic	English/ French	Primary/ University	Young/ Old	Union/ Non-Union	Quebec/ Non-Quebec	
Role of government	.025	−.010	−.093	−.038	.009	−.042	−.035	−.010
Foreign policy	.065	−.064	−.066	.022	.018	−.011	−.081	−.037
Social policy	.011	−.023	−.032	−.025	.045	.021	−.016	.000
Moral issues	−.015	−.101	−.062	.020	.043	−.001	−.055	−.021
Ties with Britain	.090	.077	.055	.000	−.014	.031	.108	.050
French-English relations	.127	−.019	−.025	.001	.043	−.028	−.063	−.022
Foreign influence	−.036	.014	−.040	.025	.049	.015	.000	−.012
Labour	−.005	−.027	−.020	−.015	.020	−.008	−.022	−.010
Immigration	−.004	.062	−.079	−.141	.009	−.011	−.027	−.005

*Table entries are obtained by subtracting 1949-69 average DIs from 1970-75 average DIs, as reported in Table 2. A positive value indicates a greater difference on a given cleavage and issue in 1970-75 than in the earlier period.

is primarily in matters to do with the character of the Canadian community that social divisions — and not just regional/provincial ones — are sharpest. The indications of convergence should not, however, be overestimated. First, our data continue to show substantial differences between social groups on many issues. Second, the data are not so much consistent with a decline of conflict, or of disagreement. Rather, they suggest a reduced tendency for policy disagreements to be correlated with social and economic position in the population. Thus, many of the emerging issues of political debate — women's rights, the environment, energy, the debate over foreign influence, and so on — do not have an obvious link with the "objective" interests of different classes, ethnic groups or religious denominations. Differences of opinion on such issues may be intense, but they are likely to be relatively unstructured and fragmented, especially in comparison with older, more established left-right dimensions.

There are significant differences in the importance of different lines of cleavage. Language divided the population most sharply in the earlier period, not only on the issues which engage the interests of linguistic groups most directly (French-English relations and ties with Britain), but also on social and economic issues such as role of government, social policy and labour. The language division dropped more sharply than any other between the two periods. It remained important, but now it only really stands out on policies concerning the relations between the groups, and on ties with Britain. On all other issues, little now distinguishes French- and English-speaking Canadians. Much the same thing happens with the division between Quebec and the rest of Canada.

Religious differences, reflecting their intercorrelation with language, were also high for French-English relations and ties with Britain. In the first period, they were also important sources of difference on foreign policy, social policy, moral issues and labour. By the 1970s, however, the distinctiveness of religious groups on all these issues had declined greatly. Only on immigration had they significantly increased, a finding which probably reflects the growth in immigration from Catholic southern Europe, which may predispose Catholics to greater enthusiasm for high levels of immigration.[18]

One of the most interesting findings is the increased salience of differences based on age, suggesting the emergence of a slight "generation gap" in Canadian society, particularly on questions relating to foreign investment, social policy, moral issues and relations with French Canada. The young have always been somewhat more liberal on social and moral questions, more opposed to foreign influence and more conciliatory towards French-Canada, but, at least on the last three, the gap has recently widened. Age was among the lowest three cleavages in the first period in seven policy categories, but was among the lowest in only three policy areas in the second.[19]

Liberal/Conservative differences provide the only other category in which the difference index has grown. Most of this increase is accounted for by sharper partisan conflict over ties with Britain and French-English relations, but there were also slight increases for the role of government, social policy and foreign policy.

Unfortunately, with no definitive indicators of class position, we cannot explore fully the changing links between class and policy preference. Nevertheless, there are clear indications of its importance. Oddly enough, the class division does not show up in the Difference Indices based on union membership, perhaps because of the relatively small proportion of Canadian workers who belong to unions, and the failure of trade unions to mobilize membership support across a range of issues. In both periods the DIs for union membership were the lowest of all categories; it was among the bottom three indices in every issue area except for questions directly aimed at labour issues.

The class cleavage is, however, evident in the policy divisions based on education, where we compare citizens with post-secondary education with those with less than high school. In the first period education ranked second only to language as a source of division; in the second it was the most important division. Education was among the top three DIs in seven of the nine areas in both time periods, and was in the bottom three only twice in the second period. Immigration generated the sharpest educational cleavage, but it was also strong on social and economic issues, including foreign influence, the role of government and others. Nevertheless, one should be cautious about these figures, since in comparing the extremes we maximized the chances of discovering an educational cleavage. And over our full time period, the proportions of citizens of different educational levels changed dramatically: in 1949, those with Grade 8 or less made up almost half the sample; by 1975 they had dropped to a quarter.

This analysis of other cleavage lines helps put the regional differences we have found in perspective. Regional differences are indeed significant; they have not disappeared. But they have declined over time, along with most other divisions. This is true not only in absolute terms, but in comparison with the other divisions. Thus in our first period the average regional DI was exceeded by those for language, education, Quebec and religion. In the second period age and party were also stronger, and region exceeded only union membership as a source of division. In no issue area was region among the top three divisions. This interpretation is supported by another recent study, which finds that regional differences are large on matters of immediate intergovernmental conflict, but that in other areas, such as aid to minorities, law and order, foreign control of the economy and support for income redistribution, the variance explained by socioeconomic variables equals or exceeds that explained by region.[20]

II. Dimensions of Regional Difference

Because of their potential importance to the discussion of future political arrangements in Canada, the nature of regional policy differences merits more detailed attention. The general picture is one of convergence, but the character of changes varies from issue area to issue area. Table 4 provides the basic material for this discussion.

For each issue area and time period we have presented the average percentage of each region's population falling into the side of the policy dichotomy indicated in the last column; the range between the highest and lowest percentages; and changes in the difference index comparing each region to the rest of Canada. In addition, to give some idea of regional variations around the national level of support or opposition to policies in a given area, we have calculated the average regional deviation from the *national* percentage on the given side of each issue area. The results are not substantially different from those obtained by recalculation using the opposite side of the dichotomy, suggesting that they are not an artifact of variations in the size of the "don't know" category.

Role of Government

For questions about the role of government the gap between the highest and lowest dropped considerably, as did the average deviation from the figure. By the later time period, the regions differed from the national population by an average of less than two points. The whole country had become more sympathetic to an expanded role for government. British Columbians were most likely to be interventionists in both periods. The province scored highest in eight of the eighteen questions asked in period one, and in nine of the fourteen in period two. The Prairies ranked second in both periods. The Atlantic provinces changed places with Quebec. The latter changed most dramatically: least interventionist before 1970, it was above average after that, while the Atlantic provinces dropped to last. In the first period, the index of difference between Quebec and the other regions exceeded .100 in seven of eighteen cases; in the second period it did so in only three of fourteen. The average proportion in favour of intervention in Quebec rose by twenty-one points between the two periods, while in all other regions it did so by only twelve points.

Social Welfare

If support for government intervention grew, support for the welfare state measures of social policy did not. In all regions favourable responses declined — most notably in British Columbia — but regional deviations from the national figure, never large, declined slightly. The average difference index remained unchanged in the two periods. The apparent erosion of support for progressive social policies is hard to interpret. The basic principle of programs like unemployment insurance is no longer widely questioned (70 per cent support in 1961, for example), but there appears to be growing concern about lax administration and about the possibility that

Table 4
The Nature of Regional Differences on Policy Questions*
1949-69, 1970-75

Issue Area	National	Atlantic	Quebec	Ontario	Prairies	British Columbia	Average Regional DI	Range**	Average Regional Deviation from Nation***	Direction of Opinion
Role of government	36.2/ 51.4	35.2/ 47.6	30.7/ 51.8	34.0/ 50.7	38.9/ 51.6	43.4/ 56.2	.088/ .078	12.7/ 8.6	3.7/ 2.0	Pro
Foreign policy	41.9/ 43.0	41.7/ 35.9	37.0/ 40.0	46.9/ 45.3	48.1/ 43.8	50.8/ 49.6	.109/ .072	13.8/ 13.7	5.0/ 4.0	Liberal
Social policy	54.8/ 47.3	48.3/ 42.8	58.8/ 50.5	57.3/ 47.1	52.7/ 45.9	59.4/ 45.5	.091/ .091	11.1/ 7.7	3.9/ 2.2	Expand, Approve
Moral issues	54.2/ 41.0	46.1/ 35.2	54.2/ 38.4	56.5/ 40.0	52.0/ 38.4	59.7/ 43.1	.118/ .097	10.4/ 7.9	3.6/ 2.6	Soft Line
Ties with Britain	55.2/ 46.2	70.3/ 65.8	36.5/ 20.0	62.9/ 55.4	58.0/ 59.9	58.4/ 48.1	.152/ .202	33.8/ 45.8	9.5/ 14.1	Maintain
French-English relations	48.9/ 50.2	45.5/ 50.2	68.4/ 68.3	44.8/ 46.0	40.6/ 36.6	37.4/ 42.2	.193/ .171	31.0/ 31.7	9.4/ 8.8	Conciliatory
Foreign influence	37.0/ 60.0	26.9/ 52.4	34.9/ 57.7	38.5/ 67.6	40.3/ 61.3	41.8/ 64.4	.102/ .090	14.9/ 15.2	4.2/ 4.6	Oppose
Labour	40.0/ 48.5	39.5/ 45.5	36.0/ 47.4	40.2/ 46.9	44.6/ 50.8	41.8/ 42.4	.087/ .077	8.6/ 8.4	2.2/ 2.8	Anti-Critical
Immigration	46.5/ 41.6	48.3/ 41.9	38.1/ 42.0	50.9/ 39.4	47.0/ 47.1	50.2/ 39.4	.088/ .083	12.8/ 7.7	3.8/ 2.1	Favour, Expand

* Table entries in columns 1-6 are percentages of respondents supporting the side of a given policy dichotomy indicated by the last column, averaged over questions within time periods. The first percentage in each pair is for 1949-69, the second for 1970-75. For example, 36.2 per cent of Canadians favoured a positive role for government in period 1, 51.4 per cent in period 2.

** The absolute difference between the highest and lowest percentages in the five regions.

***Calculated as the sum of the absolute differences between each regional percentage and the national figure, divided by the number of regions.

some people may "rip off" or misuse the programs. For example, by 1972, 53 per cent felt the UIC program was not being administered strictly enough.

Nor did all elements of social programs lose support. Gallup sought opinions on a guaranteed annual income three times — in 1966, 1972 and 1973. The results suggest what may be a common pattern: one region, in this case Quebec, takes the lead in support of a new idea, and gradually as it is discussed widely by leaders and the media, the idea becomes generalized, so that regional, and probably other social differences decline. Thus in 1966, two-thirds of Quebeckers supported a GAI, but only one-third of prairie residents did. The average regional deviation from the national mean was ten points. Six years later, when schemes for a GAI were high on the national political agenda, only eight points separated the top and bottom province and the average deviation was less than three points. The spread increased a bit in 1973, but remained much lower than in 1966.

Among the regions, British Columbia and Quebec stood out as favouring progressive social policies in the first period. By the second period British Columbia had dropped, but Quebec remained the strongest area of support, with the highest scores in eight of the thirteen questions asked. In both periods the Atlantic region appears the least supportive of progressive social policy. Both Ontario and the Prairie provinces are in the middle.

The growth of interventionist sentiment and the high levels of support for progressive policies in Quebec are confirmed in a 1977 study carried out at York University.[21] A battery of questions asked whether respondents supported more government effort in a list of policy areas. Quebeckers were more likely to call for more effort in all nine welfare related categories. The mean proportion for Quebec was 70 per cent. The Atlantic provinces, somewhat surprisingly, were at 61 per cent; the three other regions had average scores of 49 to 50 per cent. Similarly, Quebeckers, followed by Atlantic Canadians, were much more likely to "strongly agree" that government should provide jobs for the unemployed.

Labour Policy

Greater conservatism is also evident in the many questions in the third "left-right" category, labour. Here, in both periods, we find small regional differences. In both, residents of the Prairies were most hostile to labour interests in general. Quebec was the most sympathetic in the first period and British Columbia in the second. Between 1961 and 1975 twelve questions were asked about the right of various groups like teachers and civil servants to strike. Again, differences are small, with British Columbia slightly more likely to accept the right to strike and Quebeckers slightly more likely to deny it. Given the preponderant provincial jurisdiction in this area, the similarities are striking.

Foreign Influence

In no category do we find such a dramatic — and countrywide — change as in responses to questions about foreign ownership. The impact is not so much in convergence — the average index of difference declined slightly, while the average deviations from the national figure rose slightly — but rather in the striking rise in opposition to foreign influence, and in the evenness of the rise across all regions. Thus, while the investment-hungry Atlantic region was in both time periods the least hostile to foreign influence, nevertheless, negative responses here to foreign influence almost doubled, from 27 to 52 per cent.

Quebec, it is sometimes thought, is less concerned with United States domination than it is with Anglo-Canadian domination. While Quebeckers were indeed least likely to deny the need for U.S. capital in questions asked in 1972 and 1975, it was still the case that, since 1967, solid majorities of Quebeckers replied "no" to questions asking if more U.S. investment was needed, and in 1975 Quebeckers were *most* likely to agree that there is too much U.S. influence.

In this area we have the opportunity to explore changes over time in responses to substantially the same question and to whether our generalizations extend beyond 1975. Table 5 represents the percentages by region responding "enough" or "need less" in response to the question "Do you think there is enough U.S. capital in Canada now, or would you like to see more U.S. capital invested in this country?" The figures from 1977 require some qualification of our earlier generalization since opposition to U.S. investment actually dropped slightly west of Quebec, and substantially in the Atlantic provices. Opposition in Quebec, however, is even more similar to the level in the non-Atlantic regions.

It has also been suggested that concern with foreign ownership was particularly strong in Ontario, with its manufacturing base, and that in the West the desire for investment, and perhaps even cultural similarities with the United States, led to more openness to American capital and influence. Elite reactions to measures such as the Foreign Investment Review Agency tend to support this view. The data refute it: in three of six questions asked about the need for foreign capital, the Prairies were most restrictive. On four questions asking whether there is too much U.S. influence, British Columbia leads on two and is second to Quebec on the two others.

There also appears to be a substantial difference between elite and mass views on foreign investment, with the gap declining as one moves west. Thus in 1973 Garth Stevenson asked provincial legislative members a series of questions, including whether foreign investment should be restricted.[22] A similar question was asked by Gallup in 1974. In Atlantic Canada, 69 per cent of the population, but only 24 per cent of the legislators supported restrictions; in Quebec the ratio was 59 to 32 per cent, in Ontario 62 to 72; in the Prairies 64 to 71; and in British Columbia 77 to 75. In all regions citizens

Table 5
Opposition to More U.S. Investment in Canada
by Region 1959-1977

Year of Survey	Percentage Opposed to More U.S. Investment					
	Atlantic	Quebec	Ontario	Prairies	British Columbia
1959*	25.0	41.0	55.6	47.2	48.8
1963	29.2	39.2	51.4	52.0	47.8
1967	56.9	62.7	58.4	57.5	71.0
1970	53.0	48.0	70.0	68.6	64.8
1972	60.9	58.3	72.6	71.9	64.8
1975	65.6	60.8	75.9	78.2	76.3
1977	52.9	66.1	70.2	77.1	71.3

*Figures for 1959 exclude those who thought that Canadian development financed by U.S. capital was "not a good thing" or who gave qualified support, approximately 23 per cent of the sample.

were much more likely to support establishment of an investment-screening agency than were the legislators.

Moral Issues

We now turn to a set of issues which we term "moral issues." They include a variety of questions in which the natural break seems to be between permissiveness and restrictiveness, and cultural traditionalism versus progressivism: the death penalty, abortion, drug use, school discipline, the punishment of criminals, and so on — a total of fifty-two questions over the years of this study. In general we find considerable convergence among the regions, and an apparent reaction against permissiveness, though this may be accounted for partly by a toughening of the questions — from those about birth control to those about abortion, for example — and partly by hardening attitudes on questions about crime, punishment and the death penalty, which were asked more often in the second period.

Maritimers were the most traditional, or least permissive, in both time periods, followed by the Prairies and Quebec. British Columbia fulfilled its "liberal" image, leading in both periods. This is borne out in two of the dominant, and somewhat different moral issues of our time: birth control and abortion, and capital punishment. Three questions on birth control up to 1965 showed approval rose in all regions, but by far the most strikingly in Quebec. British Columbia was most liberal on all three. Since 1965 six questions on abortion have been asked: British Columbia is most permissive on four, and Ontario on two. Atlantic Canada was least permissive on four.

Nine questions were asked about capital punishment. Since the wording varies, precise trends are hard to spell out, but by 1975 very small proportions opposed the death penalty (16 per cent for political criminals, 23 per cent for murder), while in the 1950s and 1960s abolition gained much larger proportions. In recent years British Columbia and Quebec have been most liberal, the Atlantic and Prairie provinces the least.

Immigration

Immigration issues engage a complex of economic, social and cultural concerns. Here we find once again an apparent hardening of attitudes over the whole period. This is especially visible in British Columbia and Ontario — two provinces with heavy immigration — which moved from the most to the least liberal positions. Quebec, by contrast, moved from the least to the most liberal, and was the only region to become more rather than less sympathetic. In general, in these "cultural" or life style matters, Quebec's convergence is even more striking than it is on social and economic issues, suggesting that the Quiet Revolution produced attitudinal changes across a wide spectrum.

Foreign Policy and Defence

A third major policy category is foreign policy and defence. There was a considerable decline in regional variation in foreign policy: in the most recent period, indeed, the difference index was lower than in any other category. In the first period Quebeckers were most likely to express isolationist attitudes. They changed places in the second period with the Atlantic region. In both periods, British Columbians were most liberal and open to the world. Differences on defence issues were small; the only noticeable deviation was Quebec, where we see a faint echo of earlier traumas in the tendency for Quebeckers to be more reluctant to endorse an active military policy. No defence questions satisfying our criteria were asked in the 1970–75 period, limiting our ability to generalize.

The Character of the Community: Ties with Britain, Federal-Provincial Relations and French-English Relations

In each of the categories so far we find moderate and declining regional differences, and a strong tendency for regional opinion to move in the same direction, even when differences are significant. Two other categories, however, provide a very different picture: one of large, persisting and increasing difference. They are French-English relations and ties with Britain, or symbols of nationhood.

The average index of difference for ties with Britain rose sharply across our two periods, as did the range of differences in proportions supporting British links, from an average deviation of 9.5 points to 14. These differences are all the more striking since the questions asked relate not to live political controversies, but rather to much more general orientations, notably support for the monarchy rather than republican government. Here there are few differences among the predominantly English-speaking provinces, though the Atlantic provinces stand out as most monarchist. The real break is between Quebec and the other provinces. The symbols of the British connection held little appeal there; conversely, those symbols have lost little of their potency elsewhere.

Most questions on French-English relations concern various aspects of bilingualism. We do find here a very modest convergence, but the differences remain large. The convergence is explained by a small increase in support for bilingualism in English Canada, except for the Prairies, where support eroded over the period. Ontario and the Maritimes, close to Quebec and with substantial French-speaking minorities, are slightly more open to bilingualism than the West. Two questions asked in each period are even less encouraging. In all regions there was in 1961 *more* support for the compulsory teaching of French in the schools than there was in 1974. Similarly, in every region approval of bilingual package labelling dropped between 1968 and 1972.[23]

The final category, federal-provincial relations, suffers from a paucity of questions over the period, and is better explored in Chapter V. Relatively few variations appear in the Gallup questions, partly because support for the provinces is strong everywhere. In 1972 Canadians were asked for the first time whether they would approve of a larger provincial role and a smaller federal role in the area of "taxation and social security,"[24] reviving a Gallup focus on jurisdictional questions first manifested in the late 1940s.[25] There was remarkably little variation in answers to this question (average DI across regions was .089) and that which existed was largely due to a lower level of support in the Atlantic region (35.3 per cent). Support in the other regions ranged from a low of 48.7 per cent in Ontario to 57.5 per cent in British Columbia. By 1977, when the question was repeated, support for decentralization had increased in the Atlantic region by twelve points and had reached a high in Alberta of 61.4 per cent.

Quebec, as expected, is the most "provincialist," followed by the Prairies. The surprise is British Columbia, which is the most federalist — even more than Ontario — on each of the five questions asked before 1969. Only one question in this category concerns an active political dispute — over establishment of the Canada and Quebec pension plans. One quarter of Quebeckers wanted Ottawa to run it, as did just under two-thirds in the Atlantic region, Ontario and the Prairies — but in British Columbia three-quarters supported a federal plan.

These three categories thus display a very different pattern from the earlier ones. On issues which concern the meaning, symbols and character of Canada as a political community divergences are large.

Other Areas

Women's rights has emerged as a key issue area in the 1970s. As a result, only a few questions from the Gallup surveys are available. On all nine questions, the average proportion in favour of equal pay for equal work and related matters was virtually the same (about 50 per cent) for all regions except British Columbia which was noticeably more liberal.

Similarly, only a few questions related unambiguously to free speech and civil liberties, not even enough to justify the tentative aggregations produced for women's rights. On all six such questions, spread between 1949 and 1974, British Columbians were the most liberal, followed by Ontarians and Prairie dwellers. Atlantic residents were consistently the most conservative. Again, however, there is an indication of a major shift in Quebec: in three questions prior to 1971, its citizens were most "repressive," but on three questions since then, they were almost as liberal as citizens on the west coast.

Conclusions

The striking finding of this analysis of Canadian public opinion expressed over thirty years of polling by the Canadian Institute of Public Opinion is the apparent convergence of regional opinion on most important public policy issues. The populations of the Canadian regions are becoming more alike in their responses to the issues of the day. While other social cleavages are also of declining significance in shaping views on policy, the *relative* importance of the regional differences has also diminished. Even when differences remained, there was a striking tendency for all regions to move in the same direction over time; seldom did opinion move in different directions.

This is not to say that region is no longer relevant. Some important differences remain. Maritimers are, compared with other Canadians, much more committed to maintaining symbolic ties with Britain, while at the same time they are less apprehensive about foreign investment. On the moral issues, Maritimers are less permissive than others; on defence matters they are more supportive of an active military policy. All this is consistent with a region which has strong attachments to traditional values. Economic need is the most likely explanation for the greater receptiveness to foreign investment.

Ontario residents do not appear to be sharply distinctive in any policy domain. Its citizens are somewhat more concerned than other Canadians to maintain British ties, to limit foreign influence, and to discourage expanded immigration.

Residents of the Prairies are considerably less likely than others to support official bilingualism. Perhaps in reaction against recent policies to foster bilingualism, Westerners are second only to the Maritimes in defence of the British tie.

British Columbians are noticeably more liberal on the "life-style" questions tapped in moral issues, the rights of women, civil liberties, and the like. The effects of the cooperative and populist tradition in both British Columbia and the Prairies were seen in their somewhat greater than average support of state intervention and the welfare state.

The second major finding concerns the position of Quebec. Even though it remains quite distinctive on many issues, the convergence between its citizens and those of the rest of Canada is remarkable. Equally remarkable is the degree of change in Quebec opinion: it has been more volatile than opinion anywhere else. Thus it moved from least to most interventionist on issues dealing with the scope of government, it moved from the most conservative and traditional on issues like civil rights to among the most liberal — striking evidence for the pervasive effects of the rapid secularization that accompanied the Quiet Revolution.

Our third basic finding is that two clear exceptions to a generally increasing similarity stand out. Questions relating to French-English relations, while producing slight convergence, remained highly divisive. Questions about ties to Britain — symbolic, we assume, of a much wider set of views about the nature and meaning of the political community — produced wider differences in the 1970s than they did before.

With so few questions on these subjects, it is risky to read much into these data. But they are entirely consistent with findings reported in other chapters, where we found increasingly strong attachments to provincial governments, and a declining integration of national and provincial voting and party systems. They are also consistent, of course, with recent political events, especially the rise of autonomist sentiment in Quebec and the 1976 election victory of the Parti Québécois, the growing salience of federal-provincial conflict, and the inability of governments to agree on important constitutional issues.

The patterns described here demonstrate that similarity of policy preferences — of expectations about what governments should do — does not in any way necessarily imply growth in common identities or loyalties; nor does it imply consensus on which level should do it. Translated into Canadian politics, this means that a growing consensus among Canadians of both linguistic groups and all regions need not be, and is not in many cases, accompanied by a consensus on the political community.

Several explanations for this apparent paradox may be offered. First, it may be that the questions which the CIPO has asked seldom directly concern current subjects of dispute between federal and provincial governments, such as energy pricing. Similarly, few questions refer to the historic issues of regional grievance: the tariff, transportation, and so on. On such questions regional differences of opinion might have loomed larger. Nor do these questions directly examine possible differences in the agenda of political debate within provinces. Rather, most Gallup questions focus on issues which have been subjects of nationwide media attention and of debate between national parties and leaders. It is not surprising, therefore, that regional populations would respond to the same stimuli in much the same terms. Even if this is true, however, it does not explain the convergence between our two time periods.

Second, it might be argued that one lesson of this study is that regional political elites may only imperfectly represent underlying political sentiment. Thus, if concerned with their own drive for power and status, they have a strong incentive to exaggerate the degree of provincial homogeneity, and to stress points of difference, rather than similarity, in relations with other governments. Third, so long as provincial governments possess the bureaucratic and fiscal resources, then it does not necessarily follow that citizens with common interests should necessarily look to the federal government to enact them. Their interests may be satisfied just as well by a provincial government — which has the additional advantage of proximity.

Fourth, there are grounds for believing that in some circumstances growing *similarity* of aspirations and values may actually foster interregional conflict and divergent orientations to the political community. This may happen when there are pre-existing identities, with an existing political framework for mobilizing them, so that the regional community becomes a readily available "container" into which new policy aspirations or disputes can be poured, and when common interests lead to competition for similar scarce values. For example, it was once thought that ethnic conflict in Canada was largely a product of the fundamentally *different* cultural values of French and English Canadians. The implication was that as Quebec "modernized," as Quebeckers became more like their fellow citizens, then the grounds for conflict would diminish. The reverse, of course, happened. One explanation is that it does so precisely *because* of the growing similarity. For that meant that now the two groups were competing for shares of the *same* values, such as jobs in the federal civil service or in Montreal head offices. No longer could each group proceed to enact its own agenda without implicating the other. They were now on the same plane; they made the same demands on each other and on government. It would be natural for the minority group in such a conflict to turn to the government which it alone could control. This was, in Quebec, facilitated by another consequence of change, which is captured in our data. Identities based on language and culture could not take the form of a demand for *political* independence until the state was no longer regarded with suspicion and hostility. One of the most important attitudinal aspects of the Quiet Revolution was indeed such a transformation in Quebeckers' view of the state.[26] Thus there is no inconsistency between the convergence we find here and the divergence in political loyalties and conceptions of the political community.

A somewhat similar argument might apply to other regions as well. Much current intergovernmental conflict involves competing programs for regional economic development, with provinces increasingly challenging federal dominance. Such disputes — over equalization to the Maritimes, over resource rents, and so on — do not so much represent different goals as they do competition over where development will occur, who will benefit from it, and which level of government is best equipped to generate it.

Thus no clear lessons for constitution makers emerge from this analysis. In few areas do the goals of regional populations diverge greatly. Regional differences are declining in many areas. In most areas other sources of identification and policy interests weigh more heavily than does region. In most cases greater provincial autonomy would not likely result in pursuit of radically different policies. Nor would further centralization likely mean that the *policy* preferences of many territorially defined groups would be frustrated by the national majority. The debate about the division of powers, it appears, is not really a debate about the uses to which power will be put. It is, instead, a debate about political community, and to a lesser extent about the efficiency with which various policies will be provided.

But much more evidence would be necessary to make the case decisively. Few of the issues in the distribution of powers which have arisen in recent constitutional debate — natural resources, fisheries, communication, and so on—have been probed in CIPO questions. Hardly any questions have been asked about which level of government citizens would prefer to provide particular services. Nor is similarity of viewpoint a necessary reason for centralization of responsiblity. If all governments face the same preferences from their citizens, then policy is likely to be very similar in all provinces even without overriding federal power.

In general the findings here must qualify the stress on regionalism and provincialism which dominates Canadian political discourse. There does appear to be an incongruence between a set of institutions and policy processes based largely on the primacy of the territorial cleavage and a set of policy attitudes in which the territorial base, while important, appears to be declining on many issues and to be less significant than other potential divisions. Elite political conflict does exaggerate, and perhaps even artificially create, perception of the dominance of regional differences which are not reflected strongly in mass opinion. Real as regional conflicts are, they take place against a background in which on most matters of substance Canadians in Vancouver, Toronto, Montreal and Halifax share broadly similar beliefs about what it is their governments should do.

Notes

1. See, for example, Task Force on Government Information, *To Know and Be Known*, vol. 2, Research Papers (Ottawa: Queen's Printer, 1969), pp. 52-57.

2. S. M. Lipset and Stein Rokkan, eds., "Cleavage Structure, Party Systems and Voter Alignments," in their *Party Systems and Voter Alignments: Cross-National Perspectives* (New York: Free Press, 1967), especially pp. 9-26.

3. For a survey see Milton J. Esman, ed., *Ethnic Conflict in the Western World*, (Ithaca, N.Y.: Cornell University Press, 1977).

4. See Michael Hechter, *Internal Colonialism: The Celtic Fringe in British National Development, 1536-1966* (London: Routledge and Kegan Paul, 1975); Tom Nairn, *The Break-up of Britain* (London: Humanities Press, 1977).

5. See J. A. Corry, "Constitutionalism Trends and Federalism," in *Evolving Canadian Federalism*, ed. A. R. M. Lower et al. (Durham: Duke University Press, 1958), pp. 92-125.

6. Samuel Beer, "The Modernization of American Federalism," *Publius*, 3 (1973): 49-95.

7. See Alan Cairns, "The Governments and Societies of Canadian Federalism," *Canadian Journal of Political Science*, 10 (December 1977), 695-726; Richard Simeon, "Regionalism and Canadian Political Institutions," in *Canadian Federalism: Myth or Reality?* 3rd. ed., ed. Peter Meekison (Toronto: Methuen, 1977), pp. 292-303.

8. For a survey, see Jeffery Evenson and Richard Simeon, "The Roots of Discontent," in *The Political Economy of Confederation*. Proceedings (Ottawa: Economic Council of Canada and Institute of Intergovernmental Relations, 1979), 165-196. For attempts to devise a division of powers suited to present conditions, see *Towards a New Canada*. A research paper for the Committee on the Constitution, The Canadian Bar Association, (Montreal: 1978); Ontario Advisory Committee on Confederation, *Second Report* (Toronto: Government of Ontario, 1979).

9. For a superb assessment and critique of recent proposals, see Alan Cairns, "Recent Federalist Constitutional Proposals: A Review Essay," *Canadian Public Policy*, 3 (Summer, 1979),

pp. 348-365. See also W. P. Irvine, "Liberté, Egalité, Fraternité: Respecifying the Federal Role," in *Must Canada Fail?* ed. Richard Simeon (Montreal: McGill-Queen's University Press, 1977), pp. 169-76; Canada. Task Force on Canadian Unity, *A Future Together* (Ottawa: Supply and Sources, 1979); Government of Alberta, *Harmony in Diversity: A New Federalism for Canada* (Edmonton: 1977).

10. For a survey of other criteria, see Richard Simeon, "Criteria for Choice" (Paper presented at Workshop on the Political Economy of Confederation, Kingston, November 1978).

11. We are most grateful to the Canadian Institute of Public Opinion, Toronto, for permission to use the data on which this study is based. The CIPO is in no way responsible for the analysis, for its presentation or interpretation, or for any conclusions reached. Data from the Gallup surveys of 1976 and 1977 were made available from the University of British Columbia Data Library.

12. Mildred Schwartz, *Public Opinion and Canadian Identity* (Berkeley: University of California Press, 1967) is the only study of Canadian public opinion of comparable scope. She does not restrict her attention to policy issues as we have defined them, but does explore the degree of cross-regional and cross-party consensus on groups of issues for different periods of time until 1962. Norval D. Glenn and J.L. Simmons, "Are Regional Cultural Differences Diminishing?" *Public Opinion Quarterly* 31 (Summer 1967): 176-193, examine the proportion of "liberal" responses to a variety of questions in eight issue areas given by younger and older people. Like us, they are interested in the degree to which age groups differ over a range of questions rather than on a particular question.

13. Most of these classifications are self-explanatory, as are the types of people excluded from a given division. Party support was ascertained using the standard Gallup question: "If a federal election were held today which party's candidate do you think you would favour?" Beginning with the July 1971 Gallup poll (No. 348), eighteen- to twenty-year-olds were included in the under-thirty age group. Prior to that time the youngest respondents were twenty-one. For a few surveys in the 1950s, English and French speakers were distinguished from bilinguals. In the remainder of the period "English," "French" and "other" responses were determined using the question: "What was the language you first spoke in childhood and still understand?"

14. See Norval D. Glenn, "Massification versus Differentiation: Some Trend Data from National Surveys," *Public Opinion Quarterly*, 46 (December 1967): 172-180. Glenn also follows the strategy of comparing differences between opinion distributions for a variety of cleavage groups. However, he restricts his coverage to pairs of questions with essentially the same wording separated in time by periods varying from eight and one-half to twenty-three years.

15. An extensive literature developed along this line in the 1960s. Prominent examples are Daniel Bell, *The End of Ideology* (New York: Collier Books, 1961); and Robert E. Lane, "The Politics of Consensus in an Age of Affluence," *American Political Science Review*, 49 (1965): 874-895. Other examples are cited in Glenn, "Massification versus Differentiation."

16. See Robert Alford, *Party and Society* (Chicago: Rand McNally, 1963); Mildred Schwartz, *Politics and Territory* (Montreal: McGill-Queen's University Press, 1974); Donald Blake, "The Measurement of Regionalism in Canadian Voting Patterns," *Canadian Journal of Political Science* 5 (March 1972): 55-81; Michael Ornstein, H. Michael Stevenson, and Paul Williams, "Region, Class and Political Culture" (Paper presented to the Canadian Political Science Association, June 1979).

17. Mildred Schwartz, *Public Opinion and Canadian identity*, p. 251, qualifies this conclusion by suggesting that "views on symbolic questions are becoming less divergent between English and French Canadians." But she anticipates one of our clearest findings, noting that questions tapping ties to Britain are a major exception. Schwartz also anticipates our finding of declining regional differences and increasing opposition all over Canada to U.S. investment and to immigration.

18. A detailed examination of this question is not possible here. For an excellent exploration of the perspectives of different ethnic groups on Canadian immigration policy, see John R. Wood, "East Indians and Canada's New Immigration Policy," *Canadian Public Policy* 4 (Autumn 1978): 547-67.

19. We cannot, in any event, address the question of whether age trends are the result of generational changes or of changes associated with aging. For an ingenious attempt using American Gallup poll data and age differences to explore the possibility that regional cultural differences in the United States are diminishing, see Glenn and Simmons, "Are Regional Cultural Differences Diminishing?" The authors compare the percentage "liberal" responses among younger and older people over a range of questions. Their reasoning was that if cultural differences are to diminish, between-region differences of opinion should be less for younger people than for older people. They conclude (p. 181) that "The data fail to support the belief that regional differences have declined appreciably; instead, they suggest that many kinds of differences have increased." Unfortunately, they cover only the period 1953 to 1961, limiting the possibility of comparing the United States and Canada.

20. See Michael D. Ornstein, H. Michael Stevenson, and Paul Williams, "Region, Class and Political Culture," *Canadian Journal of Political Science*, 13 (June 1980), 227-272. Their data are from a 1977 survey conducted as part of the "Social Change in Canada" project based at York University.

21. The data were made available by W.P. Irvine and the documentation unit, Department of Political Studies, Queen's University.

22. See Garth Stevenson, "Foreign Direct Investment and the Provinces: A Study of Elite Attitudes," *Canadian Journal of Political Science*, 7 (December 1974): 630-647.

23. If anything, positions seem to have hardened in this area, since 1972. When asked in July 1977 whether Quebec should have a "special status," defined as "more powers than other provinces," fully 91 per cent of Canadians outside Quebec expressed opposition. However, this was also true of 72 per cent of Quebec residents. Even assuming most English Quebeckers are opposed to special status, this is still a large figure. Only 3.3 per cent of the sample did not have an opinion on this question. The Quebec/not Quebec difference score on this question was .191.

24. The exact question was: "As you may know, provincial governments are asking for more responsibilities in such areas as taxation and social security measures — like welfare, pensions, and so on. Would you approve or disapprove if the provincial governments had more power in these fields and the federal government had less?"

25. In a series of surveys conducted between 1943 and 1948, approximately 45-50 per cent of Canadians expressed opposition to further transfers of power to Ottawa and to Ottawa's retention of its extra wartime powers. See Schwartz, *Public Opinion and Canadian Identity*, p. 93, Table 32.

26. See for example, James de Wilde, "The Parti Quebecois in Power," in Simeon, ed., *Must Canada Fail?*

IV

The Horizontal Mosaic: Immigrants and Migrants in the Provincial Political Cultures

David J. Elkins

Immigrants assimilate, to one degree or another, when they settle in a new place. But to what do they assimilate — to Canada, to provincial or regional norms, to the standards of a local ethnic group, or what? Does it matter more for the development of their political culture that they have come from a particular background or that they have migrated to a particular place? Persons who grew up in one region of Canada but move to a new province might be expected to exhibit the same degree of diversity as does Canada. But will they retain the political culture of their province of origin or will they acquire norms more appropriate to their new home?

Theories of socialization and of personality development suggest that people have quite definite patterns of thought and behaviour even before full adulthood. Therefore, since most immigrants to Canada and most migrants from one province to another are adults, it stands to reason that their political cultures should reflect the areas in which they grew up. Consequently, migration into Canada from abroad and across provincial boundaries should have the effect of homogenizing Canada's regional diversity, since movement of different types of people into each region would make the composition of regions more similar. Paradoxical as it may seem, to make each region more diverse would serve to make Canada less diverse from one region to the next.[1]

These speculations about the homogenizing effects of migration may be strengthened by practical considerations about why people who move to the various Canadian regions might have more "national" orientations and be less "provincial" in outlook. Most immigrants would come from countries which are less regionally divided than Canada. The largest single group comes from Britain, of course, which has a unitary form of government and may also be less "provincialized," though Scotland, Wales and Northern Ireland are quite distinct from England. Furthermore, immigrants deal

106

mainly with the federal government, and hence they might think of that level as more important than the provincial.

Migrants from one province to another might be more nationally oriented, since leaving an area implies less commitment to it than is exhibited by those who stay. Only if there is a national community with common economic and political processes can such mobility occur; hence migrants might become more aware of the national level of politics than nonmigrants.

Many of these speculations find support in our data. In Chapter I we reported, for example, that migrants are more federally oriented on several of our measures, and that migrants generally are more critical of governments than nonmigrants, suggesting that "broadened horizons" and willingness to compare, contrast and criticize institutions are products in part of exposure to varied circumstances. We also saw that native-born Canadians were more "provincial" than immigrants, and that immigrants became more provincial in orientation the longer they resided in any Canadian region. In addition, country of birth and country of ancestors play virtually no part in explaining the scores on the Canadian national identity index, except that those of French origin score slightly lower and those of British origin score slightly higher.[2]

All of these observations support the hypothesis that over time there should be a decline in regionalism and provincial distinctiveness in political cultures.[3] The alternative hypothesis is that the provincial political cultures are stable or becoming even more distinct, and that they exert an independent influence on immigrants and migrants. If people moving into an area assimilate to the norms of that area, this would explain the persistence of provincial cultures. It would also provide indirect proof that Canadian provincial cultures are creatures of long standing and not temporary anachronisms.

It might be argued, however, that the provinces diverge so much in political characteristics because they differentially attract people with one or another kind of orientation. While it is implausible that most immigrants know enough about regional political differences to choose their residence on that basis, some migrants from other regions might seek out places with a particular party or a special "style" of politics. Selective migration on the basis of political characteristics seems less plausible when we recall that many migrants choose their destination on the basis of kin ties, friendship networks and job opportunities. We will present some evidence which might reflect a degree of selective migration, but most of the evidence supports our contention that the regional political cultures have long existed as stable and relatively autonomous normative forces.

Selective migration, if it occurs, does not invalidate the influence of political cultures. It simply specifies the means by which provincial differences are maintained. If political culture areas attract certain types of citizens, this certainly constitutes evidence of their strength.

A related avenue of investigation concerns what kinds of provincial cultures might have existed if there were no immigration or internal migration. We will construct various "hypothetical provinces," based on a knowledge of who has always lived in a province, who has recently arrived and who arrived from what other backgrounds. Again, the evidence will clearly support only one interpretation: with or without migration, the provinces would manifest distinctive political cultures.

The title of this chapter should recall John Porter's famous metaphor of Canadian society as a vertical mosaic.[4] While we take exception to some of Porter's analysis, our emphasis on horizontal diversity rather than vertical is intended to supplement his analysis and is not a criticism of him. His demonstration of linkages among ethnicity, class and power need to be considered in the context of independent cleavages such as province of residence and political culture. Nevertheless, within each region, power is distributed quite unevenly on ethnic and class grounds.

Patterns of Immigration and Migration

It is a cliché that Canada is a land of immigrants. Even for the native peoples, one must assume a migration from Asia. But for the vast majority of Canadians immigration is a recent event, if not personally, then for a parent or a grandparent.

Cliché or not, it is well to remind ourselves of this feature of Canada. There are important differences between people born in different countries, and the mixture of backgrounds — the mosaic — is a visible feature of Canadian society. In Table 1, we present the simple tabulation of the proportions of foreign-born residents of Canada in recent decades and the countries and areas of the world from which immigrants have come. The merged data sets which we will analyze below reflect this diversity quite accurately. Although about 18 per cent of the samples report being born outside of Canada, which is higher than the census figures in Table 1, this discrepancy is easily explained. The sample consists of voters, hence of citizens. Since the average age of immigrants is much higher and the proportion of children is lower than for the native-born, the proportion of *voters* who are foreign-born should be higher than their proportion of the total population.[5]

The overwhelming majority of immigrants have been from European countries and from the United States. Recently, however, there has been a slight decline in the European proportion and an increase in the Third World and particularly in the Asian proportion of immigrants. Although French-speaking immigrants from France and elsewhere continue to arrive, it is clear that they are greatly outnumbered by non-French. This is, of course, one major source of concern among Francophones, especially in Quebec: the "dominant" English group has grown by immigration much faster than the French, and there is no reason to expect any substantial change in that trend.[6]

Table 1
A. Immigrants to Canada, 1946-71

Source	Numbers
United Kingdom	982 288
France	110 314
All other European	1 778 571
Australia, New Zealand	60 886
United States	384 137
Other western hemisphere	183 093
Asia	263 278
Africa	63 120
Oceania (islands not included in Asia, South America, Australia or New Zealand)	17 276
Total	3 842 963

Source: Canadian Government, Department of Manpower and Immigration, *Immigration and Population Statistics* (Ottawa: Information Canada, 1974), pp. 32-37. Reproduced by permission of the Minister of Supply and Services Canada.

B. Foreign-born in Canadian Population at End of Decade

Period	Number (in thousands)	Percentage of total population
1941-51	2060	14.7
1951-61	2844	15.6
1961-71	3269	15.3

Source: From *Canada: A Socio-Political Report* by Ronald Manzer, p. 118, based on figures supplied by Statistics Canada. Copyright© 1974, McGraw-Hill Ryerson Limited. Reprinted by permission.

Table 2
Percentage of Regional Populations Which Are Foreign-born, 1951, 1961 and 1971

	1951	1961	1971
Atlantic (includes Newfoundland)	3.4	3.5	3.6
Quebec	5.6	7.4	7.8
Ontario	18.5	21.7	22.2
Prairies	22.9	19.1	15.4
British Columbia	29.1	26.0	22.7
Territories	10.6	12.4	9.0

Source: 1951-1961: From *The Demographic Bases of Canadian Society* by Warren E. Kalbach and Wayne W. McVey. Copyright© 1971, McGraw-Hill Ryerson Limited, p. 143. Reprinted by permission.
1971: Statistics Canada, Population Census, vol. 1, part 5.

Not only is Canada's population rich in diversity of backgrounds, but the provinces are quite varied in their patterns. Table 2 contains data on the percentage of each province or region which was foreign-born in the 1951, 1961 and 1971 censuses. The figures reveal wide variation from area to area, with Ontario and the West hosting high proportions of foreign-born and Quebec and the Atlantic region low proportions of immigrants. Although eastern Canada appears to have a stable foreign element, Ontario's proportion of immigrants is rising while those in the West have declined over this period. In part this decline of foreign-born in the West is deceptive, since it reflects mainly the greatly enhanced rates of in-migration (in Alberta and British Columbia principally) from other provinces, rather than a real decrease in foreign immigrants. This, then, is one way in which immigration might prove *not* to be a homogenizing force, since the immigrants are unevenly distributed geographically.[7] Furthermore, the provinces differ in terms of the relative proportions of their immigrants who come from eastern Europe, western Europe, Asia and the Americas.

There is also regional variety among the Canadian populace in terms of interprovincial mobility. In Table 3 we see the proportion of people in the period 1966-1971 who moved from any given province to each other province. Two patterns are quite clear. First, Ontario is by far the major destination of out-migrants from Quebec and the Atlantic region, while British Columbia is the target of most western migrants, with Alberta also important. Second, propinquity is a major factor in mobility. There is considerable migration within the Atlantic region; Quebec and Ontario exchange populations at a high rate; and a large proportion of Prairie residents migrate within that region or to British Columbia.

Over time these patterns have changed somewhat. Ontario has yielded somewhat to Alberta and British Columbia as a prime destination, though its predominance is still obvious. Also, intra-Atlantic and intra-Prairie mobility has increased from the 1956-1961 period to 1966-1971. Impressionistic evidence based on out-migration from Quebec and on the growth of Calgary and Edmonton as financial and resource centres suggests that these trends will continue for some time.

These patterns and trends contradict the possibility outlined above that selective migration on the basis of political styles could account for the existence of regional political cultures. If people move mainly to one province, Ontario, or if they move to contiguous provinces (within a region like the Maritimes), their chances of finding quite different political cultures more congenial to them are minimized. Selective migration may happen, but it must occur on a limited scale.

In Table 4 we summarize the net effect of these various forces. Provinces clearly differ in rate of population growth. They diverge in rate of natural increase, but most notably they exhibit enormous variation in the rate of net migration (which here includes both foreign migration and interprovincial migration).

Table 3
Intra-Canadian Migrants Five Years and Over, by Province of Residence in 1966, for Canada and the Provinces, 1971*
(Vertical Percentages)

Province of Origin (1966)

Province of Destination (1971)	Newfoundland	P.E.I.	N.S.	N.B.	Quebec	Ontario	Manitoba	Saskatchewan	Alberta	B.C.	Yukon and N.W.T.	Ratio of out-migrants to in-migrants	Index of instability
Newfoundland	—	2.4	4.4	2.6	1.4	3.4	0.2	0.2	0.4	0.6	1.8	2.13	.132
P.E.I.	1.2	—	3.7	2.9	0.5	1.6	0.5	0.1	0.2	0.4	0.1	1.12	.150
N.S.	11.9	23.1	—	18.7	4.1	10.1	2.1	0.8	1.9	3.4	2.0	1.17	.146
N.B.	6.0	14.1	14.2	—	6.3	6.7	1.6	0.5	1.1	1.6	2.3	1.21	.142
Quebec	7.7	6.7	8.1	17.8	—	25.9	5.3	1.5	3.2	6.4	3.4	1.91	.152
Ontario	61.6	37.7	47.7	41.7	66.9	—	27.4	11.3	16.8	28.6	17.3	0.77	.160
Manitoba	2.3	2.8	3.1	3.0	2.9	9.8	—	15.7	6.9	8.5	5.4	1.53	.157
Saskatchewan	1.0	1.3	1.1	1.1	1.1	3.7	10.9	—	10.1	8.2	3.6	2.87	.168
Alberta	2.8	5.3	6.1	4.8	5.2	12.6	20.1	40.1	—	37.4	26.5	0.82	.195
B.C.	5.0	6.3	11.3	7.0	11.3	25.4	31.0	28.7	56.2	—	33.7	0.38	.245
Yukon and N.W.T.	0.6	0.4	0.4	0.4	0.4	0.9	0.9	1.2	3.3	4.9	—	0.74	.272
CANADA	13 585	8470	46 165	36 890	77 895	241 180	56 900	36 355	127 555	194 195	12 210	851 495	.168

*(a) Source: Statistics Canada, Population Census, vol. 1, part 2, Table 32 (November 1974).
 (b) Omitted:"place of residence not stated in 1966," which amounts to 7.7 per cent of total intra-Canadian migration.
 (c) "Canada" row is the total number of 1971 residents, by province, who in-migrated during the period 1966-1971.
 (d) Index of instability = (intraprovincial migrants + interprovincial in-migrants) ÷ total population (1971).

Table 4
Change in Population as a Result of Natural Increase and Net Migration,
Canada, by Province, 1951-71

	Population		Percentage change, 1951-71		
	1951	1971	Natural Increase	Net Migration	Total
	(Thousands)		(Per cent)		
Newfoundland	361	522	60	−16	44
Prince Edward Island	98	112	32	−18	14
Nova Scotia	643	789	35	−12	23
New Brunswick	516	635	40	−17	23
Quebec	4056	6028	43	6	49
Ontario	4598	7703	40	28	68
Manitoba	776	988	34	− 7	27
Saskatchewan	832	926	36	−25	11
Alberta	939	1628	53	20	73
British Columbia	1165	2185	36	52	88
Canada	14 009	21 568	41	13	54

Source: Estimates by the Economic Council of Canada, based on data from Statistics Canada, published in *Living Together: A Study of Regional Disparities* (Ottawa: Supply and Services, 1977), p. 175.

Our samples of respondents reflect these patterns. Somewhat over half of the respondents in our studies claim they have always lived in the same province. The question specified that visits or brief stays in another province did not count; a relatively permanent move was required for classification as living in another province. Nearly a quarter of the respondents satisfied these criteria, and are counted as having lived in more than one province for a substantial period (usually their childhood). The remainder consist of immigrants, people who could not recall which provinces they had inhabited, or who refused to say. Hence the numbers of mobile Canadians and the wide variety of regional backgrounds allow us to compare people in terms of the permanence of their residence and in terms of the provinces of origin. As we shall see, current province of residence exerts its influence clearly on the mobile Canadians' expressions of political culture.

Country of Birth

Turning first to a comparison of Canadians born here or abroad, we present in Table 5 the data for their scores on our measure of political efficacy. Oddly, native-born Canadians have, on the average, slightly lower scores on efficacy than immigrants. This provides an object lesson in the dangers of generalizing from national patterns, since half the provinces follow the national pattern and half follow the opposite. There are several hopotheses which could account for this mixture of patterns, at least at the provincial level. For one, the provinces where immigrants appear more efficacious than

Table 5
Country of Birth by Efficacy Scores for the Province-Language Groups
(Merged Data, 1968 and 1974)

	Mean Scores (N)		
	Born in		All
	Canada	Elsewhere	Respondents
Nation	1.71	1.75	1.72
	(3256)	(713)	(3969)*
Atlantic Provinces**	1.56	1.77	1.57
	(429)	(13)	(442)
Quebec French	1.53	1.67	1.53
	(891)	(21)	(912)
Quebec Non-French	1.77	1.63	1.71
	(120)	(63)	(184)
Ontario	1.86	1.81	1.85
	(940)	(329)	(1272)
Manitoba	1.74	1.62	1.72
	(163)	(29)	(192)
Saskatchewan	1.77	1.48	1.73
	(159)	(29)	(188)
Alberta	1.76	1.57	1.71
	(236)	(84)	(321)
B.C.	1.99	1.83	1.94
	(253)	(121)	(375)
Non-Quebec French	1.50	1.50	1.50
	(107)	(4)	(111)

* Ns for born in Canada and born elsewhere may not add up to those for all respondents, because some people answered "don't know" or did not answer.
** In Tables 5 to 11, the Atlantic provinces have been combined because of the small numbers of immigrants in each.

persons born in Canada have very small numbers of immigrants; hence the means based on a few cases may be unstable. This seems implausible since one would not, in such circumstances, expect such a consistent pattern. Another possibility concerns the logical relation of political efficacy to a general sense of efficacy. By emigrating from their native country, immigrants to Canada often demonstrate some disenchantment with their circumstances and a sense that they can take action to deal with these dissatisfactions. If they are, by this measure, more efficacious or self-reliant, perhaps they would be expected to score higher on our measure of political efficacy.

More to the point, we suspect that selective migration among native-born Canadians helps to account for the observed pattern. If people with higher efficacy scores leave areas (like the Atlantic provinces or Quebec) with relatively low average efficacy scores, then those "donor" provinces will have even lower scores, while "receiving" provinces will manifest higher average scores. The provinces or language groups in which those born here score lower than immigrants are precisely the provinces with the highest rates of out-migration. "Receiving" provinces, on the other hand, reveal a pattern where native-born Canadians are much more efficacious than immigrants. Further evidence supporting this speculation will be found later in this chapter.

The French, whether in Quebec or outside, are not as highly migratory as Maritimers, though many have gone to Ontario to seek jobs. Therefore, we hypothesize that low levels of education and affluence probably contribute to the low efficacy scores among Francophones, especially in Quebec.[8] The political culture of Quebec itself cannot be the primary explanation, since the non-French, native-born residents there score higher than immigrants and have much higher education and income levels.

In short, there are reasonable grounds so far for thinking that provincial norms are operative. The variation among immigrants on the efficacy dimension is large and follows regional norms closely. In conjunction with

Table 6
Country of Birth by Trust Scores for the Province-Language Groups
(Merged Data, 1965 and 1968)

	Mean Scores (N)		
	Born in		All Respondents
	Canada	Elsewhere	
Nation	1.74 (4020)	1.77 (864)	1.75 (4876)
Atlantic Provinces	1.61 (420)	1.48 (25)	1.60 (445)
Quebec French	1.68 (1168)	1.57 (23)	1.67 (1191)
Quebec Non-French	1.74 (140)	1.71 (66)	1.73 (206)
Ontario	1.83 (1222)	1.82 (398)	1.83 (1620)
Manitoba	1.78 (206)	1.92 (50)	1.81 (256)
Saskatchewan	1.69 (183)	1.62 (45)	1.68 (228)
Alberta	1.76 (290)	1.66 (115)	1.73 (405)
B.C.	1.86 (238)	1.80 (136)	1.84 (374)
Non-Quebec French	1.71 (153)	1.33 (6)	1.70 (159)

selective migration, most of the variation in native-born and immigrant scores on efficacy can be accounted for by political culture norms at the provincial level.

The scores on political trust in Table 6 reveal an even clearer pattern of regional norms. In nearly every area west of the Ottawa River, immigrants approximate closely to the provincial norms on trust. Where divergence occurs, principally in the Atlantic provinces and among the French, the low-scoring immigrants cannot be viewed as responding to the national rather than regional norms, since they score even further below the national average than do the Canadian-born residents. (The fact that the national average for immigrants exceeds that for the Canadian-born reflects the preponderance of numbers of high-scoring immigrants in Ontario and British Columbia.)

Political involvement varies so little among province/language groups that it provides scant evidence for or against any hypothesis. However, immigrants vary in the same general way as do the native-born, to the extent that either group does. To save space, we have not presented these data on involvement.

Comparing the findings for all three of our indicators of political culture, we can tentatively conclude that immigrants assimilate to provincial, regional or language norms and not to national norms. Given the limited numbers of immigrants to the Atlantic provinces, it has not been possible to compare regional to provincial effects there. In any case, there is relatively little variation among these four provinces when compared to Ontario or the rest of Canada. Also, due to the small numbers, we have not presented tables on the specific countries in which immigrants were born; but later in the chapter an analysis of variance of country of ancestral origin suggests that this variable has at best a modest impact on the learning of provincial norms of political culture.

Period of Immigration

A logical hypothesis on the basis of general models of assimilation would state that the longer an immigrant resides in his new home, the closer he will approximate to the local norms. We know, however, that over the last few decades there have been changes in the relative proportions of immigrants from different backgrounds. There has been an increase in eastern and southern Europeans and Asians, and there has been a shift from interwar and postwar political refugees to persons in the 1950s and 1960s seeking better jobs or more pleasant surroundings. Hence an equally plausible hypothesis would state that the type and degree of assimilation will depend on the motives for emigration, skill and education levels, and place of origin of the immigrants. The two hypotheses can be combined to state that *within each type of immigrant* length of residence correlates positively with assimilation.

Tables 7 to 9 present the mean scores on our three indicators of political culture, by region and language groups, for Canadian-born respondents, for those who immigrated here before or during World War II, and for those who immigrated since then. The data lend credence to the above hypotheses, although the limited numbers of cases preclude some kinds of test we deem relevant.

Table 7
Year Immigrated to Canada by Efficacy Scores for Province-Language Groups
(Merged Data, 1968 and 1974)

	Mean Scores (N)		
	Born in	Immigrated	
	Canada	Before 1946	1946-73
Nation	1.71	1.62	1.84
	(3256)	(300)	(402)
Atlantic Provinces	1.56	1.80	1.75
	(429)	(5)	(8)
Quebec French	1.53	1.33	2.00
	(891)	(9)	(11)
Quebec Non-French	1.77	1.50	1.65
	(120)	(16)	(46)
Ontario	1.86	1.72	1.85
	(940)	(109)	(215)
Manitoba	1.74	1.48	2.00
	(163)	(21)	(8)
Saskatchewan	1.77	1.40	2.00
	(159)	(25)	(4)
Alberta	1.76	1.39	1.84
	(236)	(51)	(32)
B.C.	1.99	1.81	1.84
	(253)	(59)	(61)
Non-Quebec French	1.50	1.00	1.50
	(107)	(1)	(2)

For efficacy, in Table 7, the more recent immigrants differ noticeably from immigrants of longer residence, but the differences do not generally support the simple hypothesis of assimilation as a direct function of time in Canada. Even leaving aside the cells with small Ns, which may yield unreliable estimates, it appears that recent immigrants have assimilated more closely to provincial and language-group norms on political efficacy. This is surprising, and it supports the second hypothesis above, namely, that different types of immigrants follow different assimilation paths.

At the same time, we must point out that the "deviant" prewar immigrants follow regional lines of demarcation; the problem is rather that

Table 8
Year Immigrated to Canada by Trust Scores for Province-Language Groups (Merged Data, 1965 and 1968)

	Mean Scores (N)		
	Born in Canada	Immigrated Before 1946	Immigrated 1946-73
Nation	1.74 (4020)	1.71 (448)	1.83 (408)
Atlantic Provinces	1.61 (420)	1.46 (13)	1.55 (11)
Quebec French	1.68 (1168)	1.56 (9)	1.54 (13)
Quebec Non-French	1.74 (140)	1.55 (22)	1.80 (44)
Ontario	1.83 (1222)	1.79 (164)	1.86 (233)
Manitoba	1.78 (206)	1.94 (38)	2.00 (10)
Saskatchewan	1.69 (183)	1.59 (39)	2.00 (5)
Alberta	1.76 (290)	1.59 (79)	1.86 (35)
B.C.	1.86 (238)	1.77 (81)	1.85 (55)
Non-Quebec French	1.71 (153)	1.33 (3)	1.50 (2)

they have done so less closely than more recent immigrants. Unfortunately, given the number of cases (except in Ontario), we cannot further subdivide the immigrant groups by occupation, education and other relevant control variables.

The data on political trust, in Table 8, follow the same lines as for efficacy. The two types of immigrants again differ markedly, with the more recent ones closer to provincial norms than the earlier ones. As with efficacy, however, both groups of immigrants vary across province/language groups in ways more consistent with regional norms than with national norms. The early immigrants, while relatively "deviant" compared to their province of residence, would be even more deviant if compared to the norms of contiguous regions. In general, then, this variable reinforces the hypothesis that assimilation is a function of both length of residence and type of background.

Only when we turn to our measure of political involvement, Table 9, do we find substantial confirmation of the simple assimilation hypothesis. This fits the more general pattern that overt behaviour may be more easily modified than attitudes like efficacy or trust.

Table 9
Year Immigrated to Canada by Involvement Scores for Province-Language Groups
(Merged Data, 1965 and 1974)

| | Mean Scores (N) | | |
| | Born in Canada | Immigrated | |
		Before 1946	1946-73
Nation	1.90	1.88	1.89
	(2748)	(276)	(284)
Atlantic Provinces	2.00	1.71	2.00
	(365)	(14)	(7)
Quebec French	1.93	1.75	2.00
	(819)	(8)	(12)
Quebec Non-French	2.01	1.89	1.85
	(100)	(18)	(26)
Ontario	1.89	1.88	1.90
	(786)	(101)	(142)
Manitoba	1.77	1.96	1.67
	(149)	(25)	(6)
Saskatchewan	1.82	2.05	2.60
	(118)	(20)	(5)
Alberta	1.73	1.76	1.65
	(194)	(38)	(23)
B.C.	1.82	1.85	1.92
	(159)	(46)	(48)
Non-Quebec French	2.00	3.00	—
	(100)	(2)	(0)

Analysis of Variance

Immigrants and native-born Canadians clearly differ to some degree in political culture as we have assessed it. Yet both types of respondents gravitate around provincial, regional and language-group norms. In this section, we make a tentative estimate of which source of variation is most significant by means of analysis of variance procedures analogous to those used in Chapter II. Not only can we see the relative importance of these two types of variation, we can also check on their joint effect by means of the interaction terms in two-way analysis of variance.

Table 10 presents a brief summary of salient features of these analyses for province/language groups when compared, respectively, to country of birth, country of ancestors and year of immigration to Canada. The smaller the F-probability, the more significant the variation accounted for by the independent variable in question. A probability of .05 is the standard cut-off line between significant and nonsignificant.

The first noteworthy feature concerns the significance of province/language groups. Except for efficacy in the comparison of province/language and country of ancestors, province/language variation is highly significant in every case. Indeed, the overall impression reinforces strongly our contention that provincial political cultures constitute a fundamental fact of Canadian life, perhaps the most salient cleavage system.

Conversely, despite the large variations in Tables 5 to 9 among immigrants and between them and nonimmigrants, most of the tests of significance for country of birth and year of immigration are clearly below the standard level of significance. Again we interpret this to mean that provinces are more meaningful lines of cleavage than are origins or place of birth.

Country of ancestral origin, however, does display several significant F-tests. By itself this variable plays a substantial role, almost equal to province/language groups, in our three measures of political culture. Interestingly, in the one case (trust) where ancestry seems to lack significance, there is a significant interaction between it and the province/language variable. This means that there is some significant variation among Canadians in the trust dimension according to where their ancestors originated, but the variation is different in different provinces. No other interaction terms are close to significance.

Table 10
Analysis of Variance — Country of Birth, Country of Ancestors, and Year Immigrated to Canada by Province-Language Groups* — Efficacy, Trust, and Involvement as Dependent Variables (Merged Data)

	F-probabilities		
	Province	Birth	Interaction
A. Province-Language by Country of Birth			
1. Efficacy (N = 4029)	.001	.516	.217
2. Trust (N = 4885)	.001	.087	.638
3. Involvement (N = 3380)	.012	.136	.207
	Province	Ancestors	Interaction
B. Province-Language by Country of Ancestors			
1. Efficacy (N = 4029)	.474	.017	.729
2. Trust (N = 4885)	.036	.435	.045
3. Involvement (N = 3380)	.048	.022	.345
	Province	Year	Interaction
C. Province-Language by Year Immigrated			
1. Efficacy (N = 4029)	.003	.001	.141
2. Trust (N = 4885)	.007	.156	.822
Involvement (N = 3380)	.028	.227	.376

*The Atlantic provinces have been combined because of small Ns in some cells.

It is well known that support for political parties varies widely between provinces and language groups. This will be documented in later chapters for both federal and provincial levels. In addition, ethnic groups and citizens of different national backgrounds diverge in their party support patterns. Blake has shown, further, that which party a group supports depends on the province or region of residence; there is a significant interaction between province and national or ethnic origin.[9]

Table 11
Analysis of Variance — Country of Birth, Country of Ancestors, and Year of Immigration with Strength of Party Identification as Dependent Variables (Federal and Provincial) — Merged Data Sets (1965, 1968, 1974)

	F-probabilities		
	Province	Birth	Interaction
A. Province by Country of Birth			
1. Strength of federal party identification (N = 7062)	.064	.806	.008
2. Strength of provincial party identification (N = 6956)	.131	.456	.035
	Province	Ancestors	Interaction
B. Province by Country of Ancestors			
1. Federal (N = 7062)	.056	.033	.003
2. Provincial (N = 6956)	.014	.400	.087
	Province	Year	Interaction
C. Province by Year of Immigration			
1. Federal (N = 7062)	.145	.257	.002
2. Provincial (N = 6956)	.320	.360	.011
	Province	Ancestors	Interaction
D. Canadian-Born Respondents — Province by Country of Ancestors			
1. Federal (N = 5837)	.089	.491	.131
2. Provincial (N = 5762)	.015	.079	.297

In Table 11 we introduce two new variables, strength of federal and provincial party identification. Neither is a measure of political culture, and they do not assess support for particular parties. Instead they measure the extent to which types of citizens report some degree of psychological attachment to any political party.[10] If immigrants assimilate, then we expect them to develop these attachments, regardless of whether they come to support the same parties as Canadian-born respondents or different ones. Because the party systems, especially at the provincial level, are determined by provincial boundaries, we have used province, rather than province/ language groups, as our independent variable here. As a check, we repeated these analyses of variance with province/language as a variable; almost identical results emerged.

Although there are relatively few F-tests with probabilities less than .05, eight are significant and several others are close to significance. Country of ancestors by itself and in interaction with province is closely related to the strength of federal party identification. Year of immigration, on the other hand, interacts significantly with province to explain variation in both federal and provincial strength of party identification. We are unsure how much weight to place on these findings. It may be, however, that for certain people arriving in Canada, issues and political leaders of special appeal have been decisive in stimulating political party involvement. For some groups, in some regions, provincial issues and leaders have proven important, while for others, federal issues and leaders have been crucial.

Except for strength of party identification at the federal level for Canadian-born respondents, province plays a significant part in all of these analyses, sometimes by itself and sometimes in conjunction with another variable. The presence of several significant interaction terms underlines the importance of background and current residence in acculturating to the party systems.

As we shall see in later chapters, the provinces have quite distinct party systems. These significant interactions between province and other background variables, we hypothesize, emphasize the degree to which immigrants and native-born Canadians have acculturated to provincial party systems rather than to a single national system.

A Land Without Immigrants

If there had never been any immigration to Canada, there would obviously be no Canada. But it is plausible to imagine that immigration might end or that it might have been much less extensive in the past than it was. What would our regional cultures be like then?

Suppose that only persons born in Canada were citizens, and suppose that most of the nearly one in five citizens in our sample who were born elsewhere had never been admitted. Would we manifest such extensive regional variation as we have so far documented? We have just shown that immigrants are not always carbon copies of the native-born respondents, and that the types of immigrants have changed over the last few decades. Hence the question has real implications.

To try to answer hypothetical, counter-factual, speculative questions, of course, belies our scholarly caution. In order to make sense of the data on Canadian-born respondents alone requires that we make some strong assumptions which readers may not share. If so, they may disregard these few pages. But is it plausible to assume that with no immigrants in the last few decades, citizens here would have converged on national (or more broadly regional) norms? Is it any more plausible to think that native-born Canadians develop attitudes like efficacy or trust *because* of the presence of immigrants? We think not; in fact, we think the data in Tables 12 and 13 can be taken at face value: regional and provincial variations have, if anything, been muted by the vast numbers of immigrants to Canada, even though these new arrivals have not actually reduced to insignificance the variation in provincial cultures.

In Tables 12 and 13 we have replicated the relevant parts (Part B) of Tables 10 and 11. Obviously, we cannot assess for the Canadian-born the influence of place of birth (no variation) or year of immigration; but we can assess the role of their ancestral national origins relative to current province of residence.

Although there are no significant F-tests for involvement, province is significant for efficacy and for trust. In addition, country of ancestor plays a

Table 12

Analysis of Variance — Country of Ancestors by Province* for People Born in Canada — Efficacy, Trust, and Involvement as Dependent Variables (Merged Data)

| | F-probabilities | | |
	Province	Ancestors	Interaction
A. Efficacy (N = 3128)	.057	.001	.811
B. Trust (N = 3882)	.010	.199	.335
C. Involvement (N = 2757)	.125	.143	.911

*The Atlantic provinces have been combined because of the small numbers of persons in some cells.

Table 13

Analysis of Variance — Country of Ancestors by Province* — with Strength of Federal Party Identification and Strength of Provincial Party Identification as Dependent Variables (Canadian-Born Respondents Only) (Merged Data)

| | F-probabilities | | |
	Province	Ancestors	Interaction
A. Strength of Federal Party Identification (N = 5431)	.020	.479	.177
B. Strength of Provincial Party Identification (N = 5431)	.015	.092	.242

*The Atlantic provinces have been combined because of small Ns in some cells.

significant independent role for efficacy. There are no significant interaction terms.

In the case of party identification, country of ancestors plays no part, either alone or in interaction. Province does, however, relate significantly to the development of strength of attachment to parties at both the federal and provincial levels. This means that *provincial* arenas differ in their residents' attachment to the *federal* level of parties.

The conclusion we draw from this brief excursion into our hypothetical past is simple: provincial political cultures are creatures of considerable age and would have been at least as diverse today if there had been no immigration for the last two generations.

A Land Without Mobility

Just as we can compare Canadian-born respondents and immigrants from outside Canada, so we can compare persons who have always lived in a given province, persons who used to live there but now reside permanently in another province, and persons who have moved to a province. By doing so we can again test notions of assimilation in a crude way and we can speculate on what the political cultures might have looked like if there had been no interprovincial mobility in recent decades.

Our findings parallel in most respects those on immigrants, and our conclusion is similar. Permanent residents of the provinces differ more than migrants; they clearly form an important base for the provincial political cultures. At the same time, selective migration of people "deviant" in one area to another area where they would be less deviant may have contributed — along with simple assimilation — to the maintenance of distinctive provincial cultures. If persons leave an area in which they are or feel deviant and settle in

Table 14
Mean Scores on Efficacy for Respondents Who Have Always Lived in the Same Province and Who Have Previously Lived There (1974 Data)

	Mean Scores (N)		
	Always Lived in Province	Used to Live in Province	Moved to Province
Newfoundland	1.67 (39)	1.56 (9)	1.60 (10)
Prince Edward Island	1.66 (32)	1.33 (3)	1.67 (18)
Nova Scotia	1.86 (63)	1.57 (14)	1.92 (24)
New Brunswick	1.74 (47)	1.95 (21)	1.74 (19)
Quebec	1.62 (297)	1.95 (43)	1.86 (44)
Ontario	1.95 (243)	1.79 (87)	1.93 (101)
Manitoba	1.72 (39)	1.98 (40)	1.50 (20)
Saskatchewan	2.03 (36)	1.90 (48)	1.94 (16)
Alberta	1.73 (51)	1.91 (46)	1.83 (36)
British Columbia	2.12 (58)	1.80 (46)	1.93 (69)

an area in which they are less deviant, this process will *increase* the differentiation between the areas. This process works in conjunction with assimilation, since the migrant may not fully "fit in" when he arrives in his new home but may assimilate more easily and quickly because he is less deviant than if he were elsewhere.

The reader will notice in Tables 14 through 18 that we use *provinces* rather than province/language groups as our basic variable. Partly this reflects a lack of data on changes in linguistic competence. Mainly, however, it derives from our belief that in this hypothetical reconstruction physical residence is the more meaningful indicator of mobility. We are not here interested in reconstructing hypothetical linguistic patterns — as though, for example, Quebec were wholly Francophone. Instead, we want to know what kinds of interprovincial differences would have existed with the current populations relocated in their native provinces.

In every province, there are substantial differences between the mean efficacy score of permanent residents and that of former residents. Although the numbers of cases in some cells of Table 14 are small, for most provinces we can rely on the estimates.

The first major observation about Table 14 concerns the scores of people who have left the Atlantic provinces and Quebec. (As we saw in Table 3 above, about half the migrants from any given Atlantic province move to another province in that same region. Similarly, migrants to one of these provinces often come from elsewhere in the region.) Allowing for the small numbers in Newfoundland and Prince Edward Island, we speculate that most of the out-migrants had more sense of efficacy than those who remained behind. Nova Scotia is interesting, of course, since it has received most of the migrants from elsewhere in eastern Canada, and these may have been even more efficacious than the permanent residents. Other "receiving" provinces, especially Ontario and British Columbia, reveal patterns in which the locals are more efficacious than the out-migrants. (These patterns are even clearer in the case of trust; see Table 15.) Overall, it is clear that the migrants differ across provinces less than do permanent residents, but such variation is still evident.[11]

Were the out-migrants' efficacy scores the same upon leaving their previous province, or have they changed upon settling in a new area? Let us explore these options conceptually, since we obviously do not have measures of political culture at the time of mobility.

Suppose the forty-six former residents of British Columbia used to have efficacy scores higher than they do now, indeed perhaps even as high as the permanent British Columbians. Since these migrants have moved to the Prairies or to Ontario, all of which have lower mean scores than British Columbia, the logical deduction would be that their scores dropped in order to reflect assimilation to new provincial norms. This scenario of high scores while in British Columbia and lower scores while in provinces with lower average scores would demonstrate doubly the influence of provincial political culture norms: once when growing up and subsequently after mobility.

The converse scenario is also plausible. Suppose the former British Columbians always had scores lower than the British Columbia average. They might therefore have felt less involved in British Columbia, have been more willing to accept employment elsewhere (or have been less successful in British Columbia), and have fitted in better in their new province, whose average approximately matched their own. This pattern would suggest a form of selective migration. Of course, we do not wish to imply that the primary reason for mobility could be awareness of efficacy norms, nor do we imply that all "deviant" scorers on efficacy have moved. But, logically, there is a possibility of selective migration, although this is no more than a hypothesis given the limitations of the present data.

Table 15
Mean Scores on Trust for Respondents Who Have Always Lived in the Same Province and Who Have Previously Lived There (1965 Data)

	Mean Scores (N)		
	Always Lived in Province	Used to Live in Province	Moved to Province
Newfoundland	2.24 (21)	1.92 (13)	2.33 (3)
Prince Edward Island	1.45 (20)	2.33 (3)	1.50 (4)
Nova Scotia	1.88 (42)	1.79 (34)	1.84 (31)
New Brunswick	1.42 (78)	1.71 (31)	1.60 (30)
Quebec	1.67 (544)	1.76 (72)	1.82 (99)
Ontario	1.83 (549)	1.82 (124)	1.86 (174)
Manitoba	1.69 (77)	1.69 (55)	1.74 (53)
Saskatchewan	1.43 (53)	1.79 (90)	1.66 (41)
Alberta	1.84 (87)	1.79 (77)	1.80 (84)
British Columbia	1.79 (43)	1.81 (96)	1.73 (85)

The first scenario has more intuitive plausibility than the second, and readers can no doubt suggest even more complex possibilities. One reason for this hunch is our suspicion that high political efficacy is related to general efficacy, and more highly efficacious individuals would be more likely to be mobile. While the mobile Canadians appear, on average, to be slightly more efficacious, they are hardly a homogeneous group converging clearly on a national norm, despite the fact that geographic mobility might otherwise be expected to have that effect by "broadening horizons" and encouraging respondents to consider issues and circumstances more cosmopolitan than those of a single province. The conclusion we prefer to draw, therefore, is that either changing efficacy scores after moving or selective migration constitute indirect evidence of the importance of provincial or regional norms.

Turning to Table 15, we find the data on trust are consonant with the speculations just outined. Mobile Canadians are slightly more homogeneous than nonmobiles, but still quite various in their orientations. In most provinces the movers are more trusting than permanent residents; but this is truer of the provinces with large out-migrations historically than of provinces like Ontario, British Columbia and Alberta, which have traditionally been the recipients of interprovincial migrants. Those who have moved to a province appear very similar to its permanent residents.

The data on political involvement in Table 16 are more ambiguous. As we have noted before, there is less differentiation among the provinces on this dimension than on the others. Furthermore, the high involvement provinces are, by and large, lower in their mean scores on efficacy and trust. If a form of selective migration occurred, then the permanent residents would be the ones more involved than the out-migrants (true of Quebec and the Atlantic provinces); and the migrants who may have left because of the attractiveness of other locales could be expected to become more involved in settings more congenial to them (true of Ontario, Alberta, Manitoba, and perhaps British Columbia).

Table 16
Mean Scores on Involvement for Respondents Who Have Always Lived in the Same Province and Who Have Previously Lived There
(Merged Data, 1965 and 1974)

	Mean Scores (N)		
	Always Lived in Province	Used to Live in Province	Moved to Province
Newfoundland	1.90 (60)	1.82 (22)	1.85 (13)
Prince Edward Island	2.25 (52)	2.00 (6)	2.09 (22)
Nova Scotia	1.94 (105)	1.73 (48)	2.07 (55)
New Brunswick	1.97 (125)	1.96 (52)	1.98 (49)
Quebec	1.93 (841)	1.90 (115)	1.97 (143)
Ontario	1.90 (792)	1.95 (211)	1.87 (275)
Manitoba	1.83 (116)	1.91 (95)	1.82 (73)
Saskatchewan	1.94 (89)	1.86 (138)	1.79 (57)
Alberta	1.71 (138)	1.76 (123)	1.75 (120)
British Columbia	1.88 (101)	1.87 (142)	1.82 (154)

All of these speculations about hypothetical pasts lack firm and unambiguous evidence. We are the first to admit that. But we note that the evidence can be interpreted in this way, and the data could have turned out in many ways which would have precluded inferences about selective migration or the role of provincial norms of political culture. Therefore we feel free to offer these hypotheses in the hope that other scholars will be able to shed more light on them, whether confirming or disproving them.

Before leaving this intriguing topic, however, we have a further approach to the question of whether the provincial political cultures could have existed without migration between provinces. We present analyses of variance for several dimensions of mobility in relation to our measures of political culture (Table 17) and our indicators of psychological attachment to the party systems (Table 18).

Table 17
Analysis of Variance — Province, Always Lived in Province, Reconstructed Provinces,* and Mobile Respondents — with Efficacy, Trust, and Political Involvement as Dependent Variables (Merged Data)**

	F-probabilities		
	Efficacy (N=)	Trust (N=)	Involvement (N=)
A. Province***	.001 (1262)	.001 (2118)	.001 (3380)
B. Always lived in same province	.001 (905)	.001 (1514)	.001 (2419)
C. "Reconstructed provinces"	.001 (1262)	.001 (2109)	.001 (3371)
D. Used to live in province	.218 (357)	.903 (595)	.543 (952)
E. Moved to province	.091 (357)	.623 (603)	.050 (961)

   * "Reconstructed provinces" are hypothetical regroupings of the people who have always lived in a province plus those who used to live there.

  ** Since the 1968 study did not ascertain which other provinces a respondent had lived in, these figures refer to the 1965 (trust), 1974 (efficacy) or 1965 and 1974 merged data set (involvement).

*** The Atlantic provinces have been combined in all of the analyses of variance reported here because of small numbers of cases in parts D and E.

Table 18
Analysis of Variance — Province, Always Lived in Province, Reconstructed Provinces and Mobile Canadians — with Strength of Party Identification as Dependent Variables (Merged Data: 1965, 1968, 1974)

	F-probabilities	
	Strength of Federal Party Identification	Strength of Provincial Party Identification
	(N=)	(N=)
A. Province*	.000 (4405)	.000 (4262)
B. Always lived in same province	.000 (3168)	.000 (3083)
C. Always lived in province plus used to live in province ("reconstructed provinces")	.000 (4396)	.000 (4253)
D. Used to live in province	.516 (1228)	.904 (1170)
E. Moved to province	.260 (1237)	.311 (1179)

  * The Atlantic provinces have been combined in each analysis of variance reported here.

In all cases, provinces as they now exist account for a very significant amount of variation. (In Table 13, we obtained slightly different significance levels, .020 and .015, for federal and provincial party identification, respectively. The difference reflects a two-way analysis of variance in Table 13, but only a one-way analysis here. In the former case, country of ancestors explained part of the variance; and that table was restricted to native-born Canadians, wereas a few immigrants are included among the mobiles in Table 18.) Similarly, "provinces" hypothetically restricted to permanent residents are significantly different on all five of our indicators, as are the "reconstructed provinces" consisting of permanent residents plus people who used to live there but now reside elsewhere.

When we examine people who have *moved away* from their native province (part D, "Used to live in province"), we find no significant F-tests for any dependent variable. Likewise, except for a barely significant F-test for political involvement, there is no significant provincial variation among people who have *moved to* their current province. These two sets of findings are not surprising if we assume that provincial norms influence individuals both while growing up and while residing in a new home elsewhere as adults. In that case, some respondents would have their scores "raised" by new contextual norms, while others would become *less* efficacious, trusting, and so on because of provincial norms at their destination. The net effect would be to "flatten" the interprovincial differences, as seems to be the case in Tables 17 and 18. Of course, we must qualify these inferences, as we did above, by the tenuousness of our assumptions about the dynamics of selective migration. In the absence of better data, however, we feel it worth hypothesizing that the provincial cultures were important influences on residents before they moved. The lack of significance of the variables "used to live in province" and "moved to province" suggests to us that the mobile Canadians are influenced also by their new provinces of residence, and the "cross-pressures" of these old and new norms reduce the variation within this large group.

Conclusion

This excursion into geographic mobility and our hypothetical pasts intended to accomplish two things, both of which we believe to be consonant with the data presented here. First, we hoped to show that immigrants and migrants who settle in a province take on certain norms and patterns of behaviour characteristic of that province, rather than approximate to a uniform national standard. Of course, the mobile Canadians do differ across provinces somewhat less than do permanent residents of the provinces, because of "cross-pressures," broader horizons and new experiences. They still diverge, however, in the same general way as the "core residents" of each province. In this sense, we argue that the provincial political cultures have an independent normative force which serves to provide an assimilative framework for new arrivals from abroad or from another province.

Second, we attempted to demonstrate that, if anything, immigration and internal migration have dampened the distinctiveness of the provinces on the variables examined here. If there had been no immigration or migration, the provincial differences in political culture would have been at least as great as they are now, and perhaps even greater. In short, the provincial political cultures have existed for several decades at least, and they show very little sign of disappearing.

At this level of general attitudes, Canada consists of many "small worlds." This fact does not, of course, entail the lack of integration of Canada, since the very existence of extensive mobility demonstrates how many Canadians think of "their world" as broader than a province or region. On other variables, as we shall see below, the provinces share many features in common; and by comparison with Britain, France, the United States and other countries, Canada is distinctive. One of the distinctive features of Canada, we allege, is this pattern of powerful normative forces at the provincial level within a broader national framework.

Notes

1. For a sensitive discussion, see Anthony H. Richmond, "Immigration and Pluralism in Canada," in *Social and Cultural Change in Canada*, ed. W.E. Mann (Toronto: Copp Clark, 1970), pp. 81-96.

2. For data on Toronto using a somewhat different measure of identification with Canada, see John Goldhurst and Anthony H. Richmond, "Factors Associated with Commitment to and Identification with Canada," in *Identities: The Impact of Ethnicity on Canadian Society*, ed. Wsevolod Isajiw (Toronto: Peter Martin, 1977), pp. 132-153.

3. There are, of course, other reasons besides immigration and migration for the decline of regionalism. We ignore these other aspects in this chapter. Interested persons should see the review of the literature in Mildred A. Schwartz, *Politics and Territory: The Sociology of Regional Persistence in Canada* (Montreal: McGill-Queen's University Press, 1974), chap. 1; and S.M. Lipset, "Political Cleavages in 'Developed' and 'Emerging' Polities," in *Mass Politics: Studies in Political Sociology*, ed. Erik Allardt and Stein Rokkan (New York: Free Press, 1970), pp. 23-44.

4. John Porter, *The Vertical Mosaic: An Analysis of Social Class and Power in Canada* (Toronto: University of Toronto Press, 1965).

5. For age comparisons of native and foreign born, see Warren E. Kalbach and Wayne W. McVey, *The Demographic Bases of Canadian Society* (Toronto: McGraw-Hill, 1971), p. 137.

6. Anthony H. Richmond, "Immigration, Population, and the Canadian Future," *Sociological Focus*, 9 (April 1976): 125-136.

7. For further discussion, see Richmond, "Immigration, Population, and the Canadian Future."

8. Recall our findings in Chapter II, above; when we controlled for education and other variables, this accounted for part of the lowness of Francophone scores on political efficacy.

9. Donald E. Blake, "The Measurement of Regionalism in Canadian Voting Patterns," *Canadian Journal of Political Science*, 5 (March 1972): 55-81.

10. Each variable has been recoded as zero = no party identification; one = not very strong; two = fairly strong; and three = very strong.

11. Although we do not present the data because small Ns make the interpretation no more than suggestive, we have another approach to mobility and political culture. We cross-tabulated "province of origin" (or previous residence) with "province of destination" (current residence), and within each cell calculated the mean scores of respondents on efficacy, trust, involvement and strength of federal and provincial party identification. For those cells with a reasonable number of cases (unfortunately, less than half the cells) there is a fairly clear pattern: variation occurs along both dimensions (former province and current province), but people who have *moved to* a province are more similar to the permanent residents of their current province than to the permanent residents of their former province. Unfortunately, we do not know how long the mobile respondents have resided in their current residence or whether they intend to remain there. These two aspects would no doubt help to clarify the nature of the assimilation process at work.

V

Federal and Provincial Voting:
Contemporary Patterns and Historical Evolution

Richard Johnston

Canadians' political attitudes differ greatly between provinces and, within each province, Canadians evaluate their national and provincial societies in complex ways. In part, these differences and complexities are the inevitable product of geography, economics and history. But political institutions must make an independent contribution. Some institutions may sharpen interprovincial and federal-provincial differences, while other institutions may mitigate them. In this chapter, I shall focus on political parties. I shall investigate them only briefly as organizations and as sources of policy, for the most part examining them indirectly, by looking at voters. But why examine parties at all?

Parties as Political Stimuli

The party's role may be either integrative or disintegrative. What a party actually does will reflect its size, its growth possibilities, the relative size of the provinces, each province's party contest and the party members' feelings about regional appeals per se. Lurking behind many of these factors are the tactical dilemmas posed by the single-member plurality electoral system.

Parties, in linking the fates of politicians from different provinces, may be an integrative force. It is true that a party's seemingly homogeneous and disciplined public face masks considerable internal, geographically based conflict. Each member's chances of re-election must be partly contingent on his party's treatment of his constituency and region, and so the member must lobby for policies whose benefits are localized. But national shifts of opinion about the party and its leader also affect the member's re-election chances.[1] The member's chances for promotion to or within cabinet (and for patronage after retirement or defeat) are contingent on the fate of the whole party. And members from relatively poor regions may also be financially dependent on party sources in rich regions.[2] For these reasons, members will strive to reach a bargain satisfactory to members in other regions. To the extent that politicians from different regions have a joint stake in their party's advancement, they should present a reasonably common front, and invite voters in one region to respond in the same way and to the same issues as voters elsewhere.

But making the same appeal in different provinces will not necessarily evoke a geographically undifferentiated response. In a country with sharp underlying regional policy conflicts, maintaining a consistent policy stance is potentially as divisive as running on different policies in different regions. In any case, whether or not a party adopts regionally divisive policies will reflect its tactical circumstances. Where regions are similar in size and similar in their party contests, a party with a serious chance of victory might try to effect a regional policy synthesis, or appeal to the region whose policy interests differed at least from the interests of other regions.[3] But where regions differ markedly in size, the party might find it tactically wise to give large regions correspondingly great weight in its policy calculations, at the expense of some smaller regions. Similarly, if the party has little hope of success in some region, whatever the region's size, it might write the area off and not couch appeals to its interests. Under a single-member plurality electoral system, the very size of the party could be a factor in these calculations. A small party may seek to consolidate its base at the expense of its growth possibilities. Where its base is geographically confined, the party might profit from inflaming regional sentiment. Doing so would be the best means of increasing the number of seats the party wins per vote. A large party, conversely, may benefit from a pan-regional appeal.[4]

Whatever the conflicts between regions, the very existence of a federation creates conflicts between governmental levels. Groups and interests affected adversely by the creation of a national economy or by policy decisions at the national level will attempt to shelter behind the constitutional barriers to national government action. Beneficiaries of national action or of the breakdown of trade barriers within the federation will naturally take the other side in the constitutional struggle, and may be joined by local groups which have lost in provincial policy battles. What would otherwise have been an ordinary struggle between rival interests may thus be transmuted into a more fundamental conflict over the nature of the federal polity.[5] Provincial politicians' ambitions may themselves be a centrifugal force, as Hamilton observed long ago:

> . . . in every political association which is formed upon the principle of uniting in a common interest a number of lesser sovereignties, there will be found a kind of eccentric tendency in the subordinate or inferior orbs, by the operation of which there will be a perpetual effort in each to fly off from the common centre. This tendency is not difficult to be accounted for. It has its origin in the love of power.[6]

Countervailing these centrifugal tendencies will be the centralizing ambitions of national politicians.

Again, parties can increase or decrease the conflict.[7] What parties actually do reflects, among other things, their finances, the career paths of their members and the parties' very success at the polls. The more unitary the party's finance system, the more the party should try to act as an integrative agent. This should be especially true if the initial collection of funds is centralized, as it traditionally has been for the Liberals and Conservatives.[8] Conversely, if a party's federal and provincial budgets are separate, the wings may act relatively independently of each other. The degree to which provinces have regulatory leverage, independent of Dominion regulatory powers, over potential campaign fund donors will affect the ability of provincial parties to raise funds on their own.

Ambition can assist money in cementing federal and provincial parties together. The party is potentially a chain of career opportunities spanning both levels. Provincial politicians hoping to enter federal politics and federal politicians with provincial experience may mute their attacks on each other; politicians can move from federal to provincial politics as well, of course. The frequency of shifts between levels reflects, among other things, the relative likelihood, for politicians of a given party, of gaining cabinet office at each level. Such likelihood reflects, in turn, the relative electoral strength of the party's national and provincial wings.

How a party acts in the present may also be affected by its relative federal and provincial success in the recent past. A party much stronger in some provinces than in the Dominion as a whole may become a champion not just of its provinces of strength but of provincial rights in general.[9] This tendency will be reinforced if, within some provinces, the party is stronger in provincial elections than in federal ones. A party stronger provincially than federally in some provinces, but elsewhere relatively strong in federal politics, may even turn against itself.[10]

The last observation suggests a more general dilemma facing parties as integrative agents: actions which seek to reduce differences between provinces may exacerbate conflict between levels. The policies parties adopt to win national elections would not win elections in any single province, with the possible exception of Ontario, as the electorates in question, obviously, differ. A province in which a party's federal and provincial wings do similarly well or poorly is often a province very distinct from the others in federal voting. If both wings do well, it is often because the federal wing is resigned to opposition. If both do poorly, the provincial wing may be a pathetic appendage of a federal party itself little more than a vehicle for federal patronage.[11]

In sum, expectations for the integrative role of parties must be equivocal. Parties can mute differences between provinces or increase them. Parties can integrate the federal and provincial politics of a province, or they can pull the levels apart. We should let the evidence speak for itself.

In this chapter the evidence describes not parties themselves, but voters. Most of the data come from official returns in national and provincial elections; some come from the merged survey file used elsewhere in this book. Throughout the chapter the prevailing themes will be convergence and divergence, between provinces and levels. In the first part, I shall assess interprovincial differences in the vote and ask whether such differences have increased or decreased historically. In the same section, I shall examine the role of the electoral system. The second part of the chapter will consider federal-provincial differences. I shall describe the differences as they are now, and again ask whether they have historically grown or shrunk. I shall also examine some of the individual sources of aggregate federal-provincial differences: do the differences come from citizens selectively abstaining at one level or the other or from direct switching between parties? Are the individuals who make the difference between levels politically relatively involved or relatively apathetic? And do particular social groups produce the federal-provincial differences or do the differences fall across the board?

The Provincial Bases of National Elections
The Electoral System

Why begin with the electoral system? First, the system is an important element in the parties' tactical setting. Seats are the real currency in the parliamentary game, and votes are important principally as they affect the probability of winning and losing seats. As a result, not every vote is equally valuable to a party. Parties may orient much of their policy and campaign effort to the especially important votes, the ones in closely contested seats. In necessitating such tactical decisions, the electoral system biases party politics toward some regions and against others and, in general, forces parties to reason in geographic terms.[12] Second, the system distorts our perceptions of the geography of Canadians' votes. A major purpose of this chapter is to correct some of those misperceptions.

National elections in Canada are now fought under a single-member plurality electoral system. The national system has always used the plurality formula, but has not always used only single-member constituencies. Double-member constituencies were fairly common in the nineteenth century and two such constituencies, one each in Nova Scotia and Prince Edward Island, persisted to 1965.

The most important effects of the plurality electoral system are variants of the following basic one: the expansion, as votes are translated into seats, of size differences between parties. Just as differences are magnified, so are changes between elections in a party's vote as they become seat changes. And so, by the same logic, are magnified many parties' differences between provinces. Within each province, large parties are made to seem even larger and small parties even smaller than their respective votes would indicate, just as happens in the national election as a whole. The fewer the constituencies in a province, the more pronounced is the effect. Thus, many provinces are made to seem relatively homogeneous partisan blocs. In turn, each party becomes a regional rump or a collection of a few such rumps. These generalizations hold more strongly for large parties than for small ones; the electoral system bias against small parties often makes their seat shares small even in their provinces of greatest strength. A final point: a party's ability to win seats in a province reflects not just the party's own size but the number and relative size of the other parties.

Table 1 documents the electoral system's effects for the 1965–1974 period. The two bottom rows illustrate this section's most general argument: that the system exaggerates major party vote differences between provinces. The rows do so by comparing, by election and party, the standard deviations across provinces of seats and votes. The standard deviation indicates the average magnitude of differences between provinces. It can also be viewed as a measure of geographic concentration. The more uniform the party's geographic distribution, of either seats or votes, the more closely its provincial seat or vote shares will cluster around the national mean, and thus the smaller will be the standard deviation. For the Liberal and Conservative parties, the standard deviations of seat shares are three to four times as great as the standard deviations of vote shares. Clearly, major parties are made to seem more concentrated in a small number of regions than the parties "really" are. The system's treatment of small parties is, as expected, more equivocal. In three of the four elections NDP vote differences do expand as they are translated into seat differences. But the seat differences are not spectacularly greater than the vote ones and, in 1974, seat differences are actually smaller than vote ones. For Social Credit, seat-share differences were slightly smaller than vote-share differences in three of four elections. Social Credit is typically so small outside Quebec that misrepresentation of the party's provincial base is next to impossible.

The rest of Table 1 tells a story mainly about the large parties, and does so especially by comparison with the vote-share evidence in Table 2 below. In most provinces, major party seat shares are either very large or very small. The Liberals typically win three Ontario seats in five and three Quebec seats in four. The only other provinces to give the Liberals respectable seat totals are Newfoundland, New Brunswick and British Columbia, and those provinces do so only occasionally. The Conservative picture complements the Liberal one almost exactly. The Conservatives typically win overwhelming seat shares in Prince Edward Island, Nova Scotia and the Prairie provinces. But neither major party wins as many votes in its strong provinces or as few votes in its weak provinces as its seat shares would indicate. Further, a given vote share gains a party more seats in some provinces than in others. The Liberals get proportionately as many votes in the Atlantic provinces as in Ontario. Yet Ontario yields strong Liberal seat majorities, while the Atlantic

Table 1
National Election Seat Shares 1965-1974, by Province and Party

	Party															
Province	Liberal				Conservative				NDP				Social Credit			
	Election				Election				Election				Election			
	1965	1968	1972	1974	1965	1968	1972	1974	1965	1968	1972	1974	1965	1968	1972	1974
Newfoundland	100.0	14.3	42.9	57.1	0.0	85.7	57.1	42.9	0.0	0.0	0.0	0.0	0.0	0.0	0.0	0.0
Prince Edward Island	0.0	0.0	25.0	25.0	100.0	100.0	75.0	75.0	0.0	0.0	0.0	0.0	0.0	0.0	0.0	0.0
Nova Scotia	16.7	9.1	9.1	18.2	83.3	90.9	90.9	72.7	0.0	0.0	0.0	9.1	0.0	0.0	0.0	0.0
New Brunswick	60.0	50.0	50.0	60.0	40.0	50.0	50.0	30.0	0.0	0.0	0.0	0.0	0.0	0.0	0.0	0.0
Quebec	74.7	75.7	75.7	81.1	10.7	5.4	2.7	4.1	0.0	0.0	0.0	0.0	14.7	18.9	20.3	14.9
Ontario	60.0	72.7	40.9	62.5	29.4	19.3	45.5	28.4	10.6	6.8	12.5	9.1	0.0	0.0	0.0	0.0
Manitoba	7.1	38.5	15.4	15.4	71.4	38.5	61.5	69.2	21.4	23.1	23.1	15.4	0.0	0.0	0.0	0.0
Saskatchewan	0.0	15.4	7.7	23.1	100.0	38.5	53.8	61.5	0.0	46.2	38.5	15.4	0.0	0.0	0.0	0.0
Alberta	0.0	21.1	0.0	0.0	88.2	78.9	100.0	100.0	0.0	0.0	0.0	0.0	11.8	0.0	0.0	0.0
British Columbia	31.8	69.6	17.4	34.8	13.6	0.0	34.8	56.5	40.9	30.4	47.8	8.7	17.6	0.0	0.0	0.0
Canada	49.4	58.7	41.3	53.4	35.8	27.3	40.5	36.0	7.9	8.3	11.7	6.1	5.3	5.3	5.7	4.2
Standard deviation of seat shares	36.3	28.7	23.5	25.9	39.1	36.5	27.8	28.0	13.8	16.7	18.1	6.5	7.2	6.0	6.4	4.7
Standard deviation of vote shares	12.7	7.1	8.3	9.9	11.8	13.6	11.7	10.9	10.8	12.4	12.1	9.0	8.8	5.2	7.4	5.2

Sources: Chief Electoral Officer *Reports 1965-1974* (Ottawa: Supply and Services). Reproduced by permission of the Minister of Supply and Services, Canada.

Table 2
National Election Results 1965-1974

Province	Liberal				Conservative				NDP				Social Credit			
	Election				Election				Election				Election			
	1965	1968	1972	1974	1965	1968	1972	1974	1965	1968	1972	1974	1965	1968	1972	1974
Newfoundland	64.1	42.8	43.0	46.3	32.4	52.8	47.0	43.2	1.2	4.4	4.5	9.4	1.6	0.1	0.1	0.1
Prince Edward Island	44.1	45.0	40.5	46.2	53.9	51.8	51.9	49.1	2.0	3.2	7.5	4.6	0.0	0.0	0.1	0.0
Nova Scotia	42.0	38.0	33.9	40.7	48.6	55.2	53.4	47.5	9.1	6.7	12.3	11.2	0.0	0.0	0.3	0.4
New Brunswick	47.5	44.4	43.1	47.2	42.5	49.7	44.9	33.0	9.4	4.9	5.7	8.7	0.6	0.7	5.6	2.9
Quebec	45.6	53.6	49.1	54.1	21.2	21.4	17.4	21.2	12.0	7.5	6.4	6.6	17.5	16.4	24.4	17.1
Ontario	43.6	46.6	38.2	45.1	34.0	32.0	39.1	35.1	21.7	20.6	21.5	19.1	0.4	0.0	0.4	0.2
Manitoba	31.0	41.5	30.9	27.4	40.7	31.4	41.6	47.7	24.0	25.0	26.3	23.5	4.3	0.2	0.7	1.1
Saskatchewan	24.0	27.1	25.3	30.7	48.0	37.0	36.9	36.4	26.0	35.7	35.9	31.5	1.9	0.0	1.8	1.1
Alberta	22.4	35.7	25.0	24.8	46.6	50.4	57.6	61.2	8.2	9.4	12.6	9.3	22.5	0.0	4.5	3.4
British Columbia	30.0	41.8	28.9	33.3	19.2	19.4	33.0	41.9	32.9	32.7	35.0	23.0	17.4	0.0	2.6	1.2
Canada	40.2	45.5	38.5	43.2	32.4	31.4	35.0	35.4	17.9	17.0	17.7	15.4	8.3	4.4	7.6	5.1

Sources: see Table 1.

provinces have recently been something of a Liberal graveyard. In Ontario, the non-Liberal vote is split between the Conservatives and the NDP. In the Atlantic provinces the Conservatives pick up almost all the non-Liberal vote. The Conservatives get proportionately as many votes in Ontario as in Saskatchewan. But Ontario typically yields the Conservatives proportionately only half as many seats as Saskatchewan.

The net effect of the system is stark. Most central Canadians are made to seem Liberals and most Liberals, central Canadians. Most Canadians in the Atlantic and Prairie provinces are made to seem Conservatives and most Conservatives, residents of the Atlantic and Prairie provinces. British Columbia seems to swing wildly between three parties. The real heterogeneity of each region is masked and British Columbia's volatility is exaggerated. Whatever its other merits, the electoral system fails, in translating votes into seats, as an integrative mechanism. Rather, the system makes Canadian voting seem more regionalized than it really is. How, then, do Canadians in each province vote?

Locating the Federal Vote

Table 2 reveals the regional character of the federal vote. The elections from 1965 to 1974 are, of course, the four spanned by the national election surveys, although the data here are from official returns. In addition to the vote in each province, the table contains the national returns.

Some might object to a concentration on the vote in a section which purports to describe enduring features of elections. Instead of the vote, I might have examined responses to the "party loyalty" or "party identification" probe in the national surveys. By such means I would have tapped a factor which predisposes many individuals' votes, but which is less subject than the vote itself to ephemeras and distractions. Two considerations deterred me from using party loyalty data. First, later sections of this chapter will consider time series data from elections before 1965. For the earlier elections, no party preference data other than actual votes are available. To enhance the comparability of this section with those to come, I decided to concentrate on the vote. Second, the national surveys greatly overestimate Liberal support and underestimate support for other parties. The magnitude of misestimation varies from province to province. This happens whether the indicator of support be the party identification measure or the respondent's recall of his or her vote in the last election. Such estimation error would muddy comparisons between provinces and parties. I am forced, then, to use official sources, which, of course, record only votes. I must emphasize, however, that my rejection of the party identification data in this chapter represents no rejection of the concept to which the data refer. The stability of the returns in Table 2 cautions against such a rejection. Even more to the point, my very attempt to generalize across elections would be theoretically groundless if I did not believe that most voters most of the time had stable and enduring party loyalties.[13]

I shall begin with the shape of Liberal support. It will come as no surprise that, in most elections, Liberal support is greatest in Quebec. But Quebec is hardly homogeneous: only about half the total vote goes to the Liberal party. The Liberals benefit, though, from the fragmentation of the rest of the vote. And the Liberals are only modestly stronger in Quebec than in several other provinces. The party typically receives over 40 per cent of the popular vote in Newfoundland, Prince Edward Island, New Brunswick and Ontario, and nearly 40 per cent of the vote in Nova Scotia. The fact that the Liberals are as strong in many Atlantic provinces as in Ontario is, of course, masked by the electoral system. West of Ontario, the Liberal position is shaky, but not everywhere as bleak as often assumed. The party gets about 30 per cent of the vote in Manitoba, Saskatchewan and British Columbia, and about 25 per cent in Alberta. Note, however, that Saskatchewan and British Columbia are rather tightly contested three-party provinces. The Liberal position in Conservative-dominated Manitoba is weak (and apparently getting more so) and the party's position in Alberta is truly desperate.

Like the Liberals, the Conservatives are strong in Atlantic Canada, but elsewhere the Conservatives are strong where the Liberals are weak, and vice versa. The Conservative party typically gets over 45 per cent of the vote in Prince Edward Island and Nova Scotia, and between 40 and 45 per cent of the vote in Newfoundland and New Brunswick. Western Canada is often perceived as as much a Conservative stronghold as Atlantic Canada. In fact, the West is complicated, internally heterogeneous and, in places, unstable. The Conservatives are unequivocally strong (and may even be strengthening) in Alberta, with more than half that province's popular vote. The party also does well in Manitoba, where it gets over 40 per cent of the popular vote, and may be growing there. Saskatchewan and British Columbia are more difficult cases. The party appears to have shrunk in Saskatchewan and now enjoys only a modest province-wide plurality. In British Columbia, the party has grown rapidly and in 1974 won just over 40 per cent of that province's votes. Even so, the legendary volatility of federal voting in British Columbia makes me reluctant to describe the province as a Conservative stronghold in any enduring sense. In Ontario the party gets very nearly its national average popular vote. If we do not perceive Ontario as an important source of Conservative votes, we have been fooled yet again by the electoral system. Quebec, of course, is usually the party's weakest province. But even there the party receives about one-fifth of the popular vote, a much larger proportion than it receives of seats. In 1965 and 1968 the party actually received a proportionately larger vote in Quebec than in British Columbia. And in three of the four elections, the Conservative party received more votes in Quebec than did Social Credit.

There are few surprises in the NDP evidence. The party is typically strongest in Saskatchewan and British Columbia (notwithstanding 1974 reverses in the latter province), in each of which it usually gets about one-third of the total vote. In Manitoba and Ontario the party gets from 20 to

25 per cent of the vote. Elsewhere the party's situation is dismal. The only province other than the four just mentioned in which the NDP gets more than 10 per cent of the vote is Nova Scotia.

There are fewer surprises still in the Social Credit data. Of course, the only province in which the party has any strength is Quebec, and events since the 1974 election make even that foothold uncertain. The last traces of erstwhile Social Credit federal strength in Alberta and British Columbia disappeared between 1965 and 1968.

Table 2 does reveal some change, most notably in Newfoundland, Alberta and British Columbia. In Newfoundland, the Liberals·dropped and the Conservatives gained sharply between 1965 and 1968. Since 1968 the Liberals have restored their position somewhat, but the essential effect endures: Newfoundland is no longer a secure Liberal stronghold but is now a competitive two-party province. In Alberta, the change from 1965 to 1974 made the province even less competitive than before. In 1965 the Conservative dominance of Alberta was partly a result of the fragmentation of the rest of the vote. In 1974, however, the Conservatives captured more than 60 per cent of the popular vote, making Alberta much the least competitive province. The growth of the Alberta Conservatives was largely at Social Credit expense. British Columbia's Conservatives also gained at Social Credit expense, although in doing so they did not achieve remotely as commanding a position as their Alberta counterparts. And some of the British Columbia Conservative growth from 1972 to 1974 was at the expense of the NDP. As such, it may have been a short-term expression of discontent with the then NDP provincial government.

Less spectacular changes occurred in three other provinces. In New Brunswick, the Conservative vote dropped ten points from 1972 to 1974. This may only have been a short-term phenomenon.[14] In Manitoba, the Conservatives and Liberals moved in complementary ways from election to election. From 1965 to 1968, the Liberals gained and the Conservatives lost sharply, followed by a complete restoration of the original 1965 position in 1972. Then, from 1972 to 1974, the Liberal position weakened and the Conservative position strengthened still further. Whether 1974 represents a new alignment or only a temporary aberration (as 1968 was) remains to be seen. Saskatchewan contradicts the trends in its immediate neighbours. In Saskatchewan, the Liberals and New Democrats have strengthened and the Conservatives have declined, yielding the competitive three-party system described above.

The Historical Pattern of the Federal Vote

In the last section I gave the impression of great provincial differences. But the differences, though substantial, may be on a path to disappearance. Several arguments, which I shall sketch in a moment, point to such a prediction. So do the examples of the United Kingdom (at least before 1974) and the United

States. As it happens, however, Canada runs against the grain: her regional differences have not shrunk but grown.

What social processes might produce a convergence of provinces' voting patterns? The literature on political geography suggests at least three such processes: interregional mobility, recruitment into organizations trading widely or with membership spanning the regions, and exposure to mass media of communication.[15] The first two processes are especially important in their effects on the political character of the other individuals with whom a given individual interacts; the burden of much voting research is that individuals are powerfully affected by such personal influence, by face-to-face contacts.[16] The third process, mass media exposure, taps, almost by definition, impersonal influences. But the mass media also feed political stimuli to networks of personal influence and so help define the groups of friends and acquaintances among whom face-to-face influence operates.

What, then, of interregional mobility? A key observation here is that transportation costs have decreased mightily, reducing barriers to movement between provinces. As transportation costs have fallen, the spatial scale of migration should have increased. The more frequent intermingling of hitherto geographically separated and politically disparate individuals should have helped break down political differences between locales. In Canada immigrants from abroad may have helped the process along.[17]

Organizations have increased the spatial scale of their operations. Trade now often spans great distances, and many voters are employees of firms with a geographically very dispersed labour force. Large corporations have in turn spawned national and international unions. Voluntary associations recruit across provincial and even national boundaries. Information flowing along organizational lines is now quite likely to have originated outside the receiver's province. Thus even personal influence networks transmit political cues common to a number of provinces. This ebb and flow of political discourse between regions may have made voters in the different provinces less disparate than before in their response to the national parties.

Just as the costs of transportation between regions have declined, so have the costs of communication. The telephone and telegraph, radio and television have worked to homogenize across provinces the political information available to individuals. Conceivably, as the audience exposed to common stimuli has become spatially more dispersed, the responses of audiences in different places will have become commensurately more homogeneous.

These expectations seem to have been confirmed in the United States and the United Kingdom. In this century local and regional differences in those countries' voting patterns have diminished. Average differences between regions are now relatively small and response to short-term political forces, the interelection "swing," relatively more uniform across locales.[18] Could the same now be true in Canada?

Powerful arguments predict the opposite, however. Social and political forces may have increased or, at least, maintained differences between Canadian provinces. In Canada interregional migration and patterns of employment, trade and voluntary association membership have evolved in equivocal ways. Further, arguments which focus on only these factors ignore real and abiding conflicts of interest between regions.

One argument pointed to the increasing spatial scale of interregional migration, an increase attributable to declining transportation costs. This argument ignores the role of factors other than cost in migration decisions, and in any case diverts us from the fact that, in a proportionate sense, interregional migration in Canada has not increased, but decreased.[19] At the turn of the century a massive westward shift of the native population accompanied the high levels of migration to the West from abroad. Seventy years ago many more western Canadians had ties of recollection, affection and kinship to the older provinces than presently do. To the extent that such links work in both directions, Canadians in most regions were then less provincial in their personal influence ties than they are at present. Further, migration to and from Quebec may have added a peculiar twist to the general migration story. Migrants to that province are disproportionately likely to be French, while those from it are disproportionately likely to be English. The net effect of migrant exchanges between Quebec and elsewhere has been to reinforce the dominant language of the destination: Quebec is now more homogeneously French, and the rest of Canada more homogeneously English than each used to be.[20]

The second argument pointed to the geographic spread of organizations. It is certainly true that as Canadians have moved off the farm, larger and larger numbers of them have entered occupations tying them to networks of interaction transcending the immediate locale. At the same time the voluntary association life of the country has become richer and deeper. Even so, it is easy to overstate the degree to which the links so created cross provincial boundaries. Much economic activity is carried on within the provinces by provincially chartered companies. An increasing proportion of extra-provincial trade has been with adjacent regions of the United States, rather than with other parts of Canada.[21] Union and voluntary association activity is usually organized along provincial lines, even where the organizations are nominally national.

Changes in communications must have had similarly equivocal effects. It is easy to overstate the degree to which Canadians have come to attend to common sources of information and entertainment. Newspapers are still quite local in character, however much wire copy they carry. Broadcast media are much the same. The principal national network, the CBC, has seen its audience dwindle in the face of locally (or, in some cases, regionally) based commercial broadcasters. The common programs Canadians now receive are more often than not American. And of course the growth of the mass media has proceeded in parallel: it has not broken down, but may even have reinforced the segregation of the official language communities.

Even these admissions do not go far enough. All three arguments imply that contact between individuals and groups lessens differences between them, and that the necessary interregional contact simply has not been forthcoming in Canada. But the effect of contact on group differences is much more complex. The *nature* of contacts profoundly conditions the impact of their simple frequency. In Canada interaction between regions has often embodied severe conflicts of interest. Interregional migration of language groups may have sharpened linguistic conflict, and to the extent that language use was geographically differentiated in the first place, made linguistic questions into geographic ones. Politicians in Quebec and in other provinces have faced incentives to identify their own province uniquely with one or the other official language. Economic rivalries and grievances have also been real, of course. Different provinces have fundamentally different stakes in common economic policy instruments. The regionally differentiated effects of the tariff, for instance, simply cannot be willed away by migration or the CBC. Even where provincial economies resemble each other, the possibility of rivalry exists. And, of course, these conflicts achieve institutional expression through the very existence of provincial governments.

The social and demographic changes of this century may only have exacerbated the interregional conflicts of interest. Urbanization may have heightened linguistic conflict; language groups may coexist much more happily when dispersed in the countryside than when forced into dense urban neighbourhoods and when made to share a common division of labour.[22] The rapid economic development of the Canadian West introduced yet another axis of political conflict.

How exactly might I tap regional convergence or divergence? I shall approach the matter along two paths. First, I can examine differences between provinces in each national election: are differences greater or smaller now than before? Historical comparisons of the standard deviation of each party's vote across the provinces, supplemented by direct examination of national and provincial vote series, will be my basic activities here. Second, I can look at differences between provinces in short-term change. Provinces may be far apart in their average proportions supporting a party, but may respond to short-term influences (issues, leaders or the nature of the times) in quite similar ways. Although there is no necessary relationship between historical change in these two phenomena, the arguments I have just made seem applicable to both.

Table 3 presents the standard deviation of each party's vote across the provinces for each federal election the party contested from 1878 to 1974. The number of provinces entering the calculation increases from the beginning of the series to the end. Until 1896 only six provinces had competitive party politics. In British Columbia and the territories that were to become Saskatchewan and Alberta, federal electoral politics were "ministerialist," in that great efforts were made to ensure that the region voted with whoever won the genuinely partisan battle to the east.[23] Only in 1896 do we see something resembling party politics in British Columbia federal voting, and not until 1908 can we examine federal voting in Alberta and Saskatchewan. Of course, Newfoundland enters the calculation only in 1949.

The historical pattern is unmistakable: far from declining, provincial differences in the federal vote, as indicated by the standard deviation, are now much greater than they were a century ago.

From 1878 to 1911 inclusive, the average standard deviation of the Liberal vote was 4.6 points, while for the Conservatives the average was 3.7 points. The peak of geographic homogeneity was achieved in 1887. In that

Table 3

The Geographic Concentration of the National Vote, by Party, 1878–1974

Election	Party			
	Liberal	Conservative	NDP	Social Credit
1878	5.4	4.4	—	—
1882	4.4	4.7	—	—
1887	2.1	1.8	—	—
1891	4.7	1.8	—	—
1896	6.5	2.2	—	—
1900	2.3	3.2	—	—
1904	3.2	4.6	—	—
1908	6.5	4.9	—	—
1911	6.3	6.1	—	—
1917	16.0	16.2	—	—
1921	19.6	11.1	—	—
1925	12.3	12.3	—	—
1926	11.6	10.8	—	—
1930	7.1	8.0	—	—
1935	12.0	7.2	12.1	16.0
1940	8.5	12.8	11.8	11.3
1945	10.5	12.7	14.0	11.7
1949	11.0	10.8	14.1	11.7
1953	11.7	13.0	14.5	14.1
1957	13.9	10.5	12.4	13.0
1958	13.9	5.3	10.6	7.0
1962	11.9	9.0	9.2	10.8
1963	12.8	11.6	9.2	10.3
1965	12.7	11.8	10.8	8.8
1968	7.1	13.6	12.4	5.2
1972	8.4	11.8	12.1	7.4
1974	9.9	10.9	8.9	5.2

Entries are standard deviations. Sources: 1878–1958: Howard A.Scarrow, *Canada Votes* (New Orleans: Hauser, 1962); Chief Electoral Officer, *Reports 1962-1974* (Ottawa: Supply and Services). Reproduced by permission of the Minister of Supply and Services Canada.

year such modest provincial differences as had appeared before began to reverse themselves, and provinces passing each other in opposite directions each gave the parties remarkably similar proportions of their popular vote. By 1891 the system was again about as geographically differentiated as in 1882. With the initiation of party politics in British Columbia and with the creation of Alberta and Saskatchewan, the system's geographic variation increased a bit more. Even so, the 1908 and 1911 elections, the first two with party politics in nine provinces, yielded vote distributions that were geographically remarkably uniform.[24]

This tightly contested, geographically fairly homogeneous system ended with a bang in 1917. Only one major party standard deviation since 1917, the Conservatives' one in 1958, was lower than the very highest one before 1917. The average standard deviation over the 1917–1974 period was 11.7 points for the Liberals and 11.0 points for the Conservatives. The major parties' regional concentration varies from election to election, of course. In general, the major parties' geographic concentration is a direct function of the size of third parties (1917 is a major exception to this rule). Thus Conservative and Liberal standard deviations are especially large in the early 1920s, the period of greatest Progressive strength. From 1921 to 1930, however, the Progressives ebbed and major parties flowed back into areas of temporary Progressive strength. As the major parties did so, they became geographically more homogeneous. But in 1935 and 1940, the old parties were rolled back into sectional strongholds, as new third parties, Social Credit and the CCF, established what was to be a lasting and growing base in the West. The Liberals remained about as regionalized throughout the period after 1935 as they were in that particular year. The Conservative case has been slightly more complex. In 1935 the Conservatives seemed actually less regionalized (that is, the standard deviation of their vote across provinces was smaller) than in the essentially two-party 1930 election. Conservative losses from 1930 to 1935 were disproportionately in areas of previous strength. But thereafter the party settled into a pattern even more regionalized than that of the Liberals. The election of 1958 was a major exception to this. Over the period 1953–1957–1958 the Conservatives grew disproportionately where they had hitherto been weak. The party's 1958 return was thus geographically extraordinarily uniform; the party's standard deviation, 5.3 points, was below the Conservative average for the 1878–1911 period. In 1962 and after, however, the party returned to its highly sectionalized ways.

Tables 4 and 5 give the particulars of Liberal and Conservative geographic strength and weakness for the full 1878–1974 series. The tables confirm the importance of the 1917–1921 and 1957–1963 periods. Note, however, that in 1917–1921 the only truly major shift in the *direction* of differences involved Alberta. In its first two elections as a province, 1908 and 1911, Alberta was quite heavily Liberal. It did not return to the Liberal fold after 1917–1921, and has remained ever since sternly out of step with the rest. Otherwise, while the explosions in 1917 and 1921 greatly expanded the magnitude of differences between provinces, they did not much disturb the direction of differences. True, the exact rank order of provinces may have shifted from, say, 1908 to 1930, but the parties did largely preserve, in exaggerated form, their earlier regional character. The Conservative party remained a party heavily of Ontario and the Atlantic provinces; its weak regions remained Quebec and the Prairies. The Liberals remained a party of the Atlantic provinces and Quebec, with greater strength than the Conservatives on the Prairies.

The 1957–1963 "Diefenbaker interlude"[25] affected the party system as profoundly as the 1917–1921 period did. But where the first realignment

Table 4
Liberal Party Federal Election Vote Shares, by Province, 1878–1974

					Province					
Election	New-foundland	P.E.I.	N.S.	N.B.	Que.	Ont.	Man.	Sask.	Alta.	B.C.
1878	—	43.2	44.2	55.0	40.1	47.3	50.4	—	—	—
1882	—	51.5	45.0	45.5	40.7	49.0	52.3	—	—	—
1887	—	53.5	47.4	48.9	49.1	49.5	48.6	—	—	—
1891	—	51.5	45.0	37.7	45.4	49.1	46.9	—	—	—
1896	—	51.0	48.8	44.3	53.5	40.2	35.0	—	—	49.1
1900	—	51.3	51.7	51.9	56.3	49.8	51.8	—	—	49.1
1904	—	49.1	54.5	51.0	56.4	49.5	55.5	—	—	49.5
1908	—	50.4	51.0	53.8	57.3	47.1	45.4	56.6	50.2	35.9
1911	—	48.9	50.8	50.8	50.7	43.1	44.8	59.4	53.3	37.5
1917	—	50.2	45.5	40.6	72.7	34.1	20.3	25.9	35.5	25.6
1921	—	45.7	52.4	49.4	70.2	29.8	10.9	20.7	15.8	29.8
1925	—	52.0	41.9	40.3	59.4	31.0	20.3	41.9	25.9	34.7
1926	—	52.7	43.5	46.1	62.3	38.9	37.9	56.8	24.5	37.0
1930	—	50.0	47.5	40.6	53.2	43.9	37.2	46.5	30.0	40.9
1935	—	58.2	52.0	57.2	54.4	42.7	40.5	40.8	21.2	31.8
1940	—	55.3	50.6	54.6	63.3	50.8	47.8	43.0	37.9	37.4
1945	—	48.4	45.7	50.0	50.8	41.1	34.7	32.7	21.8	27.5
1949	71.9	49.1	52.7	53.8	60.4	45.7	47.9	43.4	34.5	36.7
1953	67.2	51.1	53.0	52.7	61.0	46.9	40.2	37.7	35.0	30.9
1957	61.9	46.6	45.1	48.1	57.6	37.1	26.1	30.3	27.9	20.5
1958	54.4	37.5	38.4	43.4	45.7	32.6	21.6	19.6	13.7	16.1
1962	59.0	43.3	42.4	44.4	39.2	41.7	31.1	22.8	19.4	27.3
1963	64.5	46.4	46.7	47.3	45.6	46.3	33.8	24.1	22.1	32.3
1965	64.1	44.1	42.0	47.5	45.6	43.6	31.0	24.0	22.4	30.0
1968	42.8	45.0	38.0	44.4	53.6	46.6	41.5	27.1	35.7	41.8
1972	44.8	40.5	33.9	43.1	49.1	38.2	30.9	25.3	25.0	28.9
1974	46.7	46.2	40.7	47.2	54.1	45.1	27.4	30.7	24.8	33.3

Sources: see Table 3.

expanded regional differences without altering their direction, the later changes did exactly the opposite: the parties emerged in 1963 about as regionalized as before, but their actual regional composition had shifted enormously. The Liberal party underwent fewer changes in the period than the Conservative party. The Liberal vote dropped, to a greater or lesser degree, in every province but Alberta and Ontario. The party's position in Alberta, however, was no more desperate after 1963 than before 1957. But Ontario, by remaining about as Liberal as before, became one of the very strongholds of the party, with a Liberal vote share often rivalling that in Quebec. Quebec, of course, remains the heart of Liberal support. Even so, the party's advantage in that province is not remotely as overwhelming now as it was before 1957. Before 1957, the party often received over 60 per cent of the

Table 5
Conservative Party Federal Election Vote Shares, by Province, 1878–1974

Election	New-foundland	P.E.I.	N.S.	N.B.	Que.	Ont.	Man.	Sask.	Alta.	B.C.
1878	—	56.8	52.3	45.0	56.4	52.2	49.6	—	—	—
1882	—	48.5	55.0	54.5	59.3	51.0	46.7	—	—	—
1887	—	46.5	50.2	51.1	50.6	50.5	51.4	—	—	—
1891	—	48.5	54.0	59.3	52.0	49.4	53.1	—	—	—
1896	—	49.0	50.4	49.0	45.8	45.0	49.0	—	—	50.9
1900	—	48.2	48.3	47.8	43.5	49.7	48.2	—	—	40.9
1904	—	50.9	44.5	48.8	43.4	50.3	41.8	—	—	38.8
1908	—	49.6	49.0	46.2	40.8	51.4	51.5	36.8	44.4	46.8
1911	—	51.1	48.8	49.2	49.2	56.2	51.9	39.0	42.5	58.8
1917	—	49.8	48.4	59.4	25.1	62.3	79.7	74.1	61.0	68.4
1921	—	37.2	32.3	39.4	18.4	39.2	24.4	16.7	20.3	47.9
1925	—	48.0	56.4	59.7	33.7	57.0	41.3	25.4	31.8	49.3
1926	—	47.3	53.7	53.9	34.3	54.1	42.2	27.5	31.5	54.2
1930	—	50.0	52.5	59.4	44.7	54.4	47.7	37.6	33.9	49.3
1935	—	38.4	32.1	31.9	28.2	35.3	26.9	18.8	16.9	24.6
1940	—	44.7	39.8	43.4	19.8	42.7	26.0	14.1	13.0	30.5
1945	—	47.4	36.8	38.3	8.4	41.7	24.9	18.8	18.7	30.0
1949	27.9	48.4	37.5	39.4	24.6	37.4	22.0	14.4	16.8	27.9
1953	28.1	48.1	40.1	41.9	29.4	40.3	27.0	11.7	14.5	14.1
1957	37.8	52.3	50.4	48.7	31.1	48.8	35.9	23.2	27.6	32.6
1958	45.2	62.2	57.0	54.1	49.6	56.4	56.7	51.4	59.9	49.4
1962	36.0	51.3	47.3	46.5	29.6	39.3	41.6	50.4	42.8	27.3
1963	30.1	52.0	46.9	40.4	19.5	35.3	42.3	53.7	45.3	23.4
1965	32.4	53.9	48.6	42.5	21.2	34.0	40.7	48.0	46.6	19.2
1968	52.8	51.8	55.2	49.7	21.4	32.0	31.4	37.0	50.4	19.4
1972	49.0	51.9	53.4	44.9	17.4	39.1	41.6	36.9	57.6	33.0
1974	43.6	49.1	47.5	33.0	21.2	35.1	47.7	36.4	61.2	41.9

Sources: see Table 3.

Quebec vote. Now it typically receives about 50 per cent.[26] From 1921 to 1957, the Atlantic provinces were usually important sources of Liberal support. They remain so even today, but now typically give the party about the same proportion as Ontario does. Although Manitoba and Saskatchewan were not major sources of Liberal strength before 1957, the party's vote in those provinces was at least respectable (especially as the non-Liberal vote was usually quite fragmented). In both, the Liberal vote rivalled that in Ontario. But the party never really recovered from its 1957–1958 collapse on the Prairies. Now, Saskatchewan and Manitoba give the Liberals only a slightly larger vote than does Alberta.

Still, the Liberal changes pale beside the Conservative ones. Only in the Atlantic provinces did pre-1957 Conservative patterns hold in 1963 and after; those provinces were before and continue to be important sources of Conservative support. Everywhere else major changes occurred. Before Diefenbaker, Ontario often returned the largest Conservative vote. Indeed, the party's pre-1957 caucus usually seemed little more than an Ontario rump. In 1963 and after, however, only Quebec, and occasionally British Columbia, gave the Conservatives proportionately fewer votes than Ontario. Quebec, it should be noted, became the weakest Conservative province only in the Diefenbaker period. Before 1957, the party often received about one-third of the Quebec vote, a much larger proportion than in Alberta, Saskatchewan and (often) British Columbia. After a surge in 1958, the Conservative vote in Quebec fell from its earlier one-third to its present one-fifth. The greatest change of all, however, happened in the Prairie provinces. Before Diefenbaker, the Conservative position there was truly desperate. From 1935 to 1953, the party never received more than 30 per cent of the Manitoba vote and 20 per cent of the Alberta and Saskatchewan votes. Since 1958 the Conservatives have never received less than 40 per cent in Alberta and 30 per cent in Saskatchewan and Manitoba.

We certainly cannot conclude that differences between provinces in parties' vote percentages have diminished. Indeed, the historical record shows the opposite. But what of *short-term fluctuations* in the vote? It could be that, even as provinces have diverged from each other, the critical blocs of changeable voters in each province have come to attend more and more to common political stimuli, and to move back and forth between parties in concert.

To test this possibility, I shall correlate each party's vote in each province with its vote in each other province. I shall present correlations separately for each of three periods. If interelection flux has become geographically more homogeneous, the correlation between different provinces' series should be greater in later periods than in earlier ones. [27] The periods of comparison seem reasonably obvious. Tables 3, 4 and 5 suggest that the first party system ended in 1917. Elections from 1921 to 1957 add up to a second period, even though there is a circulation of minor parties from the beginning of the period to the end. Elections in and since 1958 constitute a third period. The 1917 election presents a knotty problem. The party battle was nonexistent in many English-Canadian ridings, and might as well have been in many French-Canadian ones. Many Canadians were thus not choosing in any meaningful way between parties. Compare this with the 1958 election which, while certainly a watershed in Canadian political history, was unequivocally a party battle. The peculiarities of 1917 moved me to drop it entirely from the calculations. Thus the first electoral period will end in 1911, while the second will begin in 1921.

Tables 6 and 7 present evidence for the Liberal and Conservative parties respectively. The story is different for each. Short-term fluctuations in the Liberal vote have become geographically more homogeneous, and the historical increase has been quite smooth. Even so, the Liberal pattern in the late period is no more homogeneous than the Conservative one. Response to the Conservative party has evolved in a much more complex way. In the 1878–1911 period the Conservative pattern resembled the Liberal one and was quite heterogeneous. In the 1921–1957 period, short-term fluctuations in the Conservative vote became extraordinarily homogeneous. In that period the Conservative vote fluctuated greatly, but did so in very similar ways in each province. In the 1958–1974 period, the Conservative pattern became rather heterogeneous again. In short, the passage of time has not made the geography of short-term response to Canadian parties unambiguously more integrated.

Some specifics of each period merit attention. The secular realignment between about 1887 and 1904, in which the Liberals supplanted the Conservatives as the dominant party, is responsible for some of the weakness in the 1878–1911 coefficients. The realignment was effected, as a practical matter, in Quebec and Nova Scotia. Across much of the period the Liberals were growing and the Conservatives were declining in those two provinces, somewhat independently of fluctuations elsewhere. This is reflected in the strongly positive correlations between the Quebec and Nova Scotia series and the weak to negative links between each of those provinces and most of the others. As it happens, New Brunswick, which reveals no trend for the 1878–1911 period, is also strongly associated with Quebec and Nova Scotia. New Brunswick's very location between Quebec and Nova Scotia may be reason enough, however, for the statistical association. Not all of the weakness in the early period is attributable to the realignment, of course. Inspection of Tables 4 and 5 uncovers a fair amount of just plain randomness. Prince Edward Island, which underwent no long-term change in the period, was particularly out of step.

Conservative and Liberal patterns ceased to mirror each other in the 1921–1957 period. This became possible, of course, as after 1921 the two old parties no longer exhausted the total party space. In this period, short-term response was geographically much more diverse for the

Table 6
Correlations Between Provinces' Liberal Party Vote Series,
by Period

	P.E.I.	N.S.	N.B.	P.Q.	Ont.	Man.	Sask.	Alta.	B.C.
A. 1878–1911									
P.E.I.		0.15	−0.52	0.33	0.15	−0.14	—	—	—
N.S.			0.40	0.91	−0.06	−0.08	—	—	—
N.B.				0.26	−0.07	0.29	—	—	—
P.Q.					−0.14	−0.20	—	—	—
Ont.						0.87	—	—	—
B. 1921–1957									
P.E.I.		0.10	0.35	−0.19	0.45	0.55	0.59	0.22	0.44
N.S.			0.74	0.31	0.45	0.31	−0.30	0.21	0.08
N.B.				0.11	0.53	0.49	−0.19	0.16	−0.21
P.Q.					−0.28	−0.34	−0.23	−0.03	0.07
Ont.						0.94	0.42	0.77	0.35
Man.							0.63	0.71	0.44
Sask.								0.42	0.71
Alta.									0.35
C. 1958–1974									
Nfld.	0.13	0.79	0.51	−0.75	0.06	−0.19	−0.53	−0.57	−0.33
P.E.I.		0.60	0.77	0.28	0.98	0.60	0.69	0.55	0.80
N.S.			0.75	−0.40	0.51	0.08	−0.07	−0.23	0.09
N.B.				0.11	0.68	0.10	0.41	0.07	0.35
P.Q.					0.32	0.27	0.76	0.68	0.56
Ont.						0.75	0.68	0.69	0.89
Man.							0.39	0.87	0.89
Sask.								0.70	0.76
Alta.									0.94

Entries are Pearson product-moment correlation coefficients.
Sources: see Table 3.

Liberals than for the Conservatives. Even so, the Liberal pattern was less diverse in this period than in the first one. Two principal contrasts appear in the Liberal data. One pitted Nova Scotia and New Brunswick against Saskatchewan and Alberta. Correlations within each province pair are strongly positive, while those between pairs are weak or negative. This reflects vote swings in roughly the first half of the period. From 1921 to 1930 the Liberals declined in Nova Scotia and New Brunswick, while in Saskatchewan and Alberta the Liberals recovered as the Progressives decomposed. Then, from 1930 to 1935, the Liberals gained sharply in the Atlantic provinces; on the Prairies the Liberals, like the Conservatives, were beaten back by the second wave of regional minor parties. After 1935, vote differences between the two pairs of provinces persisted but interelection fluctuations began to move in concert. Quebec was also out of step, especially in 1940 and 1945, in which

Table 7
Correlations Between Provinces' Conservative Party Vote Series,
by Period

	P.E.I.	N.S.	N.B.	P.Q.	Ont.	Man.	Sask.	Alta.	B.C.
A. 1878–1911									
P.E.I.		−0.02	−0.52	0.25	0.37	−0.12	—	—	—
N.S.			0.56	0.80	−0.08	0.47	—	—	—
N.B.				0.42	−0.17	0.21	—	—	—
P.Q.					0.21	0.13	—	—	—
Ont.						0.20	—	—	—
B. 1921–1957									
P.E.I.		0.70	0.59	0.38	0.56	0.48	0.36	0.43	−0.05
N.S.			0.95	0.71	0.97	0.90	0.73	0.86	0.58
N.B.				0.71	0.97	0.91	0.78	0.87	0.69
P.Q.					0.63	0.82	0.71	0.69	0.37
Ont.						0.93	0.80	0.90	0.72
Man.							0.92	0.93	0.68
Sask.								0.92	0.72
Alta.									0.80
C. 1958–1974									
Nfld.		0.08	0.77	0.36	0.10	0.15	−0.11	−0.76	0.64	0.32
P.E.I.		0.65	0.73	0.87	0.88	0.64	0.49	0.26	0.49
N.S.			0.78	0.50	0.55	0.14	−0.24	0.50	0.34
N.B.				0.65	0.60	0.07	0.27	−0.05	−0.08
P.Q.					0.92	0.73	0.48	0.27	0.65
Ont.						0.83	0.40	0.44	0.78
Man.							0.37	0.55	0.89
Sask.								−0.53	−0.04
Alta.									0.81

Sources: see Table 3.

years conscription and the wartime role of the language communities figured prominently. The 1921–1957 story for the Conservatives is much simpler. Differences between provinces emerged in 1921 and persisted throughout the period. But swings from election to election were very much in phase across the provinces. The only exception to this generalization is the correlation between the British Columbia and Prince Edward Island series, which is effectively zero.

In the last period each old party is about as heterogeneous as the other. The Liberal pattern of short-term fluctuations is less diverse than in the period before, but retains important regional contrasts. Newfoundland, Nova Scotia and New Brunswick Liberal swings are at odds with or unrelated to swings in Quebec, Manitoba, Saskatchewan, Alberta and British Columbia. Inspection of Table 4 suggests that the correlation pattern reflects shifts after 1965. Quebec and the four western provinces swung toward or away from the Trudeau-period Liberal party somewhat together, while the three Atlantic provinces resisted national trends. For the Conservatives, the most striking contrast is between Saskatchewan, on one hand, and Newfoundland, Nova Scotia, Alberta and British Columbia, on the other. Table 5 suggests that Saskatchewan and the other provinces diverged markedly after 1965. When Stanfield replaced Diefenbaker, the Conservatives became much less appealing in Saskatchewan, but rather more so elsewhere.

In sum, evidence for a decrease in the geographic diversity of short-term vote swings is weak. Although short-term response to the Liberals has become geographically more homogeneous, the same cannot be said for the Conservatives. And although the Conservative evidence is important in its own right, it also raises the possibility that the apparently smooth increase in Liberal geographic homogeneity represents not the unfolding of ineluctable demographic or other processes, but is as much a series of historical accidents as the Conservatives' history seems to have been. Realignments, in which regional considerations figured prominently, in all three periods produced weak correlations between some provinces. In the 1878–1911 period, Liberal growth in Nova Scotia and Quebec was linked to a surge of provincialist sentiment in both places. In the 1921–1957 period, the complicated Liberal pattern reflected the intensity of grievances in the Atlantic and Prairie provinces together with the entirely different partisan expression of those grievances in each region. In the 1958–1974 period, the West-East alternation of Conservative leaders provoked geographically differentiated swings in both parties' fortunes.

Neither the short-term change evidence nor the cross-sectional standard deviation evidence points unequivocally to a diminution of provincial differences in the vote. The change evidence is ambiguous, while the standard deviation evidence reveals an actual historical increase in the importance of geographic differences.

The Relationship Between the Federal and the Provincial Vote: Historical Evolution

Could a major factor in the regional disintegration of national politics have been the very existence of provinces as political entities? Most Canadians, after all, belong to not one, but two major electorates, and the same individuals voting in quick succession at different levels may come to respond at both levels according to common criteria. Voting in federal elections could reflect judgments on provincial politicians and issues, and vice versa. The existence of an essentially similar party system at both levels and the reliance of voters on parties to simplify the political world could produce a convergence of vote patterns between levels. But as time passes each province's provincial politics may get progressively more out of phase with each other province's politics. Thus part of what pulls provinces away from each other in national elections may be the several autonomous rhythms of their respective provincial elections. The question in this section, then, is: as provinces have diverged from each other at the federal level, what has happened to the relationship, within each province, between levels? In particular, have federal and provincial voting become more, less or no more and no less integrated with each other as time has passed?

History reinforces common sense in leading us to expect *some* relationship across levels. We can think of major realignments occurring more or less simultaneously at both levels, as with the growth of third parties in the West. We can also think of provincial elections that were virtual referenda on national issues, such as the 1939 Quebec election. Conversely, some federal shifts seem to have reflected judgments on provincial politics, such as British Columbia's marked swing away from the NDP in 1974. Organization strength or weakness at one level can affect the party's chances at the other. Provincial patronage is often thought to be a factor in a party's federal chances, and the flow of benefits can be reversed, especially in poor provinces.

At the same time, however, much evidence suggests that federal and provincial politics are diverging. In many provinces federal and provincial party organizations consist of quite different people, even where the same nominal organization fights elections at both levels. In some provinces, of course, even the formal organizations are now separate. Donations to parties are no longer channelled through a small number of federally oriented sources. Instead, increasing amounts are collected directly by provincial parties, a phenomenon connected to provincial jurisdiction over natural resources and to growing provincial regulatory power. The gradual spread of the public funding of parties will promote the financial independence of provincial parties still further. Meanwhile, the chain of career opportunities spanning both political levels is breaking down, as fewer provincial politicians seek federal office, and vice versa.[28] Finally, the correspondence between federal and provincial party systems varies enormously between provinces, a fact which must affect both parties and voters even as it is itself a consequence of party and voter action. In a province a party's ideological and power positions may differ radically between provincial and federal levels, and, to be consistent, a voter may have to switch between parties.[29]

In short, my expectations for the historical evolution of ties between provincial and federal voting are not simple. Some provinces may reveal an historical divergence between levels; others may reveal convergence. My equivocal expectations are mirrored by confusion in the literature on federal-provincial vote patterns. Frank Underhill, for example, has argued:

> By some instinctive, subconscious mental process, the Canadian people have apparently decided that, since freedom depends upon a balance of power, they will balance the monopolistic power of the Liberal government at Ottawa by setting up the effective countervailing power, not in

> Ottawa but in the provincial capitals . . . there must now be thousands
> and thousands of Canadian citizens who vote Liberal in federal elections
> and anti-Liberal in provincial elections.[30]

Howard A. Scarrow, on the other hand, has argued quite the opposite:

> In Canada, as in other federations, the normal presumption is that a voter
> will exhibit relatively consistent behaviour in both federal and provincial
> elections, and that alternating elections are exceptional. Party officials
> appear to act on this presumption, as witnessed by the fact that the
> Progressive Conservative victory in the 1956 Nova Scotia election was
> interpreted in Conservative circles as a favourable omen of the party's
> chances at the forthcoming federal election, or the fact that following Mr.
> Diefenbaker's 1958 victory the Ontario press speculated that Premier
> Frost would call an early election in order to take advantage of the
> Conservative tide.[31]

We might as well turn directly to the facts.

But which facts are pertinent? Dominion and provincial governments
have not obliged me with perfectly coincident election dates. Instead, the two
kinds of elections are interspersed, with two elections at one level frequently
intervening between elections at the other level. Determining which elections
ought properly to be compared between series is no mere technical question,
but requires attention to substantive issues. These issues are especially
pressing for the analyses in the second part of this section. In particular, what
should relationships between levels look like? One possible structure of
effects would have impulses from each federal election transmitted to the next
following provincial election. We could also imagine impulses travelling
from each provincial election to the next following federal one. This suggests
separate but matching federal-to-provincial-to-federal comparisons.[32] I
could then break the series into earlier and later periods to see if federal-
provincial links have strengthened, weakened, reversed sign, or whatever.
Such an approach will not do, however. A moment's reflection will show the
artificiality of enforcing a strict succession between federal and provincial
elections. For example, which federal election would we reasonably expect
the provincial outcome more to resemble, one three years before or one two
months after the provincial election in question? One two months before or
one three years after? Most processes linking federal to provincial voting will
probably have greater success the closer federal and provincial elections are
to each other, regardless of which level's election happens to come first. This
should be true whether the effect in question be the impact on both federal
and provincial voting of some exogenous policy variable, the effect of party
organization or leadership, or even the effect of attempts by voters to
"balance" federal and provincial outcomes by consciously switching between
levels. Comparing provincial elections with preceding federal ones, and
federal elections with preceding provincial ones, would introduce into each

series observations which are not strictly the ones of interest. Comparisons in both directions will not really get around the problem, but would only expand the opportunity for error. What I really must do is relate federal elections to the provincial elections closest to them in time.[33] Sometimes the federal election will precede the provincial one; sometimes the opposite will happen.

As before, I shall compare series in two ways. First, I shall look at the Index of Dissimilarity between each federal election and the nearest provincial election for each province (except Newfoundland, whose series will begin in 1949), in each federal election from 1908 to 1974.[34] The index shows the minimum percentage of the province's electorate that would have to be reallocated between parties to transform the provincial outcome into the federal one, or vice versa. The index can also be read as giving the actual difference between levels as a percentage of the maximum possible difference. Second, I shall examine correlations between each province's federal and provincial series. In this section my concern will be with the federal-provincial correspondence of short-term change.

Table 8 gives the historical pattern of each province's indices of dissimilarity. No generalization covers the whole table. In the Atlantic provinces and Ontario, federal-provincial differences are small and show no sign of growth. The Prairie provinces reveal a chequered history, with marked fluctuations in federal-provincial differences. In Quebec and British Columbia, of course, federal and provincial party systems now correspond to each other hardly at all.

In the Atlantic provinces and Ontario, the two levels have held together. Federal-provincial differences are typically no greater now than fifty years ago. Occasional bursts of interlevel distinctiveness have appeared, but the differences have subsided quickly. Evidently, forces work to integrate levels in the provinces where both old parties remain strong.

On the Prairies, the story differs between provinces and periods. In Manitoba, interlevel differences surged in 1917, 1930 and 1968. Often index values were higher in Manitoba than in the English-speaking provinces to the east. But Manitoba's differences usually have been smaller than those in Quebec and in the three westernmost provinces. Manitoba's historical pattern is one of intermittent divergences followed by gradual convergence over three or four elections. Saskatchewan also reveals divergence followed by convergence. While convergence after 1917-1921 and 1935 was swift, that after 1957-1958 took several years. In the first instance, the Liberal party restored its federal position shortly after 1921. The years from 1935 to 1945 saw the growth of the CCF at both levels. In 1957 and 1958, the Conservative party mushroomed in federal voting but remained virtually nonexistent at the provincial level. This pattern persisted to 1972. But in 1974, the levels converged sharply.[35] Alberta reveals a pattern of its own. In 1917 and 1921, interlevel differences did emerge but not to as great a degree

Table 8

The Net Dissimilarity of Federal and Provincial Elections, by Province, 1908–1974

					Province					
Election	New-foundland	P.E.I.	N.S.	N.B.	Que.	Ont.	Man.	Sask.	Alta.	B.C.
1908	—	1.2	7.4	5.3	2.2	6.1	2.5	11.1	14.7	10.5
1911	—	9.1	3.3	9.4	6.4	3.3	1.5	2.8	4.7	18.4
1917	—	4.1	5.8	11.7	10.7	37.5	46.7	37.2	19.0	28.9
1921	—	14.3	12.1	14.9	19.0	11.1	15.5	33.1	21.6	16.7
1925	—	1.1	5.3	6.6	3.4	11.9	16.0	13.4	10.7	19.5
1926	—	0.4	6.8	2.3	2.3	20.0	31.9	13.6	8.6	4.2
1930	—	1.7	2.2	7.0	1.8	12.1	48.5	5.7	26.4	3.4
1935	—	3.6	15.9	10.5	14.0	9.7	23.6	38.9	21.7	8.4
1940	—	2.3	5.6	1.9	29.7	3.7	16.6	15.0	50.5	7.9
1945	—	3.4	7.4	6.9	22.4	14.6	9.6	12.3	40.5	31.8
1949	2.1	2.7	1.9	7.2	53.9	16.5	6.2	16.3	33.4	7.3
1953	3.5	3.9	3.8	8.2	44.8	16.8	13.7	11.2	25.3	17.3
1957	6.2	8.4	3.2	5.2	45.0	6.3	14.6	21.4	17.3	29.8
1958	20.4	11.6	9.9	2.7	52.4	10.4	16.0	49.6	36.1	46.6
1962	1.6	6.1	8.9	9.0	60.4	7.3	9.1	37.8	30.3	27.7
1963	6.3	3.0	9.4	12.3	54.0	13.5	5.9	40.5	35.0	28.7
1965	4.1	6.4	3.9	9.9	50.4	12.7	2.3	32.7	32.0	31.6
1968	21.3	13.3	3.8	6.5	42.2	16.0	18.7	27.4	51.3	48.7
1972	11.0	13.4	15.1	9.2	38.3	11.1	17.1	36.6	36.9	33.6
1974	13.8	8.9	9.4	14.2	35.0	10.7	20.1	9.9	20.9	64.3

Entries are indices of dissimilarity between the distribution of the vote across parties in the indicated federal election and in the nearest provincial election.

Sources: see Table 3 and note 33.

as in Manitoba and Saskatchewan; the UFA-Progressives dominated both levels. After 1930, however, interlevel differences expanded quickly and persisted. From 1935 to 1971, Social Credit dominated provincial politics but had much less strength at the federal level. This was especially so after 1958. The extraordinary federal Conservative growth from 1953 to 1958, unaccompanied by corresponding province-level growth, expanded the already substantial interlevel difference. The difference reached its maximum in 1968. In that year, Social Credit collapsed in federal voting, while the federal Conservative vote grew still more. But Social Credit's federal collapse was soon followed by a provincial one. The 1971 provincial election, won by the Conservatives, signalled a convergence between levels. The index value for 1974, 20.9, is well below the average for the six federal elections immediately before 1974. Alberta, with a strong provincial Social Credit party, still has greater federal-provincial differences than every English-speaking province to its east, but may be on a path to convergence between levels.

No such conclusion is indicated by evidence from British Columbia and Quebec. Before 1953, British Columbia revealed a pattern of divergence-convergence, rather like that on the Prairies. Since 1953, however, federal-provincial differences have been huge and may even have grown. The emergence of Social Credit in the provincial elections of 1952 and 1953 was matched only weakly at the federal level. The federal Social Credit vote, such as it was, collapsed in 1968. The Liberal and Conservative parties, meanwhile, have respectable, if highly unstable federal vote shares. But in provincial elections the two old parties do very poorly. By 1974, nearly two British Columbians in three would have had to switch parties to transform the 1974 federal outcome into the 1975 provincial one.

The differences in Quebec rival those in British Columbia and are of even longer standing. Before 1940, Quebec voting was remarkably consistent across levels. But the differences expanded with the rise of the Union Nationale and remained large as the Parti Québécois partially supplanted the older nationalist party. The Social Credit presence, much stronger in federal than in provincial politics also contributed to the interlevel differences. In five federal election years out of ten, from 1949 to 1974, at least one Quebec voter in two would have had to shift between parties to make the two levels identical.

Does the evidence permit any conclusion about the party system's ability to integrate federal and provincial voting? Generalizations are possible only if they are highly qualified. In five provinces, interlevel differences have not expanded. And even the Prairie provinces give evidence of pressures toward interlevel integration. While the differences that emerged on the Prairies around 1958 (earlier in Alberta) persisted for a dozen years or

Table 9
Correlations Between Federal and Provincial Vote Series, by Province and Period

Province	Liberals		Conservatives		NDP	Social Credit
	1908–1945	1949–1974	1908–1945	1949–1974	1949–1974	1949–1974
Newfoundland	—	0.75*	—	0.42	—	—
P.E.I.	0.76*	0.28	0.36	0.49	—	—
Nova Scotia	0.69*	0.28	0.82**	0.34	—	—
New Brunswick	0.44	0.51	0.66*	0.51	—	—
Quebec	0.62	−0.64*	—	—	—	0.36
Ontario	0.83**	−0.29	0.34	0.46	0.67*	—
Manitoba	0.10	0.32	0.61	0.74*	0.64*	—
Saskatchewan	0.27	−0.30	0.68*	0.42	0.72*	—
Alberta	0.54	0.13	0.91**	0.81**	—	0.69*
B.C.	−0.29	0.01	0.70*	0.00	0.33	0.31

*p < .05

**p < .01

Entries are Pearson product-moment correlation coefficients.

Sources: see Table 3 and note 33.

so, recent evidence suggests a convergence. In Alberta and Saskatchewan, the provincial party systems have come to resemble the federal ones. In Manitoba, the federal system has come to resemble the provincial one. But the Prairie provinces' newly similar federal and provincial systems are themselves markedly distinct from the systems elsewhere, and are different from each other. While the Conservatives are now strong at both levels in each Prairie province, just as they are in the eastern Anglophone provinces, the other major parties in the Prairies' systems, the NDP in Manitoba and Saskatchewan and Social Credit in Alberta, do not have as much strength in the eastern provinces. Quebec and British Columbia are not only different from the rest, but continue to differ radically between levels.

It is still possible, even though some provinces now reveal marked interlevel differences in any given election, that shifts between successive elections at each level will move in phase. The next obvious questions, then, are: do swings between successive federal elections correspond to those between adjacent provincial elections, and has the degree of correspondence changed historically? Table 9 gives the pertinent evidence: correlations between each party's federal and provincial vote series in each province for each of two periods, 1908-1945 and 1949-1974.[36]

In Table 9, as in Table 8, the story differs between provinces and parties. Both major parties reveal a marked decline in the number of provinces within which short-term fluctuations correspond between levels. But in both periods the Conservatives show greater interlevel consistency than the Liberals. In the 1949–1974 period, the NDP vote was highly consistent between levels. The same was true for Social Credit in its province of origin, Alberta.

From 1908 to 1945, the Liberals' federal-provincial correspondence was strongest in the Atlantic provinces and Ontario. In the West, in contrast, interlevel correspondence was weak to negative. The relatively high coefficient for Alberta reflects the Liberals' collapse at both levels in 1917 and 1921. From 1949 to 1974, federal Liberal votes were incredibly detached from provincial ones. Only in Newfoundland did the two move together. In the other Atlantic provinces and Manitoba, the coefficients are weakly positive. In Alberta and British Columbia, each level has been utterly unrelated to the other. In both provinces this must reflect, in part, the lack of variance in the Liberal provincial series: votes which hardly exist cannot fluctuate much. In Saskatchewan, Ontario and Quebec, federal and provincial Liberal votes have actually moved against each other. In Saskatchewan, the provincial Liberals grew in the first part of the 1949-1974 period and then declined, while the federal Liberals did the opposite. In Ontario, the 1949–1974 picture has been one of a modest Liberal growth in federal politics and decline in provincial politics. In Quebec, the provincial Liberal surge of 1960 and 1962 coincided, more or less, with the federal Liberals' very nadir in 1958 and 1962.

From 1908 to 1945, the Conservative vote was remarkably consistent across levels. Only in Ontario and Prince Edward Island was the correspondence very weak. In the 1949-1974 period, in contrast, the correspondence between levels was strong only in Manitoba and Alberta. In both provinces in this period the party was reborn at both levels. In every other province but British Columbia, the coefficients were weakly positive. In British Columbia, the levels corresponded to each other not at all.

Together, Tables 8 and 9 suggest that patterns of short-term change need not correspond at all to patterns of dissimilarity in specific elections. It is true that the provinces with the smallest interlevel correlations in Table 9, Quebec and British Columbia, also frequently have the highest indices of dissimilarity. Voters' response at one level in each of these provinces is detached in almost every way conceivable from response at the other level. But the same is not true of Alberta and Saskatchewan. Until 1974, at least, Saskatchewan and Alberta yielded indices of dissimilarity quite as large as those in British Columbia and Quebec. But in Alberta and Saskatchewan, at least one party's vote shifts between elections corresponded closely across levels, as was also true in Manitoba. In the Atlantic provinces and Ontario, short-term change corresponded only weakly across levels, however much those provinces' federal and provincial party systems resemble each other in a given election. Of course, some of the weakness in Ontario and Atlantic coefficients may stem from the relatively low variance in provincial and federal vote series; these are, after all, provinces with relatively stable party systems.

Is any summary judgment possible? Comparing the party system's ability to integrate levels with its ability to integrate provinces within the federal level is rather like comparing apples and oranges: for at least one pertinent comparison, no common standard of measurement exists. My general sense, however, is that, with the major exceptions of Quebec and British Columbia, the system has done a better job of holding levels together within provinces than of holding provinces together within levels. In the old English-speaking provinces, dissimilarity between levels seems no more than should be expected of elections whose dates do not coincide. No dynamic seems to push levels apart for more than an election or two. Even the Prairie provinces seem to indicate the system's ability to integrate levels. While the interlevel differences beginning in 1958 persisted for some years, they now seem on a path to disappearance.[37] Differences between provinces, in contrast, are now much greater than they were at the turn of the century. There is no reason to suspect that those differences will soon disappear.

The Relationship Between the Federal and the Provincial Vote: Individual Sources of Aggregate Differences 1965-1974

Who actually produces the interlevel differences just analyzed? This question can be made more specific in a number of ways. First, I shall investigate the possibility that few Canadians actually switch parties between levels. Rather, certain groups of voters may selectively abstain at one level or the other.

Accordingly, I shall examine the relative contribution to net interlevel shifts from direct switching between parties and from selective abstention. The second question is about the "quality" of net shifts: do the shifts come principally from apathetic citizens or from highly involved ones? The suggested answers in the literature on voting are contradictory. The third question is about the socioecononic or demographic composition of change: do particular occupations or ethnoreligious groups contribute disproportionately to interlevel differences, do changes occur among the party's most marginal voters, or is change, where it occurs, simply, across the board? Such questions undoubtedly weigh on politicians' minds.

Behavioural Sources

We often forget that electorates change from year to year. The eligible population changes as some voters die and others come of age, and as migrants move between nations and provinces.[38] And, more to the point, only about two-thirds to four-fifths of the eligible voters actually turn out in a typical election. Many nonvoters never vote, of course, but many others fail to turn out in some particular election for idiosyncratic reasons, ones not likely to inhibit voting in other years. Such variations in abstention occupy my attention here.

The fact that turnout fluctuates raises the possibility that some of the variation in parties' vote shares stems from the selective migration of voters in and out of the electorate. Some citizens may specialize in voting at only one level. Supporters of a party at one level may be repelled by its equivalent at the other level, but may find it difficult to switch labels. Or where a party has been historically much weaker at one level than at the other, some of its supporters may get discouraged and withdraw from political involvement at the weak level and, in doing so, may reinforce the pattern initially discouraging them. At least one study has suggested that such selective abstention plays a large role in explaining the marked federal-provincial vote differences in Ontario.[39] Could this be true more generally? If it were, it would make citizens in places like British Columbia and Quebec seem more "consistent" than we might otherwise imagine them to be.

I want, then, to calculate the relative contribution of selective abstention and of direct switching between parties to net federal-provincial party size differences. If, in each level's election, we take the party's percentage of the whole electorate (rather than just that of the total votes cast), the difference between the two percentages will be arithmetically identical to the party's percentage point gain or loss through exchanges with the other parties plus the party's percentage point gain or loss through exchanges with abstention.[40] Note that by calculating percentages in this way I make parties seem smaller than they otherwise seem to be. I also introduce a type of net change that we do not ordinarily notice and may not much care about: if turnout increases from one election to the next, all parties may gain yet no change in their strengths relative to each other need occur. Thus we must be on our guard for net change in parties' sizes and contributions to the total net change which are, in this sense, spurious.

We have to be on our guard for other measurement problems as well. The fact that I can separate direct switching from selective abstention only with recall data from a survey creates problems of bias, of which at least two kinds infect my data. First, where respondents misremember their past behaviour, they are more likely erroneously to report past behaviour as consistent with present behaviour than as inconsistent. This self-directed bias leads me to underestimate the volume of gross and net change, but need not lead me to misestimate the relative contributions of direct switching and selective abstention to the change we do observe. The second bias is more serious. Surveys typically overestimate the size of the winning party. The overestimation is greater the more distant in time the election. The winner's inflated margin comes largely at the expense of reported nonvoting, as numbers of apolitical respondents give the socially approved response. The effect of this bias on my analysis depends on whether or not the same party won at both levels. If the same party won, then I may underestimate total change. If different parties won, then I may *over*estimate change, as each party's margin at its winning level is exaggerated. Further, in the latter case I may be led to overestimate the contribution of direct switching to the total net change, as I might count as direct switchers respondents who in fact voted at neither level.

In spite of these problems, the estimates in Table 10 of total net change from the last provincial election to the federal election indicated conform really quite closely to estimates from official returns. Net shifts do not seem exaggerated in provinces with non-Liberal provincial governments or in provinces in which party standings differ greatly between levels. This aggregate correspondence between survey and official electoral data does not allow me to dismiss the possible overestimation of individual-level direct switching, but does make such overestimation seem less threatening. I feel reasonably confident, then, in interpreting the table straightforwardly.[41]

The picture is really quite clear. Where change worthy of note occurs, it comes overwhelmingly through direct switching. Again, provinces do not differ in obvious ways in the degree to which this is true. And the observation holds even in Ontario; evidently, Wilson's and Hoffman's argument does not apply even to their own province. Where selective abstention seems to make an important proportionate contribution to net change, the effect is rather bogus. The instances where this occurs are ones of small total change. The change, further, is mostly of the kind mentioned a few paragraphs above: an across-the-board increment or decrement in all parties' sizes rendered by a net change in the amount of abstention, a quirk of my accounting system.

In sum, although federal and provincial electorates do not consist always of the same people, this fact does not suffice to explain aggregate

Table 10
Sources of Net Change from Provincial to National Elections, by Party and Province 1965–1974

Election

Province	1965 Exchange with Other Parties	1965 Exchange with Abstention	1965 Net Change	1968 Exchange with Other Parties	1968 Exchange with Abstention	1968 Net Change	1974 Exchange with Other Parties	1974 Exchange with Abstention	1974 Net Change	Merged Exchange with Other Parties	Merged Exchange with Abstention	Merged Net Change
Newfoundland												
Liberals	0.0	0.0	0.0	−15.0	−15.0	−30.0	+6.0	−8.4	−2.4	−0.7	−9.0	−9.8
Conservatives	0.0	−4.8	−4.8	+15.0	−5.0	+10.0	−8.4	−4.8	−13.3	−0.7	−4.9	−5.6
NDP		(21)			(40)		+2.4	0.0	+2.4	+1.4	0.0	+1.4
								(83)			(144)	
Prince Edward Island												
Liberals	0.0	+4.3	+4.3	−5.9	−5.9	−11.7	−4.8	+2.4	−2.4	−4.1	+1.7	−2.5
Conservatives	0.0	0.0	0.0	+5.9	+5.9	+11.8	+5.9	−2.4	+3.6	+4.9	−0.8	+4.0
		(23)			(17)			(83)			(123)	
Nova Scotia												
Liberals	+9.1	+1.5	+10.6	+1.0	−2.9	−1.9	−2.5	−4.4	−6.9	+1.0	−2.8	−1.8
Conservatives	+1.5	0.0	−10.6	−1.01	+2.0	+1.0	+0.7	0.0	+0.6	−2.2	+0.6	−1.5
NDP	+1.5	0.0	+1.5	0.0	0.0	0.0	+1.8	−1.3	+0.7	+1.2	−0.6	−10.6
		(66)			(102)			(160)			(328)	
New Brunswick												
Liberals	−6.1	−4.0	−10.1	+0.8	0.0	+0.8	+5.4	−3.6	+1.8	+0.3	−2.7	−2.4
Conservatives	0.0	−1.0	−1.0	−1.2	−1.1	−2.3	−9.9	−1.8	−11.7	−4.1	−1.4	−5.4
NDP	+5.1	0.0	+5.1	0.0	+1.1	+1.2	+1.8	0.0	+1.8	+2.4	+0.3	+2.7
Social Credit	+1.0	0.0	+1.0				+0.9	−0.9	0.0	+0.7	−0.3	+0.4
Other							+1.8	0.0	+1.8	+0.7	0.0	+0.7
		(99)			(87)			(111)			(297)	

Quebec												
Liberals	−9.2	−1.3	−10.4	+7.2	+3.9	−3.1	+0.9	−6.6	−5.7	+0.2	−3.7	−3.7
Conservatives	+4.1	+1.3	+5.5	+1.3	−1.0	−2.2	+7.6	0.0	+7.5	+4.1	−0.4	+3.7
NDP	+4.5	+2.8	+7.3	+2.0	+2.0	0.0	+4.5	+0.4	+4.8	+3.5	+1.0	+4.6
Social Credit	+7.9	+0.4	+8.2	+3.9	+4.3	+0.2	+0.1	−1.2	−1.1	+3.9	−0.3	+3.8
Other	−7.3	−2.1	−9.3	−14.4	−17.8	−3.3	−13.1	−5.2	−18.4	−11.7	−3.5	−15.3
(N)		(536)				(636)		(557)			(1729)	
Ontario												
Liberals	+7.3	+3.1	+10.4	+12.4	+12.4	0.0	+8.5	+0.7	+9.3	+9.7	+1.2	+10.8
Conservatives	−10.5	−1.1	−11.6	−11.7	−13.3	−1.7	−6.8	−3.0	−9.8	−9.9	−1.8	−11.8
NDP	+3.5	+0.4	+4.0	−0.7	−1.4	−0.7	−1.5	−0.6	−2.1	+0.4	−0.3	+0.2
(N)		(628)				(809)		(540)			(1977)	
Manitoba												
Liberals	+1.7	+0.9	+2.6	+7.0	+5.2	−1.7	+6.4	−1.1	+5.3	+4.9	−0.6	+4.3
Conservatives	−7.9	+2.6	−5.3	−9.6	−9.5	0.0	+7.3	0.0	+7.4	−3.9	+1.0	−3.1
NDP	+6.2	+3.5	+9.7	+0.8	+0.9	0.0	−13.7	−7.4	−21.1	−1.5	−1.0	−2.5
(N)		(113)				(116)		(95)			(324)	
Saskatchewan												
Liberals	−8.4	−4.8	−13.2	+1.6	+0.8	−0.8	+5.5	−4.2	+1.4	−0.3	−2.8	−3.2
Conservatives	+15.6	+2.4	+18.0	+7.1	+7.1	0.0	+13.9	+2.8	+16.7	+11.2	+1.4	+12.7
NDP	−8.4	−4.8	−13.2	−7.9	−7.8	0.0	−20.8	−8.3	−29.2	−11.3	−3.5	−14.9
(N)		(83)				(127)		(72)			(282)	
Alberta												
Liberals	+8.8	−2.7	+6.1	+27.0	+27.9	+1.0	+11.8	+0.7	+12.4	+17.3	−0.2	+17.0
Conservatives	+21.8	+2.0	+23.8	+13.8	+16.2	+2.4	−2.1	−5.9	−8.1	+11.6	0.0	+11.7
NDP	0.0	+2.0	+2.1	−0.5	−0.5	0.0	−0.7	−0.7	−1.5	−0.4	+0.4	0.0
Social Credit	−30.6	−6.1	−36.7	−39.3	−44.6	−5.4	−9.6	−3.7	−13.2	−28.3	−5.1	−33.4
(N)		(147)				(204)		(137)			(488)	
British Columbia												
Liberals	+16.3	+2.6	+18.9	+20.7	+24.3	+3.7	+12.8	0.0	+12.9	+16.6	+2.0	+18.6
Conservatives	+9.5	+3.4	+12.9	+3.7	+3.7	0.0	+24.2	+2.7	+27.0	+13.1	+1.8	+15.0
NDP	−1.7	+1.7	0.0	+1.7	−0.5	−2.4	−19.2	−4.6	−23.9	−7.3	−2.3	−9.6
Social Credit	−24.1	−1.7	−25.9	−26.1	−31.4	−5.1	−17.8	−0.9	−18.8	−22.4	−2.7	−25.2
(N)		(116)				(214)		(218)			(548)	

federal-provincial differences in the vote. Most of the net differences between levels come from direct exchanges of voters between parties. The schizophrenia of many provinces' politics is not just collective, but individual. Now, what kinds of individuals actually produce the federal-provincial differences?

Psychological Sources

Are the people who make the differences between levels relatively involved in politics or relatively apathetic? The literature on this question yields contradictory expectations. One strand, which draws upon theories of psychological consistency, predicts that vote switchers should be typically uninvolved and apathetic. The other strand, drawn largely from economic thought, predicts the opposite. I shall review each briefly.

The marked federal-provincial differences in Canadian voting may have been made possible by a reserve army of the apathetic. This would be an implication of work on the behavioural and attitudinal effects of inconsistency. Such inconsistency is said to generate tension in individuals, a drive state whose reduction requires shifts in attitude or behaviour in the direction of consistency, or avoidance of the field altogether.[42] Specifically political evidence in support of this contention comes from studies of "cross pressure." An individual whose socioeconomic and ethnoreligious characteristics predispose him in conflicting partisan directions is relatively likely to claim a lack of interest in politics and to delay making a choice, or even to withdraw from the choice and not vote altogether.[43] The same allegedly is true of individuals whose political attitudes contradict each other.[44] Other political evidence comes from studies of the "floating voter." Such studies claim that interelection and intracampaign voting changes are made disproportionately by relatively uninformed and uninvolved voters.[45] The role of information, according to these studies, is to reinforce initial commitments, not to disturb them. Otherwise, the information is shunned. Thus in equilibrium the electorate should contain relatively involved, informed and consistent voters at one end of a continuum and relatively uninvolved, uninformed and inconsistent voters at the other. Large aggregate federal-provincial vote differences may indicate that many voters are psychologically distant from Canadian politics.

Not every student of voting makes such an argument, however. An investment theory of the vote, gaining currency in recent years, suggests that it is rational to acquire political information only if the information has a serious probability of altering one's decision.[46] Otherwise, costs of acquiring the information are incurred with little corresponding benefit. As elections are collective decisions, beyond the capacity of any single voter greatly to alter, few voters may really have much reason to search for political information. Voters who do change should be relatively well informed.[47] Some support for this expectation exists in the literature on attitude formation and change. There it is found that persons who are relatively likely actually to acquire contradictory information are, for the same reason, relatively tolerant of ambiguity.[48] In sum, I can find arguments which predict that the citizens who produce aggregate federal-provincial inconsistency will be far from apathetic, but instead will be the electorate's most informed and involved members.

Both arguments are plausible and evidence can be found for each. For this reason, a net prediction for the effect of information and involvement on vote change would be premature. Such a prediction would be premature for another reason as well: while I want to examine *net* change, all of the studies mentioned above examined gross change, the probability that individual voters will change, regardless of the direction of change. Now, the arguments predicting frequencies of gross change may also hold for net change, but to the best of my knowledge, the empirical relationship between the two kinds of change has never been studied. It is true that the more the gross change, the more the net change that is arithmetically possible. But this does not necessarily mean that more net change actually occurs. It is conceivable that the individuals most susceptible to persuasion are at the same time the least exposed to the systematic factors working in the election to produce net, aggregate change. Such individuals may respond instead to factors not strictly related to issues or the appeals of candidates, but to "random" factors, such as conformity pressures in the immediate social milieu. In the end, though, I just do not know how gross and net change fit together.

The net change measure I shall use here is exactly that used above with aggregate data, the index of dissimilarity. Unlike in the section on "behavioural sources" of net change, algebra does not force me here to analyze party shares of the total eligible electorate. Instead, I can go back to net change in party shares of votes actually cast. In Table 11, then, I present indices of federal-provincial dissimilarity for respondents with different levels of political involvement. The index of political involvement is exactly that used in Chapter II and needs no further explication. Table 11 gives evidence for 1965, 1974 and the merged file. The index was not available for 1968. The table gives the Atlantic provinces' results for the region as a whole, as cell sizes in those provinces would otherwise have been too small. By merging the four provinces, I do, unfortunately, reduce estimates of net change in the region. Party systems differed too greatly between Prairie provinces to permit a merger. I could make no entries for those provinces in 1974, as cell sizes were too small.[49]

As it happens, Table 11 is anti-climactic. No consistent pattern appears and net change differences between involvement levels are never astounding. The largest differences appear where cases are fewest, and even there the differences are not obviously monotonic. The most parsimonious interpretation of Table 11 is that political involvement has little obvious and interpretable effect on the magnitude of net federal-provincial differences.

Table 11
Political Involvement and Federal-Provincial Dissimilarity

Province/ Region	Election 1965 Political Involvement			Election 1974 Political Involvement			Merged Political Involvement		
	Low	Medium	High	Low	Medium	High	Low	Medium	High
Atlantic Provinces	8.0 (56)	5.0 (105)	9.0 (98)	2.0 (47)	3.0 (94)	4.0 (73)	5.1 (103)	3.4 (199)	6.4 (121)
Quebec	22.6 (176)	18.0 (216)	32.2 (194)	23.8 (58)	16.0 (134)	21.9 (77)	23.5 (234)	18.6 (350)	26.2 (221)
Ontario	13.7 (216)	13.1 (252)	20.9 (160)	20.9 (65)	7.9 (129)	8.1 (76)	15.5 (281)	10.9 (381)	16.7 (236)
Manitoba	14.8 (37)	13.2 (52)	8.0 (24)	—	—	—	4.6 (53)	3.5 (78)	12.3 (34)
Saskat- chewan	23.4 (29)	29.8 (29)	20.0 (25)	—	—	—	27.4 (29)	27.6 (46)	15.7 (36)
Alberta	50.3 (64)	34.3 (55)	46.9 (28)	—	—	—	44.9 (87)	24.7 (81)	31.3 (44)
British Columbia	33.3 (43)	32.1 (42)	37.9 (31)	56.0 (38)	32.6 (49)	36.2 (23)	43.4 (81)	31.8 (91)	32.7 (54)

The citizens who create the aggregate vote differences within provinces come from all levels of psychological commitment to politics, from the most active and involved to the most apathetic. To mix metaphors, the federal-provincial schizophrenia is not a fit of absent-mindedness.

Social Sources

Do particular economic or social groups tip the balance between levels? We can imagine a range of possibilities. At one extreme, interlevel switching would be socially localized. Most groups would remain consistent across levels, but some particular ones might swing sharply. At the other extreme, switching between levels could be across the board, such that an individual voter would have roughly the same probability of interlevel switching whatever the social or economic group to which he belonged.

Where should we look for group differences in switching? Two variables, occupation and religion, come immediately to mind, each for different reasons. Two reasons recommend occupation. First, in English Canada, the net circulation of parties between levels usually involves parties other than the NDP. To the extent that occupation marks NDP voters off from those of other parties it may also affect interlevel vote switching. Second, a particular economic group, farmers, are often alleged to be a critical voting bloc. Religion, meanwhile, suggests itself as the most powerful predictor of Canadians' votes. I shall expand the arguments for each variable, beginning with occupation.

The New Democratic Party assembles much the same geographic coalition in federal elections as in provincial ones, and federal-provincial shifts in some provinces (notably British Columbia, Saskatchewan and Ontario) seem to exclude the NDP. This suggests that vote-switching is essentially a middle-class phenomenon, as white-collar voters steer strategically around the NDP to whichever other party has the best chance of winning each level's election.[50] The alleged issuelessness of Liberal, Conservative and Social Credit appeals may help white-collar voters in switching between those parties.

Another set of arguments singles out farmers as an especially volatile group. Much has been made of farmers' detachment from the old parties, especially in the West, since about 1920.[51] The massive and sudden changes in the Prairie provinces' voting suggests that farmers, the predominant group in the region when most of the changes occurred, are detached not just from the old parties but from *all* parties.[52] American arguments and evidence also support such an expectation. In the United States, farming regions often have supported minor parties. On occasion an agrarian region has supported an extreme left-wing party only to swing to an extreme right-wing party shortly thereafter.[53] Such swings have moved observers to argue, and to find survey evidence corroborating their argument, that farmers really are not psychologically very involved in politics and thus are prone to erratic electoral behaviour.[54] Other observers argue that the volatility of the farm vote indicates not that farmers are apolitical, but the opposite.[55] Whatever the interpretation, farmers appear as a swing group in American elections. Cursory inspection of the historical record suggests that they have played the same role in Canadian federal and provincial politics. Could it be, then, that farmers supply the critical shifts *between* levels?

Table 12 gives the net change from provincial to federal elections by party and in toto in four occupation groups. Each province appears separately, except again for the Atlantic provinces, which appear as a region. Sampling variance and economy of presentation moved me to present a single table using the merged file. The table thus "synthesizes" federal-provincial turnover for 1965, 1968 and 1974.[56] The fourfold occupation classification is relatively straightforward. The "nonmanual" group embraces professional and managerial respondents as well as clerical workers. Treating such diverse occupations as a single group is not completely satisfactory, in view of the marked status and income differences within the group, but is indicated by work elsewhere on the political effects of class. Where occupation differences in the vote do exist, they are in fact greatest between white-collar and blue-collar workers, regardless of "objective" differences within and between groups in income.[57] The manual, or blue-collar, group

Table 12
Net Provincial-Federal Change Within Occupation Groups, by Region (Merged File)

Region	Occupation	Party					Index of Dissimilarity	(N)
		Liberal	Conservative	NDP	Social Credit	Other		
Atlantic	Nonmanual	−0.5	−0.3	+1.3	0.0	−0.5	1.3	(221)
	Manual	−0.5	−1.7	+1.9	0.0	+0.2	2.2	(443)
	Farm	−1.3	0.0	0.0	0.0	+1.3	1.3	(78)
	Other	−8.2	+4.4	+2.6	+1.3	0.0	8.3	(82)
Quebec	Nonmanual	+4.0	+4.8	+8.8	+2.5	−20.1	20.1	(629)
	Manual	−0.3	+4.9	+4.7	+8.0	−17.3	17.6	(731)
	Farm	+2.5	+8.9	+1.2	+7.3	−19.8	19.9	(106)
	Other	+3.2	+5.9	+2.2	+6.3	−17.4	17.5	(154)
Ontario	Nonmanual	+19.8	−19.3	−0.2	−0.1	−0.1	19.8	(855)
	Manual	+11.3	−12.2	+1.3	−0.3	0.0	12.6	(851)
	Farm	+3.5	−1.3	−2.1	0.0	0.0	3.5	(130)
	Other	+8.5	−12.6	+3.6	+0.6	0.0	12.7	(172)
Manitoba	Nonmanual	+13.2	−8.0	−5.1	−0.1	0.0	13.2	(119)
	Manual	+2.9	−0.9	−3.5	+0.7	0.9	4.5	(115)
	Farm	−1.1	−12.7	+10.9	+0.2	+2.6	13.8	(41)
	Other	+1.1	−2.2	+4.9	−4.0	0.0	6.1	(37)
Saskatchewan	Nonmanual	−3.8	+19.8	−15.0	−1.3	0.0	19.7	(78)
	Manual	+3.3	+3.7	−5.8	+0.2	−1.3	7.2	(79)
	Farm	−7.2	+20.6	−14.7	+1.2	0.0	21.9	(80)
	Other	+0.9	+22.6	−23.5	0.0	0.0	23.5	(29)
Alberta	Nonmanual	+26.7	+4.0	−0.2	−30.5	0.0	30.7	(185)
	Manual	+24.7	+17.2	+0.2	−41.3	−0.6	42.0	(160)
	Farm	+7.9	+33.4	0.0	−41.4	0.0	41.4	(65)
	Other	+14.4	+37.7	+2.7	−54.8	0.0	54.8	(34)
B.C.	Nonmanual	+19.4	+20.6	−11.1	−29.0	0.0	40.1	(231)
	Manual	+26.3	+14.4	−16.0	−24.7	0.0	40.7	(217)
	Farm	+27.5	+17.9	−7.7	−37.9	0.0	45.5	(13)
	Other	+20.8	+14.1	+9.1	−44.0	0.0	44.0	(57)

includes the residue of nonfarm occupations. Farmers, of course, are an occupation group in their own right. The "other" group is heterogeneous, and includes housewives, retired persons and the unemployed.

The general impression given by Table 12 is one of very modest occupation differences, where any appear at all. The degree and direction of occupation differences varies between provinces. Not much need be said about the Atlantic provinces. There, net shifts are generally so small that group differences are not interpretable. In Quebec, the volume of change varies hardly at all between groups, but the direction of change does so vary. The net change in each group embraces about one in five of its members. From provincial to federal elections, nonmanual Quebecois shift disproportionately to the Liberals and the NDP, while manual respondents move to Social Credit, and farmers move to Social Credit and the Conservatives. In Ontario, in contrast to Quebec, groups differ not in the direction but in the volume of net change. All Ontario groups reveal provincial-federal shifts to the Liberals from the Conservatives. But the nonmanual shift is half again as large as the manual one, and farmers swing hardly at all. In Manitoba, the relatively volatile groups are nonmanual respondents and farmers, but each volatile group circulates in a different direction. Nonmanual respondents move between the provincial Conservative and federal Liberal parties, while farmers move between the provincial Conservatives and the federal NDP. In Saskatchewan, manual workers resist interlevel change; in each other group, the net change embraces about one voter in five. As in Ontario, however, all four groups move in approximately the same direction: from provincial to federal elections, the NDP loses and the Conservatives gain. In Alberta, change is massive and across the board, with even the least change-prone group, nonmanual respondents, more volatile than any group in any province to the east. In each Alberta group, the provincial-federal shift is to the Liberals and Conservatives and from Social Credit. Nonmanual respondents are the most likely to move to the Liberals, however, while farmers and the "other" group shift overwhelmingly to the Conservatives. Manual respondents also shift disproportionately to the Liberals, although less extremely so than do nonmanual respondents. In British Columbia, the volume of shifting is great in each group. Net change in each group embraces about two voters in five. In each group, from provincial to federal elections Social Credit and the NDP lose and Liberals and Conservatives gain. British Columbia does reveal an occupation bias in the direction of shifts, but the bias is much weaker than in Alberta and in the opposite direction. In British Columbia, blue-collar workers, farmers and others move somewhat disproportionately to the Liberals, while white-collar respondents move, again only somewhat disproportionately, to the Conservatives.

Summary descriptions of Table 12 must be couched in negatives. Blue-collar workers are never the most volatile group, while each other group claims that honour at least once. But blue-collar workers are not everywhere the least volatile. Further, in no province is only one group especially shift-prone. Where group differences appear, at least two groups will be relatively changeable. More often, three or even all four are similarly shift-prone. The isolable group, if any, is the one that *resists* change. In some provinces, groups differ in the partisan destination of provincial-federal shifts; but the same group does not move to the same federal party in every province. In some provinces, every group moves in the same direction. In other provinces, groups move at odds with each other. Thus, just as patterns of overall change-proneness differ between provinces, so do the directions in which particular groups shift.

What of the variable that differentiates the vote most powerfully — religion? Roman Catholics and Jews are disproportionately Liberal, and Protestants of every denomination disproportionately Conservative. Those without religion are relatively likely to support the NDP.[58] Even when occupation, language and place of birth are controlled, the religious differences persist.[59] Religion might be a good variable, then, with which to assess where in a party's coalition federal-provincial shifts occur. Is the shifting greatest in the group with the smallest vote for a party, in the group with the largest vote for the party, or in the groups in between? Or is the shifting in and out of parties simply not differentiated by religion?

Table 13 gives the net provincial-to-federal shifts, by party and in toto, for religious groups within provinces. The religious breakdown differs between provinces, as a reflection of the number of cases. Roman Catholics and Protestants appear in every province, Ukrainian and Greek Catholics appear in Ontario, Manitoba and Saskatchewan, respondents with no religion appear in Ontario, Alberta and British Columbia, and Jews appear in Ontario and Quebec. Historically, Protestant denominations differed importantly from each other in party preference,[60] but examination of federal and provincial voting in the 1965, 1968 and 1974 surveys suggest that these historical differences have largely evaporated; accordingly, I treat Protestants as a single group.

Religious differences do appear in Table 13, but they are no more impressive than the occupation differences in Table 12. Differences between provinces within religious groups generally exceed those within provinces between denominations. Again, the party destinations of each group's provincial-federal shifts vary from province to province. Where they appear in significant numbers, Ukrainian and Greek Catholics are the most volatile. In Ontario, Manitoba and Saskatchewan, the group reveals total net change proportionately twice as great as that in the other denominations. But the pattern of Ukrainian and Greek Catholic shifts varies greatly between provinces, and generally reflects (and enhances) the pattern dominant in the province. Roman Catholics, in contrast to Greek and Ukrainian ones, are the least volatile. In most provinces, Roman Catholics are simply bound to the Liberals at both levels. In Ontario, Roman Catholics move between the major

Table 13

Net Provincial-Federal Change Within Religious Groups, by Region (Merged File)

Region	Religion	Party					Index of Dis-similarity	(N)
		Liberal	Conservative	NDP	Social Credit	Other		
Atlantic	Rom. Catholic	+1.8	−2.5	+1.0	0.0	−0.3	2.8	(312)
	Protestant	−3.9	+1.2	+2.1	+0.2	+0.4	3.9	(499)
Quebec	Rom. Catholic	+3.1	+4.5	+5.7	+6.4	−19.8	19.8	(1468)
	Protestant	−13.6	+14.3	+4.3	−0.1	−4.9	18.6	(113)
	Jewish	−4.9	+3.6	+10.0	0.0	−8.7	13.6	(28)
Ontario	Rom. Catholic	+12.7	−14.0	+1.5	−0.2	0.0	14.2	(544)
	Protestant	+12.8	−13.5	+0.8	0.0	0.0	13.6	(1275)
	Jewish	+15.0	−21.8	+6.8	0.0	0.0	21.8	(40)
	Ukrainian & Greek Catholic	+29.7	−35.2	+0.2	−0.4	0.0	32.8	(42)
	None	+18.3	−13.2	−3.6	−1.4	0.0	18.3	(80)
Manitoba	Rom. Catholic	−1.0	+0.9	+2.0	−1.9	0.0	2.9	(63)
	Protestant	+5.6	−3.6	−2.8	+0.3	+0.5	6.4	(204)
	Ukrainian & Greek Catholic	+3.2	−9.7	+3.3	0.0	+3.2	9.7	(31)
Saskatchewan	Rom. Catholic	−0.2	+13.8	−13.8	+0.2	0.0	14.0	(67)
	Protestant	−4.3	+17.7	−12.7	0.0	−0.6	17.7	(168)
	Ukrainian & Greek Catholic	+17.9	+13.5	−31.5	0.0	0.0	31.5	(20)
Alberta	Rom. Catholic	+29.4	−7.5	+2.1	−24.1	0.0	31.6	(87)
	Protestant	+19.4	+22.5	+0.8	−41.9	−0.7	42.7	(306)
	None	+20.8	+14.9	−7.2	−29.2	+0.6	17.7	(24)
B.C.	Rom. Catholic	+27.1	+11.6	−7.1	−31.8	0.0	38.8	(58)
	Protestant	+21.4	+18.1	−9.6	−30.0	0.0	39.6	(358)
	None	+19.7	+12.3	−15.3	−16.7	0.0	32.0	(63)

172 / Small Worlds

parties at the same rate as Protestants do, but at a much smaller rate than the remaining groups. Only in Alberta and British Columbia do Roman Catholics reveal great volatility. In those provinces, however, Roman Catholics are no more volatile than the provincial norm, and their provincial-federal shifts are overwhelmingly to the party they would probably support in provincial politics, were it a credible force at that level: the Liberals. Protestants have on average less fixed commitments than Roman Catholics, but are not outstandingly volatile. Typically, total net changes are a few points greater among Protestants than among Roman Catholics, although in some provinces Protestants are actually the least volatile group. Not surprisingly, Protestants' provincial-federal shifts are more likely than those of Roman Catholics to favour the Conservatives.

Table 13 does suggest that federal-provincial shifts are differentiated by religion, but only to a modest degree. The religious groups with the longest history in Canada of mutual antipathy, Roman Catholics and Protestants, are the least available for switching between levels. In that sense, then, the core of the old parties' support holds across levels, where opportunities permit, and the flux between levels is greatest in groups whose arrival in large numbers is more recent, or for whom the religious struggles have been irrelevant: Greek and Ukrainian Catholics, Jews (in Ontario, but not in Quebec) and those without religion. But none of the foregoing applies to two provinces where federal-provincial differences have been especially great, Alberta and British Columbia. And, even where the arguments (more or less) apply, the numbers outside the major denominations never suffice to account for very much of the total federal-provincial difference. Roman Catholics and Protestants, numerous as they are, still make most of the difference.

Conclusions

Most of this chapter's evidence points in the same direction: in voting, as in other ways, Canadian politics are becoming less national and more provincial. Vote differences between provinces are now greater than they were at the turn of the century. Short-term movements in each major party's vote remain geographically diverse. Within provinces, the evidence is more mixed and varies from province to province. In the Atlantic provinces and Ontario, federal and provincial levels have not diverged in the distribution of the vote across parties. There has, however, been a decline in those provinces in the interlevel correspondence of short-term vote change. In the Prairie provinces, federal and provincial voting have often diverged markedly, but divergences typically have been followed by convergences. Further, swings between elections on the Prairies have become more integrated between levels. British Columbia and Quebec are hard cases. Not only is each of those provinces markedly distinct from others in federal voting, but federal voting in each is very distinct from provincial voting; this observation holds for specific elections and for swings between elections. Whatever the province, where federal-provincial differences occur, they are socially ubiquitous. We cannot identify critical occupation or ethnoreligious groups as sources of such differences. Rather, the social unit in which federal-provincial change-proneness must be said to inhere is the province as a whole. With the major exceptions of British Columbia and Quebec, then, provincial party systems have not become unambiguously less consistent across levels. Evidence suggests, rather, that divergences between levels engender tensions which in turn promote eventual convergence. But, as the Prairie provinces indicate, the convergence between levels can leave the province internally consistent in its distinctiveness from other provinces. The forces for integration, within parties themselves or in the social and economic environment of parties, seem to be stronger between levels within provinces than between provinces within the federal level.

Are the parties responsible for the provincialization of the vote? My evidence, of course, has been only about the vote itself. It is possible that parties have been neutral or positively integrative in their endeavours, and have been only conduits for or prisoners of underlying social and economic processes. Still, we can ask whether parties are *likely* to have played a disintegrative role. In the introduction, I discussed briefly finance, careers and the geographic distribution of the vote itself as factors affecting the likelihood that a party will adopt an integrative or disintegrative strategy. Further, I examined some effects of a major constraint on parties, the electoral system. The system magnifies and distorts vote differences between provinces. It creates regionally homogeneous blocs in Parliament and, in doing so, may engender cumulative regional policy biases within parties. The electoral system encourages voters and even party activists to see parties in exaggerated regional terms. The electoral system also encourages parties to discriminate between locales in search of the few votes necessary to swing closely fought seats. In short, thinking about the circumstances of electoral competition leads me to suspect that parties, responding to their tactical setting, have made an independent contribution to the provincialization of the national and provincial popular vote.

Sir John A. Macdonald may have hoped that provincial governments would wither away and that political life would become more uniform throughout the Dominion, but the cumulation of evidence indicates otherwise. Parties may have played a major role in frustrating his expectations:

> ... How soon the new provincial identities would begin to crystallize was seen in the Toronto *Globe* in July, 1867. Party politics tended to make the local governments a weapon against the central government; this was so in Nova Scotia, and if Brown had his way it would be so in Ontario. Party established the nucleus about which would soon cluster the old provincial loyalties.[61]

Notes

1. On the relative importance of national, regional and local effects in Canada, see Robert W. Jackman, "Political Parties, Voting, and National Integration," *Comparative Politics*, 4 (1972): 511-36. For the role of leader images, see Gilbert R. Winham and Robert B. Cunningham, "Party Leader Images in the 1968 Federal Election," *Canadian Journal of Political Science*, 3 (1970): 37-55.

2. Khayyam Z. Paltiel, *Political Party Financing in Canada* (Toronto: McGraw-Hill, 1970).

3. This is a geographic implication of the argument in Anthony Downs, *An Economic Theory of Democracy* (New York: Harper & Row, 1957).

4. Alan C. Cairns, "The Electoral System and the Party System in Canada, 1921-1965," *Canadian Journal of Political Science*, 1 (1968): 58-60; Richard Johnston and Janet Ballantyne, "Geography and the Electoral System," *Canadian Journal of Political Science*, 10 (1977): 857-66.

5. The best statement of this perspective on Dominion-provincial relations is J.R. Mallory, *Social Credit and the Federal Power in Canada* (Toronto: University of Toronto Press, 1954).

6. Alexander Hamilton, John Jay, and James Madison, *The Federalist* (New York: Random House Inc.), No. 15. Authorship of No. 15 is usually attributed to Hamilton. See also Alan C. Cairns, "The Governments and Societies of Canadian Federalism," *Canadian Journal of Political Science*, 10 (1977): 695-725.

7. Indeed, William H. Riker argues that parties are the most important influence on centralization-decentralization. See his *Federalism: Origin, Operation, Significance* (Boston: Little, Brown, 1964), pp. 129-35.

8. A party finance system can be unitary even when collection is decentralized. The New Democratic Party, for example, transfers funds between provinces and levels at least as readily as the major parties do, but relies heavily on small, individual donations to create the fund. See Paltiel, chap. 3.

9. This certainly describes the position of the Liberals before 1896 and of the Conservatives in recent years.

10. In the 1930s, the harshest attacks on the Mackenzie King Liberal government were made by Mitchell Hepburn, the Liberal premier of Ontario. See H. Blair Neatby, *William Lyon Mackenzie King: The Prism of Unity 1932-1939* (Toronto: University of Toronto Press, 1976). In the 1960s, Ross Thatcher, the Liberal premier of Saskatchewan, played much the same role as Hepburn in attacking the federal Liberal government. See David E. Smith, *Prairie Liberalism: The Liberal Party in Saskatchewan 1905-71* (Toronto: University of Toronto Press, 1975), p. 291ff.

11. The Alberta Conservative and Liberal parties respectively (at least, before the 1979 national election) illustrate the last two propositions nicely.

12. Johnston and Ballantyne, "Geography and the Electoral System." See also John M. Munro, "Highways in British Columbia: Economics and Politics," *Canadian Journal of Economics*, 8 (1975): 192-204, and Donald E. Blake, "LIP and Partisanship: An Analysis of the Local Initiatives Program," *Canadian Public Policy*, 2 (1976): 17-32.

13. The role of the party loyalty in Canada is very much in dispute. See Paul M. Sniderman, H. Donald Forbes, and Ian Melzer, "Party Loyalty and Electoral Volatility: A Study of the Canadian Party System," *Canadian Journal of Political Science*, 7 (1974): 268-88; Jane Jenson, "Party Loyalty in Canada: The Question of Party Identification," *Canadian Journal of Political Science*, 8 (1975): 543-53; and David J. Elkins, "Party Identification: A Conceptual Analysis," *Canadian Journal of Political Science*, 11 (1978): 419-35.

14. A large part of the decline is attributable to the "independent" candidacy of Leonard Jones, formerly mayor of Moncton and until 1979 Member for the constituency of that name. Jones

had been nominated as the Conservative candidate but was repudiated by the national party.

15. Kevin R. Cox, "The Spatial Evolution of National Voting Response Surfaces: Theory and Measurement" (Paper given at the Annual Convention of the American Political Science Association, New York, 1969).

16. Elihu Katz and Paul Lazarsfeld, *Personal Influence* (New York: Free Press, 1955).

17. On the political effects of migration, see Chapter IV.

18. Donald E. Stokes, "Parties and the Nationalization of Electoral Forces," in *The American Party Systems: Stages of Political Development, ed.* William N. Chambers and Walter Dean Burnham, (New York: Oxford University Press, 1967), pp. 182-202; David Butler and Donald Stokes, *Political Change in Britain* (London: Macmillan, 1974), chap. 6; and Angus Campbell et al., *The American Voter* (New York: Wiley, 1960), chap. 16.

19. Leroy O. Stone, *Migration in Canada: Regional Aspects* (Ottawa: Dominion Bureau of Statistics, 1969), pp. 42-47 and p. 137ff.

20. Richard J. Joy, *Languages in Conflict* (Toronto: McClelland and Stewart, 1972). See especially chaps. 5, 7 and 14.

21. W.A. Mackintosh, *The Economic Background of Dominion Provincial Relations* (Toronto: McClelland and Stewart, 1964; originally Appendix III to the Report of the Royal Commission on Dominion-Provincial Relations, 1939); R.E. Caves and R.H. Holton, *The Canadian Economy: Prospect and Retrospect* (Cambridge, Mass.: Harvard University Press, 1959).

22. See, for example, H.D. Forbes, "The Effects of Contact on Ethnic Prejudice and Discrimination" (Manuscript, University of Toronto, 1976); J.A. Laponce, "The City Center as Conflictual Space in the Bilingual City: The Case of Montreal," in *Center-Periphery*, ed. J. Gottmann (Beverly Hills: Sage, forthcoming).

23. Escott M. Reid, "The Rise of National Parties in Canada," in *Party Politics in Canada* ed. Hugh G. Thorburn (Scarborough, Ont.: Prentice-Hall, 1972), pp. 15-22.

24. This is not to say, of course, that geography was not a major factor in the politics of the period. Regionalism and Dominion-provincial relations figured very conspicuously and divided the parties. The vote differences between regions were magnified greatly as they were translated into seat differences, quite as happens at present. Even so, the differences of the period are very modest in comparison with those of the present. Each major party was highly competitive with the other in each province.

25. The expression is Peter Regenstreif's. See his *The Diefenbaker Interlude: Parties and Voting in Canada* (Don Mills, Ont.: Longman, 1965).

26. The Liberal vote share in Quebec has been greater since 1968 than it was from 1958 to 1965 inclusive. In Quebec, as in Saskatchewan and Nova Scotia, a party's vote share does seem to be influenced by whether or not that party's leader comes from the province in question. Even so, Trudeau was not able to gather in Quebec majorities as overwhelming as those given to St. Laurent.

27. The use of correlation coefficients in Tables 6 and 7 may make some readers uncomfortable. Correlation coefficients are very sensitive to the variance in each series, to the extent that some of the differences between province-pairs and periods may stem not so much from differences in the "real" magnitude of association as from differences in series variance. I have decided to risk this possibility and draw attention to it in places and periods where variances are small. I am concerned to avoid any imputation of asymmetry in the flow of causation between provinces and, further, have concluded that the goodness of fit (the attribute actually indicated by a correlation coefficient) is close to the phenomenon of interest.

Some of the differences between province-pairs and periods may be the result of variation in autocorrelation in the series. The more autocorrelated observations in a series are, the larger will seem statistical associations between series. Autocorrelation typically indicates some kind of linear or nonlinear secular change in the series, for example, a gradual growth or decline in a party's vote share. There is, in fact, significant autocorrelation in a number of the series reported in Tables 6 and 7. I have decided, however, not to attempt to remove it and so create series "purified" of secular change. If a party's secular growth or decline in one province does not correspond to its growth or decline in another province, I should want my evidence to reflect this fact. The reader should be aware, however, that my data indicate gradual party growth or decline over several successive elections as well as shifts between pairs of elections.

28. The points in this paragraph are taken from Donald V. Smiley, *Canada in Question: Federalism in the Seventies* (Toronto: McGraw-Hill Ryerson, 1976), chap. 4.

29. On this, see Chapter VII.

30. Frank H. Underhill, "Canadian Liberal Democracy in 1955," in Underhill, *In Search of Canadian Liberalism* (Toronto: Macmillan, 1960), p. 237.

31. Howard A. Scarrow, "Federal-Provincial Voting Patterns in Canada," in *Voting in Canada* ed. John C. Courtney (Scarborough, Ont.: Prentice-Hall of Canada, 1967), pp. 84-85.

32. See, for example, Bill Reeves and Roger Gibbins, "The Balance Theory: An Empirical Look at the Interdependency of Federal-Provincial Electoral Behaviour" (Paper given at the Annual Meeting of the Canadian Political Science Association, Quebec City, May 1976).

33. The choice of federal elections, rather than provincial elections, as units is arbitrary. I have made the choice purely for convenience in the presentation of data. Shifting to provincial election units would alter my conclusions not at all. Provincial election data are from Loren Simerl, "A Survey of Canadian Provincial Election Results, 1905–1976," in *Politics: Canada*, 4th ed., ed. Paul W. Fox (Toronto: McGraw-Hill Ryerson, 1977), pp. 599-637.

34. The formula for calculating the index is:

$$\text{Index of Dissimilarity} = \tfrac{1}{2} \sum_{k} |(\text{Pik} - \text{Pjk})|,$$

where Pik is the percentage of the federal vote in a province won by party k; and Pjk is the percentage of the total vote won by party k in the closest provincial election to the indicated federal election. For a formal account of the index's properties, see O.D. Duncan and B. Duncan, "A Methodological Analysis of Segregation Indices," *American Sociological Review*, 20 (1955): 210–217.

My use of the index is very close to that in Harold Clarke et al., *Political Choice in Canada* (Toronto: McGraw-Hill Ryerson, 1979), Table 5.1. The Clarke et al. calculation uses proportions as units, while my calculation uses percentage points. The index in this chapter can be seen as a special case of the more general formula given below in Chapter VI. In that chapter the index is generalized to the comparison of more than two distributions.

35. Although Table 8 makes the Saskatchewan convergence seem to occur between 1972 and 1974, the critical year is actually 1975. In that year's provincial election, the Conservative vote mushroomed. The 1978 provincial election confirmed the trend toward Conservative provincial growth.

36. In part the choice of periods was dictated by the availability of data. The provincial election data collected by Simerl (see above, Note 33) go back only to about 1905. Splitting the series between the 1945 and the 1949 elections yields ten observations in each half-series.

37. For many purposes, of course, the federal-provincial vote dissimilarity is not the critical property. One might usefully examine whether or not the same party is in power in Ottawa and in the provincial capital. One might also investigate the federal-provincial dissimilarity in seats, rather than votes. The plurality electoral system typically expands federal-provincial differences as votes become seats. Thus even the Atlantic provinces and Ontario, with their rather small federal-provincial vote differences, yield seat distributions that differ markedly between levels.

38. Incoming cohorts of voters are often major contributors to swings between elections. For British and American evidence, see Butler and Stokes, *Political Change in Britain*, chaps. 10 and 11, and Kristi Andersen, "Generation, Partisan Shift, and Realignment: A Glance Back to the

New Deal," in Norman H. Nie, Sidney Verba, and John R. Petrocik, *The Changing American Voter* (Cambridge, Mass.: Harvard University Press, 1976), chap. 5. See also Jon H. Pammett, et al., "The Perception and Impact of Issues in the 1974 Federal Election," *Canadian Journal of Political Science*, 10 (1977): 93–126. See, in particular, pp. 98–101. Unfortunately, of the surveys in our merged file, only the 1974 one records eligibility in the last provincial election. In the 1974 survey, only six respondents claimed to have been ineligible in the last provincial election.

39. John Wilson and David Hoffman, "The Liberal Party in Contemporary Ontario Politics," *Canadian Journal of Political Science*, 3 (1970): 177–204. The Wilson and Hoffman argument is consistent with the analysis of swings between on and off-years in the U.S. Congressional vote. See Angus Campbell, "Surge and Decline: A Study of Electoral Change," in Campbell et al., *Elections and the Political Order* (New York: Wiley, 1966), chap. 3. But see Carole J. Uhlaner, "Independence of Canadian Governmental Levels: An Examination of its Manifestation in Participatory Behaviour" (1976), mimeographed.

40. For calculation identities, see Butler and Stokes, *Political Change in Britain*, chap. 12.

41. The only outstandingly bad estimate in Table 10 is that for Saskatchewan in 1968. Liberal losses and Conservative gains from the preceding provincial election are underestimated by about twenty points.

42. Leon Festinger, *A Theory of Cognitive Dissonance* (Stanford: Stanford University Press, 1957); Milton J. Rosenberg et al., *Attitude Organization and Change* (New Haven and London: Yale University Press, 1960).

43. Paul F. Lazarsfeld, Bernard R. Berelson, and Hazel Gaudet Erskine, *The People's Choice* (New York: Columbia University Press, 1948).

44. Bernard R. Berelson, Paul F. Lazarsfeld, and William N. McPhee, *Voting* (Chicago: University of Chicago Press, 1954), p. 19ff; Campbell et al., *The American Voter*, p. 77ff.

45. R.S. Milne and H.C. Mackenzie, *Straight Fight* (London: The Hansard Society, 1954) and *Marginal Seat, 1955* (London: The Hansard Society, 1958); Butler and Stokes, *Political Change in Britain*, 1st ed. (New York: St. Martin's, 1969), p. 220ff.

46. Downs, *An Economic Theory of Democracy*, pt. 3; Samuel Popkin et al., "Comment: What Have You Done for Me Lately? Toward an Investment Theory of Voting," *American Political Science Review*, 70 (1976): 779-805.

47. For an early finding consistent with this prediction, see Campbell et al., *The American Voter*, p. 142.

48. Peter W. Sperlich, *Conflict and Harmony in Human Affairs: A Study of Cross-Pressures and Political Behavior* (Chicago: Rand McNally, 1971); William J. McGuire, "Personality and Susceptibility to Social Influence," in *Handbook of Personality Theory and Research*, ed. Edgar F. Borgatta and William W. Lambert (Chicago: Rand McNally, 1968), pp. 1130-87.

49. The self-directed and socially approved response biases, mentioned above, operate here as well. But their net effect is uncertain. I expect relatively uninvolved respondents to be more prey to the biases than relatively involved respondents. Where party strengths differ greatly between levels, we might expect relatively uninvolved respondents to overreport switching and so to create a spurious negative association between political involvement and net interlevel change. Conversely, uninvolved respondents are also relatively likely erroneously to claim to have behaved consistently and, in doing so, to create a spurious *positive* association between political involvement and net interlevel change. The ultimate effect of these two biases' joint operation is not known. The reader should have these biases in mind, however, as he approaches Table 11.

50. Wilson and Hoffman, "The Liberal Party in Contemporary Ontario Politics," 195-96.

51. W.L. Morton, *The Progressive Party in Canada* (Toronto: University of Toronto Press, 1950); C.B. Macpherson, *Democracy in Alberta: Social Credit and the Party System* (Toronto:

University of Toronto Press, 1953); S.M. Lipset, *Agrarian Socialism* (Garden City, N.Y.: Doubleday, 1968).

52. Indeed, anti-party rhetoric figured prominently in Prairie, especially Alberta, politics. See Macpherson, *Democracy in Alberta*, chap. 2, and Morton, *The Progressive Party*.

53. Lipset, *Agrarian Socialism*, chap. 1.

54. Campbell et al., *The American Voter*, chap. 15.

55. Popkin et al., "Comment: What Have You Done for Me Lately?," p. 791; Michael S. Lewis-Beck, "Agrarian Political Behavior in the United States," *American Journal of Political Science*, 21 (1977): 543-65; and Sidney Tarrow, "The Urban-Rural Cleavage in Political Involvement: The Case of France," *American Political Science Review*, 65 (1971): 341-57.

56. There is some risk in merging the three surveys. Where party vote shares fluctuate, merging elections can reduce the net shifts and blur differences between groups. The problem is potentially especially acute where a province's federal or provincial system has undergone a realignment between 1965 and 1974. Inspection of the occupation pattern in separate surveys suggests, however, that the merged presentation does not do violence to the facts as they emerge from the separate surveys.

57. Butler and Stokes, *Political Change in Britain*, p. 78; Robert Alford, *Party and Society* (Chicago: Rand McNally, 1963).

58. See, for example, John Meisel, *Working Papers on Canadian Politics* (Montreal and London: McGill-Queen's University Press, 1975), chap. 3.

59. Lynn McDonald, "Religion and Voting: A Study of the 1968 Canadian Election in Ontario," *Canadian Review of Sociology and Anthropology*, 6 (1969): 129-44; William P. Irvine, "Explaining the Religious Basis of Canadian Partisan Identity: Success on the Third Try," *Canadian Journal of Political Science*, 7 (1974): 560-63.

60. For a recent discussion of differences among Protestant denominations, see J.A. Laponce, "Ethnicity, Religion, and Politics in Canada: A Comparative Analysis of Survey and Census Data," in *Quantitative Ecological Analysis in the Social Sciences*, ed. Mattei Dogan and Stein Rokkan (Cambridge, Mass.: MIT Press, 1969), pp. 187-216.

61. Peter B. Waite, *The Life and Times of Confederation, 1864-1867: Politics, Newspapers, and the Union of British North America.* (Toronto and Buffalo: University of Toronto Press, 1971), p. 325.

VI
Dimensions of Variation in Electoral Coalitions, 1965–1974[1]

Mike Burke

I. Introduction

Political parties in Canada have distinct bases of group support. Each party draws the bulk of its votes from a different configuration of social groups. Each party's electoral coalition is unique. But unique in what sense? In examining patterns of group-party relations, it is important to recognize the numerous dimensions along which differences might lie. First, significant differences might emerge between *levels of government* — between the federal and provincial coalitions of a given party. Secondly, at both levels, the group composition of a party's coalition might vary by *province*. Finally, one might expect to find differences between *parties* at the same level of government. The objective of this chapter is to measure and to compare the patterns of group-party support on each of these dimensions.

The contribution of a group to the electoral coalition of a party is defined as the "proportion of a party's total votes that is provided by a given group."[2] As Robert Axelrod points out, the magnitude of any one group's contribution is a function of three factors — the size of the group, its turnout and its loyalty.[3] Other things being equal, a large group is able to contribute more votes to a party than is a small group. However, other things are not invariably equal. The turnout of the group must also be considered. If members of a large group tend to abstain from voting, then that group's contribution to any party will be minimal. Finally, group loyalty is a vital consideration. A large group may split its votes equally among a number of parties and thus minimize its contribution to the coalition of any one party. On the other hand, members of a small group may vote en masse for one particular party thereby maximizing the group's contribution. While we do not intend to replicate Axelrod's analysis,[4] it is important to keep in mind the three factors on which the magnitude of a group's contribution depends.

This chapter is partitioned into a number of sections. Theoretical concerns are examined first. That is, in the next section we discuss our reasons for focusing on the three dimensions of level of government, province and party. In Section III we briefly summarize the group composition of electoral coalitions and in Section IV the data and measurement techniques are described. In the fifth part of the chapter we examine level of goverment differences in the social profile of coalitions. Next, we compare the ways in which coalitions vary by party and by province in both federal (Section IV) and provincial (Section VII) politics. After a short synopsis of the research findings, the chapter ends with some observations on the brokerage theory of politics, the nature of parties' electoral appeals, and the process of intergovernmental relations.

II. The Dimensions of Variation

Why would one expect the composition of electoral coalitions to vary by level of government, by province and by party? The literature on the development of federalism and on voting behaviour provides numerous justifications for this view.

Canadians are at once members of two distinct political systems — the national and the provincial. And, for various reasons, we would expect citizens to be well aware of the federal nature of the polity. First, the reality of living under a federal system is not masked by the overwhelming strength of one level of government as compared to the other. Both the federal and provincial governments are major political actors with significant social and economic functions.[5]

Secondly, in the majority of provinces, the pattern of party competition differs as one moves from federal to provincial politics. In British Columbia and Quebec, for example, parties which are electorally strong at one level are either weak or nonexistent at the other. This asymmetry of party systems "probably encourages citizens to believe that they live in two relatively discrete political systems rather than an integrated system."[6]

Other factors which might contribute to voters' awareness of the distinction between levels of government could be mentioned as well. Federal and provincial election campaigns are held at different times and waged on different issues. Federal and provincial parties of the same name often expound different views. The frequency of federal-provincial conflict constantly reminds citizens that there are two governments vying for their support.

Indeed, evidence suggests that the electorate is able to distinguish between these levels. Individuals attach different degrees of importance and pay differential attention to federal and provincial politics.[7] The manner in which people identify with political parties also varies by level of government.[8] And a not inconsiderable number of electors switch their votes between federal and provincial elections.[9] In sum, given that the marked disjunction between the two political systems is reflected in the attitudes and behaviour of voters, it seems reasonable to hypothesize that the composition of electoral coalitions will vary by level of government.

The extent of variation by province is the second dimension on which we focus. The most straightforward and compelling reason for our expectation of provincial differences in electoral coalitions concerns group size. There is substantial provincial variation in the size of demographic groups — the number of Anglicans, farmers, urban residents, and so on, varies considerably from one area of the country to the next.[10] Since group size is one of the factors affecting the composition of coalitions, these interprovincial differences in the social profile of the electorate will, to some degree, be mirrored by interprovincial differences in the social profile of a given party's supporters.

But demographics is not the sole consideration. Given the differing historical and contemporary experiences of the provinces, it is not surprising to find provincial variation in the political attitudes and perceptions of the *same* social groups. The ways in which citizens orient themselves to politics in general and to parties in particular differ across provinces.[11] Likewise, the voting behaviour of some social groups varies from one province to the next.[12] These factors would also lead us to expect variation by province in the group profile of party support.

Finally, we examine the extent to which the composition of coalitions varies between parties. Variations in the pattern of group loyalty would seem to suggest the existence of interparty differences in electoral coalitions. Some groups tend to give a majority of their votes to one political party, with a correspondingly small proportion of their support distributed among the remaining parties.[13] Therefore, since group loyalty varies by party, one would expect the group profile of coalitions to vary by party as well.

It is certainly not out of place to suggest that political parties in Canada can be distinguished by the social characteristics of their supporters. As early as the election of 1867, the two national parties could be seen as coalitions of distinct groups.[14] And although the exact composition of coalitions has changed since that time, the parties' profiles remain dissimilar.[15]

In sum, there are three dimensions on which we expect the group makeup of electoral coalitions to differ: by level of government, by province and by party. However, before comparing the magnitude of variation on each dimension, some discussion of the social profiles of the different coalitions is required.

III. The Electoral Coalitions

What is the group composition of electoral coalitions in Canada? Although a detailed description of each coalition is beyond the scope of this chapter, we plan to illustrate a few of the ways in which party profiles differ. In this manner, some introductory information about the actual composition of electoral coalitions will be provided.

Most of the existing evidence about the group profile of coalitions pertains to national differences among parties at the federal level of government.[16] For instance, Catholics, French-speaking Canadians, those living in large urban centres and persons from upper- or middle-class backgrounds contribute disproportionately to the vote totals of the federal Liberal party. The Conservatives appear to be a coalition of Protestants, Anglophones, rural residents, the working- and middle-classes and the elderly. The federal NDP is a party of Protestants, people without any religious affiliation, English-speaking Canadians and of those living in metropolitan areas. Nationally, the Social Credit party[17] derives a disproportionate share of its votes from Catholics, Francophones, rural residents, the young and the working class.

Unfortunately, not much is known about the province-by-province composition of federal electoral coalitions.[18] In the broadest outline, provincial differences in the distribution of demographic characteristics are parallelled quite closely by provincial differences in the patterns of group-party support.[19] For example, each party's profile is predominantly French-speaking and Catholic in Quebec. In the other provinces, however, the parties derive a large proportion of their votes from Anglophones and Protestants.[20] In terms of ethnic origin, we find that each party relies more heavily on the support of non-British, non-French groups in the western provinces than elsewhere. Additional examples could be given, but the major point would remain the same: there is sizable provincial variation in the group composition of federal coalitions, regardless of which party we consider.

Studies of electoral behaviour at the provincial level have tended to focus on the vote preference of particular groups rather than on the group composition of particular coalitions. We know, for example, the proportion of farmers that voted Conservative in the 1971 Alberta election; but we do not know the proportion of Conservative votes that were provided by farmers.[21] Nevertheless, it does appear that coalitions vary by party and by province. In Manitoba, for instance, the Tories are much more of a rural, small town party than the NDP. As an illustration of the differences between provinces, one can point to the fact that the Liberal party receives a substantially larger percentage of its votes from the working class in New Brunswick than it does in British Columbia.

Is there any evidence which suggests that the composition of electoral coalitions varies by level of government? In British Columbia we find that those living in urban centres contribute more votes to the provincial NDP than they do to the federal NDP. In Quebec and British Columbia, the Social Credit party draws more of its support from the working class in federal elections than it does provincially. Once again, the examples could be multiplied but the conclusion would not be altered: the social profile of each party's coalition differs from one level of government to the next.

The group composition of electoral coalitions varies on each of the dimensions of party, province and level. But how does one compare the extent of variation across dimensions? Which of the differences predominate? Questions such as these pose problems in terms of the kind of data and the kind of measurements to be used.

IV. Methods and Measures

The data for this analysis are drawn from a single, merged file which combines information from each of the 1965, 1968 and 1974 Canadian National Election Studies. Given that similar kinds of questions were not always asked in the same way in each year, only those measures which possessed a relatively high degree of comparability over time were combined. The merged data set consists of one hundred variables which provide demographic, attitudinal and behavioural information on some 7400 individuals.[22]

In one sense, the use of merged data is disadvantageous because we cannot trace changes over time in the group composition of electoral coalitions. However, these data do provide us with subsamples of sufficient size for meaningful analysis. With the large number of cases on which the merged file is based, we are able to partition the analysis by province and to examine the electoral coalitions of minor parties. If one uses data from only a single election year, the provincial subsamples of minor party supporters are prohibitively small.

For each dimension — level of government, party and province — an index of dissimilarity is used to measure the magnitude of difference in the group composition of coalitions. The index is defined as

$$\frac{1}{2n} \sum_n \sum_k |P_{ik} - P_{jk}|$$

where: (a) for the index of party dissimilarity

P_{ik} is the contribution of group k to party i's total vote in a given province;

P_{jk} is the contribution of group k to party j's total vote in the given province;

n is the number of provinces.

(b) for the index of provincial dissimilarity

P_{ik} is the contribution of group k to a given party's total vote in province i;

P_{jk} is the contribution of group k to the given party's total vote in province j;

n is the number of parties.

(c) for the index of federal-provincial dissimilarity

n = 1 because only one province *and* only one party are considered and thus the index reduces to

$$\frac{1}{2}\sum_{k}\left|P_{ik} - P_{jk}\right|$$

where[23]

P_{ik} is the contribution of group k to a given party's federal vote in a given province;

P_{jk} is the contribution of group k to the given party's provincial vote in the given province.

This measure ranges from 0 (most similar) to 100 (most dissimilar) and may be interpreted as the percentage of the maximum possible variation between coalitions. A few examples may help to clarify the way in which the indices are computed.

Table 1 presents an illustration of the computation of the index of federal-provincial dissimilarity. Columns 1 and 2 demonstrate that, in Newfoundland, the federal Liberal party receives 31.4% of its votes from those 18 to 35 years of age, while provincially the party receives 28.8% of its votes from that group. The absolute difference between the two figures is 31.4% − 28.8% = 2.6%. After a similar computation is made for each age group the absolute differences are summed across all groups. Since the maximum possible variation between any two coalitions is 200%, the figure in column 4 is divided by 2 to ensure that the index ranges from 0 to 100. Finally, from column 5 we can see that, in Newfoundland, the federal Liberal coalition differs from the provincial Liberal coalition by only 2.8 percentage points out of the maximum possible difference of 100.

We also wish to measure the extent to which electoral coalitions vary by province. Column 4 of Table 2 shows that the sum of the absolute differences between the age group composition of the federal Liberal coalitions in Newfoundland and Quebec is 7.4 percentage points. But the index of provincial dissimilarity measures provincial differences across *all* relevant parties. In comparing the two provinces of Newfoundland and Quebec, we have a sufficient number of cases to examine only the Liberal and Conservative coalitions. After repeating these same calculations for the federal Conservative party, we find that the sum of the absolute differences between provincial coalitions is 12 percentage points (column 8). Thus the *overall* sum of absolute differences across groups *and* parties is 7.4% + 12.0% = 19.4% (column 9). Since our comparison involves two parties (i.e. n = 2), this figure is divided by 4 to yield an index score of 4.85. That is, the parties' coalitions in Newfoundland differ from those in Quebec by less than five percentage points. In the tables below an index of provincial dissimilarity is computed for each pairwise combination of provinces, taking account of only those parties that appear in both provinces. Given a total of ten provinces, forty-five such scores are reported in each table.

Table 1
Sample Computation of the Index of Federal-Provincial Dissimilarity*

Age	Newfoundland Federal Liberals P_{ik}	Newfoundland Provincial Liberals P_{jk}	$\|P_{ik}\text{-}P_{jk}\|$	$\sum_k \|P_{ik}\text{-}P_{jk}\|$	Index Score $\frac{1}{2}\sum_k \|P_{ik}\text{-}P_{jk}\|$
18–35	31.4%	28.8%	2.6%		
36–45	21.4	21.3	0.1	5.6	2.8
Over 45	47.1	50.0	2.9		
Column	1	2	3	4	5

* See text for explanation.

Two additional points should be made about the construction of the index of provincial dissimilarity. First, by considering only those parties that appear in *both* provinces under comparison, the index is a conservative estimate of differences. In terms of the example in Table 2, we have enough cases to examine the NDP and Social Credit coalitions in Quebec, but we do not have enough cases to examine these parties' coalitions in Newfoundland. Therefore, the two parties are not used in the calculations. If one included the NDP and Social Credit, the magnitude of the index would be increased substantially. For instance, the sum of the absolute differences between the NDP coalitions in Newfoundland and Quebec is 100, because the party "does not have" a coalition in the former province. For the same reason, the sum of the absolute differences between the Social Credit (actually Créditiste) coalitions in Newfoundland and Quebec is equal to 100. Including these two parties would increase the overall sum by 200 points, from 19.4 to 219.4. Dividing this figure by 8 because we are dealing with four parties yields an index score of 219.4/8 = 27.43, which is much larger than the score of 4.85 reported in column 10 of Table 2. By focusing on only those parties that appear in both provinces, our measure underestimates the extent of dissimilarity between provinces. But the differences we find represent real differences that are not artificially inflated by the minor status of some parties in some provinces.

Secondly, in summing the absolute differences across all relevant parties each party is treated as an individual unit and is weighted equally. Our measure is insensitive to the fact that, for each pair of provinces under comparison, the size of coalitions varies by party. In Table 2, for example, we do not take into account that, in terms of raw numbers, the Liberal coalitions in Newfoundland and Quebec are larger than the Conservative coalitions in those provinces. The magnitude of the Newfoundland-Quebec index score is unaffected by the differential size of parties' coalitions.[24]

Table 2
Sample Computation of the Index of Provincial Dissimilarity*

| Age | Federal Liberals | | | | Federal Progressive Conservatives | | | | Newfoundland-Quebec Index Score | |
| | Nfld. | Que. | | | Nfld. | Que. | | | | |
	P_{ik}	P_{jk}	$\lvert P_{ik}-P_{jk}\rvert$	$\sum_k \lvert P_{ik}-P_{jk}\rvert$	P_{ik}	P_{jk}	$\lvert P_{ik}-P_{jk}\rvert$	$\sum_k \lvert P_{ik}-P_{jk}\rvert$	$\sum_n\sum_k \lvert P_{ik}-P_{jk}\rvert$	$\dfrac{1}{2n}\sum_n\sum_k \lvert P_{ik}-P_{jk}\rvert$
18-35	31.4%	35.1%	3.7%		42.3%	36.3%	6.0%			
36-45	21.4	19.9	1.5	7.4	19.2	19.2	0	12.0	19.4	4.85
Over 45	47.1	44.9	2.2		38.5	44.5	6.0			
Column	1	2	3	4	5	6	7	8	9	10

* See text for explanation.

Table 3
Sample Computation of the Index of Party Dissimilarity*

| | Newfoundland | | | | | Liberal-Progressive Conservative Index Score |
| | Federal Liberals | Federal Progressive Conservatives | | | | |
Age	P_{ik}	P_{jk}	$\lvert P_{ik}-P_{jk} \rvert$	$\sum_k \lvert P_{ik}-P_{jk} \rvert$	$\sum_n \sum_k \lvert P_{ik}-P_{jk} \rvert$	$\frac{1}{2n} \sum_n \sum_k \lvert P_{ik}-P_{jk} \rvert$
18-35	31.4%	42.3%	10.9%			
36-45	21.4	19.2	2.2	21.7	179.6	8.98
Over 45	47.1	38.5	8.6			
Column	1	2	3	4	5	6

* See text for explanation.

The final dimension of comparison concerns differences between parties at the same level. In the fourth column of Table 3 we find that, in Newfoundland, the federal Liberal coalition differs from the federal Conservative coalition by a total of 21.7 percentage points. Since the index of party dissimilarity measures differences between parties across *all* relevant provinces, the calculations are not yet complete. We have enough cases to compare the Liberal and Conservative coalitions in every province. Column 5 shows that, summed across all provinces, the absolute difference between the two parties' coalitions is 179.6 points. This sum is then divided by 20 because we are dealing with ten provinces (n = 10), yielding a dissimilarity score of 8.98 out of 100 maximum. In like manner, all parties are compared in a pairwise fashion. With a total of four parties — Liberal, Conservative, NDP and Social Credit — six indices of party dissimilarity are presented in each table.

In computing the party index, we consider only those provinces that are relevant to *both* parties under comparison. This presents no problem for the Liberal-Conservative pair because all ten provinces enter into the calculations. However, for comparisons involving the NDP and Social Credit, not every province is used. For example, in measuring the extent of dissimilarity between the federal Liberal and NDP coalitions, absolute differences are summed across the provinces of Quebec, Ontario, Manitoba, Saskatchewan and British Columbia. There are not enough cases to examine the NDP profile elsewhere. In each of the provinces where the NDP coalition is "nonexistent," the absolute difference between the NDP and Liberal coalitions is 100 points. In order not to inflate the magnitude of the index, these provinces are eliminated from the computations. Like the provincial index, then, the index of party dissimilarity is a conservative estimate.

For each pairwise combination of parties, the size of coalitions varies by province. The Liberal and Conservative coalitions, for instance, are larger in Quebec than in Newfoundland. But in summing the absolute differences across all relevant provinces, we ignore this variation and weight each province equally.[25]

In addition to the age variable, the social composition of each coalition is defined for class, community size, linguistic and religious groups.[26] The extent to which the group profile of coalitions varies between levels of government is considered in the next section.

V. Variations by Level of Government

Given that we expected to find differences between the federal and provincial coalitions of any one party, it is surprising to learn that there is in fact minimal variation by level of government. Consider the data in Table 4. With a few notable exceptions, the index scores are extremely small for most of the parties in most of the provinces. In terms of social class, the federal coalition of each party closely resembles its provincial counterpart. In five of the six cases where the index is greater than ten, the federal wing receives a larger percentage of its votes from the working class than does the provincial party. Only for the Conservatives in Saskatchewan is this trend reversed.

At the bottom of the table we can see that the mean index score is 5.74 — a relatively small figure when compared to what we will encounter on the party and province dimensions. Furthermore, the overall pattern found in Table 4 — for groups defined by social class — is essentially the same as that for groups defined by community size, age, religion and language.[27] This reinforces our earlier impression of the minor differences between levels of government.

Why is there not more variation between the federal and provincial coalitions of a given party? Recall that the magnitude of a group's contribution to an electoral coalition is determined by the three factors of size, turnout and loyalty. Within any one province, group size is a constant regardless of the level at which an election is held. In addition, turnout is relatively invariant across levels — those who vote in provincial elections are likely to vote federally and vice versa. Thus group loyalty is crucial. But even this factor does not produce much variation in the cross-level composition of coalitions. There are a number of reasons why this is the case.

There is little evidence of the wholesale desertion of specific groups. For instance, members of a group do not vote unanimously for a party in provincial elections and then totally reject that party federally. In provinces where a party is strong at one level but weak at the other, *all* groups tend to desert the weaker party in *almost equal* proportions. Finally, some of the effect of those who do switch their votes between federal and provincial elections is tempered by group members who switch in the opposite direction.

Table 4
Index of Federal-Provincial Dissimilarity by Province:
Subjective Social Class

	Liberal	Progressive Conservative	NDP	Social Credit
Newfoundland	3.10	12.70	—*	—
P.E.I.	0.95	2.05	—	—
Nova Scotia	6.40	4.60	—	—
New Brunswick	2.45	0.50	—	—
Quebec	1.90	2.45	—	18.65
Ontario	3.15	3.90	2.80	—
Manitoba	3.30	1.50	2.10	—
Saskatchewan	1.05	13.70	8.65	—
Alberta	14.30	4.65	—	10.30
B.C.	7.90	7.15	1.50	13.15

$\bar{X} = 5.74$
S.D. = 5.00
*Insufficient N.

VI. Variations at the Federal Level

Although there is not much variation in electoral coalitions by level of government for any given party, at each level the patterns of group support may differ by party and/or by province. Our focus here is on the relative magnitude of these differences at the federal level of government.

While each particular figure in the tables below is worthy of comment, for the most part we will restrict our discussion to a comparison of the variation between dimensions. For such a purpose, the index means are especially helpful. For example, Tables 5 and 6 demonstrate that, in terms of age groups, there is little difference between the variation by party ($\overline{X} = 9.83$) and the variation by province ($\overline{X} = 9.29$). On each dimension, electoral coalitions differ to a similar extent; each mean is larger than the average difference between levels of government in Table 4.

The community size profile of federal coalitions shows a slightly different picture. Here, the patterns of group support differ less by party (Table 7) than they do by province (Table 8). Social Credit contributes disproportionately to the magnitude of the mean index of party dissimilarity. Not surprisingly, that party is much more rural-based than are the Liberals, the Conservatives or the NDP.

On the provincial dimension we find consistently large differences between almost all pairwise combinations of provinces. To some extent this pattern is a function of the way in which the community size variable was categorized. There are no cities with a population greater than five hundred thousand in Atlantic Canada, Saskatchewan or Alberta. In each of these provinces, then, the size of the group defined in such terms and therefore the group's contributions are equal to zero. But, in Quebec, Ontario, Manitoba and British Columbia the size and contributions of this group are considerable. In comparing across these two sets of provinces, the magnitude of the index scores is inflated by the extreme discrepancies in group size.[28]

For coalitions defined by linguistic groups, the provincial differences are greater than those between parties. As can be seen from Tables 9 and 10, the mean index of provincial dissimilarity ($\overline{X} = 24.35$) is three times as large as the mean index of party dissimilarity ($\overline{X} = 7.64$). But the cell entries of Table 10 indicate that the largest provincial differences are found on comparisons involving Quebec. This, of course, is due to the unique linguistic composition of that province. If one eliminates Quebec from the analysis, the mean provincial index score is reduced from 24.35 to 10.66. Thus, by removing Quebec, we are left with an almost equal amount of variation by party and by province; both dimensions reveal an average difference approximately twice that found between levels of government.

In Canada, the variable of religion is among the most powerful predictors of individual vote choice.[29] Does the religious composition of federal coalitions vary by party? Table 11 demonstrates that there are

Table 5
Index of Party Dissimilarity: Age (Federal Level)

	Liberal	Progressive Conservative	NDP	Social Credit
Liberal				
Progressive Conservative	8.98			
NDP	7.18	13.11		
Social Credit	10.62	9.43	9.63	

$\bar{X} = 9.83$
S.D. $= 1.97$

Table 6
Index of Provincial Dissimilarity: Age (Federal Level)

	Newfoundland	P.E.I.	Nova Scotia	New Brunswick	Quebec	Ontario	Manitoba	Saskatchewan	Alberta	B.C.
Newfoundland										
P.E.I.	12.63									
Nova Scotia	10.53	8.40								
New Brunswick	10.43	7.35	7.95							
Quebec	4.85	10.53	8.63	7.13						
Ontario	9.48	10.10	8.30	5.05	9.05					
Manitoba	9.60	6.23	6.28	1.78	14.07	7.52				
Saskatchewan	7.80	8.93	3.18	8.28	15.00	11.32	8.90			
Alberta	12.58	16.20	14.40	10.65	9.67	6.10	12.43	12.63		
B.C.	12.48	10.65	10.35	3.30	13.00	4.23	8.18	13.22	8.83	

$\bar{X} = 9.29$
S.D $= 3.26$

Table 7

Index of Party Dissimilarity: Community Size (Federal Level)

	Liberal	Progressive Conservative	NDP	Social Credit
Liberal				
Progressive Conservative	9.92			
NDP	10.81	16.97		
Social Credit	30.28	21.22	40.78	

$\bar{X} = 21.66$
S.D. $= 11.98$

Table 8

Index of Provincial Dissimilarity: Community Size (Federal Level)

	Newfoundland	P.E.I.	Nova Scotia	New Brunswick	Quebec	Ontario	Manitoba	Saskatchewan	Alberta	B.C.
Newfoundland										
P.E.I.	8.85									
Nova Scotia	6.55	13.20								
New Brunswick	6.85	2.00	11.20							
Quebec	37.20	45.25	37.95	43.25						
Ontario	32.80	40.05	28.40	38.05	15.50					
Manitoba	34.60	37.60	34.60	36.85	12.65	9.45				
Saskatchewan	6.75	14.20	1.00	12.20	44.30	29.40	35.92			
Alberta	31.95	40.80	27.60	38.80	31.33	29.60	38.35	26.60		
B.C.	52.85	59.50	52.85	57.50	12.56	21.07	18.55	50.47	43.28	

$\bar{X} = 29.12$
S.D $= 15.78$

Table 9
Index of Party Dissimilarity: Language (Federal Level)

	Liberal	Progressive Conservative	NDP	Social Credit
Liberal				
Progressive Conservative	6.97			
NDP	6.75	3.46		
Social Credit	9.88	9.60	9.18	

$\bar{X}=7.64$
S.D. $=2.45$

Table 10
Index of Provincial Dissimilarity: Language (Federal Level)

	Newfoundland	P.E.I.	Nova Scotia	New Brunswick	Quebec	Ontario	Manitoba	Saskatchewan	Alberta	B.C.
Newfoundland										
P.E.I.	5.75									
Nova Scotia	5.10	5.35								
New Brunswick	30.00	25.25	24.90							
Quebec	83.90	78.95	78.80	53.90						
Ontario	7.60	9.45	5.10	26.70	80.35					
Manitoba	11.28	10.23	6.73	25.13	80.17	3.32				
Saskatchewan	8.15	7.70	6.50	28.35	81.98	4.47	5.58			
Alberta	6.13	6.83	4.28	28.18	86.62	3.83	5.75	2.28		
B.C.	3.85	6.70	4.45	29.35	87.16	4.37	6.85	3.50	4.82	

$\bar{X}=24.35$ (10.66)
S.D. $=29.19$ (9.22)
Figures in parentheses calculated without Quebec.

Table 11
Index of Party Dissimilarity: Religion (Federal Level)

	Liberal	Progressive Conservative	NDP	Social Credit
Progressive Conservative	20.04			
NDP	14.94	17.00		
Social Credit	22.02	17.90	20.03	

$\bar{X} = 18.66$
S.D. = 2.54

Table 12
Index of Provincial Dissimilarity: Religion (Federal Level)

	Newfoundland	P.E.I.	Nova Scotia	New Brunswick	Quebec	Ontario	Manitoba	Saskatchewan	Alberta	B.C.
Newfoundland										
P.E.I.	28.45									
Nova Scotia	23.40	22.80								
New Brunswick	36.88	30.78	27.03							
Quebec	60.48	52.03	62.43	41.65						
Ontario	24.50	26.00	20.40	36.23	64.05					
Manitoba	24.60	24.40	21.60	39.78	67.97	18.30				
Saskatchewan	25.10	18.55	19.55	36.43	64.43	18.20	12.73			
Alberta	30.13	20.91	15.33	34.80	71.47	15.93	13.18	10.73		
B.C.	23.53	36.58	24.43	43.30	80.81	21.82	28.55	29.65	24.20	

$\bar{X} = 32.76$ (25.24)
S.D = 17.42 (7.92)
Figures in parentheses calculated without Quebec.

substantial differences between each pair of parties; but these appear small when compared to the variation by province (Table 12). The mean provincial score ($\overline{X}$ = 32.76) is almost twice the size of the mean party score ($\overline{X}$ = 18.66). As was the case with language, however, the Quebec figures are considerably higher than the provincial average. Calculated without Quebec, the mean index of provincial dissimilarity decreases by some seven percentage points. Nevertheless, the overall differences by province remain somewhat larger than those between parties.

On the province dimension, there is an additional comparison which might be drawn between coalitions defined in terms of language and religion. As we have seen, the elimination of Quebec reduces the mean provincial score in both instances. However, the two distributions remain significantly different. For language, the standard deviation (9.22) is almost as large as the mean (10.66), reflecting the comparatively high scores found in the New Brunswick comparisons and the low scores found elsewhere. For religion, the standard deviation (7.92) is only one-third the size of the mean (25.24), which suggests that the scores are clustered around the midpoint of the distribution. Computing coefficients of variation, we find that the *relative* dispersion of the language scores is two and one-half times that of the religion scores.[30] In other words, the religious composition of electoral coalitions differs relatively consistently across all areas of the country. Coalitions defined by language display a more uneven pattern — some pairs of provinces are very similar, some are very dissimilar.[31]

The degree to which political parties are differentiated along class lines has provoked considerable controversy. Alford suggests that Canada is an example of "pure non-class politics," while Chi maintains that the nature and extent of the class cleavage have been seriously underestimated.[32] As the figures in Table 13 indicate, the class composition of party coalitions varies considerably. The profiles of the NDP and Social Credit are more working class than are those of the two major parties except in Quebec, where the NDP draws the bulk of its votes from the middle class. Class profiles also vary by province, with a mean index of provincial dissimilarity ($\overline{X}$ = 14.89) almost equal to that found on the party dimension ($\overline{X}$ = 16.66).[33] Surprisingly, New Brunswick stands out as the most unusual of provinces. There, both the Liberals and the Tories receive a much larger percentage of their votes from the working class than they do elsewhere.[34]

In sum, federal electoral coalitions vary by party and by province. In terms of age groups, the variation on both dimensions is relatively small and approximately equal. On the other hand, we find large differences for coalitions defined by community size and religion, with considerably more variation by province than by party. The pattern for social class groups stands somewhere in between these two poles. Like the variables of religion and community size, differences in the class composition of coalitions are

Table 13
Index of Party Dissimilarity: Subjective Social Class
(Federal Level)

	Liberal	Progressive Conservative	NDP	Social Credit
Liberal				
Progressive Conservative	6.02			
NDP	15.43	19.72		
Social Credit	21.88	18.27	18.63	

$\bar{X} = 16.66$
S.D. $= 5.62$

Table 14
Index of Provincial Dissimilarity: Subjective Social Class (Federal Level)

	Newfoundland	P.E.I.	Nova Scotia	New Brunswick	Quebec	Ontario	Manitoba	Saskatchewan	Alberta	B.C.
Newfoundland										
P.E.I.	18.83									
Nova Scotia	11.25	9.73								
New Brunswick	9.85	27.48	20.50							
Quebec	19.40	16.48	9.25	28.65						
Ontario	21.60	9.18	10.60	30.85	16.93					
Manitoba	16.20	9.68	9.15	24.70	16.73	5.53				
Saskatchewan	15.35	9.63	8.65	22.45	19.28	6.02	2.85			
Alberta	20.10	10.58	12.20	29.35	7.60	3.15	4.70	6.90		
B.C.	29.18	10.95	17.93	38.43	14.93	6.22	9.95	11.73	9.47	

$\bar{X} = 14.89$
S.D $= 8.30$

comparatively large. Like the pattern found for age groups, the extent of dissimilarity on the party dimension is approximately equal to that on the province dimension.

Coalitions defined linguistically differ substantially across provinces. As was mentioned above, however, eliminating Quebec from the analysis reduces the mean provincial score. In other words, most of the variation between provinces on the linguistic variable is due to the unusual character of coalitions in Quebec. Surprisingly, the language profiles of *parties* differ hardly at all. How, then, would one account for the image of the Liberals as the party of Francophones and the image of the Conservatives as the party of Anglophones?

The finding that political parties do not differ in language bases is partly a result of the way in which the party index was constructed. Recall that the index sums differences across all relevant provinces and that each province is weighted equally. Therefore, our measure does not take into account the fact that party coalitions are larger in some provinces than in others. If provinces are differentially weighted according to the size of a party's coalition, then we find relatively large differences in the language profiles of the two parties — the Liberal party is much more Francophone-based than are the Tories. Of course, weighting the provinces in this manner does take into account the fact that the Liberals draw a disproportionate share of their votes from Quebec.

However, even though the national language profiles of the parties may be more dissimilar than our measure suggests, one should not neglect the role that institutional factors have played in exaggerating this linguistic distinctiveness. We know, for example, that most of the voters in Quebec and most of the MPs from Quebec are French speaking. And the Liberal party usually receives a larger percentage of seats from that province than it does votes. Therefore, because of the peculiarities of the electoral system, the Liberal party in Parliament is more French speaking than the Liberal party in the electorate. The reverse obtains for the Conservative party — proportionately it receives more votes than seats from Quebec.[35] While the Liberal profile is more Francophone than that of the Conservatives across the nation as a whole, such institutional factors as the electoral system tend to underscore this difference.

VII. Variations at the Provincial Level

In this section we examine the composition of coalitions in provincial politics and compare the variation *by party* aggregated across provinces to the variation *by province* aggregated across parties. Earlier we demonstrated that, in each province, the federal and provincial profiles of any given party were almost identical. For this reason differences in the social composition of coalitions at the provincial level are similar to those found federally. Therefore, much of the data presented in this section can be dealt with fairly briefly.

Table 15
Index of Party Dissimilarity: Age (Provincial Level)

	Liberal	Progressive Conservative	NDP	Social Credit
Liberal				
Progressive Conservative	10.31			
NDP	6.68	11.63		
Social Credit	20.20	12.58	13.55	

$\bar{X} = 12.49$
S.D. = 4.47

Table 16
Index of Provincial Dissimilarity: Age (Provincial Level)

	Newfoundland	P.E.I.	Nova Scotia	New Brunswick	Quebec	Ontario	Manitoba	Saskatchewan	Alberta	B.C.
Newfoundland										
P.E.I.	14.08									
Nova Scotia	10.68	8.95								
New Brunswick	9.18	8.10	6.40							
Quebec	3.18	13.10	10.25	6.65						
Ontario	6.73	10.55	7.70	3.55	3.90					
Manitoba	10.63	14.40	6.85	10.80	9.70	6.66				
Saskatchewan	3.33	12.25	8.75	9.60	4.90	10.60	10.83			
Alberta	15.25	25.18	20.23	18.78	18.52	15.98	19.03	18.48		
B.C.	13.83	13.00	11.75	5.40	17.25	6.00	11.03	15.77	12.57	

$\bar{X} = 11.12$
S.D = 5.05

In terms of age, Tables 15 and 16 demonstrate that the average party difference ($\overline{X} = 12.49$) is essentially equal to the mean variation between provinces ($\overline{X} = 11.12$). Social Credit is the most distinctive party, having a younger profile than the Liberals and Conservatives in Quebec; but it is an older party compared to the Liberals in Alberta and British Columbia, to the Conservatives in Alberta, and to the NDP in British Columbia. Alberta is the only province whose scores are uniformly higher than the overall provincial average. Both the Liberals and the Tories draw a larger proportion of their votes from the younger cohorts in Alberta than elsewhere. In contrast, those over forty-five years of age contribute more votes to the Social Credit coalition in Alberta than in Quebec.

Unlike the pattern on the age variable, coalitions defined in terms of community size differ much more by province ($\overline{X} = 29.71$) than they do by party ($\overline{X} = 15.51$). At the provincial level of government, as at the federal, the Social Credit profile is heavily weighted towards rural support. On the province dimension, Table 18 shows that the index scores within Atlantic Canada are relatively small. But for comparisons between the Atlantic and other provinces, the magnitude of the scores indicates a high degree of dissimilarity. Once again, this is due to the nonurban nature of the Atlantic region.

Tables 19 and 20 display the index scores for language groups. The extent to which coalitions defined linguistically vary on the dimensions of party and province is by now a familiar story. The variation by party is minimal ($\overline{X} = 5.19$) because each party's profile is predominantly French speaking in Quebec[36] and predominantly English speaking elsewhere. Although differences between provinces appear substantial ($\overline{X} = 24.81$), removing Quebec from the analysis reduces considerably the extent of provincial dissimilarity ($\overline{X} = 10.61$).

Comparing the religious composition of electoral coalitions, we find almost identical index scores for each pairwise combination of parties. The provincial Liberal party is more Catholic than the Conservatives in New Brunswick, Ontario and the West but less Catholic in Quebec, Newfoundland and Prince Edward Island. In British Columbia, those with no religious affiliation contribute three times as many votes to the NDP total as they contribute to Social Credit. In terms of the variation by province, coalitions are much more Catholic-based in Quebec than they are in the rest of the country. Eliminating the discrepancies produced by the singular position of Quebec, however, still leaves a substantial amount of dissimilarity between provinces ($\overline{X} = 23.56$).

Without Quebec, the extent of provincial dissimilarity for linguistic and religious groups is reduced. But, as was the case federally, the pattern of differences between pairs of provinces is more uniform on the religion variable than it is on the variable of language.[37]

Table 17

Index of Party Dissimilarity: Community Size
(Provincial Level)

	Liberal	Progressive Conservative	NDP	Social Credit
Liberal				
Progressive Conservative	7.73			
NDP	11.38	20.13		
Social Credit	17.38	16.40	20.05	

$\bar{X} = 15.51$
S.D. = 4.98

Table 18

Index of Provincial Dissimilarity: Community Size (Provincial Level)

	Newfoundland	P.E.I	Nova Scotia	New Brunswick	Quebec	Ontario	Manitoba	Saskatchewan	Alberta	B.C.
Newfoundland										
P.E.I.	7.95									
Nova Scotia	5.15	13.10								
New Brunswick	7.95	2.40	13.10							
Quebec	41.78	46.83	39.23	46.83						
Ontario	31.95	39.90	28.50	39.90	11.58					
Manitoba	32.65	34.15	31.45	35.35	13.03	15.85				
Saskatchewan	6.25	12.90	6.30	12.90	39.18	30.23	40.15			
Alberta	36.25	44.20	31.10	44.20	31.12	31.90	42.35	31.30		
B.C.	50.85	56.35	48.30	56.35	17.20	22.27	16.55	50.03	40.28	

$\bar{X} = 29.71$
S.D = 15.35

The final characteristic we examine is that of subjective social class. The overall variation on the party dimension ($\overline{X} = 14.35$) is approximately equal to the average difference between provinces ($\overline{X} = 16.48$).[38] Generally, the NDP and Social Credit coalitions are more working class than are those of the Liberals and Conservatives. And, as we found at the federal level, the latter two parties derive a larger percentage of their votes from the working class in New Brunswick than they do in the other nine provinces.

VIII. Summary

Table 25 summarizes much of the data presented in the two preceding sections. In both federal and provincial politics, the largest differences between parties are found on the variables of community size, religion and subjective class. On the province dimension, there is also considerable variation in coalitions defined by language.

Table 25 also indicates that, at both levels of government, the overall variation by province is greater than the overall variation by party. Though eliminating Quebec from the computation of the means for linguistic and religious groups reduces the differences between provinces, the provincial variation remains substantial. Perhaps the major conclusion to be drawn is that there is considerable dissimilarity in the group composition of coalitions on each of the dimensions of party and province.[39]

Ordering each party in terms of its degree of dissimilarity — from high to low — we find that, across all possible comparisons, the Social Credit profile is the most dissimilar and that of the Conservatives the least dissimilar. The NDP ranks second and the Liberals third, but both parties are slightly closer to the Conservatives than they are to Social Credit. On the province dimension, comparisons involving Quebec exhibit the largest differences while those involving Nova Scotia differ the least from all the other provinces. The remaining provinces cluster near the low end of the scale, with New Brunswick and British Columbia occupying second and third place respectively.

Why does the composition of electoral coalitions vary by party? Quite simply, it is because of variations in the patterns of group loyalty. The same group votes for different parties in different proportions. For example, in virtually every province, a higher percentage of Catholics support the federal Liberal party than support the Conservatives, NDP or Social Credit.[40] This finding is repeated at the provincial level except in Alberta and British Columbia, where the Liberals are only a minor electoral force.

Why does the composition of electoral coalitions vary by province? Here, the most important factor is group size. Recall that both the Liberal and Tory profiles are more working class in New Brunswick than elsewhere. In terms of group size, we find that over 70 per cent of New Brunswick residents classify themselves as working class, while the corresponding figure in each

Table 19
Index of Party Dissimilarity: Language (Provincial Level)

	Liberal	Progressive Conservative	NDP	Social Credit
Liberal				
Progressive Conservative	6.85			
NDP	5.58	2.59		
Social Credit	7.32	3.72	5.05	

$\bar{X} = 5.19$
S.D. = 1.81

Table 20
Index of Provincial Dissimilarity: Language (Provincial Level)

	Newfoundland	P.E.I	Nova Scotia	New Brunswick	Quebec	Ontario	Manitoba	Saskatchewan	Alberta	B.C.
Newfoundland										
P.E.I.	6.55									
Nova Scotia	6.10	7.25								
New Brunswick	30.15	24.75	24.05							
Quebec	87.50	81.80	81.40	57.35						
Ontario	8.38	9.53	4.68	26.48	82.53					
Manitoba	11.28	8.93	7.03	25.93	81.98	3.57				
Saskatchewan	7.28	6.73	5.78	28.23	84.28	4.30	3.67			
Alberta	7.15	8.30	4.75	27.75	88.37	1.33	4.13	2.93		
B.C.	3.55	6.65	5.60	29.65	89.25	5.15	6.58	4.92	2.85	

$\bar{X} = 24.81$ (10.61)
S.D = 30.15 (9.22)
Figures in parentheses calculated without Quebec.

Table 21
Index of Party Dissimilarity: Religion (Provincial Level)

	Liberal	Progressive Conservative	NDP	Social Credit
Liberal				
Progressive Conservative	18.95			
NDP	17.81	13.58		
Social Credit	18.30	9.88	14.70	

$\overline{X} = 15.54$
S.D. = 3.49

Table 22
Index of Provincial Dissimilarity: Religion (Provincial Level)

	Newfoundland	P.E.I	Nova Scotia	New Brunswick	Quebec	Ontario	Manitoba	Saskatchewan	Alberta	B.C.
Newfoundland										
P.E.I.	25.48									
Nova Scotia	18.58	20.90								
New Brunswick	33.03	31.60	25.05							
Quebec	63.28	56.50	64.65	44.00						
Ontario	20.60	23.43	19.53	32.73	64.28					
Manitoba	24.50	23.38	21.03	37.48	70.98	16.35				
Saskatchewan	25.48	15.55	18.70	35.05	64.95	16.48	13.30			
Alberta	21.13	19.40	12.15	30.70	70.42	13.83	16.73	15.65		
B.C.	23.65	33.03	25.83	45.58	82.07	18.30	24.35	26.35	23.12	

$\overline{X} = 31.76 \ (23.56)$
S.D = 18.43 (7.48)

Figures in parentheses calculated without Quebec.

Table 23
Index of Party Dissimilarity: Subjective Social Class
(Provincial Level)

	Liberal	Progressive Conservative	NDP	Social Credit
Liberal				
Progressive Conservative	9.54			
NDP	14.10	17.30		
Social Credit	15.52	14.05	15.60	

$\bar{X} = 14.35$
S.D. = 2.64

Table 24
Index of Provincial Dissimilarity: Subjective Social Class
(Provincial Level)

	Newfoundland	P.E.I	Nova Scotia	New Brunswick	Quebec	Ontario	Manitoba	Saskatchewan	Alberta	B.C.
Newfoundland										
P.E.I.	14.63									
Nova Scotia	7.55	12.28								
New Brunswick	14.83	29.35	20.88							
Quebec	15.38	15.20	8.38	29.05						
Ontario	17.23	7.10	14.73	32.05	9.50					
Manitoba	10.90	8.83	9.35	24.38	8.43	6.98				
Saskatchewan	14.73	16.75	12.78	18.40	12.15	13.13	6.72			
Alberta	23.13	13.90	20.83	36.40	13.68	9.50	12.23	19.90		
B.C.	28.55	18.13	22.50	43.38	10.30	9.32	13.93	19.95	14.48	

$\bar{X} = 16.48$
S.D = 8.22

Table 25
Mean Index Scores

| | Federal Level | | | Provincial Level | | |
| | Party | Province | | Party | Province | |
	$\overline{X}$	$\overline{X}$		$\overline{X}$	$\overline{X}$	
Age	9.83	9.29		12.49	11.12	
Community size	21.66	29.12		15.51	29.71	
Language	7.64	24.35	(10.66)*	5.19	24.81	(10.61)*
Religion	18.66	32.76	(25.24)*	15.54	31.76	(23.56)*
Subjective class	16.66	14.89		14.35	16.48	
Overall $\overline{X}$	14.89	22.08	(17.84)*	12.62	22.78	(18.30)*

*Calculated without Quebec

of the remaining provinces is closer to one-half. In New Brunswick, the small size of the upper and middle classes limits the magnitude of the contribution that can be made by those groups. Of course, considerations of group size also account for the French-speaking nature of coalitions in Quebec.

As implied above, the loyalty of groups varies from one province to the next. For some groups this variation is considerable. As an example, in Alberta 54 per cent of those living in rural areas vote for the federal Conservative party, whereas only 26 per cent of that group support the Conservatives in British Columbia. In addition to the factor of group size, then, variations in group loyalty must also be considered when examining provincial differences in the composition of electoral coalitions.

IX. Conclusion

This chapter has demonstrated that although there is little variation in the composition of coalitions by level of government, patterns of group support differ substantially on the dimensions of party and province. What are the implications of these findings? The degree of variation by level of government qualifies our understanding of party systems; the magnitude of differences between parties affects the operation of brokerage politics; and the dissimilarity by province holds consequences for the nature of parties' electoral appeals and for the process of intergovernmental relations as well.

Numerous scholars have emphasized the separation of federal and provincial party systems. In terms of party organization, party finance, ideology, and so on, federal and provincial parties of the same name are not well integrated.[41] But, in the light of what we have found about the social profiles of parties, the extent of separation between levels appears to have been exaggerated. Within each province the federal and provincial coalitions of each party are remarkably alike. In Ontario, for example, the support base of the federal Liberal party is much the same as that of the provincial Liberals. In comparing federal and provincial party systems, then, it is important to recognize that both differences *and* similarities exist.

The brokerage theory of politics has frequenty been applied to Canada.[42] Accordingly, political parties are seen as mediators, attempting to control and to resolve the conflicting demands of divergent groups. In order to perform effectively these integrative functions, parties must draw their support from a broad cross-section of the electorate, they "must aggregate a wide spectrum of interests into a voting coalition."[43] However, as we have seen, the group composition of coalitions varies considerably from one party to the next.

In federal politics, the profiles of the two major parties are more representative of the social complexity of the country than are those of the NDP or Social Credit. But important social and political groups are underrepresented in each party's coalition. For instance, across the nation as a whole, Protestants are underrepresented in the Liberal coalition, French-speaking Canadians in the Conservative, and rural residents in the NDP coalition. The same pattern appears in provincial politics — each party has failed to aggregate a broad cross-section of the population. At both levels of government, then, not a single party has fulfilled one of the fundamental prerequisites of brokerage politics.

Coalitions differ not only between parties but also, for any one party, they differ between provinces. The magnitude of this provincial variation places strains on the types of electoral appeals that can be made by political parties. In terms of federal politics, for example, a given party must appeal to a different constituency in each province. A policy proposal geared towards satisfying the demands of coalition members in one province runs the risk of alienating those who are members of the party's coalition in other parts of the country. Confronted with such a situation the party could attempt to reach a compromise solution, but given the extent to which coalitions differ from one province to the next, it may be impossible to find middle ground. On the other hand, the dilemma might be solved by making different appeals in different provinces — a not infrequent occurrence in Canada.[44]

Provincial dissimilarity in party profiles influences the nature of federal-provincial relations as well. Consider the position of Ottawa. Although charged with the responsibility of maintaining a national perspective during negotiations, the federal government is faced with the problem of trying to satisfy clienteles whose very characteristics differ markedly from one province to the next. The difficulty that Ottawa experiences in representing these divergent coalitions must surely strengthen the position of some provincial politicians, who can cast themselves in the role of protectors of neglected interests.

In quite another sense, this variation by province is related to the dynamics of federal-provincial negotiation. It is certainly evident that the partisan-political cleavage is relatively unimportant to understanding the process of intergovernmental bargaining.[45] First ministers' conferences rarely divide on party lines; federal and provincial politicians of the same party designation are often uncooperative. But this is not to suggest that party politics are irrelevant to the study of intergovernmental relations. Governments are formed by parties and one of the fundamental objectives of a party is to secure election or to ensure re-election. Once electoral concerns are introduced, provincial differences in the composition of party coalitions become meaningful to the bargaining process.

Because the interests of each province are in some ways unique, even provincial governments of the same party label may be unable to cooperate with one another. However, we also know that at the provincial level the social profile of each party's coalition varies from one area of the country to the next. Even provincial governments of the same party label serve different clienteles. In addition to the unique interests associated with each province, then, the nature of electoral coalitions also differentiates one governing party from another. In instances where some common interest might serve as the foundation for cooperation among provinces, variations in the profiles of provincial government coalitions may tend to weaken the potential for cooperative activity. That is, a strict adherence to considerations of electoral success, wherein the satisfaction of the demands of coalition members is of overriding importance, would mean that the governing party of each province brings quite different concerns to the bargaining table. In part, this might account for the difficulty the provinces have had in presenting a united front to Ottawa — a fact that has undermined their position and strengthened the hand of the federal government.

An examination of the ways in which party coalitions are formed may help to illuminate important aspects of the Canadian political process. Brokerage politics are hindered by the unrepresentative nature of political parties. The provincial dissimilarity of party profiles encourages the use of regional appeals and reduces the prospects of intergovernmental cooperation.

Notes

1. I am indebted to David Elkins and Richard Johnston of the University of British Columbia, and to Richard Simeon of Queen's University for their comments on an earlier draft of this chapter.

2. Robert Axelrod, "Where the Votes Come From: An Analysis of Electoral Coalitions, 1952-1968," *American Political Science Review* (March 1972): 13.

3. "The size of a group is the proportion of all adults of voting age who are members of that group. The turnout of a group is the proportion that voted in a given election. The loyalty of a group to a certain party is simply the proportion of the votes of that group which are cast for that party." Ibid., p. 12.

4. There are a number of reasons, both substantive and practical, why we do not use Axelrod's approach. First, our focus is not the same as that of Axelrod. While Axelrod was interested in specifying and examining the components of a group's contribution to an electoral coalition, such concerns are peripheral to our major purpose. We focus on the dimensions of variation, on the relative magnitude of differences in electoral coalitions by party, by province and by level of government. Secondly, replicating Axelrod's analysis for ten provinces and four parties would be too cumbersome. In addition, turnout — one of the factors affecting the contribution of a group — is relatively invariant in the data used for this analysis.

5. Edwin R. Black, *Divided Loyalties: Canadian Concepts of Federalism* (Montreal and London: McGill-Queen's University Press, 1975); Richard Simeon, *Federal-Provincial Diplomacy: The Making of Recent Policy in Canada* (Toronto: University of Toronto Press, 1973). See also the growing body of literature on the theme of "province-building": Edwin R. Black and Alan C. Cairns, "A Different Perspective on Canadian Federalism," *Canadian Public Administration* (March 1966): 27-44; Thomas A. Hockin, *Government in Canada* (Toronto: McGraw-Hill Ryerson, 1976), chap. 2; Larry Pratt, "The State and Province-Building: Alberta's Development Strategy," in *The Canadian State: Political Economy and Political Power*, ed. Leo Panitch (Toronto and Buffalo: University of Toronto Press, 1977), pp. 133-62; Alan C. Cairns, "The Governments and Societies of Canadian Federalism," *Canadian Journal of Political Science* (December 1977): 695-725.

6. Donald V. Smiley, *Canada in Question: Federalism in the Seventies*, 2nd ed. (Toronto: McGraw-Hill Ryerson, 1976), p. 102.

7. Harold D. Clarke et al., *Political Choice in Canada* (Toronto: McGraw-Hill Ryerson, 1979), chap. 3.

8. Clarke et. al., *Political Choice in Canada*, chaps. 5 and 10.

9. Recall that the composition of coalitions is in part a function of loyalty. On federal-provincial vote switching see George Perlin and Patti Peppin, "Variations in Party Support in Federal and Provincial Elections: Some Hypotheses," *Canadian Journal of Political Science* (June, 1971): 280-86; J. A. Laponce, *People vs Politics* (University of Toronto Press, 1969), 167-74; John Wilson and David Hoffman, "The Liberal Party in Contemporary Ontario Politics," *Canadian Journal of Political Science* (June 1970): 177-204.

10. For a brief summary of many of the important regional differences see Mildred A. Schwartz, *Politics and Territory: The Sociology of Regional Persistence in Canada* (Montreal and London: McGill-Queen's University Press, 1974), pp. 25-50.

11. See Chapter II for a discussion of provincial differences in the distributions of political efficacy and political trust. On political parties see Harold D. Clarke et al., "Partisanship and Party Images" (Paper presented to the Canadian Political Science Association, Quebec, 1976).

12. Donald E. Blake, "The Measurement of Regionalism in Canadian Voting Patterns," *Canadian Journal of Political Science*, 5 (March, 1972): 55-81.

13. See the review in John C. Terry and Richard J. Schultz, "Canadian Electoral Behaviour: A Propositional Inventory," in *The Canadian Political Process*, rev. ed., ed. O.M. Kruhlak, R. Schultz, and S.I. Pobihushchy (Toronto: Holt, Rinehart and Winston, 1973), pp. 248-85.

14. George M. Hougham, "The Background and Development of National Parties," in *Party Politics in Canada*, 3rd ed., ed. Hugh G. Thorburn (Scarborough: Prentice-Hall, 1972), pp. 2-14.

15. John Meisel, *Working Papers on Canadian Politics*, 2nd enlarged ed. (Montreal and London: McGill-Queen's University Press, 1975), chap. 1 and app., table I.

16. Meisel, *Working Papers*, chap. 1; see also the discussion of polarization in F.C. Engelmann and M.A. Schwartz, *Canadian Political Parties: Origin, Character, Impact* (Scarborough: Prentice-Hall, 1975), pp. 196-203.

17. In this discussion and in the analysis to follow, Social Credit and le Ralliement des Créditistes are treated as a single party.

18. N.H. Chi provides a regional breakdown for class groupings in his "Class Voting in Canadian Politics," in *The Canadian Political Process*, ed. Kruhlak et al., p. 237, and "Class Cleavage," in *Political Parties in Canada*, eds. C. Winn and J. McMenemy (Toronto: McGraw-Hill Ryerson, 1976), p. 101. For data on party coalitions in the constituency of Vancouver-Burrard see Laponce, *People vs Politics*, pp. 63-66.

19. The following discussion is based on a single data set which combines information from the three Canadian National Election Studies. A more detailed description of the nature of these data will be given in the text.

20. Of course, generalizations such as these are subject to the qualification that supporters of each and every party cannot be found in each and every province. In terms of federal politics, we have a sufficient number of cases to analyze Liberal and Conservative voters in all ten provinces, NDP voters in Quebec, Ontario, Manitoba, Saskatchewan and B.C., and Social Credit voters in Quebec, Alberta and B.C. The pattern is the same at the provincial level, except that we do not have enough cases to examine NDP supporters in Quebec.

21. See, for example, J. Anthony Long and F.Q. Quo, "Alberta: Politics of Consensus," in *Canadian Provincial Politics: The Party Systems of the Ten Provinces*, 2nd ed., ed. Martin Robin (Scarborough, Ont.: Prentice-Hall, 1978), pp. 1-27.

22. This data set has been deposited in the Data Library at the University of British Columbia.

23. This formula is algebraically identical to that used in Chapter V. For a discussion of this measure see Otis Dudley Duncan and Beverly Duncan, "A Methodological Analysis of Segregation Indexes," *American Sociological Review* (April 1955): 210-17.

24. Differentially weighting the parties would introduce some party effects into our measure of provincial dissimilarity. And differentially weighting the provinces would introduce some province effects into our measure of party dissimilarity. In an effort to keep the two indices as distinct as possible, differential weighting techniques have been avoided. Each party and each province are actually unweighted or, in other words, weighted equally by a factor of one.

25. See the remarks in the preceding footnote.

26. Categorized as follows: subjective social class — upper, middle, lower/working; community size — over 500,000, 10,000 to 500,000, less than 10,000; language — English, French, Other; religion — none, Catholic, Anglican, United Church/Presbyterian, Other Protestant, Other.

27. The means (and standard deviations) are: community size = 6.44 (6.70); age = 5.07 (3.08); religion = 7.08 (4.51); language = 2.00 (2.22).

28. We decided to keep the "over 500 000" category distinct because, in terms of both votes and seats, cities of this size are of substantial political importance to parties.

29. Grace M. Anderson, "Voting Behaviour and the Ethnic-Religious Variable: A Study of a Federal Election in Hamilton, Ontario," *Canadian Journal of Economics and Political Science* (February 1966): 27-37; Richard Rose, "Comparability in Electoral Studies," and Mildred A. Schwartz, "Canadian Voting Behaviour," in *Electoral Behaviour: A Comparative Handbook*, ed. Richard Rose (New York: Free Press, 1974), pp. 17 and 579-83 respectively. On the persistence of the religious cleavage in patterns of partisanship see William P. Irvine, "Explaining the Religious Basis of Canadian Partisan Identity: Success on the Third Try," *Canadian Journal of Political Science* (September 1974): 560-63.

30. The coefficients of variation are: language = 0.86; religion = 0.31. The coefficient of variation is the ratio of the standard deviation to the mean.

31. For a comparison of religious and linguistic cleavages see Kenneth D. McRae, "Consociationalism and the Canadian Political System," in *Consociational Democracy: Political Accommodation in Segmented Societies*, ed. Kenneth D. McRae (Toronto: McClelland and Stewart 1975), pp. 238-61.

32. It should be pointed out that Alford focuses on what we have called group loyalty, whereas Chi is concerned with the group contribution to an electoral coalition. See Robert Alford, *Party and Society: The Anglo-American Democracies* (Chicago: Rand McNally, 1963), chap. 9, and Chi, "Class Voting in Canadian Politics," pp. 228-36. Clarke et al., *Political Choice in Canada*, pp. 107-19, find weak to modest correlations between several measures of social class and vote choice.

33. For income groups, the mean index of party dissimilarity = 16.08 and the mean index of provincial dissimilarity = 19.37. For educational groups, the mean party index = 18.52, the mean provincial index = 19.72. The variables were categorized as follows: income — less than $3,000, $3,000 to $4,999, $5,000 to $9,999, $10,000 to $14,999, $15,000 and over; education — 0 to 7 years, 8 to 10 years, 11 to 13 years, over 13 years.

34. Recall that we did not have enough cases to examine the NDP and Social Credit coalitions in New Brunswick.

35. Alan C. Cairns, "The Electoral System and the Party System in Canada, 1921-1965," *Canadian Journal of Political Science* (March 1968): 55-80.

36. There are too few cases to examine the NDP's provincial coalition in Quebec.

37. The coefficient of variation for language = 0.87; for religion = 0.32.

38. For coalitions defined in terms of income, the mean index of party dissimilarity = 16.33 and the mean index of provincial dissimilarity = 22.09. For education, the mean party index = 12.57, the mean provincial index = 22.19.

39. Compare the overall means in Table 25 with that on the level of government dimension $(\overline{X} = 5.27)$.

40. With the partial exception of Newfoundland, where equal proportions of Catholics vote Liberal and Conservative.

41. Smiley, *Canada in Question*, chap. 4 and the sources cited therein.

42. See the sources cited in Engelmann and Schwartz, *Canadian Political Parties*, pp. 308-309.

43. Richard J. Van Loon and Michael S. Whittington, *The Canadian Political System: Environment, Structure and Process*, 2nd ed. (Toronto: McGraw-Hill Ryerson, 1976), p. 230.

44. For a journalistic account of the ways in which party platforms differ from one area of the country to the next, see Walter Stewart's discussion of the 1972 federal election, *Divide and Con: Canadian Politics at Work* (Toronto: New Press, 1973).

45. Smiley, *Canada in Question*, chap. 4; Simeon, *Federal-Provincial Diplomacy*, pp. 31-35.

VII
The Structure of Provincial Party Systems[1]
David J. Elkins

Most scholars who analyze Canadian political parties agree that they can be arranged on a left-right continuum. That dimension is assumed to structure the parties, with the NDP on the left, the Liberals in the middle, the Conservatives just to the right of the Liberals, and the Social Credit on the right.[2] The Créditistes are more difficult to locate, not because the left-right dimension is deemed inappropriate, but because they manifest both leftist-populist elements and rightist-authoritarian components. Although unstated, the assumption apparently is also that this is a national party system.

Yet no one denies Meisel's dictum that "almost any statement made about Canadian voting behaviour as a whole can be shown to be strongly contradicted in some region or among some section of the population."[3] Could it be, therefore, that the left-right arrangement of the parties applies only to some regions or only in the eyes of some groups? Indeed, is the left-right dimension, or any single dimension, sufficient to describe the structural relations among the major Canadian political parties? Even if one dimension is adequate, do some regions or groups of people arrange the parties along the continuum in a manner contradictory to others?

A useful way of approaching these questions might be to examine in detail party pronouncements, speeches by leaders and candidates, records of party activities and votes in Parliament. While there is merit in such an approach, its difficulties outweigh the advantages at least for the purpose of analyzing Canadian elections and party competition, since actual party positions are less relevant to voting than the electorate's perceptions of the relative location of parties. This chapter will examine evidence from the 1965, 1968 and 1974 federal election studies which bears on voters' perceptions of party arrangements along a presumed left-right dimension. As in all the chapters so far, provinces provide the major lines of cleavage among party systems. Here, however, the situation is even more complex. The left-right dimension, while relevant everywhere in Canada, does not exhaust the dimensions required to describe many provincial party systems. Even in areas which are unidimensional, provincial populations disagree about the proper left-right ordering of the parties. Furthermore, supporters of any given party frequently disagree with supporters of other parties over the location of their party.

The Party Distance Model

While largely descriptive, such a study has some interesting theoretical touchstones deriving from the analysis of elections and party competition in terms of "party distances."[4] This tradition of analysis derives from economics, particularly from the theory of retail firms which rests on a spatial model of competitive behaviour. The assumption that consumers will minimize transport and travel costs to get equivalent merchandise implies that major competitors will locate near each other if the clients are distributed evenly or at least symmetrically over a Euclidean space. If one store is near the population centre and the other is on the periphery, then the former is predicted to prosper while the latter languishes.

Such an analysis can be defended in the economic domain since it is quite reasonable to interpret the distances in terms of physical coordinates and driving time, and because we have many examples of firms which are nearly identical in terms of the goods and services they offer. The Bay and Eaton's, or Simpsons and Eaton's, are generally located quite near each other in each city.

To translate this theory into the language of party competition, however, raises certain problems. Nevertheless, it has a plausible interpretation. How does a party gain votes? By winning them from other parties. Which other parties are most susceptible to raiding? The parties nearest or closest to the party trying to win them. What does closest or nearest mean in this context? At least four distinct interpretations can be given: (1) nearest in size; (2) most recent ally in a coalition; (3) most similar in ideology; and (4) most similar in types of supporters. Furthermore, closest is usually assumed (following the lead of economics) to refer to distance on a line (that is, a one-dimensional continuum like the "main street" of economic analysis). There is, however, no reason to asume that the "space," or arena, in which parties compete is unidimensional. Party space can be two-, three- or n-dimensional. This paper will test the unidimensional possibility and show that it is not adequate. Regions and groups differ in their perceptual and cognitive structuring of the party arena, and hence Canada has party systems in the plural. Precisely how many dimensions are needed to describe the divergent perceptions and which dimensions these are (beyond left-right) cannot be demonstrated with existing data. Some suggestions, however, will be offered.

While size, coalition behaviour, ideology and types of supporters might all serve to indicate distance between parties, the focus here is only on ideology, since spatial models of party competition have always interpreted distance in those terms.[5] In some cases, mention is made of types of supporters, as when Philip Converse and Henry Valen discuss the Agrarian party in Norway.[6] But a demographic characterization of parties is generally made for the purpose of inferring the ideological bases of differentiation.[7] Parties differ, it is implied, because they attract and repel different types of people.[8]

The reader will recall the lines of party cleavage inferred from client support groups in Chapter VI. There we demonstrated that such differences rival interprovincial differences and that the variations in party support by socioeconomic and ethnic groups follow closely what one would predict based on ideology and group interests.

Coalition formation may be a useful consideration in the analysis of Italian, Norwegian or other party systems, but not in the case of Canada since it is so rare.

No one, as far as I know, has suggested that parties nearest each other in size will exchange members or supporters more frequently than parties less equal in this respect.[9] Nevertheless, this will probably occur in most cases, since the largest parties are often located next to each other on other dimensions, defined by ideology or supporters, and since they are generally near the middle of the spectrum. Where the largest parties are not contiguous, however, it might be worth exploring the pattern of interchanges.

Probably the most searching criticism of party distance as a model of competition, or at least of the version formulated by Downs, is an article by Donald Stokes.[10] It will be useful to outline briefly his major concerns so that we may test them specifically or at least guard against the errors he criticises. Stokes categorizes his comments in terms of assumptions in Downs's formulation. These are the "axioms" of unidimensionality, fixed structure, ordered dimensions and common reference.

Unidimensionality is obviously important for theoretical elegance and simplicity. It is equally clear that this is a stringent demand which is rarely encountered in actual party systems.[11] One of the principal concerns in this chapter, therefore, is the extent to which Canadian parties are perceived on a single dimension (whether left-right or some other).

The axiom of fixed structure points out a related weakness. If more than one dimension characterizes the space of party competition, one cannot assume that bases of competition and evaluation are referenced to the same coordinates at two different times. Stokes points out, for example, that between 1948 and 1952 the bases for electoral evaluation changed drastically in the United States.[12] Whereas up to 1948 voters appeared to cast their ballots on the basis of economic and social issues of the New Deal-Fair Deal era, 1952 saw the decline in importance of these matters and the assertion of foreign policy as a major preoccupation. As Stokes rightly points out, this was not a substitution of one unidimensional model for another: instead, "the presence of a given evaluative dimension is often a matter of degree."[13] Hence we must not only ask how many dimensions are perceived but whether they vary in importance over time.

A Canadian example also reveals clearly the way voters may shift their frame of reference in a brief period. In British Columbia in 1952, the CCF and Social Credit parties were seen as close to each other on the dimension of "protest" parties, though widely separated on the left-right dimension. By the 1953 provincial election, however, Social Credit was the government, and the "distance" from the CCF on the "protest" as well as left-right dimensions reduced to insignificance the transfer votes between these parties.[14]

To speak of dimensionality and fixed structure implies that there are dimensions along which members of the electorate might be arrayed, and their perceptions of the parties might therefore locate the parties in a well-defined "space." Many political issues do not, however, generate a dimension at all because no one will take the opposing side. For example, everyone is opposed to corruption in government. Similarly, no one campaigns on the promise of increasing inflation or unemployment, though the voters make up their minds (at least some do) that one party will do a better job of fighting inflation than another. These examples point up a nontrivial conclusion: "The machinery of the spatial model will not work if the voters are simply reacting to the association of the parties with some goal or state or symbol that is positively or negatively valued."[15] Canadian elections, I believe, are especially prone to these "valence" issues, as Stokes calls them: instead of parties disagreeing among some set of alternatives, they often agree on policy but disagree about who could implement it better. Mr. Stanfield, in the 1972 election, for example, repeatedly stated that he would have done essentially what the Liberals had done about wages and prices, but he would have done it a few months sooner.

Given the data, this problem of valence issues cannot be adequately explored. Nevertheless, since some of the problems in characterizing the structure of the Canadian party systems may stem from it, this chapter emphasizes the need for research on political issues in Canada.

Finally, Stokes questions the axiom of common reference. "We may, in fact, have as many perceived spaces as there are perceiving actors."[16] Although he is concerned with whether party managers share a perceived space with the electorate, the present concern is with the variety of ways people in different regions or in different parties perceive relative party position. One could, of course, extend the analysis to examine the perceived party spaces of members of classes, religions, language groups, gender and age cohorts, urban or rural residents and ideologues. Due to space limitations, however, these will be ignored in favour of the subsets of the sample surveys defined by party identification and region of residence. These two classifications demonstrate that there are several party systems perceived by the Canadian electorate, and that some features vary over the decade of 1965 to 1974.

Although not mentioned in this light by Stokes, the axiom of common reference raises the question of unidimensionality in another form. In particular, multidimensionality can mean either of two things: either people ("judges" in scaling terms) agree about the nature of the space, and they perceive it to consist of n-dimensions; or each of them perceives the parties ("stimuli") on a single dimension, but different sets of people rely on different dimensions.[17] It is the latter situation which generally appears to obtain in the Canadian data presented below.

It should be clear that this chapter focuses on the structure of citizens' perceptions of the Canadian party systems and not on the structure of competition itself. The foregoing discussion indicates that perceptual structures may be relevant to the analysis of competition, and competition may in turn affect to some degree the nature of the perceptions.[18] This chapter, however, simply tests some of the "axioms" which underlie spatial models of party competition.

Data Sources and Limitations

To study the structure of the Canadian party systems at the federal level, the data analysis will be guided by assumptions and procedures drawn from scaling and measurement theory. The problem formulated in these terms is, essentially, how can we use voters' perceptions and behaviour to measure the parties' positions? How can we describe the relations among the party positions most succinctly, given such information?

As in the previous chapters, the data consist of interview responses in the 1965, 1968, 1974 and merged data sets. All three studies involved national samples. While the samples may have been adequate for studying nationwide patterns in federal elections, they are less so for provincial subsets or for provincial elections. The reader should treat the conclusions with appropriate caution. In addition, of course, the findings refer to a specific decade of Liberal dominance in federal politics.

Each survey was less than fully reliable in other respects as well, just as any survey is. For example, an important concern in this analysis is whether a voter has switched parties. Some people do not remember accurately for whom they voted, some remember but lie about it so as to appear to have voted for the eventual winner, and others claim to have voted when they did not.[19] For present purposes these are annoying but not fatal considerations, for at least two reasons. For one thing, there are half a dozen tests of the basic hypotheses, and all use different items but reach almost identical conclusions. One therefore feels more confident than if reliance were made only on one datum. In addition, memory errors and deception are assumed to be more or less randomly distributed through the party system and voter types, rather than being overrepresented in one type such as the citizens claiming to shift from party X to party Y.

Judgment Ratings

Turning now to the data, let us examine first the responses to a question which appears to be the most straightforward and directly relevant to our purposes.[20] Respondents were asked to assign each political party to a position on the left-right continuum, with "one" indicating the farthest left position and "seven" the farthest right. This is obviously a "judgment scale" and suffers from the problems typical of judgment scales (especially the assumption that respondents have sufficient information to make the discriminations). Table 1 gives the means and standard deviations for each

Table 1
Means and Standard Deviations of Canadian Political Parties on Left-Right Scale as Judged by Persons Identifying with Major Political Parties

Party identified with	Party Rated					
	PC	LIB	NDP	SC	CRED	N
1965						
Progressive Conservative	4.84(1.35)	4.16(1.46)	3.59(1.59)	3.94(1.55)	3.54(1.68)	545
Liberal	4.37(1.55)	4.72(1.50)	3.51(1.58)	3.99(1.59)	3.67(1.72)	775
New Democratic	5.15(1.49)	4.29(1.51)	3.84(1.81)	4.44(1.63)	4.05(1.87)	207
Social Credit	4.76(1.35)	4.42(1.54)	3.57(1.72)	4.67(1.60)	3.66(1.40)	90
Créditiste	3.89(1.28)	3.98(1.43)	3.81(1.05)	4.02(1.50)	4.61(1.57)	43
1968						
Progressive Conservative	4.62(1.41)	4.08(1.39)	3.50(1.43)	4.70(1.35)	4.21(1.55)	641
Liberal	4.30(1.45)	4.59(1.43)	3.44(1.53)	4.56(1.43)	3.97(1.65)	1254
New Democratic	4.64(1.57)	4.39(1.42)	3.85(1.72)	4.51(1.34)	3.60(1.92)	266
Social Credit	4.51(1.43)	4.03(1.59)	3.24(1.63)	5.06(1.48)	5.50(2.12)	78
Créditiste	3.68(1.30)	4.03(1.50)	3.85(1.12)	not asked	4.61(1.52)	40

Cell entries are mean scores; standard deviations are placed in parentheses. All figures are for the national total of identifiers, except that Créditiste identifiers are only from Quebec. The Créditistes (in Quebec) were not asked to rate the Social Credit Party in 1968.

party: that is, for the people who identify with a particular party a mean score is given for each party rated by them. For example, the Conservative identifiers in 1965 rated themselves as 4.84, the Liberals as 4.16, and so on. Figure I summarizes the position of the means presented in Table 1; this should make it easier to visualize the average distances involved. This question was not asked in the 1974 survey. In Table 2, a similar but less useful question from the merged 1968 and 1974 data set is summarized.

If these scores reflect the perceptions of different party identifiers, then there are clear contrasts between party electorates in how they perceive the

Figure I
Locations of Canadian Parties on Left-right Scale of 1–7, as Judged by Persons Identifying with Major Parties

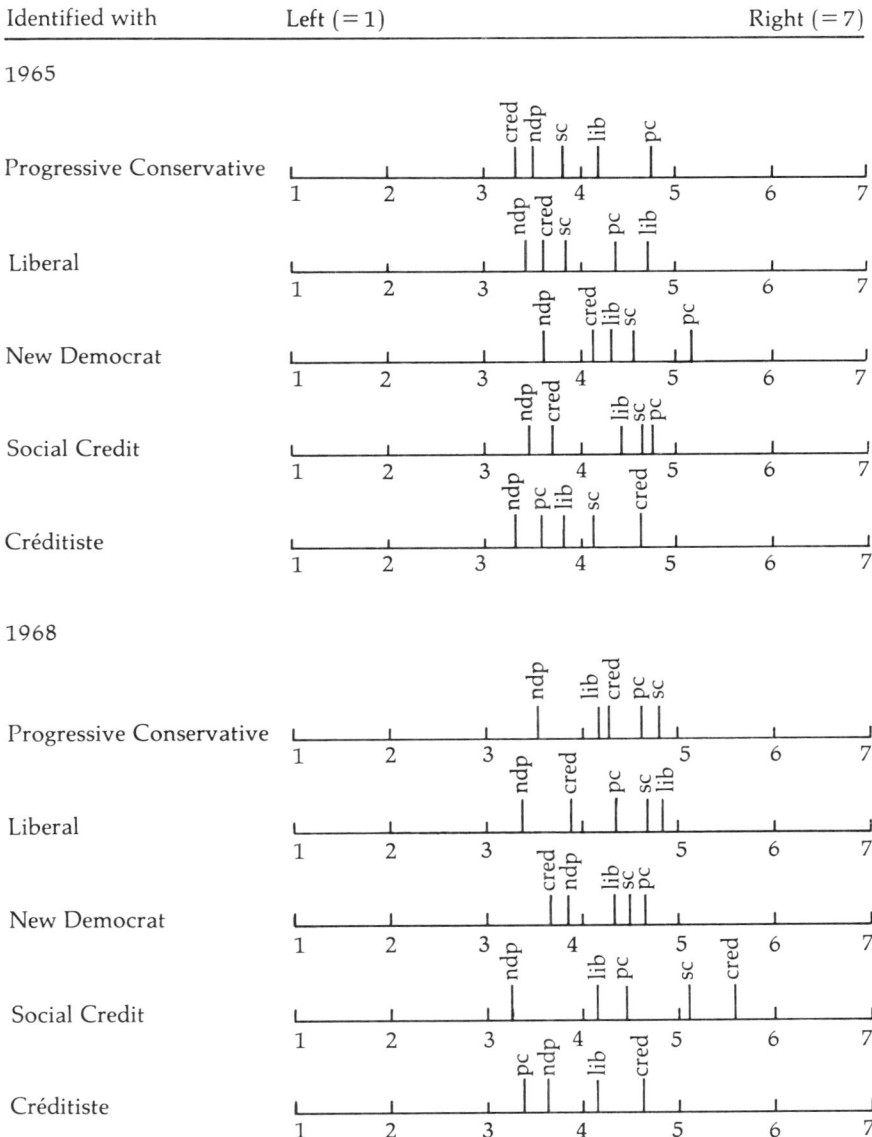

rank order and the absolute distances between parties.[21] For example, the Progressive Conservatives perceive the Créditistes as the farthest left party in 1965, while the Créditistes see themselves as the most right party.[22] Social Credit is placed in the middle (in fact, slightly to left of centre) by the Conservatives and Liberals in 1965, and yet Social Credit identifiers place themselves to the right of all parties except the Conservatives in 1965 and the Créditistes in 1968.[23]

In addition, there are some differences between 1965 and 1968. The Créditistes have generally been placed much more to the right in the latter year, except by the NDP identifiers who still see them as quite leftist. In part these shifts may reflect changes in party platforms, but more likely they indicate the unreliability of the judgments made in what must be considered a very difficult task for respondents.

Nevertheless, there is stability in the diversity. The NDP is nearly always the party ranked farthest left and is left of centre (that is, less than four) for each averaged set of identifiers. The Conservatives are usually the farthest right, though not always, and are always scored right of centre (except by the Créditistes in both years). Interestingly, Social Credit is hardly ever ranked farthest right, and is actually scored left of centre by some parties.[24]

Besides these stable points, one might note a curious coincidence which may say something about Canadian political culture: there is a clear tendency for *each* party's own identifiers to score that party farther to the right than each other party's identifiers score it. This is true for both years, and the only exceptions are that the NDP sees the Conservatives as more rightist in 1965 than PC members see themselves (and about the same in 1968), and Social Crediters score the Créditistes to the right of where the Socreds see themselves. This tendency is particularly clear in the case of the Liberals and Conservatives; each ranks itself as the most right party, as though they were vying for the position of most conservative. In Canada there may be an underlying feeling that the party on the right is somehow better or in a more advantageous position electorally.

To check on this possibility, one can see how these same groups score the party they consider "ideal." They were all asked to place such an ideal on the same one-to-seven scale along with the actual parties already discussed. Members of every party (on average) scored the ideal party as right of centre (that is, a higher score than four) in both 1965 and 1968. The rank orders of the ideal parties follow the same general left-to-right pattern as in Table 1, but with the whole system moved towards the right. Even NDP followers, on the average, placed their ideal as slightly right of centre. That they all feel their own parties are not perfect, in the sense of coinciding with the ideal, is revealed in the correlation of the score each person gave the ideal party and the score he gave his own party. The correlations (Goodman and Kruskal's gamma) range from .504 to .704, depending on year and party. These correlations also suggest, however, that the image of one's own party may be in part a reflection of one's image of the ideal party, or vice versa. Whatever the causal background, the tendency of each party to overestimate its rightward position (relative to other parties' estimates) is evident.

Table 2 presents mean scores and standard deviations on the so-called "feeling thermometer." This device requires that respondents indicate the degree of "warmth" they feel towards an object, in this case political parties. Zero indicates maximum coldness or lack of warmth, fifty equals neutral, and one hundred signifies maximum warmth. Unlike the previous exercise which specified a left-right dimension, the feeling thermometer leaves it to each respondent to define the dimensions of party evaluation underlying his degree of warmth. Unfortunately, the study did not ascertain these underlying dimensions, so we do not know to what extent "left-right" or other factors are manifested here. This table is, therefore, not generally useful, but it helps to throw light on the cultural tendency just noted to desire an ideal party different from one's own.

The first notable feature, at both the federal and provincial levels, concerns the perception of one's own party. Although it is not "ideal," one's own party is clearly rated higher than any other. Furthermore, except for Social Credit (and Créditiste) self-image at the provincial level, the ratings of one's own party are quite high, in the seventies, but not the maximum. Equally significant, the ratings identifiers of any party give to other parties

Table 2
Means and Standard Deviations of Canadian Political Parties Rated on
"Feeling Thermometer" by Persons Identifying with Major
Political Parties (Rounded to Nearest Integer)
Merged Data (1968 and 1974)

(a) Party Identified with at Federal Level:	Federal Party Rated				
	PC	LIB	NDP	SC/CRED	Range of N=*
PC	73(17)	48(21)	40(22)	38(23)	408-1139
LIB	49(19)	77(14)	42(22)	37(22)	974-2336
NDP	46(19)	49(20)	78(15)	34(22)	212-480
SC	47(20)	49(23)	37(23)	77(18)	98-157
(b) Party Identified with at Provincial Level:	Federal Party Rated				
	PC	LIB	NDP	SC/CRED	Range of N=*
PC	71(18)	52(22)	40(21)	34(22)	400-1147
LIB	49(19)	77(15)	42(22)	36(23)	800-1954
NDP	47(19)	51(22)	75(18)	35(22)	238-528
SC	54(21)	55(23)	33(23)	64(23)	268-299

*N in (a) & (b) varies according to which party is rated; generally there was the most missing data for SC/CRED.

fall below fifty in every case at the federal level, and in eight of the twelve cases provincially. Such low scores indicate considerable lack of warmth, even for parties ideologically quite close to one's own.

The other feature of these data concerns the rank orders based on warmth. For almost every set of identifiers with a party, the rank order of warmth differs from the order in Table 1. I interpret this to mean that respondents are capable of distinguishing between questions about general like or dislike ("warmth") of other parties and the left-right ordering of those parties. This is a small bit of evidence for attitudes of *real politik* among the mass publics.

In light of this differentiation between left-right and warmth, the data on "ideal" parties may be seen differently. The general rightward shift of ideal parties does not indicate a desire to be nearer any other particular party, since in many cases the party to the right is quite unattractive and viewed "coldly." Instead, the information on "ideal" parties probably reflects some deep-seated cultural belief that "right" is preferable. This finding raises as many questions as it answers, however, because the NDP preference for right of centre suggests that "correct" might be a better characterization. If "right" can mean different things for different parties, or for different survey questions, one must also question the value of the left-right dimension itself, except where these terms have been carefully specified.[25]

Leaving aside the adequacy of the definitions of left and right, that dimension clearly is insufficient in itself to account for the variations above. Thus our tentative conclusion so far must be that left-right, while probably an important element of the electorate's perceptions, reveals disagreements between groups in the use of that dimension to order these political parties.[26] Later data reinforce these views.

The "Unfolding" Technique

Since we saw in the previous section that respondents could not, for whatever reason, give absolute distance scores for the parties which were consistent for all sets of party identifiers, we now turn to other questions that require less information and prior thought. Analyzing preferences and behavioural data of this latter sort, however, requires other methodological techniques. The most promising, called the "unfolding" technique, was developed for precisely this sort of data by the psychologist Clyde Coombs.[27]

Whereas a judgment scale requires each respondent to locate himself or a stimulus object on a predetermined scale, preferential data consist of stated preferences among a set of stimuli on the basis of perceived distance from the respondent. The resulting datum indicates that subject i prefers stimulus j to stimulus k. This is assumed to mean that the distance from i to j is less than that from i to k. The analysis below does not focus on individual responses directly, however, but on groups of responses which give a unique ordering for an entire set of party identifiers or party voters in different regions. Thus the data in the tables below should be interpreted as showing that "supporters of party i prefer party j to party k."[28]

Suppose we ask three individuals (X, Y, Z) to tell us their preferences among four alternatives (such as the parties A, B, C, D). It is possible that we will get the same rank order for each. If we do, no unfolding is necessary; but if they give different orders, we ask ourselves whether there is any way to test the hypothesis that they are all responding to the same underlying structure or order but assessing it from different points of view. This obviously is a direct test of what Stokes calls the axiom of common reference. Imagine that these three persons stated the following preferences (from their most preferred to least preferred party): ABCD (for person X), CBDA (for Y) and DCBA (for Z). Note first that the preference orders for individuals X and Z are mirror images: what is most preferred for one is least for the other, and so on. That means that both rankings are consistent with the hypothesis that there is a single common dimension on which both rank the parties, but they prefer opposite ends of this dimension. The crucial question then is, can the ordering of individual Y be interpreted as also consistent with that common dimension?

To see that Y's responses are consistent with those of X and Z, note that Y's perspective may lie between those of X and Z. In other words, imagine that the common dimension on which they all rank the parties had been "folded over" by person Y; then the parties which are equally to the left and

Figure II
Hypothetical Scale

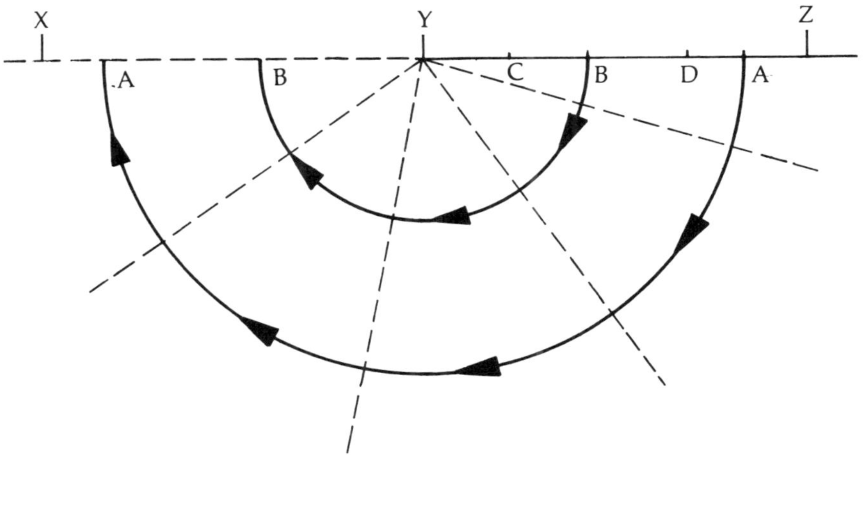

right of him would be ranked at the same point in his preference hierarchy. If one "unfolded" his ordering, these parties would then be on opposite sides of him. By examining Figure II, the reader may verify that an unfolding of the preferences for Y (CBDA) can yield the same underlying common dimension as for individuals X and Z. Since party C is the closest to Y, he ranks it first, party B is next closest (though when unfolded it may rest on the other side of Y from C), and so forth.

If we can unfold several responses to produce the same order, then we may hypothesize that all three individuals have in mind the same common dimension and, furthermore, rank the parties on *that dimension* in the same order. It will thus be seen that, depending on the perspective of the respondent based on his own place on the dimension, very different *preferences* may be clues to the same rank order on an underlying dimension (such as left-right). At the same time, there are preferences which would violate this hypothesis: for example, if Y gave as his preferred order CADB, it could not be unfolded in a manner consistent with the preferences expressed by X and Z.

A set of preferences for several people will fail to unfold uniformly if the ordering on the common dimension is different for different respondents, or if they are employing different dimensions altogether in making their judgments. In the ensuing tables, therefore, a statement that a set of responses unfolds signifies that all of the responses are consistent with the hypothesis of unidimensionality and common reference. When they do not unfold, that means that at least one set of responses failed to satisfy these requirements.

That a set of responses "unfolds" in this sense does not, of course, *prove* that each respondent in fact perceived the dimension in the same way or would order every object in this same manner if they did perceive identical dimensions. Such proof requires additional data derived from questions about the exact nature of the underlying dimension. The unfolding technique, however, does provide a stringent test of the hypothesis that respondents share a common dimension. We can, therefore, feel relatively confident, even if not certain, when several groups unfold similarly.

There are many possible variations in interparty distance which are consistent with the same ranking of parties. This is illustrated in Figure III. Obviously, both scales in Figure III, when unfolded around the point PC, have the same left-right ordering of the parties; but the intervals between the parties are different. Consequently, the folded scales (that is, the observed preference rankings for the individuals corresponding to PC) are PC-LIB-NDP-SC in Scale I and PC-LIB-SC-NDP in Scale II. The analysis that follows ignores the differences in interparty *distance* reflected in these two preference rankings (especially noticeable with regard to SC) and unfolds them both as the same left-right *ordering* of the parties. This is perfectly legitimate, but it simplifies the "party space" perceived in Canada (though not the orderings) more than would be the case if one

Figure III
Hypothetical Scales with Different Metrics

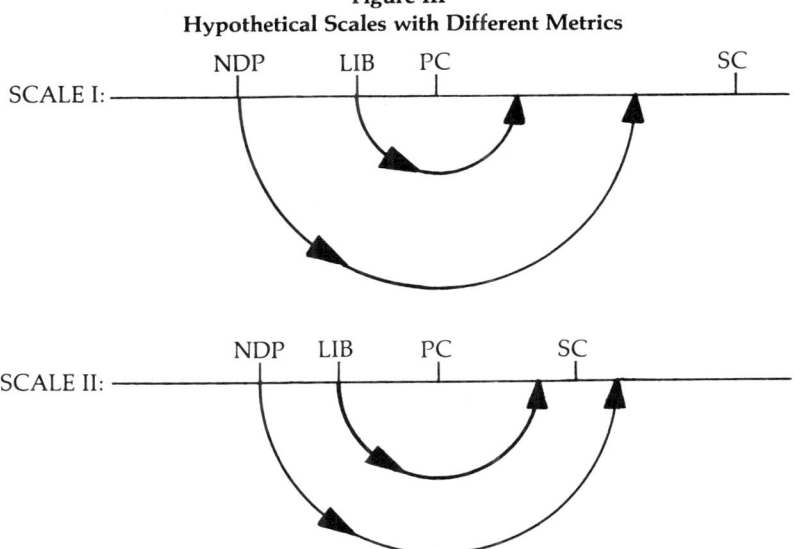

Scale I: **respondent located at PC would give his preferences as: PC-LIB-NDP-SC, by folding the scale as indicated**

Scale II: **respondent located at PC would give his preferences as: PC-LIB-SC-NDP, by folding the scale as indicated**

considers the differences between Scale I and Scale II in absolute distances. Before considering the data below, it will be well to clarify two assumptions central to this version of measurement theory.

Some of the data concern judgments which the respondents are asked to make; for example in Table 1 they were asked to assign numbers indicating the left-right location of all the parties. Other data, such as voting switches from one election to the next, are reports of behaviour. A third type of data is explicitly preferential: the respondent is asked to state his preference among alternatives, such as what his second choice of party would be if he could not vote for his first. The behavioural data are also presumed to reflect preferences; it is our task to infer these from their behavioural cocoon.

In using personal preference data, the fundamental assumption may be called the principle of least effort, or of least distance. By this is meant that if an individual cannot attain his first preference, he will shift to the next one closest to the first. It also means that if an individual is forced to choose among alternatives, he will choose the one he feels closest to at that time; and if he is asked to rank alternatives, he can be expected (unless instructed otherwise) to rank them according to their relative distance from himself, or from the alternative which corresponds to his own position. (By "distance" here, one can read "degree of similarity," "amount of favourable affect," or other appropriate paraphrases according to context.)

This assumption cannot be tested with the present data. Instead it *defines* what we mean by distance. There is, however, a good basis for this assumption in psychological theory and in its use in previous research.[29]

The import of this principle of least effort for the analysis of the structure of party systems can be vividly seen in the interpretation of switching parties in successive elections. For a voter to switch from party X to party Y means that he prefers both parties to party Z; that is, we assume that the distance between X and Y is less than that between X and Z. While there are difficulties with this inference in real elections (Social Credit runs few candidates so that a voter cannot always "reveal" his preference for it relative to other parties, and some people vote against their own party for strategic reasons), the overall analysis of several hundred switchers can be assumed to follow this general line of reasoning.[30]

A related assumption, or more exactly a convention of measurement, concerns the aggregation of these individual preference rankings. The more people who choose a particular pair of alternatives (for example, switching from party X to party Y), the more similar the alternatives are thought to be. In other words, although each person's preferences indicate only a rank order, in the aggregate they can be interpreted to define a unit of measurement (called an equal interval level of measurement). While there are some controversial features to this convention, they need not detain us.[31] For the analysis to follow I am interested only in the rank order of preferences of individuals, groups and regions, and not in the resulting metric.

Preference Rankings

Respondents were asked how they had voted in the most recent federal elections. They were also asked at a later point how they would have voted had their chosen party not nominated a candidate in their riding, and what their least favoured choice would have been. By considering the Créditistes in Quebec as part of the Social Credit party, it is thus possible to infer a rank order of all the parties for each respondent who answered all relevant questions. There are twenty-four possible ways in which four objects may be ordered, and each of the twenty-four preference orderings was expressed by someone. The number of people preferring a particular order, however, varied from one-tenth of 1 per cent of the sample to over 20 per cent. Given what was said in the previous section, it is obvious that these preference rankings cannot all be consistent with a single underlying order. Therefore, the question is which order on an underlying common scale receives the most support when each of these twenty-four observed rankings are unfolded, and how many people do not fit that unfolding.

Since we know from an earlier section that the point of clearest stability is the left position of the NDP, each of the preference orderings was unfolded in terms of the six possible rankings which placed the NDP at the left. Some of the orderings could be unfolded in only one way, while others fit more than one of these possibilities. Table 3 summarizes the results. The column entitled total percentage adds up to more than 100 per cent because some of the observed preference rankings could be counted as support for more than one ordering on the underlying dimension. The unique percentage column, on the other hand, indicates the proportion of the total sample whose unfolding was compatible with only one ranking on the common dimension. (Since the results are quite similar for each of the samples, I have presented the figures only for 1968 and for the merged data set.)

Table 3
Proportion of Samples "Unfolding" When Asked About Current Federal Vote, Second Choice and Last Choice

	Merged Data		1968	
Unfolded as:	Total percentage	Unique percentage	Total percentage	Unique percentage
A. NDP-LIB-PC-SC	64.7	12.7	69.4	9.3
B. NDP-PC-LIB-SC	57.7	5.1	59.7	2.7
C. NDP-LIB-SC-PC	21.7	4.0	22.3	5.1
D. NDP-SC-PC-LIB	32.0	0.9	42.5	0.4
E. NDP-PC-SC-LIB	16.1	7.6	15.9	9.5
F. NDP-SC-LIB-PC	32.8	0.8	39.4	0.1

Consider an example. In 1968, 21.1 per cent of the respondents indicated the preferred order: Liberal, Conservative, Social Credit, NDP. This preference ordering may be unfolded in four ways with the NDP on the left: (1) NDP, Liberal, Conservative, Social Credit; (2) NDP, Conservative, Liberal, Social Credit; (3) NDP, Social Credit, Conservative, Liberal; and (4) NDP, Social Credit, Liberal, Conservative. In each case, the scale has been unfolded around the point "Liberal" (since these were all Liberal voters in 1968), and the orders differ according to which parties have been unfolded to the left of the Liberals. Thus these respondents are counted in the "total percentage" columns corresponding to alternatives A, B, D and F in Table 3. It should be apparent that this preference ordering does not fit with unfoldings C or E in Table 3, because this would violate the relative ordering of the Conservative and Social Credit parties.

A similar logic was applied to each of the twenty-four orderings, and Table 3 summarizes this information. It will be noted first that among the six types of responses which were uniquely capable of unfolding, some represent a very small part of the total sample. This indicates that, while there is no single dimension (or ordering on that dimension) which satisfies everyone, there is only a limited amount of variability to be accounted for. (Every ordering could equally well unfold as its mirror image; but the evidence from

Table 1 shows that the NDP is on the left and not the right.) Judging by the numbers of total and unique supporters, it seems fair to eliminate alternatives D and E, that is, those rankings with the Liberals as the party farthest to the right. Hence, our task will be to decide among alternatives A, B, C and F.[32] As we shall see, regions and parties differ in terms of which unfolding fits the data.

Respondents were also asked (in 1965 only) to name the pair of parties which they believed to be most alike. (It was not specified by the interviewer or by the respondents on what dimension or dimensions the likeness was assessed.) In the case of each set of party identifiers and in the national total the Liberals and the Conservatives were overwhelmingly listed as the most similar pair. This lends support to alternatives A, B and F in Table 3. Since hardly anyone thought that the NDP and Social Credit were the most similar pair (only 2.9 per cent of the total sample) it seems reasonable to focus on alternatives A and B as the most likely basic orderings, although we shall see below that other orderings do occur among some subgroups, especially in British Columbia.

Although it is not possible with these data on similar pairs to give a definite answer to the question of whether A or B is the "correct" ordering, it may be worth noting that slightly more people "voted" for alternative A (89.5 per cent of the total sample) than for alternative B (83.0 per cent). The most plausible conclusion from these figures is that the poles of the continuum seem relatively definite (NDP on the left and Social Credit on the right), but there is considerable disagreement about the relative left-right position of the Liberals and Conservatives. This is true regardless of which set of party identifiers one examines. Hence it may also be deduced that each party is internally divided over the proper ranking.

Two additional pieces of evidence may be cited in support of the above line of reasoning. For one, respondents in 1965 were also asked to name the pair of parties *least* alike. Many respondents could not do this, indicating that it is a much more difficult task or that they did not care about that aspect of the situation. At any rate, the largest response category was NDP-Social Credit, though this category was not much larger than the others. Only the Créditiste supporters failed to render this category the largest. Secondly, for both the most alike and least alike questions, those people who stated that they had a very strong party identification revealed a pattern almost identical to the one above.

Returning to Table 3, we find alternatives A, C and F are consistent with an ordering of the three major parties as NDP-LIB-PC. Alternatives B, D and E, on the other hand, give a contrary ordering of NDP-PC-LIB. Using either total or unique percentages, therefore, the former ranking slightly exceeds the latter in all years and in the merged set. All of the evidence so far, then, favours the ranking NDP-LIB-PC (with variations in the location of SC); but the lack of unanimity warns us of the possibility that provincial samples or party groupings may have contrary views. As we shall see, both of these possibilities do occur.

Rankings Derived from Behavioural Choice

The preference data just presented, while less difficult for respondents than the judgment scales in Table 1, are still relatively demanding. The respondent must, on the spur of the moment, give a definite rank ordering which implicitly involves all of the parties. For many people, of course, this is routine since they are deeply concerned about such matters; but for most respondents one suspects that it was the first time they had ever entertained the notion of ranking the parties. Hence we turn now to data of a behavioural sort which should reflect more accurately the thought-out preferences of most voters. In particular, we compare votes in successive elections, party identification expressed at the time of the interview with any previous party identification (if different), and current party identification with current vote. In these behavioural indicators, each individual generally states a preference only among two objects, but the overall sample affords the opportunity to rank the parties according to the relative frequency with which pairs are chosen. This follows from the assumptions discussed earlier: a choice of a pair indicates that they are closest together in the eyes of that respondent, and the more respondents who see that pair as close, the closer they are deemed to be in the aggregate.

If a person is identified with a party, he is very likely to vote for that party. However, in every party there are identifiers who are willing to support another party because of the overriding importance of a particular issue or candidate presented by another party. If the respondent's party is perceived as fairly "close" to another party, the chances are greater that he will defect to that party rather than to a more distant party. Hence the rate at which party identifiers switch to a party other than the one they have identified with should indicate their perceptions of the relative distances between parties. Within a given region, there will be two, three or four rankings, depending on the number of parties whose supporters are included in the provincial sample. These rankings have been unfolded and the results summarized in part A of Table 4. Within a given party there are three (SC), seven (NDP) or ten (LIB, PC) rankings, depending on the number of provinces in which sufficient numbers of supporters of a given party were sampled. These party rankings have been unfolded and the results summarized in part B of Table 4.[33]

The most general conclusion to be drawn from Table 4 (and the following tables as well) concerns diversity: there is no single dimension or ordering upon which every province, every party or the federal and provincial levels of a province or party agree. It is impossible to say whether all respondents rely on the left-right dimension. But if they do, then it must be the case that they perceive quite different orderings of the political parties

Table 4
Party Vote Compared to Party Identification, Unfolded by
Province and by Party (Merged Data)

| | | Unfolded Scales* | |
		Federal	Provincial
A.	By Province		
	1. Newfoundland	not unique**	not unique**
	2. P.E.I.	not unique**	not unique**
	3. Nova Scotia	not unique**	NDP-PC-LIB
	4. New Brunswick	not unique**	NDP-LIB-PC
	5. Quebec	does not unfold	does not unfold
	6. Ontario	NDP-LIB-PC-SC	NDP-PC-LIB-SC
	7. Manitoba	NDP-LIB-PC-SC	NDP-PC-LIB-SC
	8. Saskatchewan	does not unfold	does not unfold
	9. Alberta	does not unfold	NDP-PC-SC-LIB
	10. B.C.	does not unfold	does not unfold
B.	By Political Party***		
	1. Liberal	NDP-LIB-PC-SC	does not unfold
	2. Progressive Conservative	NDP-PC-LIB-SC	does not unfold
	3. NDP	does not unfold	does not unfold
	4. Social Credit	NDP-LIB-SC-PC	not unique**

* Abbreviations: LIB = Liberal, PC = Conservative, NDP = New Democratic Party, SC = Social Credit and Créditiste.

** "Not unique" means the preferences can be unfolded in more than one way; except for SC, the two forms of unfolding are: NDP-LIB-PC and NDP-PC-LIB. For Social Credit at the provincial level, the two forms of unfolding are: NDP-SC-LIB-PC and NDP-LIB-SC-PC.

*** The party groupings are based on current federal or provincial party identification.

on that dimension. Equally, if not more, plausible is the assumption that more than one dimension is required to structure these perceptions. I shall explore this possibility in the next section of the chapter.

More specifically, at the federal level, Ontario and Manitoba unfold in such a way that all four parties agree on the ordering: NDP-LIB-PC-SC. Since the four Atlantic provinces can be unfolded in a way consistent with this (namely, NDP-LIB-PC), it may be fair to say that eastern Canada generally agrees on this ordering on the underlying dimension. Quebec would unfold the same way, except for the Créditistes who see the Conservatives as farthest to the right and themselves as next to the Liberals.

In the West, there is extreme variability. Manitoba, as noted, agrees with Ontario, but the other provinces disagree with that ranking and with each other. The Conservatives and NDP in Saskatchewan and the Liberals, Conservatives and NDP in Alberta and British Columbia all agree on the ordering: NDP-PC-LIB-SC; but the Liberals in Saskatchewan and Social Credit in Alberta insist on: NDP-LIB-PC-SC; and Social Credit in British

Columbia remains deviant with: NDP-SC-PC-LIB (or possibly: NDP-LIB-SC-PC). Such variety cannot be reduced to a single ordering; but it is nevertheless clear that the preponderant weight of evidence suggests quite divergent perceptions between eastern and western Canada.

Still at the federal level, the parties exhibit two clear patterns.The NDP does not unfold, indicating its internal disagreement over the rankings of the other parties; and the other three parties unfold in different ways. The Liberals and Conservatives agree that the NDP is on the left and Social Credit on the right, but disagree over their own positions in the middle. Social Credit does not grant its right wing status, insisting that the Conservatives fill that position.

The NDP's internal dissension follows exactly the east-west split noted above. In Manitoba and the East, the NDP ordering is: NDP-LIB-PC-SC, which fits with the provincial arenas unfolding that way. In Saskatchewan, Alberta and British Columbia, however, the NDP ranks the parties as: NDP-PC-LIB-SC, at the federal level.

Without other evidence, one cannot reach firm conclusions about the meaning of this east-west division. A speculation or hypothesis, however, worth pursuing concerns the general character of the two main parties. I

Table 5
Current Party Identification Compared to Previous Party Identification,
Unfolded by Province and by Party (Merged Data)

		Unfolded Scales	
		Federal	Provincial
A.	By Province		
	1. Newfoundland	not unique	not unique
	2. P.E.I.	not unique	not unique
	3. Nova Scotia	NDP-LIB-PC	does not unfold
	4. New Brunswick	NDP-LIB-PC-SC	NDP-LIB-PC
	5. Quebec	does not unfold	does not unfold
	6. Ontario	NDP-LIB-PC-SC	NDP-LIB-PC-SC
	7. Manitoba	NDP-PC-LIB-SC	NDP-PC-LIB-SC
	8. Saskatchewan	NDP-PC-LIB-SC	NDP-PC-LIB-SC
	9. Alberta	NDP-LIB-PC-SC	NDP-LIB-PC-SC
	10. B.C.	does not unfold	does not unfold
B.	By Party*		
	1. Liberal	not unique	NDP-LIB-PC-SC
	2. Progressive Conservative	NDP-LIB-PC-SC**	does not unfold**
	3. NDP	does not unfold	does not unfold
	4. Social Credit	NDP-PC-SC-LIB	not unique***

See notes to Table 4.

* The party groupings are based on current federal or provincial party identification.

** Except for Alberta, the Conservatives would also unfold as NDP-PC-LIB-SC.

*** Two possible forms of unfolding: NDP-PC-SC-LIB or NDP-LIB-SC-PC.

would suggest that the Conservatives are viewed as more centrist in the West than in the East, because they are more centrist there and the Liberals conversely are more centrist in the East. Whether the strength of the Conservatives in the West encourages their "populist" or "red Tory" nature, or vice versa, is also worth exploring.

Turning to the provincial level, we notice the same or greater degree of variety, but also some interesting differences of pattern. For one thing, Nova Scotia and New Brunswick differ in the relative placement of the Liberal and Conservative parties. Note that it is in Nova Scotia, where the Conservatives have been especially strong in recent years, that they are the more centrist party. This fits with the explanation of the east-west pattern noted above.

Even more dramatic is the federal-provincial difference in Ontario and Manitoba, which fits again the hypothesis that the Conservatives are stronger where they can occupy the centre or left of the spectrum. The success of the Big Blue Machine in Ontario may have affected the perceptions of the electorate.

The great diversity of provincial patterns, of course, should lead to internal disagreement within parties. Such is clearly the case, as none of the parties unfolds uniquely. Perhaps we should concede to Social Credit, though, the ranking: NDP-LIB-SC-PC, since that is one of the two unfoldings possible at the provincial level and it corresponds to the unambiguous federal ordering.

When one compares the orderings based on different behavioural indicators of preferences, one expects somewhat different results. Therefore, it is pleasing when the general lines of analysis coincide. In Table 5, we examine the preferences revealed by changing party identifications over time, as opposed to Table 4 which compared current identifications and current votes. The general pattern is the same: no overarching consensus; an east-west split; and federal-provincial differences (though muted ones).

If we ignore the nonuniqueness of P.E.I. and Newfoundland and count them as NDP-LIB-PC, then except for the Créditistes in Quebec, all groups in Ontario and east of there are compatible with the federal ordering NDP-LIB-PC-SC. Most but not all of the western groupings share the ranking NDP-PC-LIB-SC, with Manitoba being grouped in the West this time.

The provincial level corresponds fairly closely to the federal, where unfolding is possible. Nova Scotia, however, cannot be unfolded at the provincial level; and Quebec and British Columbia lack internal unity at both levels.

The parties unfold less clearly at the federal level than in the previous table, but about the same provincially. It is clear from Tables 4 and 5 that the large provincial differences divide most of the parties, just as they divide the country as a whole.

If switching party identification can reveal implicit orderings among the parties, then switching one's vote while retaining one's identification should

Table 6
Vote Switching Between Federal Elections, Unfolded by
Province and by Party (Merged Data)

		Unfolded Scales*
A.	By Province	
	1. Newfoundland	not unique
	2. P.E.I.	not unique
	3. Nova Scotia	NDP-LIB-PC
	4. New Brunswick	NDP-LIB-PC-SC
	5. Quebec	does not unfold
	6. Ontario	NDP-LIB-PC-SC
	7. Manitoba	NDP-PC-LIB-SC
	8. Saskatchewan	NDP-PC-LIB-SC
	9. Alberta	does not unfold
	10. B.C.	does not unfold
B.	By Party**	
	1. Liberal	not unique
	2. Progressive Conservative	NDP-PC-LIB-SC
	3. NDP	does not unfold
	4. Social Credit	not unique***

See Notes to Table 4.

  * There was no information on vote switching between provincial elections, so these results refer only to the federal level.

 ** The party groupings are based on current federal vote.

*** Social Credit can unfold two ways: NDP-LIB-SC-PC or NDP-PC-SC-LIB.

also reveal similar patterns. These patterns based on vote switching at the federal level are presented in Table 6. (None of the surveys questioned respondents about vote switching at the provincial level.)

As before, there is great diversity among and within parties and provinces. The east-west division of the provinces appears in these data, as in Tables 4 and 5, this time with Manitoba fitting the western pattern. The Liberals unfold in either of two ways (NDP-LIB-PC-SC and NDP-PC-LIB-SC) and are thus listed as having a nonunique solution. The Conservatives hold to their general pattern of putting themselves to the left of the Liberals. The NDP, as always, is too internally diverse to unfold at all. And Social Credit maintains its typical pattern of: NDP-LIB-SC-PC.[34]

It seems clear by now that the degree of consensus in parties and regions is high on some matters but not on others. The NDP is uniformly considered leftist, and, except in the West, Social Credit is on the right. However, the relative position of the Liberals and Conservatives varies by region, and sometimes by parties. Also the Atlantic provinces have fewer parties than elsewhere.

In conclusion, this set of data, like several of the previous ones, suggests that there is some tendency to use the left-right dimension to structure perceptions of the party systems in Canada, but other dimensions must also be at work or there are different interpretations of how to use the left-right continuum. At any rate, it is clear that there are regional differences which seem to be fairly stable in the way voters see the array of parties and in the way they behave in those systems.

Multiple Models

We have just seen evidence of the diversity of party rankings among partisan groups and among the provinces. Such evidence is interesting but ambiguous. It may demonstrate any of the following possibilities. (a) The reality of party policies and strategies is so different in various regions that the voters' perceptions are affected, hence accurately yielding different orderings on the left-right dimension. (b) The left-right dimension is adequate as far as it goes, but it must be supplemented by one or more other dimensions in order to handle the great diversity of perceptions. (c) The left-right dimension is totally inadequate, the variety of findings reflecting the near-random responses of electors interviewed, rather than changing reality or multi-dimensionality.

There is something to be said in favour of each of these interpretations. Party policies, leaders, strategies and other factors—which do vary widely among areas—no doubt are capable of affecting perceptions. If we did not believe that, then perceptions would hold no interest for the political analyst, only for the psychiatrist. But these variations in reality cannot account for all the variations in the data. In what way does "reality" differ for people identified with different parties but residing in the same locale? What differs, I would argue, is that partisan groups can focus on different dimensions on which to rank the parties. Or they can focus on different types of issues or policies on which to base judgments of left-right positioning (e.g., economic policies versus civil liberties). This clearly is a possible version of the second alternative above, and I shall shortly explore some multidimensional models of the party systems. The third option, randomness, may be correct for some subset of respondents; but it is unlikely to account for the generally stable patterns presented in Tables 4 to 6, particularly bearing in mind that most of the year-by-year analyses are similarly stable. The fact that there are changes between 1965 and 1974 could be due to randomness but is equally likely a result of changing events and issues and therefore perceptions.

In a nutshell, we need multidimensional models to account for all the cases. The strategy I shall pursue is this: try to find the simplest plausible model for each province and for each party; compare them; if they differ (as they do), then is there a still more complex model which can account for all of the data nationwide? To avoid undue suspense, let me note here that one can always devise a model to account for n groups in a "space" with n-1 dimensions; such models are trivial, however, and the interest centres on models of less than n-1 dimensions. In other words, with ten provinces, a nine-dimensional model by definition achieves a perfect fit to the data; but only models of fewer dimensions hold our interest. In fact, I will explore only the one- and two-dimensional models here. In the case of a province with four party groups, a three-dimensional model will always work, but will a single dimension or a two-dimensional model do as well?

Let us consider the party groups first. These are, in principle, more difficult because there are ten groups of Liberals and of Conservatives which must unfold together, seven or eight groups of NDPers (depending on which type of data) and three groups of Socreds. Despite the numbers, however, if a party has any kind of "national" ideology or structure, the provincial wings should coincide. This is, in fact, the case only for the Liberals.

There are five types of data which were summarized in Tables 4 to 6: three at the federal level and two at the provincial. With ten provinces, there are fifty rankings of the parties by Liberals (five in each of ten provinces). All fifty rankings unfold in exactly the same way: NDP-LIB-PC-SC. Of course, the reader will recall that not all subgroups unfold *uniquely* in that fashion, but all unfold in this way either uniquely or as one of two possibilities. Hence my conclusion is that the Liberals across the country all view the party system in this unidimensional manner, which corresponds to most political scientists' opinion as to the left to right order of the parties on social welfare and economic issues.

The Progressive Conservatives, on the other hand, manifest internal diversity. In Ontario, Quebec and the Atlantic provinces, all thirty (five types of data times six provinces equals thirty rankings) cases unfold the same as the Liberals: NDP-LIB-PC-SC. This is the "eastern" model.

In the four western provinces, however, a slightly different situation obtains. Saskatchewan and Manitoba agree on: NDP-PC-LIB-SC; while Alberta and British Columbia share the unfolded scale: NDP-PC-SC-LIB. We can represent, therefore, all twenty cases of western rankings by Conservatives as a two-dimensional model, but then we must decide what to call the dimensions. I prefer, however, to think of these separate rankings as two versions of the left-right dimension, with the interprovincial variations within the West (and between East and West) as responses to the varying character of the Social Credit and Conservative parties in these areas.

If this reasoning is valid, then the Conservatives all utilize the left-right dimension. They do so differently in areas where "reality" leads them to perceive the order of parties differently on that dimension.

The NDP poses some methodological difficulties. Should we disregard the data on NDP supporters in the Atlantic provinces, where the number of responses may make the rankings less reliable? Equally vexing, should we ignore cases where, in a province, only one of the five types of data "deviates" from the norm for that area? To be safe, I shall present the results both ways, excluding these cases and again including them. The general conclusion is roughly the same both ways, but it is clearer when the "deviant" exceptions are excluded.

Basically, the NDP suffers from an east-west split similar to that of the Conservatives. In Ontario and east, fifteen out of seventeen party groupings fit the "eastern" model: NDP-LIB-PC-SC. The exceptions (NDP-PC-LIB) are both at the provincial level, one in Nova Scotia and one in Ontario, both of which have stronger Conservative parties provincially than federally. In general, the eastern "wing" of the NDP fits the eastern model.

Among the twenty orderings (four provinces and five types of data) in the West, thirteen of them uniquely fit: NDP-PC-LIB-SC, which corresponds to the basic "western" model. Four exceptions occur in British Columbia, and one each in the other three provinces. Each exception in Manitoba, Saskatchewan and Alberta is an instance of the "eastern" model, as is one of the B.C. exceptions. If these are "random" fluctuations in otherwise unequivocal provincial rankings, then the western model holds except for British Columbia, of which more will be said shortly.

Social Credit can be analyzed in only three provinces (because of sample sizes), so there are fifteen rankings to consider. Fourteen of these fifteen unfold as: NDP-PC-SC-LIB. This agrees with the general western model, except for the inversion of SC and LIB. The one ranking which does not fit this comes from British Columbia, as expected, where the provincial vote compared to provincial party identification yields a nonunique solution (either: NDP-LIB-SC-PC, or: NDP-SC-LIB-PC).

Leaving aside the minor exceptions noted above, then, the four party groups yield different models in every case. In some, unidimensional models are clearly sufficient, although different for each party. For others, we must either postulate a two- or three-dimensional model, or we must assume that the real differences in party images and policies cause the perceived orderings on the left-right dimension to differ. At any rate, the parties clearly constitute "small worlds," and these are often subdivided into smaller worlds involving a party-by-province interaction effect.

Provinces, like parties, require a diversity of models. We find again evidence of different "eastern" and "western" models, although as expected the western model is more complex.

The "eastern" model of: NDP-LIB-PC-SC obtains in sixty-three of the sixty-five orderings in Ontario, New Brunswick, Nova Scotia, P.E.I. and Newfoundland. (It also holds for three of the four party groups in Quebec, but this province will be analyzed separately below.) The two exceptions are the NDP in Ontario and Nova Scotia in one of the provincial level rankings, as noted above in discussing that party. Such minor deviations can be set aside, tentatively, and we can conclude that in terms of parties and provinces there is a general, unidimensional, left-right model.

In Quebec, as mentioned, the eastern model also provides a satisfactory representation, except for the Créditistes. The five types of data involving Créditistes yield the ranking: SC-LIB-PC-NDP. Since only the left-right ranking requires that the NDP be on the left, we can consider that other

Figure IV:
A two-dimensional representation of party system structure in Quebec

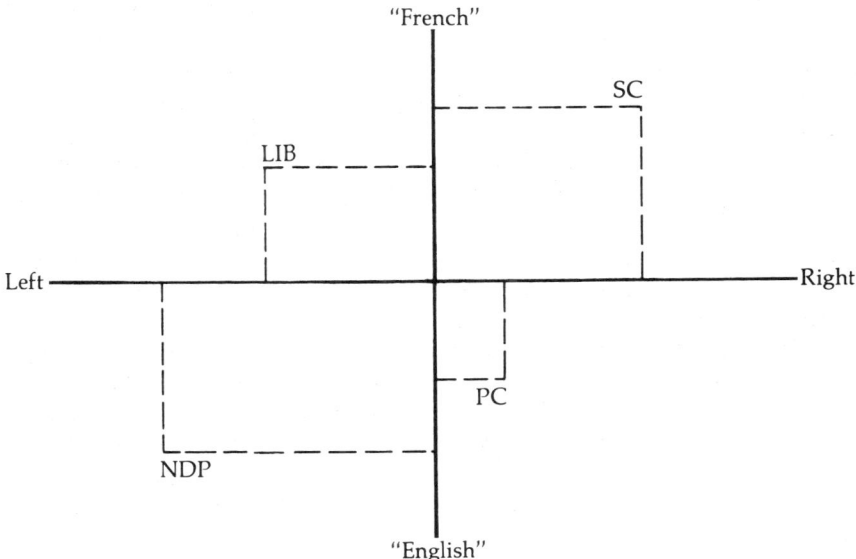

rankings on other dimensions are possible, of which the Créditiste prefer-ences are one. If they perceive the proper ordering in terms of a continuum from most "French" to least "French" (or possibly most to least Catholic), then their ranking of the parties makes sense. In that case, a two-dimensional model, shown in Figure IV, accommodates all of the Quebec data.

While this model is satisfying in the context of Quebec, it makes awkward the consolidation of Social Credit rankings presented above. If we accept Figure IV, then we must keep Créditistes separate from the Alberta and B.C. Socreds. Only future research can determine which of these interpreta-tions is correct, if either.

Saskatchewan and Manitoba can be represented by a one-dimensional model, probably interpreted as based on left-right, which corresponds to the western model: NDP-PC-LIB-SC. Twenty-seven of the thirty orderings fit this model, the three exceptions all deriving from the data on federal party vote compared to federal party identification (the Liberals in Saskatchewan, and the Liberals and NDP in Manitoba). Everyone agrees on the polar positions of the NDP and Social Credit, the disagreement occurring over whether PC is left of LIB. Since the exceptions all refer to the federal level, these may reflect some real differences between federal and provincial levels; but left-right is still the basic dimension.

Alberta takes us to the next level of complexity. Different models are needed for the federal and provincial levels, but neither fits any other models we have outlined. Federally, Albertans require a two-dimensional model, since the Conservatives and Socreds can agree on: NDP-SC-PC- LIB, but the Liberals and NDP achieve a nonunique solution (either: NDP-PC-LIB-SC, or: NDP-LIB-PC-SC). These differences cannot be reconciled, and the two dimensions cannot both be viewed as left-right. If there is a dimension other than left-right, its meaning is not obvious.

Provincially, a three-dimensional model is necessary to capture the Alberta data. At that level, the Conservative and Social Credit contingents can be made to agree on: NDP-PC-SC-LIB, which accords with their federal ordering only on the two end positions. The Liberals and the NDP, however, cannot even agree on the ends of a continuum, and so at least three dimensions are necessary provincially. For both levels together, three dimensions are also required.

British Columbia stands alone in its internal diversity. At both provincial and federal levels, three dimensions (or three versions of left-right ordering) are mandatory. If one omits the NDP, a two-dimensional model will handle the other three parties, but the interpretation of the dimensions makes no sense as left-right, as centre-periphery or as "protest" versus "establishment." In short, British Columbia is unique and uniquely complex.

Discussion and Conclusions

Before speculating on some of the implications of these findings, it may be helpful to review some observations about the nature of the questions analyzed in this report. For one thing, the use of several quite different types of data including judgment ratings, perceived preferences and behavioural manifestations, raises the chances of finding inconsistencies. We offer more hostages to fate as we increase the number and types of domains which can counter a hypothesis. Thus it comes as no surprise that there are idiosyncrasies in the findings presented here. At the same time, however, by broadening the attack we reduce our need to rely on one indicator which may be imperfect and unreliable. In fact, there are considerable consistency and stability in the patterns of data recorded above.

The clearest findings come in the behavioural indicators, and future researchers might do well to devise additional questions of this sort. For example, one might ask whether the respondent has ever considered switching parties, even though he may never have acted on it. For such persons, and for those who have changed their vote or identification, it would seem natural to ask them why, what might drive them out of one party or attract them to another. Only with more careful and detailed information can we be certain of the dimensions actually perceived. This is especially important in view of the fact that we have found it necessary to hypothesize one or even two dimensions besides the left-right in some areas. In fact, such probes would be invaluable even in the cases where one dimension proves adequate, because we are still not completely certain that the basic dimension is left-right.

When we speak of deviant provinces or parties, we must add that this deviance has been measured from only one perspective. The dimension explored has been the usefulness of left-right as a structuring principle for the party system in Canada. But the matter cannot rest with that. The real implication of finding peculiarities of perspective and behaviour in some groups or regions concerns the very adequacy of the left-right dimension itself.

It should be clear from these data that the left-right dimension is one useful organizing principle for the party systems in Canada. What is equally obvious is that at least one other dimension is required. To deny that is to admit that people are simply perceiving and behaving randomly when their answers fail to display a consistent left-right pattern. While randomness is not alien to the Canadian system, or to any other, it is a weak explanation and should be used only when all else fails.

Even without the refined data desired there are several interesting observations one can make from the information just analyzed. Perhaps most striking is the tendency for regions to unfold more frequently than parties. It appears that among party supporters, but especially the NDP, there are regional differences in perception of the party system's structure. On the other hand, we frequently found that there was consensus across parties within a given region about the perceived party space.

The contrast between "eastern" and "western" models of the party systems, while tentative, provides a fulcrum for analysis. Leaving aside a few minor exceptions, respondents in Ontario, Quebec and the Atlantic region agree on a single, left-right ordering of the parties: NDP-LIB-PC-SC. In contrast, the West was less unified in its perceptions, but the dominant view was: NDP-PC-LIB-SC, with British Columbia dissenting in several respects.

At the same time, except for the Liberals, each party revealed incipient or well-developed tendencies to divide along these same lines. The Conservatives and the NDP followed the above divisions, and so did Social Credit, if we keep Créditistes separate. As Laponce has also found, Social Credit seems to be more a middle of the road party in B.C. than elsewhere, and the distance between it and the NDP is considerably less there than elsewhere.

Although they share the model above, the eastern six provinces exhibit considerable internal variety which is partially masked by the present method of analysis. The Atlantic provinces have fewer parties, in at least two senses. They lack Social Credit identifiers (except a handful in New Brunswick), and the NDP is weak or nonexistent. Besides, when respondents are asked to rank or evaluate these two parties, they express only the vaguest awareness of their attributes.

Quebec generally fits the eastern model, except for its Créditiste identifiers, but this must be approached cautiously. We cannot examine provincial parties, such as Union Nationale and Parti Québécois, with small samples during a federal election campaign. In the light of the November 15, 1976 provincial election, changes at the provincial level may create a more complex system which may come to fit less and less the general eastern model.

Ontario, while providing the paradigm for the eastern model, is emulated exactly by no one. Each province is unique, although the variations may be centred around a specific mode.

In the West, the general model we developed fits less well the farther west one moves. By the time one crosses into British Columbia, one has left simplicity, parsimony and elegance behind: a three-dimensional model is required with *none* of the three dimensions corresponding exactly to the general model. This probably reflects the fact that the party competition of British Columbia is severe, and interparty distances generally large. Whereas most provinces, while differing from their neighbours, share across parties a common framework of analysis, such consensus is woefully absent in British Columbia and to a considerable degree also absent in Alberta.

Some of the variations we observe—especially the east-west divergence— seems to reflect accurate perceptions of differing realities. In the absence of better data gathered specifically to test this hypothesis, we should exercise caution, because reality is difficult to state categorically. That is why perceptions are interesting, and also why they are frustrating to analyze. Nevertheless, it seems safe to speculate that the Conservatives do better electorally where they are perceived as to the left of the Liberals, or more centrist. Whether this is causally accurate is doubtful; it is equally plausible that success at the polls helps to convince voters of the party's central position.

Social Credit, too, might be seen in this light. Where, as in British Columbia, it is both successful and centrist, it has been perceived as less right wing than in Ontario, Manitoba and Saskatchewan.

If there is an east-west contrast in models, this is not a centre-periphery split, as I had speculated in the earlier version of this report.[35] The Atlantic provinces are "peripheral" but fit closely the eastern model; and Quebec does not fit exactly the same model as Ontario.

Whatever we call these models, however, we can be certain that no simple, single model fits all cases. There is no *national* party system even at the federal level. Each party and each region is a small world.

There is, surprisingly, a national party—the Liberals. Although varying in strength in different regions, and although perceived in various ways by its opponents, this party shares throughout its ranks a consensus on how the four principal parties should be arrayed from left to right. One wonders whether its success derives from this nationwide framework, or whether its internal unity derives from its long-term success. Perhaps its relative lack of success in the Prairies—both federally and provincially—stems from its unwillingness to adapt to the local party systems, with an attendant mis-perception of its proper enemies and allies.

In concluding this chapter, we also end this section of the book. It is appropriate, therefore, to refresh the reader's memory about the way all of these conclusions fit together. Not only do the provinces differ in terms of the number of parties active and successful in each and in terms of the relative size of the major parties; they also differ greatly, as Johnston showed in Chapter V, in the degree to which federal and provincial levels in the same province coincide. In Chapter VI, Burke demonstrated that the parties were themselves divided along provincial lines as much as along party lines in the patterns of client-group support. Provinces, it seems, are not artificial political boundaries bridged easily by social, economic, religious and language groups in the populations.

Finally, in systemic terms, this chapter has presented the most dramatic evidence of variety among provincial party systems even at the federal level. The provinces contrast in terms of the adequacy of the left-right dimension and in terms of the stable ordering of parties on that dimension. Most important, they differ in complexity from several one-dimensional systems, a few two-dimensional systems, to two provinces requiring three dimensions to structure the perceptions of their residents.

It is important to note in closing that the regional and party contrasts which lead me to insist that there are several party systems and not one overall cognitive system are muted by the data presented here. By focusing only on perceptions of the parties and related behaviour during *federal* election campaigns, one reduces the chance of finding large and persistent differences. Yet these differences strike through these data with clarity. To conduct similar surveys during provincial elections in each region would undoubtedly sharpen the sense of disjointed political perceptions and preferences in different areas as well as reveal more vividly the exact dimensions on which divergence occurs.

Notes

1. This chapter is a revised and updated version of my article, "The Perceived Structure of the Canadian Party Systems," *Canadian Journal of Political Science*, 7 (September 1974): 502-524.

2. Robert R. Alford, *Party and Society* (Chicago: Rand McNally, 1963); John Meisel, *Working Papers on Canadian Politics* (Montreal: McGill-Queen's University Press, 1972), chap. 2; Jean A. Laponce, *People vs Politics* (Toronto: University of Toronto Press, 1969), p. 150; and the careful review of the literature in Conrad Winn, *Spatial Models of Party Systems: An Examination of the Canadian Case* (Ph.D diss., University of Pennsylvania, 1972), chap. 2.

3. John Meisel, "Conclusion: An Analysis of the National (?) Results," in *Papers on the 1962 Elections*, ed. Meisel (Toronto: University of Toronto Press, 1964), p. 286.

4. Donald Stokes, "Spatial Models of Party Competition," in Angus Campbell et al., *Elections and the Political Order* (New York: Wiley, 1966); and Anthony Downs, *An Economic Theory of Democracy* (New York: Harper and Row, 1957).

5. Ibid.; Philip E. Converse, "The Problem of Party Distances in Models of Voting Change," in *The Electoral Process*, ed. M. Kent Jennings and L. Harmon Zeigler (Englewood Cliffs, N.J.: Prentice Hall, 1966); Philip Converse and Henry Valen, "Dimensions of Cleavage and Perceived Party Distances in Norwegian Voting," *Scandinavian Political Studies*, 6 (1971): 107-52; Olavi Borg, "Basic Dimensions of Finnish Party Ideologies: A Factor-Analytic Study," *Scandinavian Political Studies*, 1 (1966): 94-120; Mogens N. Pedersen, Erik Damgaard and P. Nannestad Olsen, "Party Distances in the Danish Folketing 1945-1968," *Scandinavian Political Studies*, 6 (1971): 87-106; Gerald Garvey, "The Theory of Party Equilibrium," *American Political Science Review*, 60 (1966): 29-38; Richard Niemi, "Majority Decision Making with Partial Unidimensionality," *American Political Science Review*, 63 (1969): 488-97; Melvin Hinich and Peter Ordeshook, "Plurality Maximization vs. Vote Maximization: A Spatial Analysis with Variable Participation," *American Political Science Review*, 64 (1970): 772-91; Donald A. Wittman, "Parties as Utility Maximizers," *American Political Science Review*, 67 (1973): 490-8; Allan Kornberg, William Mishler, and Joel Smith, "Elite and Mass Perceptions of Canadian Party Location on Issue Space: Some Tests of Two Theories" (Paper presented at International Political Science Association meetings, Montreal, August 1973); and Bo Särlvik, "Mapping the Party Space: Distances, Evaluations, and Ideological Perspectives" (Paper presented at International Political Science Association Meetings, Edinburgh, August 1976).

6. Converse and Valen, "Dimensions of Cleavage," pp.114-16, 135, 147, 149.

7. See the seminal article by Vincent Lemieux, "La composition des préférences partisanes," *Canadian Journal of Political Science*, 2 (1969): 397-418, especially pp. 412-14.

8. William P. Irvine, "Voting Shifts in Canada: A Comparison of 1963-65 and 1965-68" (Paper presented to the Canadian Political Science Association meetings, Montreal, August 1973).

9. Winn, *Spatial Models of Party Systems*, pp. 76-7, 99, has suggested a "salience" dimension which is quite similar to the size criterion. Salience for Winn means likelihood of winning, and the prediction he makes is that voters will shift disproportionately to parties with better prospects of winning.

10. Stokes, "Spatial Models."

11. Referring only to material already cited, lack of unidimensionality has been demonstrated for the United States (Stokes), Finland and France (Converse), Norway (Converse and Valen), Denmark (Pedersen et al.), Canada (Kornberg et al.), and Quebec (Lemieux).

12. Stokes, "Spatial Models," pp. 168-9.

13. Ibid., p. 168.

14. David J. Elkins, "Politics Makes Strange Bedfellows: The B.C. Party System in the 1952 and 1953 Provincial Elections," *B.C. Studies*, no. 30 (Summer 1976), 3-26.

15. Stokes, "Spatial Models," p. 170.

16. Ibid., p. 175. Of course, the frame of reference of which the actor is aware may not be the one which triggers the action; but I am concerned more with describing cognitive and perceptual structures than with causes of behaviour.

17. Converse, "Party Distances," pp. 196-7, has made the same observation.

18. The article by Lemieux has some suggestive comments on the interplay of perceptions and competition in two Quebec constituencies.

19. Jean A. Laponce, "Non-Voting and Non-Voters: A Typology," *Canadian Journal of Economics and Political Science*, 33 (1967): 75-87, has a good discussion of several of the factors reducing reliability in self-reported behavioural data.

20. In fact, for our purposes, the question is ambiguous, too difficult for most respondents, and begs the question of dimensionality.

21. As small as some of the interparty ratings are in Table 1 and Figure I, most are statistically significant. This is particularly true for the Liberals and Conservatives, since ratings by them are based on quite large numbers of respondents; but even among the Créditistes, some of the differences are significant.

22. Winn, *Spatial Models of Party Systems*, pp. 164-9, also found the Créditistes difficult to pin down. Using other data, however, he found that they placed themselves on the left, while other party electorates located them on the far right. Most people find it difficult to locate a relatively new party which is active in only a few areas, since it is peripheral to their vision, interests and geography.

23. Social Credit, of course, suffers from many of the same "peripheral" problems as does the Créditiste party, since both are spinoffs of the same national party (in 1963). Some respondents were probably confused by the similarity of names, though the Francophone version of the questionnaire is the more confusing, referring to Créditistes in several different ways (Créditiste, Parti Créditiste, le Ralliement des Créditistes, le Ralliement des Créditistes de M Caouette).

24. Jean A. Laponce, "Note on the Use of the Left-Right Dimension," *Comparative Political Studies*, 2 (1970): 483-4, found the same ordering. However, in his book *People vs Politics*, chap. 7 and pp. 149-53, he found the classic ordering in most cases with the above order only in a subset of the sample. For a discussion of whether Social Credit in B.C. is left or right of centre, see Elkins, "Politics Makes Strange Bedfellows."

25. It is particularly interesting to find the left-right dimension not adequate here, since a left-right scale had been imposed on respondents. See R. L. Ogmundson, "A Note on the Ambiguous Meaning of Survey Research Measures Which Use the Words 'Left' and 'Right'," *Canadian Journal of Political Science*, 12 (Dec. 1979), 799-805.

26. The text has emphasized differences between parties, but the large standard deviations in Tables 1 and 2 and the regional differences within each party (presented below) demonstrate the lack of consensus internal to parties as well.

27. Clyde H. Coombs, *A Theory of Data* (New York: Wiley, 1964); and Warren Torgerson, *Theory and Methods of Scaling* (New York: Wiley, 1958), chap. 14. Winn has also applied the unfolding technique to Canadian party space but with different data and somewhat different results.

28. Of course, in some cases party i is also party j, as when a person who identifies with party i says he would vote for that party and no other.

29. Coombs, *Theory of Data*; see also Torgerson, *Theory and Methods*, who discusses these assumptions under the heading of the law of comparative judgment.

30. For an exceptional situation, see Gabriel Almond, *The Appeals of Communism* (Princeton: Princeton University Press, 1954). He found that some former members of the Communist party switched to right wing parties, apparently to maximize the distance from their past and perhaps to satisfy a need for authoritarian relationships.

31. The reader interested in pursuing this topic may consult Coombs or Torgerson.

32. Using the same procedures, I also analyzed the preference rankings implied by cross-tabulating party identification, second choice and last choice. The results were nearly identical to those in Table 3. Alternatives A, B and C (in Table 3) received by far the most support.

33. In the following tables, I present only the merged data; for the 1965 and 1968 results, readers may consult David J. Elkins, "The Perceived Structure of the Canadian Party Systems," *Canadian Journal of Political Science*, 7 (Sept. 1974); 502-524.

34. One must recall that I have combined the Socreds and the Créditistes. This simplifies the apparent diversity somewhat, since they are actually quite separate organizations. Nevertheless, these two groups agree on the unfolded ordering indicated in the tables.

35. Elkins, "Perceived Structure," pp. 523-24.

VIII
Regional Variations in Public Policy

Richard Simeon with E. Robert Miller[1]

So far in this book we have examined regional variations in public attitudes and political behaviour. We have looked primarily at individuals, and how their views are aggregated in voting and party structures at both federal and provincial levels. Given the interprovincial variations we have found, we should expect related variations in a great many other areas of political life, from the structure and behaviour of interest groups to legislative debating styles. In this chapter we turn to the activities of governments themselves.

Like several others, it is an exercise in comparative politics. We ask: do provinces pursue similar or different priorities in public spending? Are there significant variations in per capita government spending in the most important categories of public expenditure? In which categories are variations largest, in which smallest? And what explains the variations that we find? Do the differences arise from differences in economic structure, from differences in political formations or from historical, cultural or other differences unique to each province?

As in other previous chapters, we have given the analysis an historical character: has there been convergence or divergence over time? And, again, we have good reasons for expecting either. On the one hand, it would not be surprising to find that the cultural, party and behavioural differences we have examined, along with the increasing elite emphasis on interregional conflicts, all are associated with large and increasing interprovincial differences in the choices governments make, and in their allocation of scarce resources. Large provincial economic disparities should produce wide variations, both in the need for certain services and the ability to supply them.

On the other hand, Chapter III also suggested we should be cautious in making such inferences. There we found that attitudes on substantive policy questions differed much less than did political behaviour, identities or culturally based orientations. We also found a significant convergence of policy preferences, especially in the major fields of government activity. Moreover, comparative evidence—both across states and cities within countries, and across nations themselves[2]—suggests that differences in policy are modest, despite very large differences in history, institutions and culture. The imperatives facing government in modern industrial societies require that the state should play a similar role in all, however different the processes used to arrive at the allocation of resources.

If convergence is to be found in Canada, it could stem from two different sources—from what might be called the demand side or from the supply side, though not quite in the economist's sense of the terms. It could be that under the influence of similar living conditions, similar exposure to the mass media, and with the demonstration effects of other jurisdictions, citizen demands and expectations would come to be very similar in different political units. Greater economic development, the German economist Adolph Wagner suggested, may lead to greater demands for public services.[3] Thus governments would act alike because they face comparable political settings. On the other hand, it could be that the major constraint is not the expectations of citizens, but rather the resources available to governments to meet them. Variations in policy would in that case be better explained by the access of governments to revenues. Comparative studies of public expenditure have frequently shown that they are very highly correlated with factors roughly associated with economic development: per capita income, levels of education, urbanization, and the like. But they have not explored the "path," so to speak, through which these effects are exerted.

In Canada, we have an opportunity to examine, albeit somewhat crudely, the relative effects of the demand and supply sides. That is because the development of equalization payments to the provinces, together with extensive use of shared cost programs, makes provincial revenues (the ability to pay) substantially independent of the amount which could be produced by the productivity of the provincial economy. Provincial revenues from their own sources vary widely[4]—almost as widely as does provincial per capita income—though there are some variations resulting from different overall rates of taxation. But after transfers from other governments are taken into account, then total provincial revenues differ little, and are no longer strongly correlated with per capita income. Federal transfer programs almost eliminate the provincial variation in ability to purchase public programs. We then find that, in fact, variations in provincial expenditure also differ little, suggesting that it is indeed the ability to pay for programs which is most important. The federal government is thus an additional force which might be expected to promote convergence among the provinces, both because of its general payments to the provinces, and because of the specific inducement to provide programs such as medicare through the device of shared cost programs. We shall look at these effects in more detail.

Method and Approach
The comparative study of public policy is a diverse and complex field. Even

to describe the maze of government activity, let alone discover patterns within it, to explain how those patterns came about or to measure the impact of public activity on citizens and groups is a daunting task.[5] Perhaps only careful case studies can capture the richness of policy variation. Nevertheless, despite the pitfalls which it entails, there is much to be said for broad-scale comparative analysis of patterns of public policy such as that presented here.

The rapid growth of public expenditure in the postwar era sparked a large number of studies on the determinants of public expenditure, both among economists interested in public finance and among political scientists interested in the possible impact on policy outcomes of political factors such as which party is in power.[6]

Both groups have come to rely heavily on statistical quantitative measures of government activity, and to seek out quantitative indicators for the relevant explanatory factors. This chapter is a contribution to that literature. It presents a summary and description of provincial policies in eleven different policy areas, as measured by government expenditure. The basic data consist of variations among provinces in per capita spending, and in the proportion of total provincial spending devoted to each function for each of the nineteen years between 1956 and 1974. All figures are in constant dollars standardized to 1971, so we look at real rather than nominal changes.[7]

The primary measure of interprovincial variation is an index of dispersion. It expresses the standard deviation of the provinces around the national mean as a percentage of the mean. Low numbers indicate little provincial variation, high numbers a large deviation. Following the basic descriptive statistics we will present a regression analysis to help explain the patterns of variation.

Debate within the growing comparative literature on public expenditure has centred on the relative explanatory power of "economic" or "environmental" variables compared with political factors. For the political scientist, the question has been: does politics make a difference? Does it matter whether there is or is not a competitive party system, or whether New Democrats, Conservatives, Liberals or Social Crediters are in power? The striking conclusion of much of the literature is that it does not: that it is the wealth and economic development of cities, states or countries which is the primary shaper of policy output. As Harold Wilensky concludes in his study of social security in sixty-four countries: "Over the long pull, economic development is the root cause of welfare state development."[8] Such forces far outweigh the political factors, and, indeed, when economic factors are controlled, politics has little if any correlation with policy output. Some other studies, however, do rehabilitate the political variables, and find them especially important in explaining differences between units with similar economic conditions,[9] and in explaining variations in policies which have readily identifiable distributive effects on groups and classes. Fry and Winters conclude that in the United

States: "The political variables . . . are considerably more powerful than socio-economic variables in explaining variance in redistributive policies."[10] In one of the few Canadian studies, Dale Poel, however, concludes that two political factors—party competition and voter turnout—"show virtually no relationship to provincial policy levels."[11]

The econometric model used here attempts to sort out some of these questions. It introduces several categories of independent variables and examines the significance of each with the others controlled. First, per capita income and the proportion of the population living in urban areas are used as indicators of economic development. Second, differences in the costs of providing services in different areas are a complex problem in Canada where differences in terrain, population distribution and many other factors may be important shapers of spending needs. We have assumed that the major cost variation is found in rates of wages, and use this as our measure. Third, differences in federal transfer payments are measured by variation in equalization payments. Fourth, the political factors we explore include the proximity of elections and the party in power, grouping Liberal and CCF or NDP governments as "progressive," and Conservative and Social Credit governments as less so. Finally, we assess the residual variation of provincial characteristics not accounted for by other factors. These include differences both in demographic characteristics and in cultural and ideological character-istics. While the model does not include all the possibly relevant political or environmental variables, it does account for a high proportion of the variance, and it is sufficient to indicate the effect of different kinds of factors, which might be explored further in other studies.

The great advantage of the kinds of data used here is that they are readily available, mainly from Statistics Canada, are generally consistent over time, and allow us to compare activity in different policy areas. One must, however, be cautious about what they really mean. Public spending captures only some dimensions of governmental activity. It can tell us nothing about the actual content of what is done: two jurisdictions could spend the same amount on education but teach very different things.[12] Public spending is only one of the instruments or tools by which governments act. Others include regulation, public ownership and structural policies whose significance is not captured by the amounts which show up in government budgets. Gross amounts of spending tell us little about to whom the benefits flow or about how the burdens are distributed. Finally, expenditure figures can tell us little about the impact or effects of public policy. Ira Sharkansky identifies what he calls the "spending-service fallacy." The quality of education or the amount of learning taking place is not demonstrated by the amount spent. Indeed, he has shown that even in such a straightforward area as highways, state spending in the United States is only weakly correlated with many measures of the "output" of highways programs, such as mileage of roads built.[13] We shall not try to avoid this fallacy: it is one that all budget makers and observers themselves make. For comparative purposes, in which we are interested in differences and similarities in the amounts which governments commit to different purposes, and in which we assess the *relative* commitments of governments to these purposes, the use of measures such as those employed here is justified.

The following analysis, then, examines some dimensions of provincial public policy over the period from 1956 to 1974. It measures policy by per capita spending in constant dollars over time, and, in the descriptive summaries, by the proportion of total provincial spending devoted to a given policy field. We also examine some year-by-year changes in spending over different areas.

Gross General Expenditure and Revenues

We begin by examining trends in overall provincial spending and provincial revenues.[14] The growth in government, and of the provinces in particular is dramatically illustrated by the increase in overall provincial spending (gross general expenditure) from $186 per capita to over $1000, measured in real terms over the whole period from 1956 to 1974. Average provincial expenditures grew at 9.4 per cent a year in real terms. More important for our purposes, there was a substantial convergence among the provinces during the period. The index of dispersion reported in Table 1 has declined sharply, from 24.6 in 1956 to 9.3 in 1974. While the decline in variation across the provinces does not proceed evenly from year to year, the notable drop between 1957 and 1958, also reflected in the revenue figures, suggests the impact of the introduction of a full-fledged equalization program in 1957. In 1957, the ratio between the highest-spending province (British Columbia) and the lowest-spending (Manitoba) was two to one. By 1972, the lowest-spending province, Saskatchewan, spent almost three-quarters as much as the highest-spending one, Newfoundland.

More important, Table 2 shows a dramatic break between the wealth of provinces and their overall spending. In 1957, the three western provinces, led by relatively affluent British Columbia, were the largest spenders. The lowest four provinces in spending were also relatively poor, while the other two have-not provinces, New Brunswick and Newfoundland, were just below the average. By 1972, things had changed. The top four spenders were now the poorest provinces, led by Newfoundland and Prince Edward Island. The wealthiest provinces, Alberta, British Columbia and Ontario, were now at or below the national average. Thus there had been some dramatic changes in the rank ordering of overall spending: British Columbia from first to ninth, Saskatchewan from third to tenth, Quebec from ninth to third, Prince Edward Island from eighth to second.

Quebec, which after 1960 embarked on a large-scale program of modernization and "catching-up," did, as expected, have the highest rate of

Table 1
Provincial Government Gross General Expenditure
(1971 dollars)

Year	Mean — Ten Provinces ($/Person)	Standard ($/Person)	Dispersion Index (Percentage)
1956	186.2	45.8	24.6
1957	198.7	49.0	24.7
1958	223.2	40.2	18.0
1959	252.7	41.0	16.2
1960	272.3	35.9	13.2
1961	284.4	32.8	11.5
1962	314.6	40.1	12.7
1963	330.7	40.1	12.1
1964	357.6	49.5	13.8
1965	415.4	48.5	11.7
1966	493.9	80.7	16.3
1967	551.2	75.9	13.8
1968	578.9	60.2	10.4
1969	634.6	49.9	7.9
1970	717.7	68.0	9.5
1971	805.1	113.1	14.0
1972	839.4	81.1	9.7
1973	907.2	89.7	9.9
1974	1026.0	95.4	9.3
Absolute change 1956–1974	839.8	49.6	−15.3
Percentage change 1956–1974	451.0%	108.3%	
Avg. annual growth rate	9.4%/year		

Table 2
Rankings, by Province, of Real Per Capita
Gross General Expenditure for Selected Years
($/ Person)

1957		1962		1967		1972	
Pritish Columbia	299	Nfld.	371	Nfld.	712	Nfld.	958
Alberta	263	Alta.	350	Alta.	615	P.E.I	953
Saskatchewan	225	P.E.I.	348	N.B.	604	Que.	891
Average	*199*	B.C.	341	P.E.I.	574	N.B.	875
New Brunswick	196	Sask.	337	*Average*	*551*	Alta.	859
Newfoundland	185	*Average*	*315*	Quebec	537	*Average*	*839*
Ontario	176	Ont.	308	Sask.	522	Ont.	824
Nova Scotia	170	Que.	283	N.S.	500	Man.	779
Prince Edward Island	167	N.B.	283	Ont.	497	N.S.	772
Quebec	156	Man.	269	B.C.	492	B.C.	749
Manitoba	151	N.S.	255	Man.	460	Sask.	733

growth in government spending in the early years of the decade. For example, in each of 1960 and 1961, the province's spending increased by 20 per cent per year, compared with the provincial average of 11 and 5.7 per cent. These above average rates of growth were most strongly evident in welfare (in 1960-61), education and health, in all of which the provincial government took over activities previously dominated by church-related institutions.[15]

These changes in expenditure patterns closely parallel changes in provincial revenues. The average real per capita gross general revenue (Table 3), which includes federal transfers to the provincial governments, rose from $189 in 1956 to $1054 in 1974, an increase of 458 per cent. Alberta, British Columbia and Saskatchewan led the provinces in 1956. By 1972, the three provinces with the highest revenues were three of the poorest provinces. The dispersion index dropped from 38 per cent to 18 per cent.

The impact of federal transfers is striking when one compares changes in total revenues with changes in provincial revenues raised from their own

Table 3
Provincial Government
Gross General Revenue ($1971)

Year	Mean — Ten Provinces ($/Person)	Standard Deviation ($/Person)	Dispersion Index (Percentage)
1956	188.8	71.2	37.7
1957	197.6	64.2	32.5
1958	219.7	55.4	25.2
1959	244.3	55.0	22.5
1960	252.5	44.6	17.7
1961	268.5	41.4	15.4
1962	300.8	45.4	15.1
1963	312.5	52.1	16.7
1964	347.7	49.7	14.3
1965	410.6	55.0	13.4
1966	451.8	41.7	9.2
1967	522.6	27.8	5.3
1968	571.3	44.8	7.8
1969	695.6	42.8	6.6
1970	704.3	56.3	8.0
1971	776.1	64.7	8.3
1972	834.6	65.9	7.9
1973	929.8	82.8	8.9
1974	1053.5	187.1	17.8
1956–1974	$864.7/person	115.9	−19.9% (1956–1972 = −29.8%)
% 1956–1974	458.0%	162.8%	
Avg. annual growth rate	9.5%/year		

Table 4
Rankings, by Province, of Real Per Capita
Gross General Revenues for Selected Years
($/ Person)

1957		1962		1967		1972	
Alberta	319	Sask.	368	Que.	555	P.E.I.	970
British Columbia	294	Alta.	361	Nfld.	555	Que.	911
Saskatchewan	244	B.C.	347	Alta.	542	Nfld.	853
Average	*198*	P.E.I.	312	N.B.	542	Alta.	845
New Brunswick	191	Nfld.	302	Sask.	531	N.B.	842
Quebec	162	*Average*	*301*	B.C.	524	*Average*	*835*
Ontario	161	Ont.	293	*Average*	*523*	Man.	812
Newfoundland	156	Que.	262	P.E.I.	517	B.C.	804
Prince Edward							
Island	153	N.B.	259	Ont.	493	Ont.	782
Nova Scotia	151	N.S.	255	N.S.	485	Sask.	765
Manitoba	148	Man.	249	Man.	481	N.S.	762

(Two provinces having the same per capita revenue were ranked according to the first and second decimal places)

sources, reported in Table 5. With federal transfers removed, the dispersion index was much larger. It dropped over the period from 56 per cent to 34 per cent. Moreover, with federal transfers removed, the linking of wealth and revenue returns. Three of the top four provinces are also the three wealthiest, three of the bottom four are the poorest. Quebec, ranking first in revenue from its own sources, is an anomaly — as is Nova Scotia in overall revenues. These two examples illustrate that provincial decisions about what rates of tax to impose on their citizens also have an impact: Quebec has relatively high rates, Nova Scotia relatively low ones.

Thus the link is clearly established: federal transfers remove a high proportion of the original inequality in provincial access to public revenue, and that in turn removes much of the link between provincial per capita incomes and provincial spending. Spending overall responds to provincial needs and provincial demands, not to the original availability of funds.

One exception stands out from Table 3: the sharp rise in the dispersion index for provincial revenue from 9 per cent in 1973 to 18 per cent in 1974. The increase is accounted for by changes in provincial revenues from their own sources, notably from natural resources. A major part of the reason is the dramatic increase in oil and gas revenues following the price hikes in 1973. Between 1971 and 1974, natural resource revenue per capita rose from an average of $35 to $140, a rate of 41 per cent a year. In Alberta, it rose from $177 to $821 over the same period. Thus, while equalization and other federal transfers have reduced revenue disparities, the energy situation may have reversed the process of equalizing provincial fiscal capacities. Since 1973, the federal oil export tax and the subsidization of offshore oil imported

Table 5
Provincial Revenue from Own Sources
(Excludes All Federal Transfers) Selected Years $ 1971

Year	Mean—Ten Provinces ($/Person)	Standard Deviation ($/Person)	Dispersion Index
1957	131.7	63.0	47.8
1962	198.9	62.8	31.6
1967	342.7	94.9	27.7
1972	553.8	111.0	20.0
1974	711.1	239.4	33.7
Δ1956–1974	$584.1/person	$168.0/person	−22.5%
Δ1956–1974	459.9%	235.3%	
Average annual growth rate	9.5% /year		

Rankings, by Province, of Real Per Capita Revenue from Own Sources ($/ Person)

1957		1962		1967		1972	
Alberta	250	B.C.	283	B.C.	448	Que.	714
British Columbia	211	Alta.	282	Que.	440	B.C.	678
Saskatchewan	175	Sask.	274	Alta.	439	Alta.	673
Quebec	141	Ont.	228	Ont.	409	Ont.	631
Ontario	132	*Average*	*199*	Sask.	398	*Average*	*554*
Average	*132*	Que.	190	*Average*	*343*	Man.	550
New Brunswick	105	Man.	173	Man.	323	P.E.I.	485
Nova Scotia	80	P.E.I.	156	N.B.	291	Sask.	480
Manitoba	78	N.S.	143	N.S.	230	N.B.	477
Newfoundland	75	N.B.	140	Nfld.	226	N.S.	442
Prince Edward Island	69	Nfld.	121	P.E.I.	223	Nfld.	408

to eastern Canada have mitigated the impact of the international price changes, but in the same period, the federal government sharply reduced the degree to which natural resource revenues would be equalized across the provinces. The principle of equalization may now be threatened. Alberta, with its massive oil and gas revenues and its Heritage Fund is able to provide a very high level of services, yet can maintain significantly lower tax rates than other provinces.

What explains variations in total provincial expenditure? Table 6 presents the results of the regression analysis. It indicates that all coefficients are significant to the .01 level, with the exception of party in power which is significant only at .10. Since total spending aggregates spending across all categories the results mask considerable variation in the power of individual independent variables to explain different functions, as we shall see.

The results indicate, however, that income alone accounts for little of the overall difference. The regression coefficients can be read as saying that a dollar's increase in real per capita income increases spending by only 23 cents—with all other factors held constant. Equalization, as suggested before, is much more important: a dollar's increase in it will raise spending by $1.20. The coefficient for urbanization is high, which suggests that citizens in more complex urban environments have greater need or demand for public services.

The results of the two political variables are particularly interesting. The model shows that during election years, governments do indeed increase public spending. In election years, gross general expenditure will average

Table 6
Gross General Expenditure

GG = 0.23Y	+1.20EQ	+2.46M	+11.45U	+16.28EYR	+11.92PP
(0.03)	(0.12)	(0.75)	(2.48)	(7.11)	(8.85)
*	*	*	*	*	***

− 525.32DNLD	− 372.32DPEI	− 670.08DNS	− 576.34DNB	− 840.60DQUE
(77.75)	(46.65)	(75.05)	(70.55)	(106.44)
*	*	*	*	*

− 966.98DONT	− 798.61DMAN	− 626.19DSAS	− 750.24DALT	− 907.58DBC
(103.77)	(87.09)	(64.78)	(89.10)	(96.90)
*	*	*	*	*

GG   Gross general expenditure (1971$/person)
Y   Personal income per person (1971$)
EQ   Equalization payments per person (1971$)
M   Average manufacturing wage (1971$/week)
U   Percentage of the provincial population living in urban areas
Dummy variables:
EYR   Election year (=1 for election years, =0 otherwise)
PP   Party in power (=1 for Liberal or New Democratic Party govern-
            ments, =0 otherwise)
DNLD   Newfoundland (=for Newfoundland, =0 otherwise)
DPEI   Prince Edward Island (=1 for P.E.I., =0 otherwise)
DNS   Nova Scotia (=1 for Nova Scotia, =0 otherwise)
DNB   New Brunswick (=1 for New Brunswick, =0 otherwise)
DQUE   Quebec (=1 for Quebec, =0 otherwise)
DONT   Ontario (=1 for Ontario, =0 otherwise)
DMAN   Manitoba (=1 for Manitoba, =0 otherwise)
DSAS   Saskatchewan (= 1 for Saskatchewan, = 0 otherwise)
DALT   Alberta (=1 for Alberta, =0 otherwise)
DBC   British Columbia (=1 for British Columbia, =0 otherwise)
level of significance: :
   *   1% level   :   R-squared: 0.950
  **   5% level   :   adjusted R-squared: 0.945
 *** 10% level   :   estimated value of rho: 0.350
n.s. not significant   :

$16.28 per capita higher than in nonelection years. We would expect that the impact would be particularly visible in areas where governments have a great deal of discretion in setting spending priorities. Employment and spending in highways departments are a case in point. In the individual broad spending categories to be reported later, however, we do not easily capture these more specific effects. The largest year-by-year spending increases in the study occurred in Newfoundland in 1958, 1966 and 1971; elections were held there in 1959, 1966 and 1971. In many other cases of greater than average expenditure increases, we also found elections looming.

The political party in power, on the other hand, is only barely significant, if at all. The presence or absence of more progressive or more conservative parties does not appear to have much impact on overall expenditures or on the size of provincial budgets—though it does within some of the individual expenditure categories.

Taken together these variables explain almost three-quarters of the variation in provincial public expenditure. There remain the other characteristics of provinces not included in these five general factors. Another 20 per cent of the total variation is explained when the unique provincial conditions are taken into account. Thus beyond the variation explained by income and the other factors, each province, whether as a result of different needs or traditions, continues to vary from the others.

In overall provincial public spending, then, we confirm the findings of Thomas Shoyama, who looked at changes between 1939 and 1964 and found that despite persistent differences in income levels, the level of spending was becoming more similar. Federal aid, he argued, has indeed been an important factor in reducing interprovincial disparities in public services.[16]

Health and Hospital Care

Grants from the federal government have played an important role in the health field for many years. The National Health Grant Program was introduced in 1948 and the Hospital Insurance and Diagnostic Services Program began in 1957. Medicare was introduced in 1969, so that by then Ottawa was paying a large share of all major aspects of medical and hospital care. Given this heavy federal involvement in the health field, particularly hospital care, it would be expected that differences in per capita spending amongst the provinces would be small, that the dispersion index should be lower than that for other expenditures and that it should be declining through the period we are studying. Spending figures for both total health spending and for the hospital component were calculated separately, but only the tables for the former are presented here.

Table 7 shows that the average per capita provincial government expenditure on health rose from $33 in 1956 to slightly under $235 in 1974, more than a sixfold increase. The dispersion index for total health expenditure declined by 35.3 percentage points over the nineteen-year period. The lowest province, Quebec, spent only a third as much per capita as the highest in 1956; by 1972, the lowest was spending over 70 per cent as much as the highest. The hospital care component of health expenditure displays a similar pattern. Average per capita spending on hospital care increased from $26 in 1956 to $160 in 1974, while the dispersion index declined almost 39 percentage points. Hospital care accounted for 79.4 per cent of the per capita health spending in 1956 compared to 68.0 per cent in 1974.

The dispersion indices for health and hospital care over the 1956–74 period show considerable short-term fluctuations, despite the long-term downward trend. These fluctuations appear to result from variations in the date at

Table 7
Provincial Government
Expenditure on Health (1971)

Year	Mean—Ten Provinces ($/Person)	Standard Deviation ($/Person)	Dispersion Index (Percentage)
1957	34.6	16.7	48.4
1962	75.1	9.0	12.0
1967	117.0	14.6	12.5
1972	205.8	23.9	11.6
1974	234.9	25.2	10.7
Δ1965–74	$201.9/person	$10.0/person	−35.3%
Δ%'56–74	611.8%	65.8%	
Average annual growth rate	10.9%/year		

Rankings, by Province, of Real Per
Capita Expenditure on Health
($/ Person)

1957		1962		1967		1972	
Saskatchewan	66	Sask.	97	Sask.	143	Ont.	250
British Columbia	60	Nfld.	80	Alta.	133	Que.	236
Newfoundland	42	Ont.	77	Ont.	127	Alta.	225
Alberta	39	Alta.	79	Que.	125	Man.	207
Average	35	*Average*	75	*Average*	117	*Average*	206
New Brunswick	24	N.B.	75	Nfld.	115	B.C.	204
Nova Scotia	24	B.C.	73	B.C.	113	N.S.	193
Prince Edward Island	24	Man.	73	N.B.	109	Sask.	192
Ontario	22	P.E.I.	69	N.S.	106	N.B.	190
Manitoba	22	Que.	66	Man.	103	Nfld.	185
Quebec	22	N.S.	65	P.E.I.	96	P.E.I.	177

(Provinces having the same per capita expenditure were ranked according to the first and second decimal places).

which provinces joined federally funded programs and from considerable variation in capital expenditures, particularly for hospital construction. The latter tend to distort our view of provincial government output, since they appear as a lump sum in one fiscal year, rather than being spread over several years. The same "lumpiness" occurs in post-secondary education spending because of uneven rates of university construction.

Table 7 also shows the rankings of the provincial expenditures for health care for the years coinciding with the introduction of new federal-provincial fiscal arrangements. For each successive five-year period the lowest spending province is at a level close to that of the highest spender five years earlier. The rankings changed considerably over the period. Saskatchewan, the pioneer in medicare, fell from first to seventh place. Up to the 1960s it had to carry the burden of its advanced programs in its own budget. Quebec rose from tenth to second place in total health spending between 1957 and 1972, and Ontario from eighth to first.

How do provinces vary in the priority they accord to health care in their budgetary allocations, that is, in the proportion of their total budgets they devote to it? Across all provinces, health spending as a proportion of all expenditure rose over the period from 17 to 23 per cent. Again there was convergence, as the dispersion index on expenditure proportions fell from 29.5 per cent to 15 per cent. The introduction of hospital insurance in 1958 had a dramatic effect, reducing the index from 32 to 19 in a single year, and to 11.5 by 1961, when the program was operating in all provinces. Medicare seems to have a much less dramatic effect later on.

The rankings of spending effort in health confirm Saskatchewan's lead in the field. It was the first province to provide a universal hospital care plan, beginning in 1947, and was also the first to introduce universal medicare. In both cases innovation by one province was taken up by the federal government and extended to other provinces through shared cost programs. In 1957, Saskatchewan spent 29.3 per cent of its gross general expenditure on health, compared to a national average of 16.9 per cent. By 1972, the gap had narrowed as the national average rose to 24.7 per cent and Saskatchewan's expenditure effort fell slightly to 26.2 per cent. This may be attributed to the increasing direct federal involvement in the health field. Newfoundland and British Columbia, which alone had emulated Saskatchewan's hospital insurance before introduction of the federal program, also devoted much higher proportions of their budgets to health than other provinces did in 1957.

Between 1957 and 1972, it was the larger, richer provinces which increased their proportional spending on health care most dramatically. In Ontario, for example, it rose from 13 to 30 per cent, from near the bottom to the top. Increases in the poorer provinces were much smaller, and, in the case of Newfoundland, there was a decline. All the have-not provinces fell in the rankings between the early sixties and the seventies. This suggests that it is the wealthier provinces which have been best able to take advantage of the federal shared cost programs, though it may also be that residents of richer areas demand more elaborate and sophisticated health care than others.

Overall, however, there is strong evidence of convergence in health and medical care, influenced especially by federal conditional grants. That may change, however, under the 1977 federal-provincial fiscal arrangement which eliminated the federal cost-sharing programs in hospital insurance, medicare and post-secondary education, and replaced them with a new

Table 8
Health: Provincial Government Expenditure
Expressed as a Percentage of Gross
General Expenditure

Year	Ten Province Average (Percentage of GGE)	Standard Deviation (Percentage of GGE)	Dispersion Index
1957	16.9	5.5	32.5
1962	24.1	2.9	12.0
1967	21.5	3.7	17.2
1972	24.7	3.7	15.0
1974	23.1	3.4	14.7

Health: Rankings, by Province, of Provincial Government
Expenditure Expressed as a Percentage of Gross General Expenditure,
for Selected Years (Percentage)

1957		1962		1967		1972	
Saskatchewan	29.3	Sask.	28.7	Sask.	27.4	Ont.	30.3
Newfoundland	22.9	Man.	27.1	Ont.	25.6	B.C.	27.2
British Columbia	20.2	N.B.	26.4	Que.	23.3	Man.	26.6
Average	*16.9*	N.S.	25.5	B.C.	23.1	Que.	26.5
Alberta	14.9	Ont.	25.0	Man.	22.5	Alta.	26.2
Manitoba	14.4	*Average*	24.1	Alta.	21.6	Sask.	26.2
Prince Edward Island	14.3	Que.	23.2	*Average*	21.5	N.S.	25.0
Nova Scotia	14.1	Nfld.	21.7	N.S.	21.2	*Average*	24.7
Quebec	14.0	Alta.	21.5	N.B.	18.1	N.B.	21.7
Ontario	12.9	B.C.	21.5	P.E.I.	16.7	Nfld.	19.3
New Brunswick	12.3	P.E.I.	19.8	Nfld.	16.1	P.E.I.	18.6

transfer tied to growth in the gross national product rather than program costs. The assumption was that these were now "established" programs which would be continued with few alterations in the future. It will be interesting to see in future years whether citizens' expectations will result in maintenance of these programs at comparable levels everywhere or whether the lessening of federal influence will lead to greater divergence—as was alleged in the 1979 federal election campaign.

The regression results presented in Tables 9 and 10 show personal income to be a significant determinant of both total health spending and hospital care. Equalization is not significant for the former and not very significant for the latter. The small effects of income and equalization suggest that they have little impact on health spending. The large role of conditional grants in the field seems to outweigh them.

The cost of labour has a major impact on health spending, probably

Table 9
Total Health Spending

HE =	0.05Y	+0.05EQ	+1.51M	+1.71U	+2.37EYR	+4.19PP
	(0.007)	(0.04)	(0.22)	(0.95)	(1.92)	(2.35)
	*	n.s.	*	**	n.s.	**
—	94.74DNLD	−69.47DPEI	−101.23DNS	−96.71DNB	−129.22DQUE	
	(19.20)	(11.82)	(18.72)	(17.75)	(26.92)	
	*	*	*	*	*	
—	147.11DONT	−118.85DMAN	−106.29DSAS	−124.54DALT	−150.46DBC	
	(26.46)	(22.20)	(16.35)	(22.82)	(24.47)	
	*	*	*	*	*	

level of significance:
*   1% level   :   R-squared: 0.876
**   5% level   :   adjusted R-squared: 0.865
*** 10% level   :   estimated value of rho: 0.576
n.s. not significant   :

Table 10
Hospital Care

HC =	0.03Y	+0.06EQ	+0.54M	+2.01U	+3.06EYR	+0.81PP
	(0.005)	(0.03)	(0.16)	(0.84)	(1.37)	(1.67)
	*	**	*	*	**	n.s.
—	37.70DNLD	−29.52DPEI	−43.76DNS	−39.22DNB	−58.29DQUE	
	(12.59)	(7.89)	(12.24)	(11.76)	(17.76)	
	*	*	*	*	*	
—	66.57DONT	−54.39DMAN	−43.11DSAS	−54.28DALT	−69.36DBC	
	(17.55)	(14.73)	(10.93)	(15.25)	(16.13)	
	*	*	*	*	*	

level of significance:
*   1% level   :   R-squared: 0.729
**   5% level   :   adjusted R-squared: 0.704
*** 10% level   :   estimated value of rho: 0.690
n.s. not significant   :

because medical care is so labour intensive. Urbanization is also associated with health spending.

As for the political variables, the coefficient for the election year is significant only for hospital care, and party in power is significant only for total health expenditure. As expected, more progressive governments seem to spend more on health care. Perhaps the lack of significance for hospital spending suggests these governments concentrate more on the provision of services, and less on hospitals which are more capital intensive. Intuitively, other political factors have been crucial in health care. The CCF government of Saskatchewan endured massive political opposition when it introduced universal medical insurance and undoubtedly acted as the spur both to Ottawa and the other provincial governments. Once the schemes are in place, however, differences in spending on them are small.

Social Welfare

In the fiscal year 1972–73 the combined expenditure of all governments in Canada on social welfare was $8.66 billion, the largest of any single expenditure category. The federal government accounted for 73.4 per cent of this expenditure, while the remaining 26.6 per cent was spent by provincial and local governments. Social welfare was the largest expenditure category for the federal government and the fourth largest for the combined provincial and municipal governments after education, health and transportation and communications. In general, the federal government is responsible for the major income support programs, such as old age pensions and family allowances, while provinces (with federal assistance) concentrate on supplementary benefits and provision of services. Social welfare received the second largest share of federal conditional transfers after health. Together, the two accounted for more than 85 per cent of all federal conditional grants to the provinces in 1974: social welfare's share, almost 20 per cent, amounted to $525.8 million.[17]

Cost-sharing programs in the social welfare field have been in existence for longer than in most other areas. The Old Age Pension Act of 1927 provided for federal payment of 50 per cent of the cost of pensions for those over seventy years of age. In 1952, this was amended so that the federal government paid 50 per cent of the costs for those between the ages of sixty-five and sixty-nine years, and 100 per cent for those seventy and over. In 1956, unemployment assistance was introduced under which the federal share was 50 per cent. The Canada and Quebec Pension Plans were introduced in 1965. Several welfare programs were consolidated under the Canada Assistance Plan introduced in April 1966. Under this plan Ottawa paid 50 per cent of the cost of the programs funded by the CAP. The scheme is open ended, and the provinces determine their own rates of assistance. It is an interesting feature of the CAP that it will pay 50 per cent of the cost of improving services. This feature was designed to encourage the introduction of new services by the provinces and to equalize the level of service amongst the provinces; all the more reason to expect a higher degree of convergence in provincial social welfare spending after the introduction of the CAP.

Table 11 shows how dramatically social welfare expenditures have risen between 1956 and 1974. In 1956, the average provincial expenditure was almost $17/person. By 1974 this had risen, in real terms, more than six

Table 11
Provincial Government
Expenditure on Social Welfare ($1971)

Year	Mean—Ten Provinces ($/Person)	Standard Deviation ($/Person)	Dispersion Index (Percentage)
1957	19.4	7.4	38.3
1962	32.7	10.2	31.1
1967	62.5	22.8	36.4
1972	90.3	19.6	21.7
1974	127.4	21.5	16.9
Δ1965–74	$110.5/person	$14.6/person	−23.9%
Δ%1956–74	653.8%	211.6%	
Average annual growth rate	11.2%/year		

Rankings, by Province, of Real Per Capita Expenditures on Social Welfare ($/ Person)

1957		1962		1967		1972	
Newfoundland	34	Nfld.	52	Nfld.	102	Que.	134
British Columbia	27	Que.	44	P.E.I.	90	Nfld.	107
Quebec	25	B.C.	39	Que.	85	Alta.	92
Saskatchewan	23	Sask.	34	Alta.	68	*Average*	90
Average	19	*Average*	33	*Average*	63	B.C.	90
Alberta	17	Alta.	33	B.C.	61	P.E.I.	90
New Brunswick	16	P.E.I.	31	Sask.	46	Man.	88
Manitoba	14	Man.	28	N.S.	46	Sask.	84
Prince Edward Island	14	N.B.	25	Ont.	44	N.B.	84
Nova Scotia	13	N.S.	22	N.B.	43	Ont.	70
Ontario	11	Ont.	19	Man.	40	N.S.	63

and a half times to about $127/person. The dispersion index fell from the high level of 40.8 per cent to 16.9 per cent indicating a strong convergence in provincial spending in this field, but with considerable variation remaining. Until 1966 the dispersion index fluctuated considerably and did not exhibit a strong downward trend. But after 1965, when the Canada Assistance Plan was introduced, it fell continuously from 36.4

per cent to 16.9 per cent in 1974. In 1957, the ratio of spending by the top province to that of the lowest was 3:1, by 1972, it was about 2:1.

So far we have discussed the determinants of government spending in terms of needs or demands versus fiscal capacity. Intuitively, we would expect that in the social welfare field, need and fiscal capacity would have a strong, negative correlation: the poorest provinces would have the greatest need for welfare services and, given federal conditional and equalization grants, they would be expected to spend the most per capita. In fact, however, while Newfoundland, the poorest province, and Quebec, also a less wealthy province, ranked at the top, the other poor provinces are all below average in 1972 and Nova Scotia is last. Conversely, Alberta and British Columbia rank high. Ontario follows the expected pattern — last in the first two years, and never higher than eighth.

The relatively high positions of Alberta and British Columbia are especially striking, since their Social Credit governments throughout this period are usually thought to be conservative in most policy areas. While it is true that the B.C. government faced a threat from the left, that was not the case for Alberta. One is prompted to speculate that the rankings of all three westernmost provinces near the top of both health and welfare reflects an historical tradition of greater populism in politics and cooperative models in other areas, which are at work whichever party is in power.

It might be expected that the poorer provinces, faced with a greater welfare burden, would be forced to spend a greater proportion of their budgets on assistance, even if they could not afford to provide such high benefit levels. As Table 12, summarizing spending effort, shows, this is not the case. Again, Quebec is the top province, with welfare accounting for 15 per cent of its total budget. But the other poor provinces, except for Newfoundland, are well down the table.

Again the dispersion index has dropped sharply over the period, varying erratically at first, then dropping steadily after the introduction of the Canada Assistance Plan in 1966. Dispersion, however, remains higher than for health or for total spending.

Quebec's placing is also interesting. Since 1962, it has placed first in proportion of the budget devoted to welfare and near the top in per capita spending. It might be expected that this position is a result of the modernization and catching up in social policy which characterized the Quiet Revolution of the 1960s. That interpretation must be qualified, however. In 1957, in the last years of the Duplessis regime, Quebec also ranked near the top in both per capita spending and effort.

The regression model shows significant associations of welfare spending with both income and equalization, but the effects are relatively small. Again, the magnitude of shared cost assistance from Ottawa seems to outweigh wealth and general fiscal capacity. The cost indicator, found in wage levels, is not significant, probably because a high proportion of welfare

Table 12
Social Welfare: Spending Effort
(Provincial Government Expenditure Expressed as a Percentage of Gross General Revenue)

Year	Ten province average (% of GGE)	Standard deviation (% of GGE)	Dispersion index $(\overline{O}/\overline{X})*100$
1957	10.0	4.1	41.0
1962	24.3	2.8	27.2
1967	11.2	3.2	28.8
1972	10.7	2.0	18.7
1974	12.5	2.1	16.8

Social Welfare: Rankings, by Province, of Provincial Government Expenditure Expressed as a Percentage of Gross General Expenditure for Selected Years
(Percentage)

1957		1962		1967		1972	
Newfoundland	18.6	Que.	15.6	Que.	15.9	Que.	15.0
Quebec	16.2	Nfld.	13.9	P.E.I.	15.6	B.C.	12.0
Saskatchewan	10.2	B.C.	11.6	Nfld.	14.4	Sask.	11.5
Average	10.0	Man.	10.6	B.C.	12.3	Man.	11.3
Manitoba	9.3	*Average*	10.3	*Average*	11.2	Nfld.	11.2
British Columbia	8.9	Sask.	9.9	Alta.	11.1	*Average*	10.7
Prince Edward Island	8.3	Alta.	9.4	N.S.	9.1	Alta.	10.7
New Brunswick	8.0	P.E.I.	8.8	Ont.	9.0	N.B.	9.6
Nova Scotia	7.9	N.S.	8.8	Sask.	8.8	P.E.I.	9.5
Ontario	6.5	N.B.	8.7	Man.	8.7	Ont.	8.5
Alberta	6.5	Ont.	6.0	N.B.	7.1	N.S.	8.2

spending is in the form of transfer payments without a large role for government employees.

Modern governments do not try to win elections by manipulating welfare spending — and this is reflected in the nonsignificance of election years. There is, however, a modest relationship with party in power. Liberal and NDP governments are more likely to spend money on social welfare than Conservative or Social Credit ones. This can be shown more clearly by examining changes in welfare spending by three recently elected NDP governments in their first years in office. The Manitoba NDP increased spending in 1970, over 1969, by 45.5 per cent — compared with an average provincial increase of 16 per cent that year. In 1972, the newly elected NDP in Saskatchewan raised its welfare spending by 20 per cent compared with the average increase of 7.8 per cent over 1971. The B.C. NDP government increased welfare spending by a third in each of its first two years, while other provinces were raising theirs by only a fifth. Only in British Columbia was this effect noticeable in health care. Nor was it strong in total expenditure. The new Saskatchewan government did increase its spending twice as much as the average in 1972, and British Columbia did expand its activities at a much higher rate than others in its second year. But welfare, the most clearly redistributive policy area, is the only one where new left governments make a real impact in their first years. In all three of these cases the province was slightly below average in welfare spending before the NDP took office.

The regression model explains most of the total variance, but a large proportion of this appears to be related to characteristics peculiar to each province.

Table 13
Social Welfare

SW = 0.03Y	+0.07EQ	+0.19M	+1.61U	+0.79EYR	+3.71PP
(0.005)	(0.03)	(0.15)	(0.60)	(1.40)	(1.73)
*	*	n.s.	*	n.s.	**
− 52.97DNLD	−41.55DPEI	−77.67DNS	−68.10DNB	−82.19DQUE	
(14.66)	(8.92)	(14.26)	(13.45)	(20.37)	
*	*	*	*	*	
− 114.27DONT	−89.79DMAN	−73.20DSAS	−87.75DALT	−96.39DBC	
(19.95)	(16.74)	(12.35)	(17.16)	(18.53)	
*	*	*	*	*	

level of significance:	:	
* 1% level	:	R-squared: 0.848
** 5% level	:	adjusted R-squared: 0.834
*** 10% level	:	estimated value of rho: 0.484
n.s. not significant	:	

Education

Education is one of the most sacrosanct of the responsibilities allocated to the provinces in the British North America Act. However, as in virtually every other field, Ottawa has become involved, accounting for over one-fifth of total spending.[18] Federal contributions to primary and secondary education are very small. The major federal role occurs in post-secondary and technical and vocational education. Between 1952 and 1967, Ottawa made annual grants to universities in Canada. Under the 1967 fiscal arrangements with the provinces, the federal government agreed to pay for half the operating costs of colleges and universities through a complicated mixture of tax points and cash grants, though there was still to be no direct federal role in educational policy-making.

The contrast between minimal federal activity in primary and secondary education and significant involvement in university education is particularly useful for our purposes. If federal encouragement, through shared cost programs, is a major factor leading to convergence among provinces, then we would expect greater similarity among them in the post-secondary field. Modest support for this suggestion is found in the data presented in Tables 14 to 16.

Average real per capita expenditure on education increased sixfold over the period, from $34 to $241 per capita. Post-secondary spending increased most dramatically, from $5 to $75 per person. Convergence occurred in both categories, with the dispersion indices dropping from 40 to 27 per cent in primary and secondary education and from 43 to 21 in post-secondary education. Thus the federal presence had a noticeable effect and convergence was greater at the post-secondary level. This interpretation is reinforced by

Table 14
Provincial Government
Expenditure on Education ($1971)

Year	Mean—Ten Provinces ($/Person)	Standard Deviation ($/Person)	Dispersion Index (Percentage)
1957	37.2	12.4	33.3
1962	76.8	26.2	31.5
1967	147.6	33.7	22.9
1972	218.8	38.0	17.3
1974	241.4	42.9	17.8
Δ1956–74	$207.8/person	$32.0/person	−14.8%
Δ%1956–74	618.5%	293.6	
Average annual growth rate	10.9%/year		

Ranking, by Province, of Real Per Capita Expenditure on Education (Total) ($/Person)

1957		1962		1967		1972	
Alberta	65	Alta.	117	Alta.	208	Nfld.	260
British Columbia	49	Nfld.	111	Nfld.	190	Alta.	254
Ontario	38	Ont.	99	N.B.	171	N.B.	252
Saskatchewan	37	Average	77	Ont.	156	P.E.I.	247
Average	37	B.C.	72	Average	148	Ont.	239
Newfoundland	37	Sask.	72	Que.	147	Que.	221
Nova Scotia	35	Que.	71	N.S.	131	Average	219
Quebec	33	P.E.I.	69	Man.	131	Man.	197
Manitoba	28	Man.	57	Sask.	121	N.S.	193
New Brunswick	26	N.S.	57	B.C.	111	Sask.	173
Prince Edward Island	23	N.B.	44	P.E.I.	109	B.C.	152

Table 15
Provincial Government
Expenditure on Primary and Secondary
Education (Subcategory of Education) ($ 1971)

Year	Mean—Ten Provinces ($/Person)	Standard Deviation ($/Person)	Dispersion Index (Percentage)
1957	27.7	11.8	42.4
1962	48.4	18.2	37.5
1967	86.1	17.6	20.4
1972	136.2	32.6	23.9
1974	153.9	41.4	26.9
Δ1956–74	128.3	31.1	−13.3
Δ%1956–74	501.2%	301.9%	
Average annual growth rate	9.9%/year		

Rankings, by Province, of Real Per Capita Expenditure on
Primary and Secondary Education (Subcategory of Education) ($/Person)

1957		1962		1967		1972	
Alberta	54	Alta.	82	N.B.	119	N.B.	184
British Columbia	39	Ont.	77	Alta.	106	Nfld.	174
Newfoundland	32	B.C.	52	Ont.	93	P.E.I	162
Saskatchewan	28	Sask.	50	Nfld.	92	Ont.	151
Average	28	Nfld.	49	*Average*	86	Que.	144
Nova Scotia	25	*Average*	48	P.E.I.	84	*Average*	136
Ontario	25	Que.	42	Sask.	83	Alta.	134
Manitoba	21	Man.	38	Que.	82	Man.	118
New Brunswick	20	P.E.I.	36	Man.	74	N.S.	109
Quebec	19	N.S.	33	N.S.	65	Sask.	103
Prince Edward Island	14	N.B.	25	B.C.	62	B.C.	83

the striking change in the dispersion index for post-secondary education which followed the introduction of the fifty per cent sharing plan in 1967 — in one year the index fell from 46 to 28. No such dramatic change occurs at the primary and secondary levels.

At the post-secondary level, the dispersion index fluctuates widely, as does the spending of individual provinces. This appears to reflect large swings in capital spending, as one by one provinces undertook the massive expansion in higher education characteristic of the 1960s.

Alberta stands out as the province spending most on education. It was first in total spending throughout most of the period. By 1972, it had dropped below average in primary and secondary, but remained at the top in post-secondary. Ontario ranks near the top throughout the period, but fluctuates greatly in post-secondary spending. British Columbia began the period as one of the most generous provinces, but by 1972 ranked at the bottom. Quebec was near the average throughout the period: the often noted modernization and expansion of education during the Quiet Revolution does not show up dramatically in the data. Indeed, Quebec dropped from third to eighth in terms of the proportion of its budget devoted to education. Newfoundland and New Brunswick, where virtually all education spending is concentrated at the provincial rather than the local level, rank surprisingly high.

Table 16
Provincial Government
Expenditure on Post-secondary Education
(Subcategory of Education) (1971 Dollars)

Year	Mean ($/Person)	Standard Deviation ($/Person)	Dispersion Index (Percentage)
1957	6.4	3.5	54.3
1962	23.9	13.1	54.9
1967	53.1	24.4	45.9
1972	71.2	18.1	25.4
1974	74.9	15.9	21.2
Δ1956–74	69.6	13.6	−21.7
Δ%1956–74	1313.2%	591.3%	
Average annual growth rate	15%/year		

Rankings, by Province, of Real Per Capita Spending on
Post-Secondary Education (Subcategory of Education) ($/Person)

1957		1962		1967		1972	
Quebec	13	Nfld.	58	Alta.	97	Alta.	116
Alberta	9	Alta.	34	Nfld.	94	Ont.	79
Ontario	9	P.E.I.	24	Que.	55	Man.	78
British Columbia	6	*Average*	24	*Average*	53	*Average*	71
Average	6	Que.	23	N.S.	51	Nfld.	70
Manitoba	6	Sask.	18	Ont.	47	N.S.	69
Saskatchewan	6	N.S.	17	Man.	45	Que.	68
Nova Scotia	6	N.B.	17	B.C.	44	B.C.	65
New Brunswick	5	Man.	16	N.B.	44	Sask.	60
Newfoundland	3	Ont.	16	Sask.	32	P.E.I.	60
Prince Edward Island	—	B.C.	15	P.E.I.	21	N.B.	48

Despite the convergence, there remain large differences between provinces. In total education spending Alberta and Newfoundland spend about $100 more per person than does British Columbia. The disparities were similar at both levels of education. Further research is necessary to discover whether such variations flow from differences in numbers of pupils or from different government policy choices. Similarly, it would be interesting to know how the variations manifest themselves in different class sizes, more elaborate schools, and so on.

The commitment to education seen in Table 17 as a proportion of total government expenditure parallels the actual spending figures. The dispersion indices for the two levels of education, however, drop by roughly the same amount. Alberta and Ontario make the greatest commitment to education in general throughout the period. British Columbia, which, as we saw, dropped sharply in money spent, was always low in proportion of the budget devoted to it.

The regression model largely confirms our expectations respecting the impact of federal spending. With hospital and social welfare spending, significant coefficients were obtained with equalization, but the coefficients were small. Because these services received substantial federal conditional

Table 17
Education: Provincial Government
Expenditure Expressed as a Percentage of
Gross General Expenditure

Year	Ten Provinces Average (% of GGE)	Standard Deviation (% of GGE)	Dispersion Index (S.D. as % of Average)
1957	18.7	3.6	17.8
1962	24.2	5.8	24.0
1967	26.7	4.3	16.1
1972	25.9	2.8	10.8
1974	23.4	2.7	11.5

Education: Rankings, by Province, of Provincial
Government Expenditure Expressed as a Percentage
of Gross General Expenditure (Percentage)

1957		1962		1967		1972	
Alberta	24.9	Alta.	33.4	Alta.	33.9	Alta.	29.6
Ontario	21.4	Ont.	32.0	Ont.	31.4	Ont.	29.1
Quebec	21.2	Nfld.	30.0	Man.	28.4	N.B.	28.8
Nova Scotia	20.6	Que.	25.1	N.B.	28.3	Nfld.	27.2
Newfoundland	20.0	*Average*	24.2	Que.	27.4	*Average*	25.9
Average	18.7	N.S.	22.2	Nfld.	26.7	P.E.I.	25.9
Manitoba	18.5	Man.	21.3	*Average*	26.7	Man.	25.3
Saskatchewan	16.6	Sask.	21.2	N.S.	26.3	N.S.	25.0
British Columbia	16.4	B.C.	21.1	Sask.	23.2	Que.	24.8
Prince Edward Island	14.1	P.E.I.	19.9	B.C.	22.6	Sask.	23.6
New Brunswick	13.1	N.B.	15.5	P.E.I.	18.9	B.C.	20.3

grants, we argued that the influence of these transfers overwhelmed the effects of increased income or equalization. The results for the two levels of education provide considerable confirmation of this idea. In post-secondary education, the income coefficient is significant, but very small. The coefficient for equalization is not significant. This suggests they are overwhelmed by the direct federal payments for universities and colleges. The coefficients for these two factors are much larger and stronger for primary and secondary education where federal direct involvement is negligible. Neither of the political variables is significant for primary and secondary education. This may reflect in part the fact that provincial government discretion in education spending is limited because it consists so much of transfers to local boards of education, which are governed by rather rigid formulas. It may also be that basic primary and secondary educational systems are so old and well established that citizens of all provinces have similar standards and expectations. The expansion of university and college education is much more recent, and expectations may not have stabilized across the country. This interpretation is supported by comparison of the variance explained by the two parts of the regression model. The basic variables together explain half of the variance for primary and secondary education, leaving a fifth to be explained by specifically "provincial" characteristics. But in university education only 23 per cent of the variance is accounted for by the first group of variables; 36 per cent is explained by "province." It is most unlikely that simple variations in the size of the age group likely to attend university accounts for this.

In any case, while education is usually categorized as part of "social" policy, it does not have the obvious redistributive effects of public spending

Table 18A
Education

$ED =$ 0.03Y (0.01) * $\quad$ +0.41EQ (0.06) * $\quad$ +0.58M (0.30) ** $\quad$ +6.68U (1.36) * $\quad$ +5.34EYR (2.63) ** $\quad$ +4.01PP (3.22) n.s.

-157.26DNLD (25.94) * $\quad$ -107.66DPEI (16.03) * $\quad$ -175.29DNS (25.30) * $\quad$ -154.87DNB (24.03) * $\quad$ -225.60DQUE (36.44) *

-234.61DONT (35.86) * $\quad$ -204.19DMAN (30.09) * $\quad$ -159.74DSAS (22.17) * $\quad$ -185.07DALT (30.95) * $\quad$ -233.04DBC (33.12) *

level of significance:	:	
* 1% level	:	R-squared: 0.814
** 5% level	:	adjusted R-squared: 0.797
*** 10% level	:	estimated value of rho: 0.601
n.s. not significant	:	

in health and welfare, so we would not expect the party in power and related ideological factors to have much impact. Such qualitative elements of education as the nature of curricula in social studies and history are much more likely than overall levels of spending to be influenced by provincial political and cultural characteristics.[19]

Education displays the same pattern of convergence as the previous spending categories, but the convergence is less dramatic, and much less even. Interprovincial variation is large.

Table 18B
Primary and Secondary Education

EP =	0.02Y	+0.34EQ	+0.32M	+4.36U	+2.23EYR	+1.02PP
	(0.007)	(0.04)	(0.22)	(1.08)	(1.90)	(2.32)
	**	*	***	*	n.s.	n.s.
	−86.47DNLD	−56.88DPEI	−98.83DNS	−80.34DNB	−121.54DQUE	
	(18.09)	(11.26)	(17.63)	(16.83)	(25.49)	
	*	*	*	*	*	
	−124.44DONT	−109.78DMAN	−83.59DSAS	−101.40DALT	−123.40DBC	
	(25.14)	(21.10)	(15.58)	(21.77)	(23.16)	
	*	*	*	*	*	

level of significance: :
  *   1% level   :   R-squared: 0.728
 **   5% level   :   adjusted R-squared: 0.703
*** 10% level   :   estimated value of rho: 0.650
n.s. not significant   :

Table 18C
Post-secondary Education

ED =	0.02Y	+0.0005EQ	+0.40M	+1.90U	+2.11EYR	+2.90PP
	(0.006)	(0.03)	(0.18)	(0.78)	(1.61)	(1.98)
	*	n.s.	**	*	***	***
	−57.59DNLD	−43.06DPEI	−63.17DNS	−62.82DNB	−86.23DQUE	
	(16.23)	(9.98)	(15.82)	(14.99)	(22.73)	
	*	*	*	*	*	
	−93.75DONT	−77.52DMAN	−66.18DSAS	−68.48DALT	−92.53DBC	
	(22.34)	(18.74)	(13.80)	(19.25)	(20.67)	
	*	*	*	*	*	

level of significance: :
  *   1% level   :   R-squared: 0.625
 **   5% level   :   adjusted R-squared: 0.591
*** 10% level   :   estimated value of rho: 0.566
n.s. not significant   :

Other Spending Categories

Health, education and welfare are by far the largest categories of spending by contemporary provincial governments, and all three have substantial federal involvement. In this section we look at a group of other spending functions in which the amounts spent are much smaller and federal aid is much more limited. They are transportation and communications, which includes spending on highways, airports, communication systems, and the like; natural resources, which includes services and incentives in the management and development of resources; trade and industry, which groups programs to assist manufacturing; tourism and related activities; and recreation and culture. In 1974, average provincial per capita spending on transportation and communications, the largest of the four categories, was $106, and on trade and industry $11 — as compared with an average expenditure on health of $235. All four of these programs accounted for only 6 per cent of total federal conditional grants — while health alone accounted for 52 per cent.

We expect that the absence of federal involvement in these areas would lead to greater interprovincial variation because there would be less impetus to standardize services, and perhaps less fiscal capacity to provide them. Moreover, in these fields, variations among provincial economies, geography and other factors are likely to generate very different needs. Thus we should find higher dispersion indices, and less convergence over time. In the following sections the regression tables are omitted for space reasons, but some results are reported in the text.

Transportation and Communications

As government activity has grown, spending in the traditional function of providing highways and other transportation facilities has declined dramatically as a proportion of total spending. The average was 31 per cent of the budget in 1956 and 10 per cent in 1974. Average real per capita spending increased from $57 to $92 per person in 1972. The dispersion indices for both per capita spending and spending effort do decline somewhat, but they remain relatively large, and have been subject to wide fluctuations. The greatest divergence occurred in the middle sixties, rather than at the start of the period.

The provincial rankings show wide variations. The smaller, poorer provinces, led by Prince Edward Island in most years, spend the highest amounts, and allocate the greatest portion of their budgets to transportation; the larger, richer provinces spend smaller amounts. Moreover, the spread is large: P.E.I. and Newfoundland spend more than twice as much as does Alberta. British Columbia, whose geography dictates high road-building costs, is the only richer province to rank consistently above average. The high ranking of most of the Atlantic provinces is harder to

Table 19
Provincial Government Expenditure
on Transportation and Communications ($ 1971)

Year	Mean ($/Person)	Standard Deviation ($/Person)	Dispersion Index (Percentage)
1957	56.7	17.3	27.5
1962	60.3	21.1	35.0
1967	89.9	27.8	30.9
1972	91.6	24.1	26.3
1974	105.6	22.6	21.4
Δ1956–74	49.1	7.1	−6.1
Δ%1956–74	86.9%	45.8%	

Rankings, by Province, of Real Per Capita Expenditure
on Transportation and Communications ($/Person)

1957		1962		1967		1972	
British Columbia	85	P.E.I.	112	P.E.I.	129	P.E.I.	128
New Brunswick	73	B.C.	75	N.B.	129	Nfld.	127
Alberta	72	N.B.	67	Nfld.	123	N.B.	106
Prince Edward Island	67	Nfld.	62	N.S.	97	B.C.	99
Average	57	*Average*	60	*Average*	90	*Average*	92
Ontario	55	Alta.	56	Sask.	79	N.S.	90
Nova Scotia	55	Ont.	53	B.C.	78	Que.	87
Saskatchewan	48	N.S.	52	Alta.	76	Sask.	86
Manitoba	45	Que.	43	Ont.	70	Ont.	70
Quebec	37	Sask.	43	Que.	61	Man.	67
Newfoundland	30	Man.	41	Man.	56	Alta.	57

explain, although the regression results provide some hints. Income has virtually no effect and equalization payments are not significant. Indeed, only two of the general independent variables seem to exert much effect. They are first, urbanization, which suggests that spending will be greater when scattered rural populations must be pulled together, and, second, years in which elections are held. Highway spending is highly discretionary, can be easily varied year by year, and can be targeted precisely to individual constituencies. Duff Spafford has shown a very high correlation between highway department employment and the onset of elections,[20] and Albert Macdonald has traced out the relationship for Prince Edward Island in detail,[21] where an old political aphorism states that at election time, "If it moves, pension it; if it doesn't, pave it." Thus an orientation to patronage politics and less bureaucratized style of decision-making, both sometimes associated with the Maritime provinces, may also be important. Of all spending categories, the general factors in our model appear to explain the least proportion of the variance in transportation and communications and the province-specific factors explain the most.

Natural Resources

Primary responsibility for the development of natural resources lies with the provinces. They are responsible for the management of resources, promotion of fisheries, and have a considerable role in the mining industry. Activities range from provision of services, promotion of investment through subsidies and tax concessions, and regulation of production through licences, quotas, and the like. The federal government is also heavily involved in programs affecting natural resources, from the geological survey to development of oil pipelines to, more recently, a subsidy program for imported oil in eastern Canada. Indeed, somewhat surprisingly, given the strong defence of provincial interests in recent intergovernmental conflict, the provinces account for a declining share of total government expenditures

Table 20
Provincial Government Expenditure
on Natural Resources ($1971)

Year	Mean ($/Person)	Standard Deviation ($/Person)	Dispersion Index (Percentage)
1957	12.4	4.6	37.0
1962	15.4	5.0	32.6
1967	26.6	5.5	20.7
1972	18.8	7.0	37.0
1974	25.0	13.3	53.1

(Due to the large fluctuations the 1956–1974 comparisons are omitted)

Rankings, by Province, of Real Per Capita Expenditure
on Natural Resources ($/Person)

1957		1962		1967		1972	
British Columbia	20	B.C.	21	Man.	33	B.C.	33
Alberta	18	Sask.	20	Nfld.	31	Man.	25
Quebec	15	Man.	20	B.C.	31	N.B.	24
Saskatchewan	15	Alta.	20	Alta.	31	Nfld.	21
New Brunswick	15	Que.	17	Sask.	29	Alta.	20
Average	12	*Average*	15	P.E.I.	27	*Average*	19
Manitoba	10	P.E.I.	14	*Average*	27	Sask.	16
Prince Edward Island	9	N.B.	13	N.B.	25	P.E.I.	14
Ontario	9	Nfld.	10	Que.	23	N.S.	13
Nova Scotia	8	Ont.	9	N.S.	22	Que.	10
Newfoundland	7	N.S.	9	Ont.	15	Ont.	10

in the field: from 35 per cent of the total in 1960 to 30 per cent in 1974.

The proportion of provincial budgets spent on natural resources has also declined, from 6 per cent in 1956 to 2.4 per cent in 1974. Increased provincial involvement in the area appears to have relied more heavily on tax and regulatory measures than on the provision of services.

As expected, the dispersion indices are large and fluctuate widely from year to year. There is no pattern of convergence. Indeed, in spending effort, there is greater provincial variation in recent years. All provincial economies rely heavily on various forms of natural resources, with, of course, considerable variations in the resource base. But resources do provide a smaller proportion of the wealth of Quebec and Ontario, which rely more heavily on manufacturing. Not surprisingly, both provinces rank low in spending on natural resources. Otherwise little pattern can be found in the provincial rankings.

This is confirmed by the regression analysis. Only two coefficients are significant. Income is very weakly associated with spending and party in power is negatively related to spending. This gives some basis for suggesting that conservatively governed provinces place a somewhat higher priority on economic development activities and somewhat less on social programs, or that resource-based provinces elect more conservative governments. However, the regression model explains only 20 per cent of the variance in this category.

Trade and Industry

The other economic development category is spending on trade and industry, but it embraces only a small proportion of total government spending. In 1974, it accounted for only 3 per cent of spending by all governments combined, and only 1 per cent of provincial expenditure. There is a very large variation among provinces, and the dispersion indices have increased over time. The provincial rankings on spending effort show that the most developed provinces — Ontario, Quebec, British Columbia and Alberta — are below average, with Ontario lowest in two years. Less developed provinces are at the top of the list. The differences are large: in 1972, Ontario spent $1.77 per person on trade and industry, while Newfoundland spent $42.24.

Thus it is the less developed provinces which commit the most to promoting trade and industry. The provincial efforts are combined with those of the federal government, through the Department of Regional Expansion, which also concentrates on programs to alleviate disparities through assisting provinces in providing the infrastructure needed for development, and through assistance to individual firms. There is, however, little evidence that such programs have had much effect; regional disparities in economic development have been remarkably persistent. Economically

Table 21
Provincial Government Expenditure on Trade
and Industry ($1971)

Year	Mean ($/Person)	Standard Deviation ($/Person)	Dispersion Index (Percentage)
1957	1.0	0.3	28.7
1962	1.8	1.3	68.9
1967	5.2	4.4	85.7
1972	13.0	13.9	106.3
1974	11.4	9.3	82.2

Rankings, by Province, of Real Per Capita Expenditure
on Trade and Industry ($ 1971)

1957		1962		1967		1972	
New Brunswick	1.52	Sask.	4.93	Nfld.	16.95	Nfld.	42.24
Nova Scotia	1.43	P.E.I.	2.93	P.E.I.	6.89	P.E.I.	33.13
Newfoundland	1.20	N.B.	1.89	Man.	6.07	N.B.	17.19
Prince Edward Island	1.07	*Average*	*1.83*	N.S.	5.34	*Average*	*13.05*
Manitoba	1.05	N.S.	1.74	*Average*	*5.19*	N.S.	10.74
Average	*1.04*	Man.	1.65	Alta.	3.40	Sask.	6.82
Quebec	1.04	Nfld.	1.30	N.B.	3.05	Man.	5.81
Saskatchewan	0.98	Que.	1.29	Sask.	2.66	Alta.	5.22
Alberta	0.85	B.C.	1.04	Que.	2.60	Que.	4.84
British Columia	0.69	Ont.	1.01	B.C.	2.59	B.C.	2.71
Ontario	0.56	Alta.	0.55	Ont.	2.34	Ont.	1.77

strong provinces apparently feel less need to stimulate economic activity through government assistance; weak provinces must do so to overcome unfavourable market forces. However, as Ontario has felt its manufacturing base threatened by recent developments, it too has engaged in large subsidies to individual firms, such as $60 million to assist the Ford Motor Company to build a new plant.

Only two of the variables in the regression model are significant. Income is unrelated, but dependence on equalization is significant. Perhaps again reflecting the discretionary character of much spending in this area, election year is also associated with spending.

Recreation and Culture

Recreation and culture is another relatively small field, though one which has grown in importance from only about half of 1 per cent of total expenditure to 1.5 per cent, or from $1.38 to $15.39 per person. The dispersion index remains high—but less than trade and industry or national resources. It has also declined substantially, from over 100 in the 1950s to under 50 in the

Table 22
Provincial Government Expenditure on
Recreation and Culture ($1971)

Year	Mean ($/Person)	Standard Deviation ($/Person)	Dispersion Index (Percentage)
1957	1.20	1.29	107.5
1962	1.74	1.69	97.4
1967	8.00	4.99	62.4
1972	11.30	8.27	73.2
1974	15.39	7.31	47.5
Δ1956–74	14.01	4.91	−125.9
Δ%1956–74	1015.2%	204.6%	
Average annual growth rate	13.5%/year		

Rankings, by Province, of Real Per Capita Expenditure
on Recreation and Culture ($/Person)

1957		1962		1967		1972	
Alberta	3.54	Sask.	5.53	Man.	17.86	Man.	32.96
British Columbia	2.78	Alta.	2.82	Nfld.	13.79	P.E.I.	17.02
Ontario	1.95	Ont.	2.43	Sask.	10.78	*Average*	*11.30*
Manitoba	1.59	B.C.	2.32	P.E.I.	10.52	N.B.	10.47
Saskatchewan	1.56	*Average*	*1.74*	*Average*	*8.00*	B.C.	9.84
Average	*1.20*	N.S.	1.72	Alta.	6.16	Que.	8.42
Newfoundland							
Nova Scotia		No					
Prince Edward Island		Expenditure					
New Brunswick							
		Man.	1.37	Que.	5.28	Sask.	8.40
		Que.	1.20	B.C.	4.72	Nfld.	7.23

1960s. There still remain sharp differences: Manitoba in 1974 spent 4 per cent of its budget in the field, Ontario less than 1 per cent. Poor and wealthy provinces follow no particular order in the rankings, though income, equalization and weekly wages are all positively, if weakly, associated with spending in the field. Recreation and culture—which encompasses parks, playgrounds, aid to the arts, and so on—may be considered a "luxury" field in which we would have expected wealth to play an important role. This appears to be the case in the early years: in 1957, Alberta, British Columbia and Ontario were the top three provinces in per capita spending, and the four Atlantic provinces reported no spending in the field. By the later years, however, the pattern was broken, again enphasizing the importance of fiscal capacity, rather than differences in demand. Recreation and culture is also a relatively new field of government activity. It may well be that wealthier provinces in such areas are the pioneers, but that once expectations of government become generalized across all jurisdictions, then the relationship weakens.

In general, in the four more minor categories of government spending, we find much divergence among the provinces and rapid changes over time. In these functions, the regression model explains much less of the variance—ranging from 19 per cent for trade and industry to 50 per cent for recreation and culture. In trade and industry and in recreation, it is the basic control variables which explain the most variants, but for natural resources and transportation it is the province-specific factors which are most important; this is consistent with the widely varying conditions and endowments of provinces and with the high degree of politicization in these areas.

Conclusions

The overwhelming finding of this chapter is the very high degree of convergence among the provinces in their spending patterns over a nineteen-year period. The growing similarity is strongest in total government activity, and in the largest and most expensive fields of health, education and welfare. In other policy fields, some convergence has occurred, but inter-provincial differences remain rather high. The results here link closely with the chapter on regional policy preferences. There, too, we found that pro-vincial populations were becoming more similar to each other in their policy preferences and expectations of government. At the level of the substance of government activity, then, Canada is becoming less, rather than more, diverse.

Taken together these findings suggest a rather paradoxical mix of developments. Canada is becoming a country which is at the same time more and less regionally divided. Consider the kinds of attitudes and behaviour we have found. At the level of the most general orientations to politics, discussed in Chapter II, "Provincial Political Cultures," we find large and continuing interprovincial differences which survive all controls for other factors such as education or income levels. This level of attitudes is the most remote from day-to-day politics. At the level of identities, loyalties and attachment to different levels of government, we found a complex mix of identities, but there was considerable evidence for a relative growth in orientation to provincial governments and a decline in attachments to the centre. At the level of policy preferences, we found not only convergence on substantive economic and social policy, but also divergence in two policy areas: those relating to French-English relations, and those relating to the various symbols of nationhood. Again, then, growing similarity on the basic economic and social roles of government, but sharper division on matters which relate to the character of Canada as a political community. One link between these two sets of findings may well be found in what we have learned about elections and voting behaviour. The lack of linkage between federal and provincial elections and party systems, and the decline in the integrative ability of national political parties are both cause and consequence of the divergence in sense of community. As a result, growing convergence on *what* government should do does not centre on the federal government as the agency which should do it.

This is strengthened by the form of federal policy initiatives in many areas. In part because of the provisions of the B.N.A. Act, the emphasis has been in strengthening provincial capacity to spend through equalization and shared cost devices. Both reinforced the capability of provincial governments to provide the services demanded and were a major force in the expansion of provincial bureaucracies. There is little reason for citizens to turn to Ottawa if Ottawa itself is making it possible for provinces to act effectively.

What accounts for the convergence we have found? There are several possible reasons, all of which interact with each other. First, given the overwhelming importance of wealth in explaining differences among units in other settings, it could be that provinces have become more similar because their economic circumstances have converged. But the large and continuing regional disparities in Canada lead us to qualify this explanation. There is some evidence that richer provinces may have more freedom of action in some fields such as recreation and culture. There is also evidence that poorer provinces depend on government to promote economic development and to overcome unfavourable market forces more than do the stronger provinces. But overall differences in wealth have remarkably little to do with convergence.

The second potential force for convergence is the activity of the federal government, which, as we have seen, takes two forms, general equalization payments to the provinces and shared cost programs. The former acts to bring provincial revenues to the national average, regardless of their initial wealth; the latter, through its provision for matching funds for specific purposes, provides an incentive for provinces to act in designated fields. The overall impact of federal grants is simply to break the bond between the strength and wealth of a provincial economy and its access to public revenue. In recent years, to take the most dramatic example, total federal and provincial spending in Prince Edward Island has exceeded the province's gross provincial product. Once the link has been broken, then the poorer provinces are able to provide a level of spending comparable with the other provinces and, indeed, to respond to the greater burdens posed for welfare services and the like arising from the original poverty.

Conditional grant programs can be seen in part as an element of the general federal contribution, and in part as a more specific inducement. Again, these appear to have a marked effect. Interprovincial similarities are greatest in the fields where shared cost programs loom largest. Convergence is less in other fields, and is indeed less in primary and secondary education, where there is little federal role, than it is in post-secondary education where there is a large one. Federal aid, then, appears to be a critical force underlying the observed convergence.

Nor is the influence of the federal government restricted simply to financial assistance. It is likely that in many of the areas we have examined, federal research activities and federal influence in a wide variety of intergovernmental discussions are also important. In many cases, too, the federal government appears to have responded to provincial demands and initiatives, picking up ideas from one or a few governments and generalizing them later to the whole country. Moreover, while education, welfare and health policies probably pose distinctive issues in each jurisdiction, they are issues which tend to get discussed, in the mass media and other forums, as national issues. By contrast, natural resources or recreation and culture are relatively seldom discussed as national issues; nor is there the kind of society-wide consensus on them that we find in many aspects of social, educational and health policy. We would, therefore, expect to find wider divergence here.

This suggests the need to examine some other possible sources of convergence among provinces. One has already been mentioned: the growing parallelism of preferences, demands and expectations among regional populations which we discovered previously. Especially in social and educational policy, citizens' preferences were not sharply distinguished by region.[22] While it would be desirable to explore such questions in more detail, and while in addition to the national agenda of debate each province has its own particular agenda for discussion (whether to spray forests to protect against the spruce budworm in New Brunswick; how best to invest oil wealth in Alberta), it is probably safe to say that in broad elements of contemporary public policy examined here, it would be unlikely that citizens in different areas would demand radically different amounts or kinds of service.

If we find convergence in citizens' demands, there may also be more convergence at other levels, especially in the demands of interest groups and the expectations of economic elites. For example, labour management relations are primarily a provincial responsibility, though in the past there was considerable leadership from the federal government. We would expect law and policy in this area to reflect the balance of power between labour and capital, and thus to be more "progressive" in provinces where labour is strong or where there have been governments with a labour orientation. This may be why British Columbia and Ontario are generally conceded to have the most advanced labour laws. On the other hand, it could be argued that in all provinces, as in all capitalist societies, the role of the state is given: it must provide conditions for harmony and stability in industrial relations, by providing procedures for mediation, conciliation, and the like. Moreover, as shown in Chapter III, regional variations in public attitudes towards labour issues are relatively small. Hence it is not surprising to find that variations in labour law across the provinces are small indeed.[23]

Another source of convergence is the process of interprovincial communication and of demonstration effects. Thus in many cases innovations by one province are quickly followed by similar developments elsewhere, often using the same language and provisions. Provincial officials faced with a demand are likely first to ask what their colleagues in other provinces have done. Civil servants in particular policy fields often share many professional values and have many opportunities for personal contact. One of the most interesting elements of interprovincial variation, therefore, is in locating where new activities first take root, and examining how they then spread. Dale Poel's examination of innovation in several areas is highly instructive.[24]

The heightened rate of intergovernmental interaction, especially at the interprovincial level, together with the growth of intergovernmental secretariats, such as the Council of Education Ministers, is likely to increase the speed of diffusion of new policy ideas, leading to greater convergence.

Thus we have good reasons to expect — and the data show — that despite the high degree of decentralization in Canada, the policy differences among provinces are limited. The citizen moving from one province to another will find many details that are different, he may find higher quality education or health care in one province than another, but the differences will likely not be substantial. He will not find himself in different policy worlds.

Yet the convergence must not be exaggerated: significant policy differences were found, even though our method was one which probably tended to downplay rather than to exaggerate them. Thus had we been able to disaggregate into specific programs within the broad categories, we would probably have found more variation in some areas. Had we been able to examine some of the newest policy areas, such as consumer protection, or policy with respect to the environment, we probably would have noticed more provincial leaders and laggards. Had we gone beyond spending categories to more qualitative assessments, many differences might have been found, which while small in the overall context, might be profoundly significant to those affected.

But even without these necessary caveats and qualifications, we found much variation, though in most cases there was more in the early periods and less in the later. Table 23 summarizes the differences.

The smallest variation is in total expenditure, though even here in 1972 the lowest spending province spent only three-quarters as much per capita as the highest spending — a difference of more than $200 a person. Health and hospital care also had small indices of dispersion, and high ratios between the highest and lowest spenders. Welfare too had a small index, but there was a very large difference between the extremes: Nova Scotia spent only about half as much per person as did Quebec, even though the two presumably have similar welfare burdens. Dispersion indices were higher, but still moderate in both categories of education, and in transport and communications. Once again, however, the differences are not trivial: Alberta spent $116 for each of its citizens on higher education in 1972,

Table 23
Summary of Variation by Policy Area in
Per Capita Spending, 1972

Function	Top Prov.	Bottom Prov.	/Cap. Spending Top Prov.	/Cap. Spending Bottom	Bottom as % of Top	Top Bottom	DI 1974
Gross General Expenditure	Nfld.	Sask.	$958	$733	74.2	$225	9.3
Health	Ont.	P.E.I.	$250	$177	70.8	$ 73	10.7
Hospitals	Que.	P.E.I.	$165	$111	67.3	$ 54	12.7
Social Welfare	Que.	N.S.	$134	$ 63	47.0	$ 71	16.9
Education — Total	Nfld.	B.C.	$260	$152	58.5	$108	17.8
Primary/ Secondary	N.B.	B.C.	$184	$ 83	45.1	$101	26.9
Post-Secondary	Alta.	N.B.	$116	$ 48	41.4	$ 68	21.2
Transport & Communications	P.E.I.	Alta.	$128	$ 57	44.5	$ 71	21.4
Natural Resources	B.C.	Ont.	$ 33	$ 10	30.3	$ 23	53
Trade & Industry	Nfld.	Ont.	$ 42.24	$ 1.77	4.2	$ 40.47	82.2
Recreation & Culture	Man.	Nfld.	$ 32.96	$ 7.23	22	$ 25.73	47.5

New Brunswick only $48. Finally, in the much smaller spending categories of natural resources, trade and industry and recreation, we found very wide fluctuations by any measure: for example, British Columbia spent $33 per person on natural resources, Ontario $10; Newfoundland spent $42.40 per person promoting trade and industry, Ontario only $1.77.

Provincial profiles varied considerably. In general, we found that the Atlantic provinces tended to spend greater amounts on the economic development activities such as transportation, trade and industry and natural resources. They ranked high in overall government spending, and experienced a considerable change in this regard between 1957 and 1972. In 1957, the four provinces ranked fourth, fifth, seventh and eighth in total spending. By 1972, they ranked first, second, fourth and seventh. New Brunswick was in 1957 below average in spending in eight of the eleven categories; by 1972 it was below in only four. Among the Atlantic provinces, Newfoundland and Nova Scotia stand out but for very different reasons. Newfoundland, especially in the later period, is well above average in spending in every category except total health care, higher education and recreation and culture. Nova Scotia seems to have a much less activist government — above average in spending only on transportation in 1957, and in no category in 1972. Thus, even within the Atlantic region, there appear to be large differences in levels of government activity.

A similar difference shows in the proportions of their budgets the Atlantic provinces devote to different activities. Newfoundland was above average in education, transportation and trade and industry, and was the only Atlantic province to be above average in welfare. New Brunswick was high in education and the economic development categories. Nova Scotia, however, was the only Maritime province to rank higher than average in spending on health and universities. Despite the generally high levels in spending, none of the Atlantic provinces appears to have taken the lead in entering new policy areas. In Dale Poel's analysis of rates of adoption for twenty-five recent government programs all these provinces were well below average.

The increase in Quebec government activism is also evident. Ninth in total spending in 1957, it was third in 1972. In 1957 its spending was above average in only three categories: welfare, university education and natural resources. By 1972, it was above average in six. In 1972 it devoted an above-average proportion of its budget to health and hospital care, welfare and primary and secondary schooling—the classic welfare state activities. Ontario has been below average in total spending levels throughout the period. It stands out only in the educational and health categories. Poel found Ontario well down the list in adopting various social programs, but it was a leader in a variety of other programs. Manitoba has also been below average in its spending on most areas.

Saskatchewan underwent a remarkable change during the period. As the leader in many areas of government activity, it was, in 1957, above average in spending on eight of the categories, all except universities, transportation and trade and industry. By 1972, it was above average in per capita spending in none of the categories. It still, however, devoted a greater than average proportion of its budget to health and welfare, along with transportation. Alberta's spending was above average in most categories in both 1957 and 1972. In 1972, it devoted an above-average proportion of its budget to health, education and natural resources.

British Columbia also underwent a major drop in its relative position throughout the period: in 1957, it was a leader in ten of the eleven categories; in 1957, in only two. It moved from above to below average spending in all the major categories. Saskatchewan's change may in part be due to the defeat of the CCF in 1964, but the British Columbia government remained unchanged throughout the period. All four western provinces appear to have been policy innovators. Thus, in comparing the adoption of new policies, Dale Poel found that they had the highest scores on a variety of new social policies, with Saskatchewan first in the field in many areas.

What explains these kinds of variations? The regression model we have presented gives some very important hints, and is able to explain an impressive amount of the variance found.

First, the coefficients for *equalization* were significant for all expenditure categories except total health spending and post-secondary education, areas in which, as we saw, the Maritime provinces spend less than average levels. Equalization is the fundamental instrument by which provincial revenues become disengaged from provincial income. Partly because of different taxing regimes, and partly because equalization brings revenues up to the national average, rather than to the level of the top province, revenue differences do remain. Nevertheless differences in fiscal capacity stemming from differences in income are much reduced. Indeed, the regression model suggests that a dollar's increase in equalization increases a province's spending by even more than a dollar in the recipient provinces. This suggests that low-income provinces do indeed have high needs for certain public services — for example, welfare and industrial development programs — and that federal assistance gives the stimulus to provide them. The regression coefficients for equalization are in most cases greater than those for income, suggesting it is a more powerful determinant of spending than wealth alone.

Nevertheless, all coefficients for per capita income are also significant, suggesting that, all other things being equal, wealthier provinces do tend to spend more than poorer ones, even though the effects are small. Were it not for federal equalization payments, we would expect these associations to be very much higher. Whether income works through increasing a government's fiscal capacity, or its ability to generate revenues to purchase services, or whether it works through citizens in wealthier areas demanding a higher level of service is impossible to determine. There does appear to be some tendency for wealthier provinces to be better able to take advantage of shared cost programs, and to pay more attention to spending in such areas as higher education, which may be seen as luxuries.

Weekly industrial wages, also associated with wealth, were significant in some cases, suggesting that, especially in services with a high labour component, the costs of providing services also help explain variations in government expenditure. The level of urbanization in a province was also positively associated with levels of spending in all categories.

These four economic factors together explained a very high proportion of the variation in total government spending (about three-quarters), accounted for about half the variance in the major categories of health, education and welfare, and explained smaller proportions in the other categories. That suggests that the unique characteristics of the provinces taken individually are critically important in determining levels of spending in some specific program areas. Federal assistance, and the well-established commitment to areas like education, health care and social welfare leave little room, so to speak, for individual provincial characteristics to play a major part. It is likely that what provincial variations we do find in such programs stem in large part from what might be termed differences in need:

in proportions of poor people shaping the amount spent on welfare; proportions of school age children influencing differences in education spending, and so on. Once outside these areas, however, provincial differences are likely to be much greater. They will stem from differences such as the level of economic development and the consequent need for greater government intervention to alleviate the problems, and from different economic bases, in which the policy demands on an industrialized province like Ontario are likely to be very different from those on a resource-based economy like Alberta's, and so on.

But they may also be explained by political factors. Only two of those were explored here: changes in spending when elections loomed, and variations depending on the party in power. The former was highly significant in total spending, and there were substantial coefficients for health care, education, trade and industry and transportation. The party in power yielded substantial coefficients for health and social welfare, post-secondary education and natural resources, though in the last, the coefficient was barely significant. The ideology of the party in power *does* make a difference. This is supported by Poel's analysis of innovation, especially in social policy, and by a study of expenditure increases by John Dunfield, which finds dramatic increases in social welfare spending in British Columbia, Manitoba and Saskatchewan immediately after the accession to power of NDP governments.[25] These regimes, however, are not distinctive in other spending areas. These results are enough to show that provincial political characteristics do indeed make a difference even when environmental factors are controlled. But they only scratch the surface of the potentially important political factors. Some other political factors could be studied with the kinds of techniques used here. They include a variety of other measures to characterize the state of electoral and party politics: level of interparty competition, votes for different parties, and the like. One could also vary the measures of policy. For example, we could use performance measures, such as hospital beds per capita, pupils per teacher, and so on. Or we could examine such other factors as levels of public ownership. Advances in measuring the distributive effect of taxing and spending for different income classes also suggest a promising avenue for enquiry.[26] But these techniques are necessarily limited, especially because of the need to emphasize only easily quantifiable variables, and because of the way the small number of provincial units in Canada constrains the analytical techniques used.

Further study must move in two directions: it must make detailed examinations of provincial variations in particular policy areas, describing much more fully the quantitative and qualitative differences among provincial education systems, industrial development strategies, consumer protection legislation and a host of other fields, attempting to relate the differences found to the different constellations of political forces, parties, interest groups, and so on found in each province. Second, we need many more of the detailed case studies of individual provinces in which the interaction of social forces, political traditions, and so on can be carefully examined.[27] The policy initiatives of the CCF government in Saskatchewan, the North American pioneer in social legislation, of the Liberal government elected in Quebec at the end of Duplessis's long term, the recent Alberta government policies in resource development, the experiments of the British Columbia NDP government between 1972 and 1975, and others, all require detailed contextual study.

These examples suggest that there is room for policy innovation and variation in the provinces. But it is equally clear that the room is not unlimited, and that provincial policies are likely to vary across a relatively narrow band. All provincial policy-making takes place within the framework of ideas and needs associated with modern industrial societies. It occurs within a relatively similar set of public expectations about the role and purposes of government. Provinces differ little in the instruments that they can deploy to pursue public purposes. They face similar constraints arising out of Canada's dependence on world economic forces, though there is some variation among them. The federal government presence is likely to remain an important influence on all provincial policies, despite the recent moves away from conditional grant programs to less tied forms of financial assistance.

As in other fields we have examined, the pattern is thus one of both similarity and diversity. In public expenditure policy, however, we have shown that over the past twenty years, similarity has grown. In this we support somewhat the views of writers like J. A. Corry in postwar Canada, or Samuel Beer[28] in a more recent analysis of American federalism: that social and economic forces lead to convergence within modern political systems, They do not, however, necessarily lead to greater political unity or centralization of power.

Notes

1. The data collection and statistical analysis for this chapter were carried out by E Robert Miller. For a fuller description of the methods used, and for analysis from a rather different perspective, see his "A Study of the Determinants of Canadian Provincial Government Expenditures" (Master's Essay, Department of Economics, Queen's University, Kingston, 1979).

2. For a review of this literature, see Joyce Munns, "The Environment, Politics and Policy Literature," *Western Political Quarterly*, 2 (1975): 646-667. The best international comparison is Harold Wilensky *The Welfare State and Equality*, (Berkeley: University of California Press, 1975). Frederic Pryor, indeed, argues there is a fundamental similarity in policy output even between capitalist and Communist countries. See *Public Expenditure in Communist and Capitalist Countries* (Homewood, Ill.: Richard D. Irwin, 1968). See also Henry Aaron, "Social Security: International Comparisons," in *Studies in the Economics of Income Maintenance* ed. Otto Eckstein (Washington: Brookings Institution, 1967).

3. See Richard A. Musgrave and Alan L. Peacock, eds., *Classics in the Theory of Public Finance* (London: Macmillan, 1958), pp. 1-8.

4. For recent data see recent editions of *The Provincial Finances* (Toronto: Canadian Tax Foundation, various years).

5. For a general review of the policy literature, see Richard Simeon, "Studying Public Policy," *Canadian Journal of Political Science*, 9(1976): 548-80.

6. The best survey of the economics literature is Richard Bird, *The Growth of Government Spending in Canada* (Toronto: Canadian Tax Foundation, 1970). The political science literature began with the work of V. O. Key's *Southern Politics in State and Nation* (New York: Knopf, 1949) and Duane Lockhard's *New England Politics in State and Nation* (Princeton: Princeton University Press, 1959). The work developed with writers such as James Dawson and James Robinson, "Inter-party Competition and Welfare Politics in American States," *Journal of Politics* 25 (1963): 265-89; Thomas Dye, *Understanding Public Policy* (New York: Prentice-Hall, 1978); Ira Sharkansky, "Government Expenditures and Public Services in the American States," *American Political Science Review*, 61 (1967): 1066-72.

Critiques are found in Munns, "Environment, Politics," and John Fenton and Richard Chamberlayne, "The Literature Dealing With Relationships Between Political Process, Socio-economic Conditions and Public Policies, "*Polity* I (1969): 388-404.

7. All spending data are derived from the standardized classifications reported by Statistics Canada. Data are for provinces only and do not include municipal spending.

8. Wilensky, *Welfare State*, p.47.

9. For example, Wilensky, comparing a group of similarly advanced countries, finds that the institutional characteristic of federalism has an important effect on rates of social security spending.

10. Brian Fry and Richard Winters, "The Politics of Redistribution," *American Political Science Review*, 64 (1970): 508-22, especially p. 521.

11. Dale Poel, "Canadian Provincial and American State Policy" (Paper presented to the Canadian Political Association, Montreal, 1973) p. 15.

12. For a good general survey, see the recent study by William M. Chandler and Marsha A. Chandler, "Policy Trends," in David Bellamy et al., *The Provincial Political Systems: Comparative Essays* (Toronto: Methuen, 1976).

13.Sharkansky, especially "Government Expenditures," pp. 1068, 1070.

14. For a general discussion of provincial policy and budgetary trends, see William Chandler and Marsha Chandler, "Policy Trends," in Ronald Manzer, *Canada: A Social Political Report* (Toronto: McGraw-Hill Ryerson, 1974).

15. See Daniel Latouche, "La vrai nature de la revolution tranquille," *Canadian Journal of Political Science*, 7 (1974).

16. T. K. Shoyama, "Public Services and Regional Development in Canada," *Journal of Economic History*, 26 (1978): 498-593. The index of dispersion here follows Shoyama.

17. *The National Finance, 1975-76* (Toronto: Canadian Tax Foundation, 1976), p. 133.

18. OECD, "Education — Governments, Goals and Policy-Making," excerpted in *Canadian Federalism: Myth or Reality*, 3rd ed., ed. Peter Meekison (Toronto: Methuen, 1977), pp. 416-429, p. 419.

19. Ronald Manzer, *Canada: A Sociopolitical Report* (Toronto: McGraw-Hill Ryerson, 1974).

20. Duff Spafford, "Highway Employment and Provincial Elections" (Paper presented to the Canadian Economic Association, Fredericton, 1977).

21. Albert MacDonald, "*The Politics of Acquisition: A Study of Corruption in Prince Edward Island*" (M.A. thesis, Queen's University, 1979). He notes that P.E.I. has the lowest number of car registrations per mile of road in Canada, but has the highest proportion of paved roads and the smallest population per mile of paving. He shows a strong relationship between paving and party vote in different constituencies.

22. For an attempt to relate preferences to outcomes, see Jeffrey Obler, "The Odd Compartmentalization: Public Opinion, Aggregate Data and Policy Analysis," *Policy Studies Journal*, 7 (1979): 524-39.

23. Gail Hogarth, "Labour Policy in Canada" (Essay presented in Politics 837, Queen's University, 1979).

24. Dale Poel, "The Diffusion of Legislation Among the Canadian Provinces: A Statistical Analysis, "*Canadian Journal of Political Science*, 9 (1976): 605-26.

25. John Dunfield, "Ideology and Public Policies: Some Quantitative Indicators" (Essay presented in Politics 482, Queen's University, 1975).

26. For example, Fry and Winters, "The Politics of Redistribution."

27. For a recent example, see John Richards and Larry Pratt, *Prairie Capitalism: Power and Influence in the New West* (Toronto: McClelland and Stewart, 1979).

28. J. A. Corry, "Constitutional Trends and Federalism," in A.R.M Lower et al., *Evolving Canadian Federalism* (Durham: Duke University Press, 1958); Samuel Beer, "The Modernization of American Federalism," *Publius*, 3 (1973): 49-95.

CONCLUSION
Province, Nation, Country and Confederation
Richard Simeon, David J. Elkins

The preceding chapters have uncovered a fascinating and complex inter-weaving of different strands. Regionalism is indeed multidimensional. At some levels we find large and growing divergencies among provincial, regional and linguistic groups, at others we find growing similarity and complementarity. Wherever one slices into Canadian political life one discovers rich patterns of territorial and ethnic variation and strong local orientations, traditions and identities. But we also discover common pat-terns, and nation-wide orientations, as well as political divisions which cut across region. Images of Canada as no more than a disparate collection of regional entities, linked together by nothing more than an obsolete federal system, are as misleading as images of "One Canada."

But what follows from such observations? How is the balance and interplay between country-wide and regional forces to be given institutional form in the structure of Canadian governments? Which elements are to be mobilized and reflected in political institutions? What images of society and nation are to be expressed in the Canadian constitution and in the practices of government? We will address such questions in this conclusion. They are, of course, the central questions in the recent debate on the future of Confedera-tion and the Canadian communities. That debate arises most immediately out of the growth of Quebec nationalism and the election of a provincial government dedicated to independence. But it ranges more widely. It concerns fundamentally differing images of what the country is or should be, whether two nations, a group of strong, autonomous regional and provincial entities with a weak central government, or a strong central thrust built around a pan-Canadian vision. As Alan Cairns observes, when we talk about rearranging political institutions, we are not only talking about tax points and administrative details—we are accepting or rejecting, strengthening or weakening, conceptions of community with powerful psychic and moral implications.[1]

For most peoples at most times, the very definition and structure of the polity in which they reside is not in question: it is given, taken for granted. Canadians today cannot take the existing polity for granted; they must choose, and the outcome remains unclear. So what lessons for constitution makers grow out of our analysis of the dimensions of regional diversity? Can the materials we have explored here help explain the present crisis? Can they point to possible future alternatives? How do they relate to the constitutional debate as it unfolds in task force reports, federal-provincial conferences and other settings? Certainly no magic solution jumps out of the preceding pages. Much of the data is drawn from the period before the recent escalation in the intensity of debate which followed the Quebec election of November 1976. We have slighted several dimensions of regionalism, especially the historical and economic aspects. We have only incidentally studied the political elites at the federal and provincial levels, who do much to define and mobilize opinion and who will inevitably be the chief actors in any new constitutional settlement. Here we will look at some of these other forces which shape and express the raw material of public attitudes.

The analyses set out in previous chapters do foreshadow and illuminate recent events, and point to some of the limits and possibilities of change.

Perhaps the most important lesson is the underlining of the complexity and subtlety of the forces which must be accommodated in the constitutional debate. Constitutional proposals which fail to take account of this complexity are doomed to fail. The debate is not a black and white one, between separatism and unity, centralization and decentralization, provincial power and federal dominance. Perhaps paradoxically, Canadian citizens themselves, on our evidence, often see these alternatives not as mutually exclusive, but as complementary. They want *both* more freedom of action for their provincial communities *and* a centre which can speak for all of Canada. Regional and national loyalties are not, and need not be, in conflict. And on reflection, of course, there is no contradiction: a federal system is predicated on the existence of such multiple loyalties. This ambivalence, reflected both in differences among groups of citizens and in the opinions of individuals, extends to Quebeckers and perhaps even to the Parti Québécois itself. For example, the recent survey finding[2] that almost half of Quebec respondents who opt for sovereignty believe that Quebec would still send members to the federal Parliament probably stems not only from simple ignorance of the sovereignty program but rather from a desire *both* for independence and for the Canadian connection. Similarly, the formula "sovereignty-association" may in part be a result of the desire to avoid the economic costs of outright separation, but it may also reflect a genuine tie to the larger Canadian system. The symbolism on the cover of the P.Q. document "D'égal à égal," the basic statement of its program, was not accidental: the title was flanked by a fleur-de-lys and a maple leaf, identical in size.[3]

Patterns of Similarity and Difference

It follows that a new constitution which enshrines one model to the exclusion of others will necessarily be inadequate. The imaginative feat required is to find a way to reconcile and harmonize what may on the surface appear to be irreconcilable images, especially when stated in uncompromising terms by some political leaders. This is reinforced by our central finding: that the Canadian communities are simultaneously becoming both more similar and more different, more alike and more distinct.

In Chapter I, we found a population highly sensitized to regional differences. Canadians do indeed think of the country in regional terms—though these conceptions are highly varied, with some thinking in terms of provinces, others of groups of provinces, still others of entities not tied to existing boundaries.

"The Sense of Place" also demonstrated some sharp differences in images of Canada's cultural linguistic identity. French Canadians tend to accept the "dualist" model, to see the country as a partnership of two language groups. The question then becomes: how to institutionalize this dualism? Recent spokesmen for French Canada divide on this question. French Canadians outside Quebec, along with some federalists inside the province, argue that dualism must be entrenched within national institutions, and given expression in French language rights and services across the country;[4] the P.Q. and many others in Quebec emphasize that dualism should be expressed in the relation between governments, one pole expressed through Quebec, the other through Ottawa and the other provinces.

English-speaking Canadians, however, strongly preferred the model of a multicultural mosaic. While substantial numbers of Quebeckers felt Quebec should have special consideration in Confederation—in 1968—only small minorities elsewhere agreed. Later surveys have demonstrated continued Anglophone hostility to any form of special status, a consideration which led both the Task Force on Canadian Unity and the Ontario Advisory Committee on Confederation[5] to try to blur the issue, by proposing changes which would make it possible to have special status for all, or perhaps more cynically, de facto special status without actually calling it that.

Chapter I also demonstrated a significant growth in support for and identification with provincial governments as compared with Ottawa. Only citizens of Ontario, together with the "hostage groups," French Canadians outside Quebec and English Canadians within Quebec, appear, by 1974, to attach greater weight to Ottawa. In 1965, eleven of the twelve province-language groups tended to see Ottawa as the most important government. By 1974, all but citizens of Ontario and the two hostage groups leaned to the provinces. One might have expected that the shock of the 1976 Quebec election would have provoked a tendency for residents of other regions to rally in support of the federal power. Instead, while there has been much expression of a will to preserve unity, we have seen a greater tendency to argue the provincialist position. Developments in Quebec appear to have had a demonstration effect, encouraging others to express their grievances and to claim greater autonomy for their provinces too.

Similarly, there also appears to be a growing tendency for Canadians to see Confederation in zero-sum terms—to believe that the system has favoured regions other than one's own, and that the federal government has been unresponsive, unrepresentative and unfair. Debate on this issue at the elite level has been intense, reflected in the "battle of the balance sheets" between Quebec and Ottawa,[6] and in the tendency for spokesmen of other regions to argue they have been neglected and exploited. Reading these debates, one is tempted to believe that *every* region is a loser. "Alienation,"one citizen told the Task Force on Canadian Unity, "is the one thing we all hold in common."[7] Much of this conflict stems not from different provincial values and goals, but from similar ones. For example, conflict over oil and gas prices and over the use of revenues generated by these resources turns on similar, but directly competing, drives for economic development in producing and consuming provinces. The real issue is *where* development will take place, or what the *territorial* distribution of the costs and benefits will be. And in this conflict, the crucial question becomes who is designated by the terms *we* and *ours* in the statement "We must reap the benefits of our oil resources for ourselves": Albertans? Canadians? Companies? Workers? Thus we return to questions of identity and community.

Finally, in Chapter III, our exploration of policy preferences discovered sharp and continuing regional and linguistic divergence in two policy areas: French-English relations and the national symbols of the monarchy. Again, it is the political community which is in question.

Taken together, all these findings reinforce the commonly held impression that there are increasing conflicts among provinces and language groups; that citizens' ties to the federal government are weakening while their links to the provinces are growing. Canada is becoming even more a country of regions—and the trend was evident long before the recent constitutional crisis. But this interpretation must be immediately qualified. To emphasize regionalism is to miss many common elements. Regional divisions coexist with loyalties, attitudes and behaviour associated with many other aspects of social diversity. Regional differences do not so much eliminate other sources of difference, but interact with them in complex ways. Consider some of our other findings.

First, Chapter III demonstrates that Canadians in all regions are becoming more similar to each other in their expectations and preferences with respect to most areas of public policy. They may increasingly look to their provincial governments, but they expect them to provide much the same services and programs. Even where differences remain, opinions tend to move in the same direction, in approximately the same degree, in all regions. This consequence was most striking in Quebec. On most issues, opinion there has become much more like opinion in other provinces.

Second, as Chapter VIII demonstrates, there is even sharper convergence among the provinces in their patterns of public expenditure. Powerful provinces, disposing of greater proportions of total government spending, have not used this power to move in very different policy directions from poorer provinces.

Third, in several chapters we stress that region and province by no means erode other patterns of cleavage common to modern industrial states. Class, religion, age and other factors all help shape attitudes and interests independently of region. Moreover, the correlation between these other cleavages and province of residence are, with one central exception, weak. True, there are higher proportions of poor people in the Maritimes and Quebec than in Ontario or British Columbia, and farmers make up a larger percentage of the work force in Saskatchewan or Manitoba than elsewhere, but in general demographic divisions cut across regional and linguistic lines. This tendency may well be increasing: no longer is Alberta the "one-class" society of individual farmers described by Macpherson.[8] If the Lougheed government's ambitious plans for economic diversification succeed, then the Alberta work force will in the long run look much like Ontario's.[9]

There is an important lesson for constitution makers here. It is simply not the case that on all issues the interests of Quebeckers, Ontarians or British Columbians are systematically opposed. Common interests crisscross region. Therefore, constitutional change aimed only at institutionalizing regional diversity may be dangerous. It may artificially inflate the territorial dimension and frustrate the mobilization and expression of interests otherwise defined. The exception, of course, is the strong coincidence of language and territory. The French-English division is closely aligned with the borders of Quebec and the rest of Canada, and this is what makes the conflict qualitatively different from all the other regional grievances. But even here the fit is not exact, with large minorities of French-speaking Canadians outside Quebec and of English-speakers inside. A definition of the Canadian problem, and a search for solutions, which poses the issue *either* as one of reconciling Quebec and Canada or as reconciling English- and French-speakers misses an important dimension.

Fourth, we have seen that loyalties to region and country (not to mention city, family or profession) are not necessarily incompatible. Canadians do have multiple loyalties — and this is one of the forces that sustain a federal system. Strong ties to a provincial government do not preclude support for a strong federal government. For many, if not most, Canadians a strong Canada *entails* or presumes a strong province, and vice versa. This suggests the inadequacy of two extreme positions: on one hand that regionalism or provincialism is somehow the "problem" whose solution requires that it must be replaced by an overarching Canadian loyalty; and, on the other hand, that we should fundamentally shift power to the provinces. Political institutions must reflect this dynamic interplay between region and country and see them as mutually supportive rather than destructive.

Explanations: Mobilizing Regional Cleavages

What explains these complex patterns of similarity and dissimilarity, of convergence and divergence, of integration at the level of ideology and substantive attitudes, but divergence in conceptions of community? And why is it that it is the latter force which now dominates Canadian politics, so much, indeed, that the continuation of the political regime is in question?

There are many causes, though it is impossible to weigh them with any accuracy. At the level of culture one is tempted to identify a vacuum at the centre: the lack of a common revolutionary tradition; the lack of unifying symbols; the divisive character of many symbols we do have; the pervasive pull of external cultural forces, first from Britain and France, later from the United States. The cultural poles are either beyond Canada, or subnational.

Second, resurgence of territorially based ethnonationalist movements is not restricted to Canada: related movements have appeared in much of Europe, from Britain to Spain. While the power and character of each of these movements vary greatly, there may be some common threads, such as a reaction against the complex, centralized bureaucratic state, and a search for smaller, more homogeneous and more accessible political communities.[10] In addition, the expanded scope of government activity, and its central role in allocating material benefits once allocated by a more anonymous market, brings to the fore the distributional question of who wins and loses. Where regional diversities are large and where pre-existing identities remain, then it is likely that such tensions will be expressed in territorially focused terms. Thus while the apparently ineluctable trend of modernization and of technocratic, rationalist, bureaucratic decision-making seems to point to centralization, these same forces may generate their own reaction. Thus Arend Lijphart links the rise of ethnonationalist movements to a "new wave of democratization."[11] Similarly, Sydney Tarrow argues that:

> . . . if functional centralization has had one single effect, it has been to lead citizens at the periphery to turn more and more to the local, regional and primordial identities around them. These (as in Canada) in many cases predate the national state. In the long-run therefore, the functional cleavages that many scholars saw displacing the territorial dominance in politics may actually reinforce it.[12]

More important is the impact of economic forces. Far from creating an interdependent and complementary national economy, the particular character of economic development, and modernization in general, in Canada has accentuated some regional conflicts.[13] The extent to which this development is an inevitable result of the working of market forces and of the distribution of resources or is instead a result of deliberate government policy, is a source of important academic controversy.

Economic development in Canada has been highly uneven. While Confederation greatly benefited much of Ontario and the Montreal region, and led to a rapid expansion of the West, it coincided with and appears to have accelerated a drastic decline in Atlantic Canada. The resulting regional disparities have been persistent, and are only partially alleviated by various federal redistributive policies.[14]

The *structure* of the economy varies regionally. British Columbia exists on timber, fishing and mining; Alberta on petroleum, gas and agriculture; Saskatchewan on agriculture and mining; Ontario on manufacturing, finance, mining, and so on across the country. This produces varied economic elites, class structures and economic interests, which is underlined by the Canadian dependence on primary industry and natural resources. Natural resources are, of course, located in specific geographical areas, thus contributing to a regionalized economy. This, combined with provincial constitutional control over natural resources, has led to frequent alliances between provincial governments and resource industries. Provinces see resource wealth as "theirs." Unfortunately, regional specialization does not necessarily result in regional equality. Moreover, as a trading nation, Canada's regions trade with other countries even more than they trade with each other, reducing the sense of mutual dependence.[15] Foreign ownership and dependence on foreign markets tend to accentuate these external links and thus contribute to fissiparous tendencies. The ability of central financial institutions to act as integrating forces is also undermined by direct financial links with outside sources of capital both by provincial industry and provincial governments. The regionalized economy has also led to the creation of regional metropolises, each tending to serve its own hinterland. Urbanization, as J.M.S. Careless notes, may be a national phenomenon; but it does not have nationalizing effects.[16] It is fascinating to see much of the current Canadian conflict in terms of competition among the various metropolises — the struggle between French and English for the centre of Montreal; the growth of Toronto and the decline of Montreal as the primary financial centre; and the challenge of Calgary, Edmonton and Vancouver to the central Canadian hegemony.

Regionalized economies give rise to provincially based firms and industries and to local economic elites which have strong vested interests in promoting regional development even while they have ties both to the central government and to foreign centres. They wish to use the provincial governments as vehicles for their interests, and the provincial governments have an interest in promoting such regional industries and elites. Leo Panitch has argued that the governments are reflections of conflict among elites:

. . . the persistence of provincial state power is to be understood in terms of the differing class stuctures of various Canadian regions and in terms of the regional fractions of the bourgeoisie. The dominant classes, or rather class fractions, in the provinces, often unable to constitute a unity with their counterparts either through political parties or in economic coalitions, have used the provincial state to express their interests.[17]

Pratt argues for a complementary effect:

The powers and resources of an interventionist, "positive" government are being employed to nurture the development and to defend the province-building interests, of an ascendant class of indigenous business entrepreneurs, urban professionals, and state administrators.[18]

In this vein, Vivian Nelles describes in fascinating detail the links between different sections of Ontario capital and the two levels of government.[19] One should not feel compelled to choose between a model of economic elites causing government policies versus a model of provincial governments aiding otherwise dependent elites. Both processes are at work in a continuing cycle of reinforcing causes and effects.

The most important example of this class-based interpretation of provincialism is found in Quebec. Several writers argue persuasively that the drive for greater Quebec autonomy, for a greater role for state enterprise and planning, and for measures to promote the role of French-speakers in industry is related to the emergence of a new group of middle-class professionals who found that government both in Ottawa, and more important, in the Montreal business world was dominated by Anglophones.[20] This is another sense in which modernization and economic development lead to greater rather than less territorial/ethnic conflict. Change in Quebec's class structure and value systems meant that French and English Canadians now found themselves competing in the same arenas for the same benefits.

An alternative explanation for the mobilization of cleavage on ethnic/territorial lines focuses less on cultural or economic differences. Instead, it locates the dynamic of interregional conflict in the effects of institutional factors and in the character of political elites.

The cultural, historical, ethnic and economic forces we have identified all point to the salience of regional differences in Canada and suggest that, one way or another, they must be accommodated and reconciled. But these social and economic forces are fluid enough, and the contrary forces strong enough, that their effect is not fixed. How salient they are, how intense the conflicts they generate, and whether or not new issues arise, which transcend region or divide the population along other lines, are also shaped by the way in which institutional forms shape and channel political life.

The institutional/elite explanation begins with the observation of E.E. Schattscheider:

All forms of political organization have a bias in favour of the exploitation of some kinds of conflict and the suppression of others. . . . Some issues are organized out.[21]

In this view, then, the regionalized politics of Canada is not simply a function of the prevalence of regional identities or even of the regional distribution of political opinions. It is also a result of a regionalized political structure — one which systematically underlines, reinforces and makes salient the territorial dimension, and devalues other dimensions. Federal institutions exist largely as a result of regional and ethnic forces, but they also perpetuate and enhance them. Regional identities and regional interests, to become effective, need an institutional base.

Two interacting sets of institutional factors structure the forces of regionalism in Canada. First are some characteristics of the institutions of the central government itself — all of which seriously undermine the integrative ability of federal political parties and weaken the ability of Parliament and cabinet to represent and reconcile diverse interests. Second is the federal system, which ensures that regional loyalties will be given effective political expression; other interests and cleavages are blurred, frustrated and denied a political base. These structural factors, more than the inadequacies of particular leaders or parties, account for recent political developments. The result of a decline in the integrative capacity of Ottawa and of the growth of provincial governments is that relations between governments — the federal-provincial conferences — have become the primary instruments not only for reflecting and expressing interregional and interethnic conflict but also for accommodating and managing it.

The weakness of federal institutions is most evident in the national party system. Earlier chapters have detailed many aspects of a regionally fragmented party system. Region is among the most important correlates of the vote. Voters often divide in their support for parties at each level. Federal and provincial parties of the same name often have little in common organizationally or ideologically. Provincial party systems seldom duplicate or parallel the national system. The party system thus does not knit together politics at federal, provincial and local levels, nor does it provide a channel for movement of political leaders across levels.[22]

Most important, as Richard Johnston demonstrates historically, and as the 1979 federal election results dramatically underline, there is no longer a national party system. The Liberals are frozen out across the West; the Conservatives in Quebec. This imbalance is strongly accentuated by the effects of the single-member plurality election system which systematically distorts the relationship between the proportion of votes a party wins and the proportion of seats it gains.[23] It rewards the leading party and hurts the followers: thus in 1979, the Liberal party won no seats in the North, Prince Edward Island, Saskatchewan and Manitoba, though it won more than one-fifth of the vote in all those places. In 1972 and 1974, Liberals won a quarter of Alberta's votes, but were rewarded with no seats. The reverse happens to Tories in Quebec: its 16 per cent of the vote there in 1974 yielded only three seats out of seventy-five.

Consider how different the distribution of seats would be if they were allocated proportionally: with thirteen seats in Quebec, 10 per cent of the Tory caucus would be Quebeckers. Since in previous elections the Conservative vote in Quebec was higher, so would have been the party's number of seats. The Liberals in 1979 would have won thirteen seats on the Prairies and eight more from British Columbia. In that case 15 per cent, rather than the present 2 per cent, of its caucus would hail from the West.[24]

The results of these distortions — which also badly hurt the NDP, and thus may well help frustrate mobilization on class lines — are serious. They may well encourage divisive electoral tactics by encouraging parties to invest their resources and appeals only in regions where they can succeed. It means party caucuses are unrepresentative — and thus find it more difficult to reflect interests of excluded regions. Certainly, regions frozen out of representation in the governing party and caucus, as Quebeckers were during the brief Clarke government and as Westerners have been for many years, are likely to feel their interests will be forgotten. Between 1963 and 1979, the three Prairie provinces held 18 per cent of the seats in Parliament, but never held more than 7 per cent of the seats in the governing party; in three of the five elections between 1963 and 1974, the Prairies held less than 3 per cent of the governing caucus. After the 1979 election Quebec, with more than a quarter of the seats in Parliament, had just 2 per cent of the seats in the Tory caucus. This made it be harder to build a truly representative cabinet, as Prime Minister Clark's desperate efforts to find Quebec members so clearly showed. In the British parliamentary system, which gives such broad power to the governing party and especially to the cabinet, these are crippling defects, which seriously undermine Ottawa's legitimacy and its ability to lead, to represent and to serve as a forum for accommodation. While it would be wrong to lay the blame for the decline in the integrative capacity of national parties solely on the electoral system, there can be little doubt that it has contributed to the problem, and that, in turn, has seriously undermined the potential for classical brokerage politics at the national level. In this brokerage model each major party would have roots in all major regions and groups, whose representatives would bargain with the party. For many years the Liberals came close to this ideal, but not in recent years. The model of brokerage at the centre has been replaced by bargaining between governments; the party system has been replaced by the federal-provincial conference. The Canadian party system does little to maintain "the federal bargain."[25]

Some other aspects of British-style cabinet government have similar effects. Party discipline inhibits members from acting as regional spokesmen or from forming cross-party alliances. Cabinet secrecy and solidarity have operated to reinforce "national"or "average" positions rather than to reveal regional divisions. Moreover, the growth of government has so increased the managerial and policy roles of cabinet members that their representative and public roles have been weakened. This is combined with the growth of a more prime minister-centred leadership, which downgrades the role of regional leaders with an independent base bargaining with each other in cabinet.

All these factors contribute to a weakening of integrative institutions at the national level, despite a variety of policies (the Official Languages Act, regional development policies, and so on) designed to spread benefits widely.

The regional representative role has been increasingly assumed by provincial governments. This is the second side of the institutional coin. Federalism — with the powers and resources it gives provincial governments — provides an institutional focus for regional identities and interests. A political cleavage is laid over the other cleavages in society and it tends to force them too into the territorial mould. That is, divisions which reinforce the territorial division will be highlighted; those which do not will either be defined in such a way that they do conform to the pattern or they will tend to be ignored. There are two reasons for this. At the societal, or mass level, conflicts will tend to be encapsulated at the provincial level. Because provincial governments make the decisions, groups will have to turn to them, will have to respond to provincial policies and to the demands of other groups with which they are in competition at that level. Communication with similar groups in other provinces will therefore be inhibited, and indeed be strategically wasteful. For example, labour law in Canada is largely a matter of provincial jurisdiction. The labour movement itself must take on a federated character, and provincial labour federations must be primarily concerned with fighting their own local battles. If labour laws were primarily a national concern, the national labour groups would presumably be more powerful, and there would be a strong incentive for labour groups and associated political leaders to promote labour unity across provincial boundaries. The same analysis might be made for other groups and interests in other fields. Indeed it is not so much the case that new issues, like environmentalism, have not arisen, but that, as often as not, they have done so *within* provinces. Indeed, many groups and professional associations have split along ethnic and regional lines in recent years, from air traffic controllers to political scientists — where the relationship between the Canadian Political Science Association and the Société Canadian de science politique closely resembles a working model of sovereignty-association. National groups, such as the Association of Universities and Colleges of Canada and the Canadian Union of Students, have been weakened by shifts of power to the provinces, and many others find their structures shaped by the need to adapt to the federal system.[26] Again, such developments, like those in parties, point to the weakness of integrative institutions in Canada. The federal structure thus fragments social forces and inhibits their mobilization on a national basis, perpetuating the regional difference. It places major hurdles in the way of those who would mobilize national movements or seek national solutions.

The system also generates a relationship between federal and provincial governments which might be called "competitive state-building." Governments are large, complex organizations with their own distinct organizational interests. As governments at both levels have grown and the number of persons dependent on government for employment has risen, these organizational interests have also become more salient. Provincial governments thus can be expected to seek status, power and electoral advantage; for the same reasons so, too, will the federal government. Hence, a provincial government is motivated to accentuate and emphasize the degree of internal provincial unity, to exaggerate the sense of difference from Ottawa. It will seek greater freedom of action, by resisting "federal intrusions" and by retaining control over "its" resources. It will argue that only the provincial government understands and can represent regional interests. It too will try to respond to new and popular demands by citizens.

Two factors suggest to us that this competitive state-building may have reached a plateau. While competition will undoubtedly continue, it will take different forms from the experience of the past twenty or thirty years. For one thing, there has been a growth in the 1970s of a reaction against "big government," whether federal or provincial. The most famous symbol of these popular sentiments is the tax revolt, such as the passage of Proposition 13 in California, to which Canadian politicians have responded, even though there is little evidence that such feelings are strong in Canada. Whether this is a "conservative" or "reactionary" tendency as some have alleged, the fact is that politicians no longer feel secure in promising bold new ventures requiring new forms of expenditure. Instead, political leaders compete on the basis of promises for greater efficiency, "privatization" of government enterprises, reduction of taxes and expenditures, control of government deficits, and the fight against "loose money" and inflation. We doubt that these trends will prove to be temporary fads. Indeed, they may set a tone for decades to come and thereby contribute to a new kind of competition to see which level of government can control expenditures most responsibly and efficiently.

A second factor that may ease the intergovernment bidding concerns the repeated assertions by some political leaders that "the welfare state" is now in place. Therefore, changes and reforms — and conflicts — will centre on efficient reallocation of programs and uniformity of standards (the latter being well advanced, judging by the data in Chapter VIII). Health care is nearly universal, unemployment benefits may be restricted rather than expanded in the future, there is no need to build new schools or universities, and nearly everyone is covered by one or more pension plans. As the rate of population growth declines and as the age distribution changes, some programs will decrease in cost while others expand. But the overall complex of institutions called "the welfare state" should be near an equilibrium point by now.

The result of "big government" has been rising fiscal resources and competition over tax revenues. These conflicts will no doubt continue. But the extraordinary growth rates of areas under provincial jurisdiction (such as health and education) is now over; and the popular support for massive federal intervention in economic redistribution is being challenged widely.

As governments grew, they intruded on each others' responsibilities and jurisdictions. As the levels of expenditure stabilize, competition and conflict will continue, but their focus will shift.

The emphasis in the future will be on competition for control over the levers of economic development, and the use of these levers by provincial governments to control their own economic environments, often in direct competition with either federal development policies, focused on maximizing aggregate national income, or with the development strategies of other provinces. Such conflict becomes especially intense when resource endowments differ radically and when general national and international economic conditions engender a "politics of scarcity." The tension between the country-centred values of redistribution and of maintenance of an integrated Canadian common market will be in increasing conflict with the province-centred values of using provincial resources and provincial powers to promote the growth of provincial economies and to challenge the central-Canadian dominance in the national economy.

Alan Cairns states the elite-institutional position most forcefully: the growth of regionalism and provincialism, he argues, is not the cause but the result of expansionist provincial governments. Governments, he suggests, are so large and deploy so many resources that they mould, rather than serve, the societies in which they are rooted:

> . . . the support for powerful, independent provincial governments is a product of the political system itself, it is fostered and created by provincial government elites employing the policy-making apparatus of their jurisdiction . . . such support need not take the form of a distinct culture, society or nation as these are conventionally understood. . . . Passivity, indifference or the absence of strong opposition from their environments may be all that provincial governments need in order to grow and thrive.[27]

Stated this baldly, the elite/institutional model is exaggerated. Governments' capacity to mould their environments is by no means unlimited. Expressions of provincial power are successful not only because of organizational skills and constitutional resources, but also because provincial boundaries do indeed coincide with real differences of regional identity and interest. And functional interests will often use their territorial leverage to fight out their conflicts of interest.[28] Nevertheless, it is clear that the federal system and the interests of those who man federal and provincial governments do indeed reinforce regionalism and minimize other divisions. Canadian politics does revolve around regional issues; issues which need not, in themselves, be seen as inherently regional in nature tend to be interpreted in regional terms. We have a kind of "territorial corporatism" conducted through the relations between governments, rather than the familiar European corporatism in which the interests are defined in more functional terms.

We must be cautious, however, about what we make of comparisons with other countries. It does no good to lament the fact that regionalism is more potent here than in Europe or that we lack the class-based parties and cleavages of Europe. The circumstances of history, geography and institutions cannot easily be circumvented. Similarly, we must consider the consequences of the size and number of provinces, ten in Canada of uneven size compared to fifty in the United States. How would Canadian politics be different if the two largest provinces were at opposite ends of the country — as are New York and California in the United States — rather than cheek by jowl? We cannot explore such matters in this book, but we must bear in mind that there are features such as these which we take for granted and which may have profound implications for the way political games are played and for any reforms we may undertake.

Cultural, economic and political/institutional forces, then, all tend to strengthen the forces of regionalism and to weaken those who would mobilize politics around the centre. In each province the specific pattern varies. Quebec is the clearest case of aggressive provincial state-building activities, since the provincial state is allied to the aspirations of French Canadians for whom it is to be the one instrument for collective action which they unequivocally control. In Alberta and, to a lesser extent, Saskatchewan, provincial development strategies have revolved around the desire to exploit and maintain their natural resource base. In Ontario, while its government too has expanded in scope and power, the weight of Ontario in the national government, combined with more "nationalist" identities, have somewhat muted the province-building drive. Indeed, as the province's economic strength has been challenged by a resurgent West, Ontario has recently argued strongly the case for a powerful federal government, calling for protection of the national market and redistribution of resource revenues. In Atlantic Canada, the dependency on federal assistance has also led to a less aggressive stance towards Ottawa. Availability of resources, as the Scottish case shows, is a powerful stimulus to regionalist demands. One can guess that little beyond fiscal benefits ties Newfoundland to Canada: discovery of oil off its shores would powerfully reinforce autonomist tendencies. The province's 1979 Throne Speech was a passionate statement of its intention to free itself from dependence on a "paternalistic, centralized federalism." Newfoundlanders, said the government, intend to secure "to themselves the means by which they as a people can secure their future as a distinct society." The means are to be oil, gas and a revived fishery.

Thus, if the data derived from attitudes are ambiguous or indeterminate, the institutional forces clearly push towards interregional conflict. They explain the apparent paradox we found in our data: the movement towards communities which are at once more distinct and institutionally separate, while at the same time they are more alike, and more highly interdependent in policy terms. They suggest that despite a high level of interdependence and shared goals and values, there are few institutional linkages and networks binding together the regional communities. Federal and provincial political systems have little in common and few points of political contact; rather than forming a seamless web, they are sharply differentiated. The pattern of institutional forces also means that the contemporary political crisis in Canada, whatever its roots in cultural, ethnic and economic diversity, is preeminently a crisis of the relations between *governments*, a crisis of institutions. It is governments which channel, define and mobilize the forces of regionalism and nationalism. It is the executive-bureaucratic process of intergovernmental negotiation which both expresses these tensions and, in the constitutional negotiations, is called upon to resolve them. Thus the constitutional debates turn on the division of jurisdiction, the reform of federal institutions and the like. Underlying the debates are questions of power, representation and legitimacy, and differing conceptions of community.

Alternatives for the Future

This is the context in which Canadians are now debating their constitutional future. Which of the tendencies are to be reinforced? How and where are the regional/ethnic communities to be represented, how and where are their interests to be accommodated? The alternatives can be understood in terms of a debate between three broad models: the country-building, the province-building and the Quebec nation-building. They can be used as descriptive models to show how the cultural, economic and political forces of region and nation have interacted through Canadian history. But here we use them as normative models, as conceptions, in some cases explicit but in others implicit, of Canadian community and of the Canadian state from which can be derived specific proposals for change. Conversely, such proposals can also be assessed in terms of these models: which does any given suggestion reinforce? Each of these models picks up on different strands in the data we have examined; each suggests different directions for constitutional change; each has powerful institutional support, and opposition. Each has many variants. Few Canadians — certainly not those who turned up in our various surveys — hold unambiguously to one or another: the challenge therefore is to reconcile them, and provide a framework for continuous dialogue among them.

First is what might be called the country-building,[29] or Ottawa-centred model. Country builders stress the primacy of the pan-Canadian community and of the central government. This model assumes that there is a national interest which is distinct from and transcends local or provincial interests. The national government must define and implement the national interest. Furthermore, as with the brokerage model, this one suggests that federal politicians can themselves represent regional and linguistic interests, and that federal institutions can be the arena within which these differences are reconciled. It thus rejects the identification of provincial or regional interests with those of provincial governments; it similarly denies that the Quebec government is the only or even the primary political expression for French-speaking Canadians. The central government, therefore, is not just one among eleven competing governments: it is, rather, the senior government.

A wide variety of proposals follow from this perspective, though few exponents assert them all.

First, it is argued that there is a vital need to create a stronger Canadian identity and to promote symbols and values which unify regions and language groups, rather than divide them. A common national loyalty and identity, in the words of the Liberal document *A Time for Action* "must transcend the identifications Canadians have with provinces, regions and linguistic and other differences."[30] Agencies like the Canadian Broadcasting Corporation, the Canada Council and the National Film Board reflect this impulse. So does the desire of recent federal governments to adopt symbols such as the maple leaf flag, to have a ringing declaration of faith in Canada in the preamble to a new constitution, to remove the last vestiges of colonialism by "patriating" the British North America Act, to enforce Canadian content rules in print and broadcast media, and so on. Canada-builders are hesitant to allow greater provincial power in culture and communications which might limit these activities. Some also argue that a case can be made for a greater federal role in education, since it is such a crucial agent of socialization. The federal commitment to entrench a charter of rights in the constitution, Cairns suggests, is similarly an attempt "to construct by constitutional engineering a national community defined by the rights the citizenry possessed."[31]

Country builders respond to linguistic dualism by asserting the need to assure that French Canadians can exercise full weight in the national government, and that linguistic minorities can receive education, government services and communications everywhere in the country. From this impulse stem policies such as the Official Languages Act, extension of French radio and television across the country, promoting French language education, and so on. The centrepiece of this drive has been the attempt, frustrated since 1968, to have legal guarantees of minority language rights written into the Canadian constitution and to require all provinces to respect them. This view, therefore, rejects arguments that Quebec needs special or additional powers as the guardian of French Canada, and opposes aspects of recent Quebec language legislation which are seen to limit English minority rights. The approach also rejects another, more exclusivist, form of "One Canada" sentiment represented by leaders such as James Richardson, who argues for the primacy of the English language. Failure to guarantee French language rights, said *A Time for Action* "has led them [French Canadians] to withdraw in spirit into Quebec and added strength to the separatist movement."[32]

Economically, country builders stress the need to build an integrated national economy, and assert the primacy of the federal government in economic and fiscal policy. The central government must maintain sufficient taxing power to engage in Keynesian economic management and to act as an agent of redistribution across regions and social groups. Other economic policy tools are needed to plan overall economic development and defend Canadian interests in an increasingly interdependent and uncertain world. The integrity of the Canadian common market, with free movement of people, goods and money, must be defended against provincial policies — in purchasing, agricultural marketing, regulation of labour markets and tax policies, all of which impose barriers to trade and whittle away at a true common market.[33] Again, these impulses are represented in policies and constitutional proposals. The federal share of the fiscal pie must be protected. The power to regulate interprovincial and international trade and commerce must be defended. Provincial control over natural resources should not limit the federal power over international and interprovincial trade and commerce, or prevent Ottawa from redistributing the benefits to all Canadians. Some recent proposals suggest that a "freedom of movement" clause be written into the constitution. The capacity of Ottawa to act in times of national emergency, and if necessary to override provincial interests, must remain. Hence it should preserve its emergency power under the "Peace, Order and Good Government" clause, and resist limits on its power to declare provincial activities in the national interest and therefore under federal control. Country builders thus resist provincial attempts to limit such powers and are wary of provincial development policies which threaten federal leadership or distort the common market. They are also cautious about giving the provinces a role in fields such as transportation, foreign trade and monetary policy, which are now federal responsibilities.

In social policy, too, country builders stress the importance of the national government in maintaining national standards of social services and in redistributing wealth between rich and poor.

Thus country builders, while not denying regional diversity, do wish to minimize it and to seek issues which transcend it. Rather than saying Ottawa has too much power, they worry that it already has too little — that Ottawa's capacity for initiative in policy and leadership has already been weakened too much. Many country builders also argue that if the central government is to play the lead role, then its legitimacy and political support must be enhanced. Hence they propose a revitalization of federal institutions. Here we find proposals to reform the electoral system to encourage more effective national parties, for a constitutional charter of human rights, for various reforms of Parliament and cabinet, and for development of a more regionally sensitive civil service, which would itself be deconcentrated to other parts of the country. Another alternative, proposed in June 1978 in the Liberal government's Bill C-60, is to build regional interests more fully into central government by reform of the Senate. The "House of the Federation" it proposed would have members appointed half by the federal and half by the provincial legislatures, in numbers proportionate to party support. It would also, on issues vitally concerned with language, act as a binational body, with French- and English-speaking members counting equally. This proposal therefore sought to build region and language into the centre, but in a way which would, in the long run at least, undermine rather than strengthen the provincial governments.

In federal-provincial relations, country builders seek to maintain federal power. While accepting the need for consultation, some have misgivings about moving further towards a pattern of federal-provincial interaction in which provinces would debate national policies and have a voice on matters within federal jurisdiction. Such a collaborative process, former cabinet secretary Gordon Robertson has argued, blurs the distinction between governments, enhances the status of provincial leaders as against federal ones, and undermines Ottawa's claim to speak for the national interest.[34]

This Ottawa-centred model is, in some ways, embedded in the original terms of the B.N.A. Act itself. It flowered in the days of the National Policy, and most recently during and after World War II, a period of federal fiscal and policy dominance, engendered by the experience of depression and war, and by a new consensus on the welfare state and Keynesian economics.

For many years, in the face of resurgent provinces, this view has been on shaky ground. Few believe that in present political circumstances it is realistic to argue for increased federal power. As Alan Cairns observes:

> Contemporary supporters of centralization no longer see themselves as in the vanguard of constitutional change, riding the current of favourable historical forces. . . . They do not have the luxury of regarding the provinces with contempt as did [a] previous generation. . . . Contemporary centralists fight a rearguard action to limit how much they have to give away, and to restrict the amount of provincial input into federal institutions to the unavoidable.[35]

Even the former Liberal government — which boldly declared in recent constitutional discussion it was not going to "give away the store" to the provinces, and which campaigned in the 1979 election against parochial provincial power barons — did make numerous concessions to the provinces. The federal share of taxing and spending has steadily declined; federal conditions in shared cost programs have been loosened. In February 1978, Ottawa was prepared to accept limits on its spending and declaratory powers, and to concede the primacy of provincial resource ownership over the federal trade and commerce power, except in cases of a "compelling national interest".[36]

Nevertheless, the defeated Liberal government did, in its approach to constitutional discussions, advocate a country-building approach. The coalition of other interests in support of different variants of the approach is unclear. It clearly includes Anglophones in Quebec and many French Canadians elsewhere. It appears to have much support in the business community, especially among those operating across the national market, who fear conflicting regulations and barriers to movement. Social democrats in Canada, in the New Democratic Party and elsewhere, have traditionally argued for a strong central government with fiscal resources sufficient to engage in activist social policies.[37] More recently, advocates of comprehensive "national industrial strategies" have looked to federal leadership and feel that federalism places serious constraints on federal strategies.

Second is the province-building model. If for country builders, the primary community is the country, for province builders it is the province. Provincial interests are most important and it is provincial governments which represent and speak for them. It is the province whose wealth is to be maximized, within which redistribution is to occur, and for whose benefit resources are to be used. Provincial governments are political and juridical equals of Ottawa; national majorities should not overrule provincial majorities.

Again, there are many strands to this viewpoint, and many different kinds of proposals flow from it. Much less weight is placed on the need to build common values, to engage in interregional distribution, maintain common standards in social services, or to guarantee language rights constitutionally. Instead, the emphasis is on provincial freedom to promote its own development and follow its own priorities. Increasingly these priorities have shifted to a focus on economic issues and the evolution of regional development strategies. Hence arise proposals for a greater provincial share of tax revenues, and for provinces like Alberta to retain the revenues flowing from natural resources. Provinces also argue for varying degrees of decentralization of power in many areas, ranging from fisheries to communications. They call for a much greater provincial voice in federal policies such as transportation or foreign trade which affect regional interests. They also wish to remove or limit the broad discretionary powers which now allow Ottawa to "intrude" into areas of provincial jurisdiction.[38]

Many people view advocates of the province-building approach as selfish. They point out that it is easy enough for a rich province to argue, as Alberta has, that it should be allowed to go its own way, to develop its potential fully. Poor provinces do not have that luxury. One cannot deny that many political statements are self-serving, whether those of province builders or country builders. Nevertheless, there is a charitable interpretation to many such provincial proposals. They aim to maximize economic performance in Canada by maximizing it in each province and letting the market decide how people, capital and goods should be relocated. To argue, for example, that what is good for Alberta is good for Canada may turn out to be false or self-serving, but it is not necessarily an attempt to hurt or weaken

Canada. This follows from the belief that "Canada" and "the federal government" are not synonymous. Only if they are equated, can one urge that provincial proposals taking precedence over federal ones must of necessity damage Canada (i.e., the federal government). None of the provincial Premiers, not Davis, not Lougheed, not Lévesque, have as a primary motivation the destruction of Canada or severe harm to it. The province-building perspective (or Quebec nation-building) can represent a different orientation, a different set of strategies for achieving a goal that everyone could in principle agree with: namely, the greatest good for the greatest number. Where disagreement must — and does — arise is whether this goal can best be achieved by eleven coordinate governments, by the provinces following the federal lead, or by two nations.

The province-building perspective suggests a very different conception of how the national interest is to be determined. It arises not from the central government, but from the collective interests of eleven governments. The distinction was neatly captured in an exchange between Prime Minister Trudeau and Premier Lougheed of Alberta at a recent constitutional conference. "But who," asked the prime minister, "will speak for Canada? Ottawa must do so." Mr. Lougheed replied: "We all do." This perspective implies a confederal view of Canada in which federal powers are exercised with the consent of the provinces, and the Confederation is a compact among provincial/regional communities.

It follows that the federal-provincial conference, the forum where the leaders of the communities gather, becomes a central institution in Canadian politics. *National* policies emerge from the collaboration of the two levels of government. Hence there emerge proposals for further institutionalizing intergovernmental relations. One such device, strongly advocated by the British Columbia government and by several other groups, is the creation of a House of the Provinces,[39] whose members would be direct, instructed delegates of provincial governments. Unlike the Liberals' House of Federation, this would strengthen provincial governments. Few provinces have endorsed the proposal, preferring to focus on building up the existing intergovernmental process.

Who supports the province-building drive? Few province builders go as far as the stark model we have described. Nor is it strongly supported by all provincial governments. Leaders of the Maritime provinces temper it with a realization of their dependence on federal assistance for their development. The Ontario government, perhaps the prime beneficiary of federal policies and of the Canadian market, has asserted the fundamental federal responsibility for economic policy. In particular it has supported a stronger federal role in energy, to keep prices for Ontario consumers down and to ensure the sharing of the massive western oil and gas revenues.[40] But in general, the primary source of the province-centred drive does arise from provincial governments and their bureaucracies. These elites have found increasing popular support and have tapped many of the resentments against Ottawa. They have also enlisted allies among business and professional groups oriented to provincial activities.

The Conservative government elected in 1979 did not spell out a detailed constitutional position, but in its stress on a new era of cooperation with the provinces, and its initial moves to assure provincial control over natural resources and the like, it appeared somewhat more sympathetic to the province-building impulse than its predecessor. However, it is likely that the institutional imperatives which affect all governments will lead it to limit its concessions to the provinces.[41]

The third model is "Quebec nation-building." Quebec nation builders argue that the communities and interests to be reconciled are those not of regions and provinces, but of two distinct nations. Quebec has all the attributes of a nation; it is the primary political expression of French Canadians, who can never be more than a minority in Canada or the federal government. This approach, then, argues that Ottawa can never fully represent French Canadians; only Quebec can. It pays relatively little attention to French Canadians outside Quebec: without institutional support la francophonie hors du Québec is destined to disappear. Quebec is quite different from other provinces.[42] From this perspective flows the call for greater powers for the Quebec government in social, economic and cultural fields.

Manifestations of the Quebec nation-building perspective range from outright independence to various proposals for a statut-particulier for the province. The Parti-Québécois program of sovereignty-association is perhaps its clearest expression.[43] Quebec would have sovereignty; federal administration would cease to operate in the province; Quebeckers would no longer sit in the federal Parliament. But a wide range of common policies would be decided in a joint forum in which representatives of the two countries would have equal weight.

While support for this program remains limited in Quebec, all Quebec governments in recent years have been Quebec nation builders — from the liberal government of Jean Lesage, seeking greater tax shares, negotiating "opting out" of many shared programs and the like under the slogan "maîtres chez nous"; to the Union Nationale and its Egalité ou Indépéndance; to the Liberals under Robert Bourassa with "cultural sovereignty."

Thus all three competing models point towards different changes. Each has an institutional base. Each also finds support in the Canadian population and is reflected in the data we have presented. None, in its pure form, can easily prevail. The debate among them forms the central focus of the drawn-out negotiations on the constitution between 1968 and 1971[44] and since 1976, and explains the failure to reach agreement. To restructure the institutions of Canadian federalism is to decide which of these impulses is to be enshrined in political institutions. Do we further strengthen the forces of provincialism and regionalism; or revitalize the central government? In either case, do we or do we not recognize the distinctive position of Quebec?

Most recent proposals, with the major exception of the federal Liberal program of June 1978, have at least partly accepted the strength of the province and Quebec nation-building drives. The Task Force on National Unity, the Pepin-Robarts Task Force, though appointed by the Trudeau government, premised its report on this perspective:

> The first and foremost challenge facing the country is to create an environment in which duality might flourish; the second is to provide a fresher and fuller expression of the forces of regionalism in Canada's constitutional system and power structure. Each, if ignored or left unsatisfied, has the power to break the country; and each must accept the other if a new harmony is to be achieved.[45]

Moreover, provinces are "the basic building blocks of Canadian society, . . . the primary frameworks through which regional populations can organize and express themselves."[46] Hence, the task force's criterion for judging proposals is: "to what extent does it usefully advance the recognition of duality or regionalism?"[47]

Many of the task force's recommendations lead in this direction. The national government must reflect the equality of French and English, and while provinces are encouraged to promote minority language rights, this should be a matter of provincial legislation, not constitutional fiat.

While a new division of powers is not spelled out in detail, provinces should have the primary roles in social and cultural affairs, and in promoting regional economic development. The federal powers of reservation and disallowance would be abolished; the declaratory power should be used only with the consent of the province concerned; the spending power should be used only with provincial approval. Ottawa would no longer appoint provincial lieutenant-governors and judges.

Moreover, the provinces would be built into central policy-making by a House of Provinces, made up of provincial delegates, with a variety of powers including approval of federal treaties or legislation in areas of provincial jurisdiction, ratification of appointments to the Supreme Court and major regulatory agencies such as the National Energy Board, and so on.

These proposals were designed to meet the demands of regionalism. Dualism requires that "the distinctive role of the Quebec government . . . must be recognized,"[48] and Quebec must "have the powers necessary to protect and develop its distinctive character." The stigma of "special status" would be avoided by ensuring that additional powers for Quebec would also be available to any other provinces which desired them.[49]

Thus the primary thrust of the task force is towards province- and Quebec nation-building. But there is another side. It suggests various means to strengthen a common identity. In the economic field it assigns primacy to the federal government, would constitutionally entrench equalization, and would prohibit barriers to trade. More important, the task force argues for reform of the electoral system as a means of promoting a more regionally representative party system.

The task force report, while emphasising regionalism, thus seeks to chart a path among the three drives of country, province and Quebec nation-building, making recommendations to respond to all three. As such it accurately reflects the ambiguities and complexities in underlying sentiment described throughout this study. The weaknesses in the report stem largely from the contradictions in the reality it had to respond to. Proponents of all three models can find much in it to please them, but also much to criticize. Thus some have argued that the report gives too much weight to regionalism and provincialism and provides only a grudging rationale for a more country-centred approach. Others argue that in trying to reconcile diverging tendencies, it is led to propose ingenious institutional solutions which are difficult to comprehend and of uncertain impact. Still others suggest that by offering all provinces the special powers Quebec might need, the task force promotes much more decentralization than is really desired elsewhere. The commissioners also had to blur some of the most critical issues, leaving the division of powers, for example, only sketchily outlined. Moreover, especially as it confronted questions about the role of the state in social and economic affairs, it found that the criteria of regionalism, dualism and "power-sharing" were insufficient guides. Other criteria, themselves pointing in different directions, had to be employed — "efficiency," "effectiveness," "political responsiveness," and the like.

Again, as Cairns points out,[50] with so many different kinds of criteria, almost any proposal can be criticized, or advocated from some point of view. And while it might be argued that the criterion of community, which this book has concentrated on, is the most important one in the Canadian context, it is indeed not the only one on which citizens would wish to judge a constitution and political system. Thus, in focusing on the relation between governments, the debate among these three models has paid less attention to the relation between governments and citizens, or to the role of mechanisms for citizens' representation, such as political parties and legislatures. Similarly, questions about how interests other than territorially based ones can be mobilized have taken a back seat in the debate, as have questions about effectiveness in policy-making. The mechanism for constitutional review — the federal-provincial conference — assures that this is the case and that primary focus will be on the institutional claims of governments. Thus one can sympathize with a writer such as Anthony Scott when he argues against thinking of constitutional arrangements in terms of province- or nation-building:

> It conjures up aims that may not exist. . . . It deals with constituent provinces and the nation as though they were organic minds or spirits, in search of purposes or goals. . . . It is stated in terms of reforming the

pattern or pyramid of jurisdictional units, instead of better serving the citizens with government services, goods, regulations and protection.[51]

But, as our data have shown, it is precisely community and territory, not the role of government generally and not ideology in the sense of left versus right, which generates the profound tensions now at work in Canadian politics.

As the task force recognized, the province, country and Quebec nation-building models each reflect only part of the underlying reality in Canada. Regional and ethnic communities have become more distinct; they are in conflict on a wide range of issues. There is thus a strong basis for the continued growth of provincial power, and for a policy in which the intergovernmental forum is the primary mechanism for accommodation among these interests. But the sense of national community remains strong; and in citizens' views on policy there are many opportunities for national leadership. The objective is not to destroy the strong, effective communities which now exist in Canada, but rather to provide a broader range of institutions through which they can find effective political expression.

We have argued repeatedly that citizens generally see no need to "choose sides" — to renounce either their federal or their provincial loyalties and identities. We have urged that political leaders weigh carefully any actions or policies which might lead people to feel that a choice was being forced on them — a dilemma posed in terms of "he who is not for me is against me." We believe firmly that no such final choice is necessary or desirable. There is, however, a danger that constitutional revisions, though well-intentioned, can have the effect of forcing people to take sides — and not just in Quebec.

Political leaders will have to choose and make known their preferences in the process of constitutional revision. They must choose, for example, to give certain enhanced powers to one level of government in exchange for a diminution of that level's power in other respects. The total "package" may or may not favour one level or one province more than others. But perceptions of relative advantage will play an important role, and the leaders who bargain can exercise influence over those perceptions. If leaders proclaim — truthfully and sincerely, or not — that "their" side has been cheated or has been made to pay too high a price, then citizens may line up on one side or the other, rather than maintain the balance of loyalties that now exists in all parts of Canada. The leaders of the largest, wealthiest or most powerful provinces bear, perhaps, the greatest responsibility in this regard.

Much depends, finally, on language, on how the balance of powers, jurisdictions, rights and obligations are expressed. The perceptions of citizens and the policies of governments, we have shown, reflect a balance of unity and diversity, of convergence amid divergence, of loyalties to larger and smaller units, of highly specific processes and outcomes. The tension and conflict so obvious to any observer indicate that no one view, no one loyalty, no one identity has any predominance, nor is it likely to in the near future. The language of federal-provincial and interprovincial relations, therefore, must continue to be nuanced, specific and qualified, rather than simplistic, vague and divisive.

If political debate reaches a point where many people feel compelled to vote or act as though they must make a single choice between country and province or between nation and country — as Quebeckers may in some referendum — the choice will be painful and uncertain. Many even in Quebec would unquestionably choose Canada over their own province, but a great many would surely make the opposite choice. Excruciating as that choice would be for any given individual, it would be more so for the country as a whole — and for all the provinces, too, since they would find themselves internally divided.

Such a fateful choice would be not zero-sum but negative-sum, a Hobson's choice which no one could wish to face. There is no easy way to avoid this scenario, but we hope that our analysis can contribute to a realization that the options are still open: that people can find themselves managing a complex system involving country, nation and province, or they can choose one and reject the others.

The Chinese curse — "May you live in interesting times" — is surely applicable to Canada today, as it is to many other countries as well. Part of the "Canadian crisis" partakes of worldwide trends, most of which we have had to ignore for reasons of space. This curse, however, also marks an opportunity. Change is possible only where powerful forces are at work and where discontents are focused.

The data we have summarized may soon be dated, if they are not already. But the forces which contend will be with us for a long time to come. They will not soon fade away, regardless of specific reforms. Canadians should therefore accept the basic facts of nation-building, province-building and country-building and do what they can to bend them to advantage. In this sense we feel we would not be unduly immodest to assert that descriptions of regional variety — such as our own — have served a useful purpose; but such descriptions do not need to be repeated too often. The task now is to think about regionalism in positive rather than negative terms, to fashion institutions which will reflect and channel these robust forces to goals and ends which are politically defined and socially beneficial. Paradoxically, perhaps, a greater emphasis on regionalism in several forms may in the long run weaken the centrifugal tendencies we have catalogued and allow Canada to pass through this phase into a new period in which nongeographic forces become the focus of attention or in which other levels of government regain a closer balance with the provincial. No matter how powerful the institutional forces we have discussed appear to be, much depends on how political leaders and citizens think about them. We have, if nothing else, demonstrated that Canadians are quite varied in their perceptions and feelings; and while part of the variety reflects the variety of institutions, some part reflects visions of what should be or can be, as well as what must be.

Notes

1. Alan Cairns, Speech to the Vancouver Institute, February 1979.

2. Radio-Canada poll, released June 20, 1978.

3. Le Parti Québécois, *D'égal à égal* (Montreal, 1979).

4. La Fédération des francophones hors Québec, *Face to Face With a Failing Country* (Ottawa, 1979).

5. Task Force on Canadian Unity, *A Future Together,* (Ottawa: Supply and Services, 1979), pp. 87-88. Ontario Advisory Committee on Confederation, *Second Report: The Division of Powers* (Toronto: Government of Ontario, 1979).

6. For an analysis of this debate, see Peter Leslie and Richard Simeon, "The Battle of the Balance Sheets," in *Must Canada Fail?* ed. R. Simeon (Montreal: McGill-Queen's University, 1977), pp. 243-58. Also, C.D. Howe Research Institute, *Why Do the Balances Differ?* (Montreal, 1977). The complexities of this kind of analysis are well illustrated in the papers found in Institute of Intergovernmental Relations and the Economic Council of Canada, *The Political Economy of Confederation* (Ottawa: Supply and Services, 1979).

7. Task Force on Canadian Unity, *A Time to Speak: The Views of the Public* (Ottawa: Supply and Services, 1979), p. 83.

8. C.B. Macpherson, *Democracy in Alberta: Social Credit and the Party System,* 2nd ed. (Toronto: University of Toronto Press, 1962).

9. See generally John Richards and Larry Pratt, *Prairie Capitalism: Power and Influence in the New West* (Toronto: McClelland and Stewart, 1979).

10. For a useful survey which emphasizes this perspective, see Milton Esman, ed., *Ethnic Conflict in the Western World* (Ithaca, N.Y.: Cornell University Press, 1977).

11. Arend Lijphart, "Political Theories and the Explanation of Ethnic Conflict in the Western World," in Esman, *Ethnic Conflict,* p. 56.

12. Sidney Tarrow, "Introduction" in *Territorial Politics in Industrial Relations,* ed. Sidney Tarrow, Peter J. Katzenstein, and Luigi Graziano (New York: Praeger, 1978), p. 22-23.

13. This was noted as long ago as the 1930s by the Rowell—Sirois Commission.

14. For an analysis from an economist's perspective, see Economic Council of Canada: *Living Together; A Study of Regional Disparities* (Ottawa: Supply and Services, 1977). A valuable set of essays from an historical and political economy perspective is found in *Canada and the Burden of Unity* ed. David J. Bercuson (Toronto: Macmillan, 1977), especially the articles by Paul Phillips, "National Policy, Continental Economics, and National Integration"; Ernest R. Forbes, "Misguided Symmetry: The Destruction of Regional Transportation Policy for the Maritimes"; T.W. Acheson, "The Maritimes and 'Empire Canada'"; and T.D. Regehr, "Western Canada and the Burden of National Transportation Policies."

15. For some data on trade linkages within Canada, see Government of Canada (Federal Provincial Relations Office) *Trade Realities in Canada and the Issue of Sovereignty-Association* (Ottawa, 1978).

16. J.M.S. Careless, " 'Limited Identities' in Canada," *Canadian Historical Review* 50 (1969): 1-10.

17. "The Role and Nature of the Canadian State," in *The Canadian State: Political Economy and Political Power,* ed. Leo Panitch (Toronto: University of Toronto Press, 1977), p. 17.

18. "The State and Province-Building: Alberta's Development Strategy," in Panitch, *The Canadian State,* p.133.

19. H.V. Nelles, *The Politics of Development: Forests, Mines and Hydro-Electric Power in Ontario, 1849-1941* (Toronto: Macmillan, 1974).

20. For example, Hubert Guindon, "Social Unrest, Social Class and Quebec's Bureaucratic Revolution," *Queen's Quarterly* 71 (1962): 150-62; and Charles Taylor, "Nationalism and the Political Intelligentsia: A Case Study," *Queen's Quarterly* 72 (1965): 162.

21. Quoted in Richard Simeon, "Regionalism and Canadian Political Institutions," reprinted in *Canadian Federalism: Myth or Reality?* 3rd ed., ed. Peter Meekison (Toronto: Methuen, 1977). The primary exponents of the institutional-elite perspective are D.V. Smiley, *Canada in Question: Federalism in the Seventies*, 2nd ed. (Toronto: McGraw-Hill Ryerson, 1976)); E.R. Black, *Divided Loyalties: Canadian Concepts of Federalism* (Montreal: McGill-Queen's University Press 1975); and Alan Cairns. Cairns's statement of this view is the most sweeping. See "The Governments and Societies of Canadian Federalism," *Canadian Journal of Political Science*, X:4 (December 1977): 695-725 and "The Other Crisis of Canadian Federalism," *Canadian Public Administration* 22 (Summer 1979): 175-95.

22. For a summary of these points, see Smiley, *Canada in Question*, chapter 4.

23. The most detailed examination of this problem, together with a detailed proposal for change, is William P. Irvine, *Does Canada Need a New Electoral System?* (Kingston: Institute of Intergovernmental Relations, Queen's University, 1979). The first comprehensive indictment of the electoral system in these terms is Alan Cairns, "The Electoral System and the Party System in Canada," *Canadian Journal of Political Science* 1 (1968): 55-80. D.V. Smiley has also proposed electoral reform. See "Federalism and the Legislative Process in Canada," in *The Legislative Process in Canada: The Need for Reform* ed. W.A.W. Neilson and J.C. MacPherson (Montreal: Institute for Research on Public Policy, 1978). The New Democratic Party and the Task Force on Canadian Unity have also proposed reforms.

24. Irvine, *Does Canada Need a New Electoral System?*, pp. 90-93.

25. The term is William Riker's. See *Federalism: Origin, Operation, Significance* (Boston: Little, Brown, 1964).

26. On these points, see Helen Jones Dawson, "National Pressure Groups and the Federal Government," and David Kwavnick, "Interest Group Demands and the Federal Political System: Two Canadian Case Studies," in *Pressure Group Behaviour in Canadian Politics* ed. A. Paul Pross (Toronto: McGraw-Hill Ryerson, 1975), pp. 27-58; 69-86.

27. Cairns, "The Governments and Societies of Canadian Federalism," p. 699.

28. See Meyer Bucovetsky, "The Mining Industry and the Great Tax Reform Debate," in Pross, *Pressure Group Behaviour*, for an example.

29. The terms *province-* and *country-building* appear to have been originated by E.R. Black and Alan Cairns. See "A Different Perspective on Canadian Federalism," reprinted in Meekison, *Canadian Federalism*.

30. Pierre Trudeau, *A Time for Action* (Ottawa: Government of Canada, 1978), p. 2.

31. Alan Cairns, "Recent Federalist Constitutional Proposals: A Review Essay," *Canadian Public Policy*, 3 (Summer 1979), pp. 348-365.

32. Trudeau, *A Time for Action*, p. 20.

33. The need to strengthen the common market has become a common theme in recent proposals; it is found in the Task Force on Canadian Unity report, the report of the Committee on the Constitution of the Canadian Bar Association and others. For an analysis of the issues involved, see Edward Safarian, *Canadian Federalism and Economic Integration* (Ottawa: Information Canada, 1964).

34. "The Role of Interministerial Conferences in the Decision-Making Process," in *Confrontation and Collaboration: Intergovernmental Relations in Canada Today*, ed. Richard Simeon (Toronto: Institute of Public Administration of Canada, 1979), pp. 78-88.

35. Cairns, "Recent Federalist Proposals," p. 4.

36. For a review of the course of negotiations in 1978 and 1979, see Douglas Brown, *Intergovernmental Relations in Canada: The Year in Review* (Kingston: Institute of Intergovernmental Relations, 1980).

37. For a classic statement of this perspective, see John Porter, *The Vertical Mosaic* (Toronto: University of Toronto Press, 1965), pp. 368-9 and 379-85. For a more recent statement that provincial governments represent regressive political forces and that regionalism has few roots in regional societies and cultures, see Garth Stevenson, *Unfulfilled Union* (Toronto: Macmillan, 1979).

38. Few full-scale statements of the province-building approach exist. Many of the proposals are evident in provincial positions in recent constitutional negotiations, and in provincial position papers such as the Government of Alberta's *Harmony in Diversity: A New Federalism for Canada* (Edmonton, 1978).

39. See Province of British Columbia, *British Columbia's Constitutional Proposals* (Victoria, 1978). Other advocates include the Bar Association, the Task Force on Canadian Unity, the Ontario Advisory Committee on Confederation and the Canada West Foundation.

40. See, for example, the Hon. William Davis, *Oil Pricing and Security: A Policy Framework for Canada* (Toronto: Office of the Premier, Government of Ontario, 1979).

41. See Progressive Conservative Party of Canada, Discussion Paper No. 3, *The Constitution and National Unity* (Ottawa, n.d.) and Flora Macdonald, "Towards a Revitalized Confederation," in *The Future of North America: Canada, the United States and Quebec Nationalism*, ed. Elliot Feldman and Neil Nevitte (Cambridge, Mass. and Montreal: Harvard University Press, 1979), pp. 305-18.

42. There are many statements of this approach. For a good brief survey, see James de Wilde, "The Parti Québécois in Power," in *Must Canada Fail?*, ed. Simeon, pp. 15-27. For a survey of Quebec government positions through several governments, see Government of Quebec, Ministry of Intergovernmental Affairs, *Quebec's Traditional Stands on the Division of Powers* (Quebec, 1978). See also André Bernard, *What Does Quebec Want?* (Toronto: James Lorimer, 1978). René Lévesque's views are well summarized in *My Quebec* (Toronto: Methuen, 1979).

43. The most detailed statement of this program is Le Parti Québécois, *D'égal à égal*. For a detailed summary and critique, see Peter Leslie, *Equal to Equal: Economic Association and the Canadian Common Market* (Kingston: Institute of Intergovernmental Relations, 1979).

44. For a survey of this period see Richard Simeon, *Federal-Provincial Diplomacy* (Toronto: University of Toronto Press, 1972), chap. 5.

45. Task Force on Canadian Unity, *A Future Together*, p. 20. Reproduced by permission of the Minister of Supply and Services Canada.

46. Ibid. pp. 26-27.

47. Ibid. p. 36.

48. Ibid. p. 87.

49. The Ontario Advisory Committee on Confederation used the same approach.

50. For a severe critique along these lines, see Cairns, "Recent Federalist Proposals," pp. 19-32.

51. Anthony Scott, "An Economic Approach to the Federal Structure," *Options Canada* (Proceedings of the Conference on the Future of the Canadian Federation, University of Toronto, 1977).

Author Index

Subject Index